Mac OS 8 Web Server Cookbook

David L. Hart
San Diego Supercomputer Center
UCSD 0505
9500 Gilman Drive
La Jolla, CA 92093-0505
dhart@sdsc.edu
http://www.sdsc.edu/~dhart

Philip E. Bourne
San Diego Supercomputer Center
UCSD 0505
9500 Gilman Drive
La Jolla, CA 92093-0505
bourne@sdsc.edu
http://www.sdsc.edu/~bourne

Prentice Hall PTR
Upper Saddle River, New Jersey 07458
http://www.phptr.com

ISBN 0-13-520016-4
90000
9 780135 200162

Library of Congress Cataloging in Publication Data

Hart, David L.
Mac OS 8 Web server cookbook / David L. Hart, Philip E. Bourne
p. cm.
Includes index.
ISBN 0-13-520016-4
1. Mac OS 2. Operating systems (Computers) 3. Macintosh (Computer)
4. Web servers. I. Bourne, Philip E. II. Title.
QA76.76.063H353 1998
004.67'8--dc21 98-24444
CIP

Acquisitions editor: Michael Meehan
Editorial/production supervision: Lisa Iarkowski
Cover design director: *Jayne Conte*
Cover design: *Bruce Kenselaar*
Manufacturing manager: *Alexis R. Heydt*
Editorial assistant: *Bart Blanken*
Marketing manager: *Kaylie Smith*

Prentice-Hall, Inc.
A Simon & Schuster Company
Upper Saddle River, New Jersey 07458

Prentice Hall books are widely used by corporations and government agencies for training, marketing, and resale.

The publisher offers discounts on this book when ordered in bulk quantities.
For more information, contact Corporate Sales Department, Phone: 800-382-3419;
FAX: 201-236-7141; E-mail: corpsales@prenhall.com
Prentice Hall PTR, One Lake Street, Upper Saddle River, NJ 07458.

Printed in the United States of America
10 9 8 7 6 5 4 3 2 1

ISBN 0-13-520016-4

Prentice-Hall International (UK) Limited, *London*
Prentice-Hall of Australia Pty. Limited, *Sydney*
Prentice-Hall Canada Inc., *Toronto*
Prentice-Hall Hispanoamericana, S.A., *Mexico*
Prentice-Hall of India Private Limited, *New Delhi*
Prentice-Hall of Japan, Inc., *Tokyo*
Simon & Schuster Asia Pte. Ltd., *Singapore*
Editora Prentice-Hall do Brasil, Ltda., *Rio de Janeiro*

Dave: To Mom, who always knew I could do this,
and to Casey, who agreed with her.

Phil: To our new addition, Melanie Rebbeca

Table of Contents

Preface

If you have decided it's time to serve some information, either to the whole world via the Internet or to a single organization, large or small, via an intranet, this may be the book for you. Our first job is to turn that "may" into a yes or a no. If you want a succinct—that is, short and inexpensive—guide to establishing a complete Internet server, complete with ftp, list server, and Web server, read on. If you really want a 600-page dissertation on a project that might take you about 30 minutes, then put this back before you get the cover dirty.

As we see it, there are three types of people still reading:

- Mac addicts who will use a Mac for their Internet server even if they have to write the code themselves,
- UNIX techies or Windows drones who thought they might get a cheap laugh at the Mac from this book, and
- Users who are considering Macs for their Internet server but aren't sure if Macs are up to it.

To the Mac addicts, we'd like to say: Relax. Setting up a solid, secure Mac Internet server is just as easy as installing any Mac application. It might take as little as 15 minutes (see Section 6.7.1).

To the UNIX and Windows proponents: Would you be willing to offer $10,000 to the first person in the Internet community of hackers who successfully hacks into your UNIX or Windows Web server? We've found several such hacking challenges on the Web, and all were running a Mac server. And only recently has one had to pay up (see Section 2.1.1).

And to those of you on the fence, we'll just say: If you want an Internet server that takes about 30 minutes to set up and can handle just as many hits, yet can withstand advertised hacking challenges, you might want to look closely at the Mac. Surveys have shown that the proportion of Mac servers on the Web is far greater than the overall Mac market share (see Section 2.1.1). If you want a Web server running on an operating system that requires years of training to administer, go with UNIX. If you're really looking forward to the Blue Screen of Death (BSOD), you might look into Windows®.

If you're still with us, dear Reader, you should be leaning strongly toward a Mac server. Now we just have to convince you to buy this book.

Scope

Let's begin by making sure you understand the scope of the material presented in this book.

Emphasis on Information Servers, Not Clients. Downloading a file with ftp, sending e-mail, or surfing the Web are client activities. Setting up a secure ftp environment, redistributing an incoming message to a mailing list, or making a Web home page available are server activities. Most Internet-related books deal only with the client side of the Internet. This is not a book about using Web browsers like Netscape Navigator or Internet Explorer, nor is it a book of "cool" sites. Having said that, Chapter 5 helps you install and configure client software so you can review the information on your own server.

Not Just the Web. Of the books available that do describe how to set up an Internet server, the focus is almost always on a Web server. This book is about designing and maintaining a server to support ftp (file transfer protocol), list servers (e-mail access to information), as well as the Web.

Emphasis on Organizing Your Information. From the client's perspective, a good server is not necessarily determined by fancy presentation, but rather by the quality and organization of the information. We can't help you with your information quality; however, we have included some tips and guidance to make it easier to navigate your server and find information.

Establishing a Mac OS-based Information Server. Many of the principles in this book apply to servers using any of the UNIX and Microsoft Windows variants, as well as to Mac OS servers. However, this book will have much shorter chapters on installing software, configuring the system, and administering the server.

Prerequisites

Degree of Macintosh Proficiency. In setting up a Macintosh server, you need a basic familiarity with configuring and operating the Mac OS. For example, you should understand the basics of folders, files, system extensions and control panels, and software installation. If you can perform these tasks, you can run an Internet server.

Established Local Area Networks. For those wishing to set up an Internet server on a Local Area Network (LAN), this book assumes the LAN has already been established. This book does not discuss how to set up Macintosh networks, although some pointers for further information are provided. For the most part, we provide instructions for connecting a single Macintosh (from a home or business) to the Internet.

Why This Book

If you are still reading, either you are lucky enough to have too much time on your hands, or you belong to the intended audience and have satisfied the prerequisites. The next question to ask yourself is whether the format of this book is going to help you. To answer this question, consider our motivations for writing the book.

Dave's Reasons. I have had the chance to operate UNIX systems (as a user, not an administrator), Windows systems, and Macintoshes over the past decade or so. UNIX has its advantages where you have multiuser systems, where you have armies of system administrators available if you have a problem, and where you just need to have a command-line interface. It is, however, by no means easy or fun. Microsoft Windows® I have simply learned to dislike. In my opinion, Windows simply is not as pleasant to use as the Mac OS. Macintosh did windows first and still does it better.

By co-authoring this book, I wanted to learn more about Macs so I would have even more reasons to love 'em. Not surprisingly—at least to Mac aficionados—I have confirmed all of my preconceived notions and found very few trouble spots. So that's why there is a Mac version of the book. Phil deserves the credit for getting a contract for a Mac version and for the reasons why this book is laid out the way it is.

Phil's Reasons. Over the past couple of years, I have been responsible for establishing and supporting information and information servers on UNIX and Windows NT platforms. What frustrated me in the beginning was the lack of a good overview of what software I should be installing, where I could get it, and how I could organize my information to make its presentation most effective. I would be misleading you if I said sources, either on-line or printed, are not available today to help. In fact, the opposite is true. The problem is that there is so much information, it is hard to know where to start.

My goal is to make this cookbook that place to start. You decide with our help what to cook and then gather a set of ingredients—software obtained free from the Internet, commercial software, and of course the information itself. You put these ingredients together using the right utensils and follow steps a through z. [Dave's note: On the Mac, it's usually steps a through e.] The result should be an Internet feast for a world of information consumers. The problem for me is that I have had virtually no exposure to the Mac. Nevertheless, I do recognize the need for a Mac version of this cookbook and am very grateful that Dave has agreed to provide the technical impetus. Together we hope you find this book informative and of lasting value.

The Cookbook Format

Like a cookbook, this book presents the ingredients and procedures in a recipe format. This cookbook goes one step further in that it contains a Global Recipe—a recipe of recipes—to get you to all the other recipes. You can also think of the Global Recipe as a road map. With a traditional map, you begin with something that covers a large area—the introduction in this book—and gradually homes in on where you need to go—individual chapters and sections.

Choosing the route raises questions: Do I go on the interstate? Do I take the scenic route? In Web terms, choosing your route leads to questions like: Should I support video clips? Is Gopher still necessary? Which is the most secure of the Web servers? Should I support a forms interface? Should I support Java applets for access from Java-ready browsers?

Beyond answering the global questions, each chapter takes pieces of the Global Recipe, provides a list of software ingredients and where you can get them, and describes in a step-by-step recipe how to put them together to get the job done. But getting the software installed is the beginning, not the end, of the process.

A significant portion of this book provides recipes and cooking tips for organizing your information for effective access, creating meaningful links between items of data, and effectively using graphics, frames, and clickable maps for dining on and serving the information. How sophisticated you want your server to be depends on how much you want to learn about such tools as Perl, HTML frames, Java, and JavaScript. People learn best from examples, so the book includes several scenarios, real and imaginary, to illustrate what you can do. For the real ones, code can be downloaded from the information server associated with this book and used as a template for your own information servers.

If you are still undecided about whether this book meets your needs, look at the Global Recipe (Chapter 1) and the more traditional form for presenting this recipe, the Table of Contents. You can do this by continuing to read this book or by visiting the information server. (Yes, the book's information server runs on a Mac.)

Your Obligation

Setting up an information server can be fun and rewarding if accessed by lots of folks or by the few people you really want to access it. Remember, however, that how the information is presented is a minor issue compared to the question of what information is presented. Just as we have an obligation to write the best possible book we can so that we don't take your money under false pretenses, you have an obligation to serve up the best information on your Internet server so as not to waste anyone's time. The community at large has, so far, fulfilled this obligation.

So Finally...

The World Wide Web has come a long way in a short time from its origin as a way for physicists to distribute experimental results and papers. While it may or may not be the greatest innovation since sliced bread, neither is it completely without its advantages. The Web has a lot of growing up to do, a lot of growing pains to overcome, and everyone who participates has a chance to guide its growth. We hope this book helps you make your contribution to the Web's future.

Conventions

Special Terms

Convention	Definition
http://www.sdsc.edu/Cookbook/	Uniform Resource Locator (URL) for finding information on the Web.
ftp://ftp.sdsc.edu/pub/cookbook/	A URL beginning ftp may also be accessed using anonymous ftp.
http://www.sdsc.edu/Cookbook/Mac	URLs spanning more than one line are hyphenated following a slash (/). Hyphens located elsewhere in a URL are part of the URL.
<TEXTAREA NAME="{name}" ROWS="{size}" COLS="{size}"> {optional text} </TEXTAREA>	HTML tag. The curly braces ({}) enclose material to be entered by the user and are not present in the actual tag.
List servers	Throughout this book, the first use of a new term is given in italics and is defined in the Glossary.

Mac OS Operating Systems

Depending on how old your Mac is or how religiously you've upgraded your Mac OS, you might have any one of a number of Mac OS versions on your computer. In this book, we will be working with Mac OS 8, since it is the latest version available. For those of you waiting to upgrade, however, we will try to identify differences between version 8 and versions 7.5 and 7.6. They won't be too substantial, although Mac OS 8 includes some Internet-related features, such as Personal Web Sharing, which may not be available in all of the incarnations of version 7.

Beyond Mac OS 8, the Mac OS picture is less clear at this point. In 1998, Apple is scheduled to release its next-generation operating system, code-named Rhapsody. Once Rhapsody hits the streets, Apple's publicized plans call for developing both Rhapsody and eventually Mac OS X, so Mac users will still be able to run Mac OS applications, such as those discussed in this book. There will also be Rhapsody-native applications, but because they did not exist while we were writing this book, Rhapsody and Rhapsody applications are not discussed here.

What Is an Internet-Enhanced Book?

While this book offers a concise description of building and maintaining an Internet information server, it cannot hope to stay current for long, given the speed at which the Internet is evolving. Having a CD-ROM stuck in the back helps because it provides more information than in the book, but it too becomes dated quickly. "Internet-enhanced" means, in effect, that we use the Internet as a book supplement, which can be updated continuously and made available to you long after the book has been published. The following diagram indicates how this works.

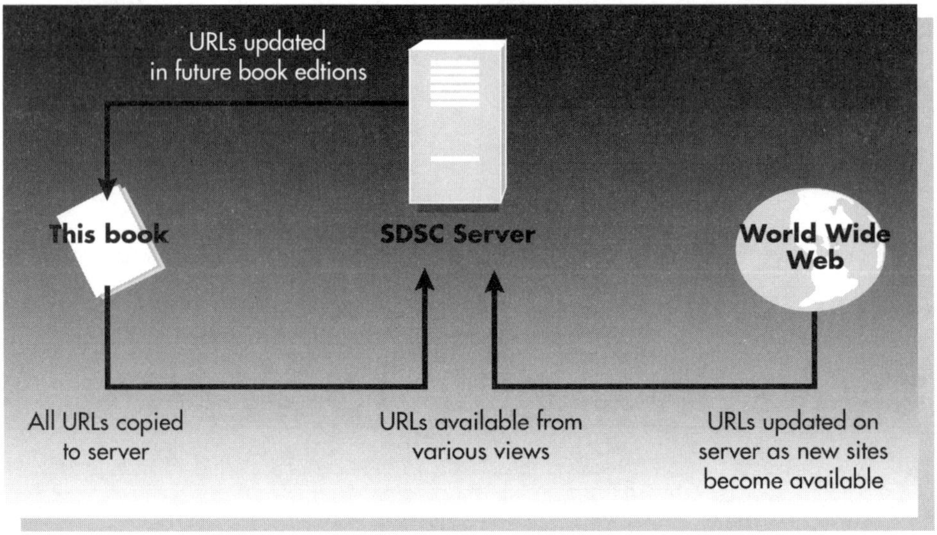

An Internet-Enhanced Book

This book summarizes lasting information on why to establish an information server and how to establish and maintain that server. It contains many pointers—in the form of Uniform Resource Locators (URLs)—to additional sources of information and to software that you will need. Those pointers, as hypertext links, are available on an Internet server at the San Diego Supercomputer Center (SDSC), a national laboratory for computational science and engineering. This serves two purposes.

First, you don't have to type these pointers each time you wish to visit a site. All you have to do is remember, or add to the hotlist of your favorite Web browser, a single pointer:

http://www.sdsc.edu/Cookbook/Mac

From there you can locate the pointer you need. If you do not have Web access but do have ftp access, you can download all or portions of this information from *ftp://ftp.sdsc.edu/pub/Cookbook/Mac*, so at least it is easy to retrieve pointers to software or information that is ftp accessible. (The meaning of an ftp archive given as a URL is discussed under Conventions.)

Second, and most important, we can keep this list of pointers on the San Diego Supercomputer Center server current! Thus, while a pointer in this book is considered the best reference at the time of writing, it may not be the best reference at the time of reading. However, the current reference is available to you simply by connecting to the SDSC server. This is important, since Internet technology is changing faster than the time it takes to provide new editions of a book. Through the information server, we can regularly supplement the book with current information.

Finding current information with the server is easy. The server provides several "views" that you can use. One view is simply the table of contents. By clicking on the section that corresponds to the one you are reading in the book, you will get a list of pointers to current information. Another view is the Global Recipe, which we introduce in Chapter 1 and which gives an overview of the steps in establishing an information server. Another traditional view is the index. The corresponding electronic view is to search by keyword.

Why don't we put the whole book on-line and update that? Maybe this will work for future generations, but for now many folks, including us, like the feel of a book in our hands and are comfortable navigating that medium. If you are reading this in the bookstore, or from someone else's copy, at this point you may be thinking: Why buy the book? I'll just jot down the pointer above and read the Web site. You are welcome to do that, of course. However, we think the combination of book and Internet server will provide the most useful and usable information.

You may also be thinking: How will they keep all the pointers to pertinent information and software current? In part, the answer is that you will help us. There is a Reader's Corner accessible on the server for you to report pointers to sites that you think should be included in the cookbook. We will frequently review these suggestions and, if appropriate, add them first to the server, and later to future editions of this book.

Involving the reader in the material they are reading, to the point where they begin to make their own contributions, seems to us a very good use of the Internet. In fact, the Internet has supported many such projects, such as Perl, VRML (the Virtual Reality Modeling Language), and others, not to mention the community of Mac OS shareware developers. The Internet has provided a communication channel between reader and author to enhance the quality and longevity of the book. In other words, the book is "Internet-enhanced."

Acknowledgments

Although it may have seemed so at the start of this endeavor, with the blank computer screen staring us in the face, no book is created completely from scratch. Especially this book, which follows the lead of the original UNIX-oriented *Cookbook for Serving the Internet*. Through their contributions to that book, many people have contributed indirectly, if not directly, to this book.

First of all, we would like to reiterate our thanks to the people who commented on the original UNIX manuscript—Brigitte Carrabin, Mike Gannis, Mike Gribskov, Pamela Puckett, Ilya Shindyalov, and Stephanie Sides. Additional thanks to Ilya Shindyalov, Rich Toscano, and Philippe Youkharibache for many discussions that made their way into the UNIX book. Many of the staff at the San Diego Supercomputer Center (SDSC) provided input, including Nancy Wilkins-Diehr, Aaron von Hungen, Joshua Polterock, Ann Redelfs, and Lynn Ten Eyck.

For the *Mac OS 8 Web Server Cookbook*, we have to thank to those who helped with this new project. Dave would like to thank Phil for publishing the UNIX version and giving him the chance to co-author the Mac version. Phil would like to thank Dave for taking nothing more than Phil's enthusiasm for a Mac version and really making it happen. Many thanks go to Mike Meehan at Prentice Hall for taking a chance with a Mac book during some tough times for Apple and for shepherding the book through the publishing house from proposal to print. Thanks also to the people who contributed their time and effort to reviewing the manuscript—John Knott, Greg Quinn, Chris Smith, Helge Weissig, and David Zimmerman.

Thanks also go out to Steve Jobs and the folks at Apple for turning Apple around after some rocky times. And as much as it pains Dave to say it, some thanks are also due to Bill Gates and Microsoft, whose timely agreement with Apple and $150 million shot in the arm helped convince Prentice Hall to go with this Mac book.

Lastly, we must thank the many people who have contributed to this book and do not even know it. The information behind the many URLs cited in this book required a great deal of time and energy to develop. A special thanks to Jon Wiederspan and his Macintosh Internet Resource Database at *http://host.comvista.com/Internet.tfm*. In many cases we are sure the effort in no way related to the developer's job requirements but was done as a community service. Thanks to you all.

CHAPTER 1

The Global Recipe

Traditional cookbooks don't bother giving you the order in which the different courses of a meal should be served. Eating a sweet dessert after a savory main course seems obvious because it is what we have learned from childhood. On the other hand, the order in which to perform tasks when establishing your information server is far from obvious. You need a Global Recipe that orders the recipes for each course.

This chapter introduces the steps you need to follow for establishing a fully functional Internet information server, and Figure 1–1 summarizes the steps even further. From top to bottom, each box in Figure 1–1 lists a specific step in the process. The numbers in the boxes represent the chapters in which each step is covered. The types of information we will encounter are shown on the left of the boxes and the types of software tools on the right.

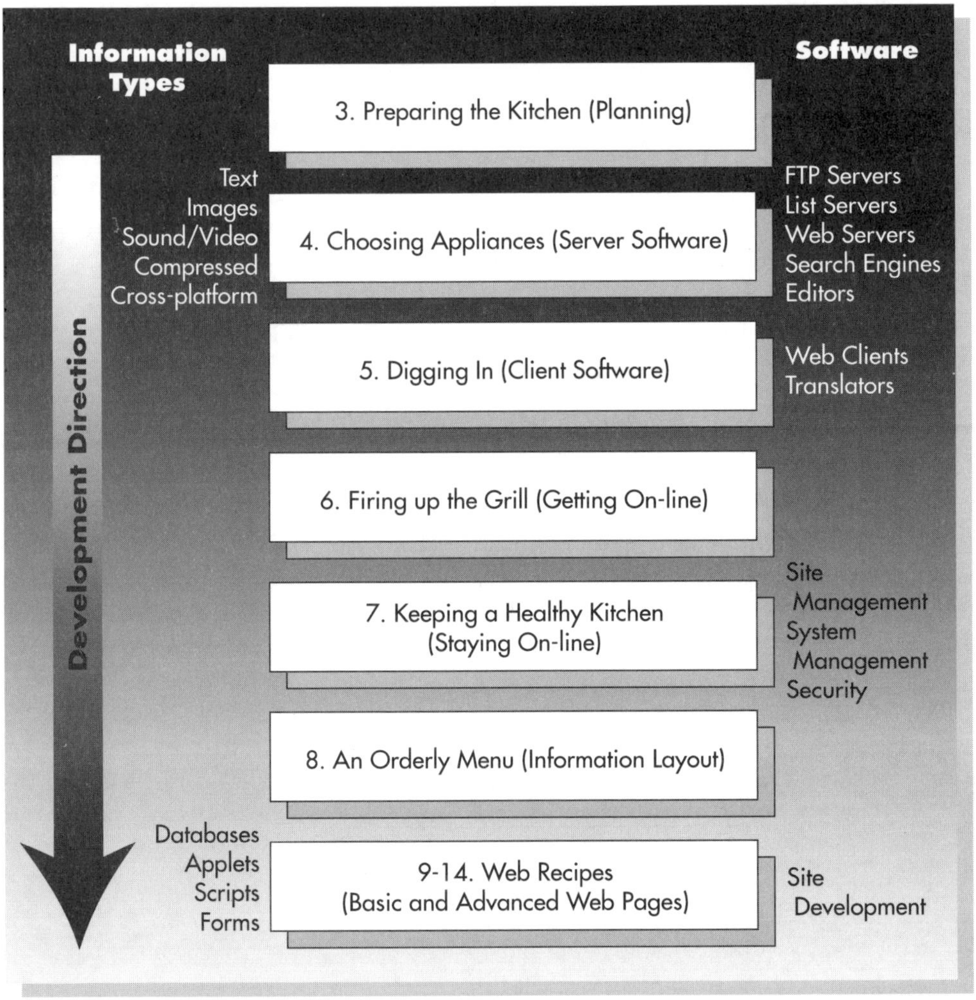

Figure 1-1 The Global Recipe

This book considers the three most common types of Internet information service in use today—anonymous ftp, list servers, and Web services using the http protocol. To reach the widest possible audience, you should support all three types of service, although your needs may be met by one or two.

- *Anonymous ftp* (file transfer protocol) is efficient at file transfer and available to a wide audience.
- A *list server* is a convenient way to broadcast e-mail messages to a list of subscribers who may not have any other service.
- A *Web server* delivers text, graphics, and other multimedia forms as well as supporting more complex interactions between a user and an information server. The server can, for example, perform some complex calculation. *Gopher* is considered to have been superseded by Web services and is not discussed.

We learned the hard way that you should follow the Global Recipe steps in the order given to get the best results when installing and maintaining these services. We recommend that you follow these steps as well. Let's look at the definition of each of these steps.

Chapter 3—Planning. First you have to decide who your audience is and, then, what information you are going to provide to your audience, and how you will provide it. Supporting sound and video, for example, requires additional server software and also will place heavy demands on your server. Planning will help you address these sorts of potential downfalls and make informed software choices from the available programs for each of the servers—ftp, list server, and Web.

A good server with lots of information also provides multiple ways for *finding* information (we call these "entry points"). During the planning process, we shall explore ways of providing useful entry points. The most direct way is providing the equivalent of an index. You will need to decide whether to provide an index and what tools to use to generate, maintain, and browse that index.

By far, the most important piece of planning for an Internet server is getting Internet access. We shall consider briefly how to obtain Internet access if you do not already have access, and how to manage it on your Mac OS machine once you are connected. In planning an information server, you also need to consider the demands it will place on a computer. The most immediate concern is likely to be sufficient disk space to store all the information. If your server becomes popular, you need to ensure that memory, file transfers, network bandwidth, and, to a lesser extent, processor power don't limit the rate at which you can serve information. We shall consider what these demands are and when in the development cycle they are likely to occur.

Chapter 5—Digging In. With the planning done and suitable hardware and software selected, you are ready to start building your information server. First you need to install the client components of all the software for which you will provide the server components. You will be the first to use your server to test whether the server functions as expected and the information is presented the way you want. We briefly discuss installing client software components, including a Web browser such as Netscape Navigator, Internet Explorer, or CyberDog, that you are likely to need. As is true of all discussions in this book, we will make good use of reference material available on the Internet.

Chapter 6—Getting On-line. A basic ftp and list server each require a single piece of software and take a few minutes to set up (plus the time to set up mailing lists and to organize files for transfer). Installing a Web-based server requires one or several pieces of software, depending on the types of information you want to serve.

In this book, we will discuss the options (yes, there are quite a few Mac OS options) from commercial software, shareware, and freeware for each type of server. We will show you how to install and configure NetPresenz, a shareware ftp server. Among list servers, we will cover AutoShare and Macjordomo, popular list servers for Mac OS platforms. We will also install and configure two Web servers, the commercial WebSTAR and the freeware Quid Pro Quo. Finally, you may also want to provide an index to the information on your server. We will show you how to install and configure Phantom and Search-Server, both of which include a gatherer, indexer, and search engine.

Chapter 7—Staying On-line. Running a Web server, from any computer, requires that you practice safe computing. For the most part, this involves the same tasks that you already know you *should* be doing for your computer— backups, disk management, security, and virus protection, for example—but that you've been putting off. Particularly if you're running a commercial site for your business, you *need* to start doing them. Other tasks include gathering access statistics, anticipating future needs, and monitoring error logs and usage of system resources. We will cover some of the available tools to help you with these jobs.

Chapter 8—Organizing the Menu. How you organize the various types of information on your server becomes important as the amount of information grows. The tricks are to (a) avoid duplication, (b) provide easy file retrieval, and (c) provide a suitable path for growth as your Internet server evolves. Yes, this requires more planning. (Sound familiar?)

This is perhaps the most critical part of the whole book! How you organize the information so it is accessible, readable, useful, and easily maintainable is paramount. Anyone can provide a server with little effort—even if it doesn't appear so from what we've said so far; however, the usability and value to the intended audience of the server require work.

Chapters 9–14—Web Recipes. Creating the information you want to serve could take a couple of hours to several months, depending on the complexity of the information being served. For this step, you need a different set of tools. For basic Web pages, you might choose to use SimpleText to write HTML files from scratch or use HTML and graphics editors and format converters to turn existing documents into HTML. If you are going to provide sound and video, you will need tools for producing, editing, and browsing these formats.

Servers range from support of simple text and graphics pages with limited links to a large server that joins a hybrid of databases and various file types. We will cover the latest in Web technology, including clickable maps, server-side includes, Java applets, and HTML frames. We will dissect information organization on a couple of real and imaginary servers to see what makes them tick.

Epilogue—Internet information servers involve rapidly changing technology and you need to keep abreast of developments that may affect your server. We will point you to some interesting sources of information on these developments, and, of course, give you some thoughts of our own.

CHAPTER 2

The Ingredients (Introduction)

Ingredients

- The Mac OS
- The Internet and intranets
- How to behave—the canon of conduct
- Clients and servers
- Basic cooking tools

From the Global Recipe you now have a basic idea of what you will be able to cook using this cookbook. It is now time to get to know your kitchen a little better, a prerequisite to cooking and serving a fine meal.

2.1 The Mac OS

Even though you're already using a Macintosh or Mac OS clone, a few words about the Mac OS as an Internet server are in order. If you are wondering if a Mac can handle the Internet—or need to convince someone else that it can—this section will give you some reasons to go with Mac. We'll also discuss the various Mac OS versions and the use of Macs in a mixed-platform environment (and why a Mac server might be the best choice).

2.1.1 Why Use a Mac?

There are any number of reasons to use a Mac to serve the Internet. First and foremost, if you are a Mac user already, it doesn't make much sense to learn the ins and outs of Windows or UNIX—a chore that some people spend years learning—just to run an Internet server. In the Windows and UNIX world, these people are called "system administrators." A Mac office might need a network administrator, who typically can support far more computers than his or her UNIX or Windows counterparts, but if you can add or remove system extensions and adjust a control panel, you've already mastered the skills of a Mac "administrator." With a Mac, serving the Internet is really not much different than running your word processor or desktop publishing software.

2.1.1.1 The Mac OS Advantage

For those of you that need more convincing, Table 2–1 provides a list of URLs where you can find more reasons to use a Mac as your Internet server. A 1997 Georgia Tech survey found that the number of Mac servers may far outstrip (because of how the survey was conducted, we can only say "may") the reported Macintosh market share; the survey showed nearly 20 percent of respondents used Mac servers. (There were more Mac servers than Windows NT servers.) And for developing Web sites, Macs hold a 64 percent market share among U.S.-based professional Web-site design firms, according to the October 1996 *Web Week Magazine.*

Table 2-1 The Mac OS Advantage

Location	Description
http://applenet.apple.com/text/server_study.html	Independent study by the Business Research Group
http://w.avaloncity.com/MacToday/MacJack/Factpg.html	Mac Today's Mac Facts page
http://www2.apple.com/whymac/advantage.html	Apple's 75 Mac Advantages
http://www.evangelist.macaddict.com/-market_internet.html	Mac EvangeList Internet Advantages
http://www.jointsolutions.com/mis/mis.html	A marketing firm's reasons for using Mac servers.
http://www.dol.net/~Ragosta/complmac.htm	The Complete Macintosh
http://www4.zdnet.com/pccomp/features/fea0797/nt/	"NT Lies"
http://www.mackido.com/Reference/MacOrNT.html	MaKiDo's Mac/NT Comparison
http://www.cc.gatech.edu/gvu/user_surveys/-survey-1997-10/graphs/webmaster/Which_Server.html	Georgia Tech Internet Survey

Because maintaining an Internet server requires effort above and beyond that required in normal desktop operation, the Mac's ease of use and ease of maintenance also provide a distinct advantage. A 1995 study by the consulting firm Norris and Wong Associates found that Windows 95 users can "expect system maintenance to be a more complex, costly and painful process than will be experienced by Macintosh users." Macintosh "plug and play" capabilities, compared to Windows "plug and pray," make it easier to add new components.

Mac OS systems also have the lowest initial costs, installation costs, content creation costs per page, server management costs, and training costs, according to a June 1997 study by the Business Research Group.

In addition to easier troubleshooting and recovery from system failures, Mac OS systems are also more secure Internet servers. Several companies and organizations have offered widely publicized Internet hacking challenges, with rewards of $10,000 or more to the hacker who could break into a Mac Internet server (Table 2–2). You don't see too many Windows or UNIX Web sites *daring* people to break in. Only one such Mac server, the second Crack-a-Mac challenge, was successfully broken into. The security loophole was in the server's Common Gateway Interface (CGI) software and the company that produced the CGI software released a patch for the loophole within 24 hours and paid the hacking prize.

Table 2-2 Mac Internet Hacking Challenges

Location	Description
http://hacke.infinit.se/resumeng.html	Crack-a-Mac Challenge
http://www.vanhacking.com/index.html	The Van Hacking Challenge
http://www.digitalforest.net/advanced/-securitychallenge.html	Digital Forest Hacking Challenge

2.1.2 Which Mac OS Version?

Although Mac OS 8 is the most current version of the Mac operating system, you might still find copies of versions 7.5.5 or 7.6 on the shelves, depending on where you shop. Chances are you'll buy the latest version, but version 8 isn't compatible with some older Macs. So if you want to use your Mac IIsi as a Web server—which you can do—you'll have to stick with version 7.6. (While you might turn your trusty IIsi into a Web server, see Section 3.4 for some hardware recommendations.)

Unlike the radical underlying differences between Windows 3.1, Windows 95, and Windows NT, the various Mac versions have more in common than not. However, Mac OS 8 does have nice features for Internet users, including Personal Web Sharing (see Section 2.1.3). In this book, we'll assume that you're using Mac OS 8 to set up your Internet server, and try to point out where the version 7 systems are different.

2.1.3 Personal Web Sharing

By far, the fastest way to get your Mac on the Web—though not necessarily the most efficient or most flexible way—is through software that comes with Mac OS 8 called Personal Web Sharing (PWS). *Although it comes packaged with Mac OS 8, Personal Web Sharing can be purchased separately and will work with Mac OS 7.5.3 and later versions.*

Personal Web Sharing works much the same way as File Sharing on AppleTalk networks. However, instead of using the Chooser to access shared folders on other Macs, anyone can use a Web browser to access a shared Web folder (which may also be shared through File Sharing) on your Mac, as long as it has an Internet address (see Chapter 3).

If you've already installed Mac OS 8 and have an Internet address, the Mac Setup Assistant probably helped you set up Web Sharing, but for the record, here are the steps:

- Open the Control Panels folder, and open the Web Sharing control panel—or use the Apple menu to select Web Sharing from the control panels.
- Click the first "Select..." button to choose the folder you want shared over the Web.
- Click the second "Select..." button to choose a default home page. If you don't choose a home page, the Mac displays the contents of the Web-shared folder as a clickable list of files to download.
- Click "Start." You can also choose whether to give everyone read-only access or use the File Sharing and Users & Groups control panels to limit access.

You may not want to run your company's Web server through Personal Web Sharing (PWS) for various reasons. For example, PWS does not allow you to restrict access based on IP address, although you can restrict access to certain individuals with Apple File Sharing. But it is a quick way to get started, share files on an intranet, or let a colleague (or perhaps your mom) look at Web pages in progress. If you don't have Mac OS 8, you can download the commercial release of PWS from *http://www.software.net*.

2.1.4 What about Rhapsody?

Beyond Mac OS 8, however, Apple's operating system strategy can seem a little complicated. In parallel with the continued development of the Mac OS you know and love, Apple has announced plans for a new, industrial-strength operating system, code-named Rhapsody. You might be wondering whether to wait for Rhapsody before starting your Mac Internet server. We don't claim to have an inside scoop on the technical details of Rhapsody. From what we've heard, Rhapsody will be a very impressive operating system if it lives up to its many claims, particularly the cross-platform promises. Because Rhapsody is being built on an existing operating system, NeXT's OpenStep (formerly NextStep), there seems good reason to believe it will work.

However, there is one reason not to wait for Rhapsody: the wait. According to Apple's timetable, Rhapsody will not ship until the middle of 1998 or later, and even then Rhapsody-native application software may not yet be widely available.

In the rapidly changing world of the Web, the wait could be a lifetime, particularly if it's your business's Web presence. Section 14.1 discusses the future of the Mac OS in a little more detail.

2.1.5 Macs in Mixed-Platform Environments

The advantages that Macs have over Windows and UNIX systems suggest that Macs should be considered as Internet servers whether your network is Mac-only or a mixture of Macs, PCs, and UNIX workstations. There is certainly no reason not to at least consider using a Mac to serve the Internet.

In addition to handling all of the data formats on the Web (see Section 3.3), Macs offer an additional advantage in their ability to handle file types from multiple platforms. The Mac OS can read and write files from PC disks and download from the Internet and read many UNIX and Windows files. In addition, the Mac can save files in formats readable by other platforms. Translation software for the Mac simplifies the task of passing information from any platform to your Web server.

2.2 Internet Ingredients

Since we've already shown you how to start serving Web pages with Apple's Personal Web Sharing software, now would be a good time to introduce you to the Internet. If you have been using the Internet for some time, that is, you have been downloading files via ftp, sending mail, or surfing the Web, then much of this may be familiar. At the very least we urge you to read the Canon of Conduct (Section 2.2.3), so that we may all continue to use the Internet in a community-minded way.

2.2.1 Internet versus Intranet

The Internet. Attempting to answer the question, "What is the Internet?" leads to a variety of detailed discussions, some technical, some philosophical. You can find examples of these discussions at the URLs in Table 2–3.

For our purposes, it is enough to know that the Internet is a conglomeration of computer networks. While size, accessibility, management, and so on are all variables within these networks, the one thing they share is a common set of protocols, namely *TCP/IP*, the Transmission Control Protocol/Internet Protocol. Without getting technical, this means these networks all communicate with each other, creating a vast global network, and can put a user on any Internet computer in contact with the information and resources on your soon-to-be-established Internet server. Worldwide accessibility to vast quantities of information at very low cost has the potential to change the dynamics of our society—government, education, commerce, and so on. That change has begun, and you will soon be contributing to that change.

Table 2-3 The History of the Internet

Location	Description
http://www.yahoo.com/Computers_and_Internet/History/	A definitive list of sites.
http://www.isoc.org/	Detailed discussion of Internet philosophy.
http://www.baylor.edu/baylor/Misc/timeline	Time line of Internet history, including growth patterns.

Intranets. The term "intranet" has come into vogue lately as people realized that the same technology that enabled information sharing on the Internet could be used to share information within an organization, whether that organization is a few offices, an entire building, or the distributed facilities of a multinational corporation. In essence, an intranet is a private section of the Internet, accessible by only the intended audience.

Your office's AppleTalk network, then, is an example of an intranet without the Web interface. Larger intranets can also be created with commercial Web server software by, for example, refusing access to users based on their Internet address or protecting a network with passwords. In describing available Internet server software for the Mac OS, we will indicate those that allow you to establish an intranet.

2.2.2 Serving the Internet

If you are interested in using and serving the Internet, you are not alone. Consider the following statistics from the past few years and what these statistics imply (indicated in bold).

- There were more than 29,600,000 Internet hosts, up from 213 in August 1981, according to the January 1998 Network Wizards Internet Domain Survey.
- As of January 1997, 194 countries had joined the Internet, according to Matrix Information and Directory Services. About 80 percent of the world's countries have at least one Internet domain.
- The April 1998 Netcraft Web Server Survey counted 2,215,195 sites, up from 18,957 hosts in July 1995.

  The growth of the Internet is phenomenal.
- More than 27 percent of Internet hosts were registered in .com as of January 1998, according to Network Wizards, compared to the 13 percent registered in the .edu domain.

  The Internet is no longer restricted to universities and other nonprofit institutions but is driven by economic factors and open competition.
- In a 1997 Georgia Tech Web survey, 84 percent of the respondents reported that they consider access to the Web indispensable, nearly the same percentage as those who feel e-mail is indispensable.

- Date of the first known Internet message sent by a head of state: March 2, 1993, by President Bill Clinton.

  The Internet has become as much an accepted form of communication as radio and TV.

- Round-trip time from Colorado to McMurdo, Antarctica: 640 milliseconds; number of hops: 18.

  The Internet is an inexpensive, fast, and global form of communication.

These numbers illustrate the amazing growth of the Internet—perhaps faster than anything in history—as well as its rapid, versatile, and commercial nature. The sources of these and more statistics, including a variety of graphical representations, are given in Table 2–4.

Table 2-4 Sources of Internet Statistics

Source	Description
http://www.yahoo.com/Computers_and_Internet/-Internet/Statistics_and_Demographics/	The definitive starting point for finding statistical information.
http://www.nw.com/zone/WWW/top.html	Network Wizards Internet Domain Survey.
http://www.netcraft.com/Survey/	Netcraft Web Server Survey.
http://www.gvu.gatech.edu/user_surveys/	Georgia Tech's Graphic, Visualization & Usability Center's WWW User Surveys.
http://www4.mids.org/mmq/	Matrix Information and Directory Services, Inc.
http://www.anamorph.com/docs/stats/stats.html	A fun site that speculates on the number of Web sites at any given point in time.

One statistic that the last of these sources provides is that Web usage alone is doubling every 10 weeks and the number of servers as of January 1, 1996, was 1.7 million, or one server for every 3,600 people on the planet. This growth rate is likely to accelerate as telephone companies, cable TV companies, and other communications companies become more active in providing Internet services and make it easier to serve the Internet for those who are less computer- and communications-literate. Everyone will be able to serve on the Internet.

2.2.3 Canon of Conduct

It is *people* who make valuable information available on the Internet. The technology is simply the vehicle that makes it happen; hence, the Internet is about people, what they contribute, and how they behave. We would be negligent in our duty if we did not discuss the generally accepted "Canon of Conduct" for operating an information server. Like most issues relating to the Internet, there are no official policies, just an honest and common-sense way to behave that makes sense to a community. There are so-called Acceptable User Policies (AUPs), which can be accessed at

ftp://nic.merit.edu/michnet/policies/acceptable.use.policy.html

Following is our own interpretation for how to behave; parts may be covered by law in various countries. This interpretation is sure to contain shortcomings and omissions, but does provide the general idea we want to get across.

1. Information on an Internet server should be considered a form of publication and should be governed by the same rules that govern good publications—no lies, no misleading statements.
2. Do not make available copyrighted information and software without permission from the creator or creators. It is advisable to have written confirmation.
3. Properly protect information you want accessed only by specific groups of people. Do not lead others into temptation.
4. Do not make available any information that is offensive to a subset of the community. If you feel strongly that the information should be available, include a warning that the information may be offensive to some people.
5. Do not attempt to profit from the Internet, unless it is clear that this is what you are doing (a fine line). A good analogy are those bits of junk postal mail which come disguised as checks or bills in an effort to make you open and read them.
6. Strive to make the information the best it can be—comprehensive but easily navigated and understood. Above all, keep it current.

If we all obey these simple rules the Internet will continue to be a wonderful place to work and play.

2.2.4 Internet Addresses

(If you are familiar with concepts like IP addresses and name servers, then you might want to skip this section.)

As we have mentioned, the conglomeration of individually managed computer networks that comprise the Internet share only one feature: They all support TCP/IP—the Transmission Control Protocol and Internet Protocol. For our purposes, it is enough to know that computers that support TCP/IP

(a) are able to communicate,

(b) are potentially able to recognize each other,

(c) are capable of making decisions about how to route information to each other, and

(d) support other protocols that are used by the Web and other information sharing tools.

Item (b) requires a little more explanation at this point, since it covers the basics of addresses—the feature that makes each computer unique—and name resolution. Each TCP/IP-based host has a unique address referred to as an *IP address*. This is of the form `nnn.nnn.nnn.nnn` where `nnn` is a number in the range 0-255 (a byte of information) with certain integers reserved, notably 0 and 255. In simple terms and with numerous exceptions, the first integer of the four-integer address defines the network, the second integer the institution, the third the department or division, and the fourth the individual computer. Since it is simpler for a human to remember words rather than numbers, the four-integer address maps to a name; for example, common Web addresses map to *www.company.com*. This mapping of integer addresses to names is called *name resolution*, and a computer (or program) that performs the resolution is a *name server*.

Since each computer on the Internet must have a unique address, *you cannot arbitrarily assign an address to a machine that is attached to a public network.* Section 3.5.2 discusses how to get an Internet IP address.

The name is usually defined in the reverse order to the number, that is, of the form

```
computer.division.institution.domain
```

or

```
computer.institution.domain
```

While you might be able to maintain on your Internet server a short list of local or popular host addresses and corresponding names, there's no way you could maintain the mapping for *all* the hosts on the Internet. Luckily, you don't have to. Mapping is handled transparently through a hierarchy of Internet servers, called *Domain Name Servers* (DNSs), or name servers for short. A name server's primary function is to dynamically maintain tables that map host names to address numbers.

So, when you enter a host name, for example, to access a Web site with your Web browser, your local name server searches its table for that name and corresponding address. If that mapping is not found, the computer will contact a designated name server. If that name server does not have the mapping, it will contact yet another name server higher in the hierarchy until the name is resolved and the information passed back to the requester. Section 3.5 discusses how you determine whether your server's Internet connection and name server are functioning correctly. Table 2–5 contains useful sources of more detailed information on name servers.

Table 2-5 Understanding Domain Name Services

Location	Description
http://oac3.hsc.uth.tmc.edu/staff/snewton/tcp-tutorial/-sec5.html	Brief introduction.
http://eeunix.ee.usm.maine.edu/guides/dns/dns.html	Comprehensive and easy to follow tutorial.
http://www.dns.net/dnsrd/	DNS Resources Directory.
http://www.yahoo.com/Computers_and_Internet/-Information_and_Documentation/Protocols/DNS/	Links to DNS information.

The Mac OS provides a TCP/IP Control Panel that handles most of these details for you. The control panel lets you specify how your computer is connected, your IP address, your first choice of name server, and other information (subnet mask and router address) for dealing with outgoing and incoming Internet requests (see Section 3.5.4).

Different Internet services use name-based addresses that extend the basic IP address scheme. Table 2–6 summarizes the basic address types by example. As we shall see, most of these addresses are used by Web browsers. They serve us humans as a guide for recognizing different types of information as it is found on the Internet. Several of these address types—http, ftp, telnet, and gopher—define protocols that are part of, or layered on top of, the *TCP/IP protocol stack*.

Table 2-6 Types of Internet Addresses

Address	Description
pauline.sdsc.edu	A specific Internet host.
bourne@pauline.sdsc.edu	A user's e-mail address at a specific Internet host.
bourne@sdsc.edu	A user's e-mail address defined uniquely in a subdomain (the most convenient form of mail address).
http://www.sdsc.edu/	The simplest form of Uniform Resource Locator (URL) for accessing a Web page using the http protocol. The Web server at the host www.sdsc.edu will serve a default file.
http://www.sdsc.edu:70/	As above, but on a specific port number, in this instance 70. The default port number for http is 80.
ftp://rosebud.sdsc.edu/pub/	An ftp archive accessed from a Web browser using a URL.
telnet://info.cern.ch/	A telnet session started from a URL.
gopher://gopher.micro.umn.edu/	A gopher site URL.
mailto:bourne@sdsc.edu	A mail address invoked as an HTML hyperlink.
news:comp.infosystems.www.providers	A news group invoked as an HTML hyperlink.

2.2.5 Server Access

The next question to answer is, what happens on the information server when, for example, a Web browser requests access to information using one of the addresses shown in Table 2–6? That's where your ftp server, Web server, or list server software come in. If the software isn't running—surprise!—nothing happens. If the program (or programs) is running, it receives incoming requests and performs the appropriate action—returning a Web page, transferring a file, or forwarding a message to a mailing list.

The number of possible requests raises some interesting points that we shall come back to later in the book. First, your system has finite resources—there is a limit on how many requests you can support. You may have already run into this situation in your ftp access: A popular server refused to let you in because of the large number of existing connections. If you are lucky enough to have your server become that popular, most software lets you control the number of simultaneous requests for a given service.

If you were expecting a long tutorial on configuration files, Internet daemons, and other such esoterica of the Windows or UNIX worlds, we're sorry to disappoint you. But if you wanted to serve information on the Internet, you're well on your way.

2.2.6 "Content"

There is one last Internet ingredient that deserves a quick mention, along with our preliminary discussion of the Internet and intranets, host names and addresses, TCP/IP, servers, and DNS. All these elements combine to enable you and the world to shuffle around heaps of information—so-called Internet "content."

How the Internet handles the many types of "content" will be discussed later in Section 3.2, for starters. But one of the authors (Dave) felt the need to explain why you won't be seeing the term "content" too much in this book. Take it away, Dave.

"Content" is a euphemism that is used mainly to describe "stuff at a Web site," as if every bit were created equal by virtue of being a zero or one. Before the Web, you rarely heard the word "content" to describe the information in newspapers or even television. Newspapers have stories, photographs, ads, and comics. TV has dramas, sitcoms, news, and commercials. Just because the diverse elements are all produced with paper and ink (in the newspaper) or electrons streaming through a vacuum tube (on television), they do not become equivalent or interchangeable—particularly in the crucial creation phase. Picture a city news desk at your local paper trying to produce a zany network sitcom.

The term "information" is admittedly not much better. Where possible, I will be as specific as possible about the type of information being presented on your Internet server. And I will revisit this issue when we encounter the term "authoring" in Section 9.1.

2.3 The Internet Restaurant (Client-Server Interaction)

In this section, we will introduce the types of tools we will discuss throughout this book. These tools can be summarized as follows.

Server Tools:

- ftp server
- list server
- Web server
- search engine

Client Tools:

- ftp software
- e-mail
- Web browsers
- news readers
- Internet chat

Information "Cooking" Tools:

- basic editing tools and format converters
- advanced development tools for WYSIWYG (What-You-See-Is-What-You-Get) Web page creation and programming
- maintenance tools

2.3.1 Clients and Servers

Let's take a step back and define what we mean by the terms "client" and "server." *Client-server computing* is a much used and much abused term. At the risk of adding to the abuse, let us ask you to consider the simple-minded definition used throughout this book. A *client* makes a request of a *server* for a particular resource, which the server dutifully provides to the client—subject to any security and resource constraints. That resource could be information or computer resources. We use the term "client" interchangeably for the software making the request, such as a Web browser, and the computer from which the request was made. The same is true for the term "server."

A simple example is a client Web browser requesting information from a server containing HTML-based documents. Figure 2–1 illustrates the basics of client-server in this scenario.

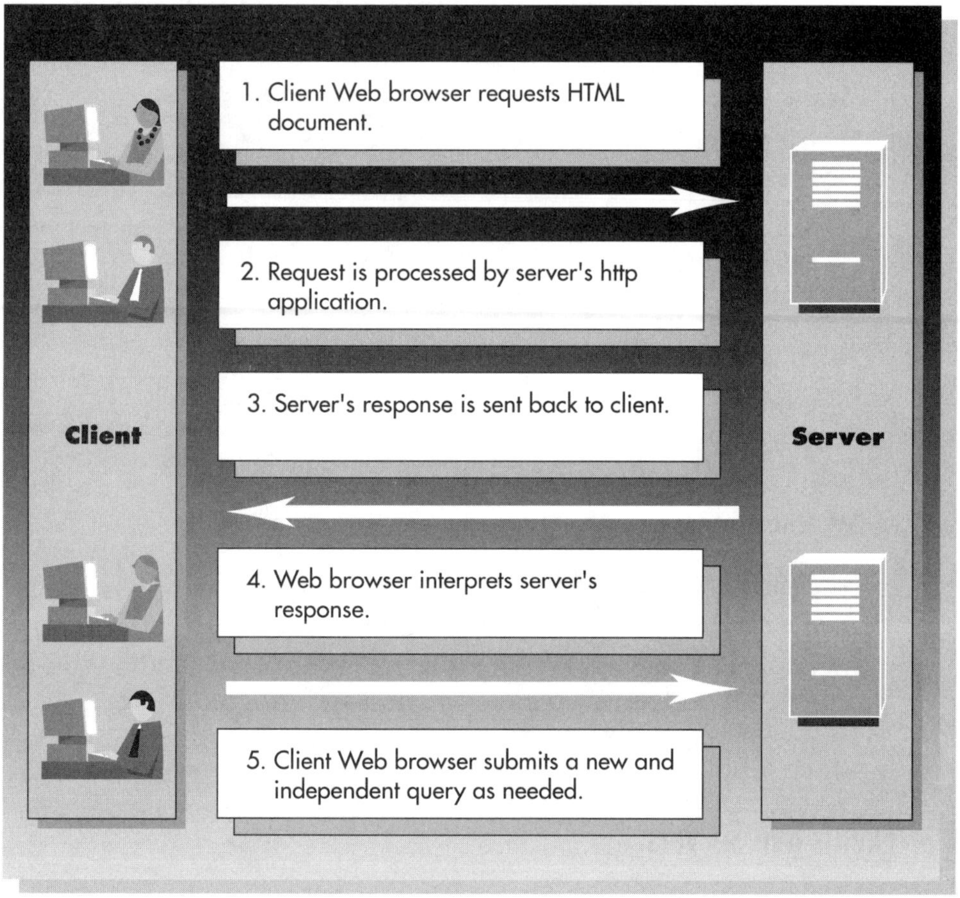

Figure 2-1 Client-Server Architecture Made Simple

The key here is what types of information the server can deliver. As we shall see, server software can variously serve text, images, sound, video, and methods (code to perform specific tasks on the client).

2.3.1.1 E-mail as an Example

Purists may not consider the sending of e-mail a client-server activity, but it does illustrate the interaction between a sender (in this case, the server) and the receiver (in this case, the client). Besides, given the importance placed on e-mail services in this book, it does not hurt to have some background information on how e-mail functions. Here is the recipe:

- A Mail User Agent (MUA)—this would be your e-mail software—is used to compose the message on the server (the computer serving the e-mail message to a remote user). The same MUA is used to read incoming messages (at which time the computer is acting as a client). Some popular commercial MUAs for Macs are Eudora Pro and Claris E-mailer, which are described in Table 2–7.

Table 2-7 Examples of Mail User Agents (MUAs)

Location	Description
http://www.eudora.com	Eudora Pro from Qualcomm
http://www.apple.com/products/claris	Claris E-mailer and E-mailer Lite from Apple's Claris software house

- The MUA passes the message and the so-called envelope data (header information containing sender, recipient, etc.) to a Mail Transfer Agent (MTA) on the server.
- The MTA will contact the MTA of the remote client for transfer. Having passed the message to the client MTA, the server MTA disconnects.
- The client MTA delivers the message to the addressee, and it is then up to the user on the client to read the message using his or her own favorite MUA.
- If the client MTA does not respond, typically you will get a warning message that your server will continue to try to send the message

over the next three to five days. If after that period the message was not delivered, you will get the message back along with a transcript of the session showing the efforts to send the message.

It should be obvious from this discussion of how e-mail works that it is easy to confuse which is the client and which is the server. Often a computer (and a piece of software for that matter) can be both the client and the server. We will try to make the distinction as clear as possible as we work through the recipes in this book. In this example, a mail message is being served to a user on a remote client. However, as we shall see in our discussion of list servers, an e-mail message may be sent to a special server from which it is broadcast to a number of client users.

2.3.2 Internet Serving

We have encountered in passing most of the concepts behind Internet servers, but we will summarize them again here.

2.3.2.1 FTP Server

File transfer protocol (ftp), which originated on UNIX systems, is used to transfer files back and forth between client and server. An ftp server responds to ftp requests, which allow you to exchange files in any format between any platform that supports ftp, which is most of them. Apart from all UNIX platforms, ftp is available on most operating systems, including Mac OS, DOS, Windows NT, Windows 3.1, Windows 95, OpenVMS, and OS/2. With an ftp service, a Mac can store and distribute compressed data files, Windows documents, or UNIX programs, since the server itself need not be able to interpret the file content.

2.3.2.2 List Server

If your goal is to reach a worldwide audience, the value of electronic mail services should not be underestimated, even with the explosion in graphics-oriented information services. This point is underscored in Section 3.2.2 when we plan the services that your Internet server will support. For now, let's consider the two major kinds of mail services:

- Information Service: user A ⇒ server ⇒ user A
- List Service: user ⇒ server ⇒ list of subscribers

An *information service* lets a user send an e-mail message to the server, whereupon some automated and predefined response is made based on the contents of that e-mail message. This is useful, for example, in automatically distributing information about a specific product or program. A typical scenario might be that a user sends a message containing the one word "HELP." The information server responds by returning an itemized summary of all available information. This works fine for small amounts of ASCII text, but is not the best way to transmit large executable files, graphics images, sound files, and so on.

Another use of an information service is to get files that are accessible by ftp, even when the user does not have access to ftp, but only mail. In this case the body of the mail message contains the ftp commands necessary to connect to the remote ftp site and download the files. This is not discussed further in this book.

In a *list service,* a user sends an e-mail message to a list server, which then broadcasts that message to anyone who has registered their interest in that topic, that is, subscribers to the list. This service can be automatic or *moderated*. A moderated list means that someone, the moderator, decides whether a particular message should be broadcast to subscribers. This prevents the wide distribution of irrelevant or offensive messages.

2.3.2.3 Web Server

As stated earlier, a Web server responds to requests sent via the hypertext transfer protocol (http). Unlike ftp, however, clients—usually Web browsers—try to display or execute the data in files sent by http. Thus, Web files are generally platform independent and can be served to any client that is running the appropriate software. A substantial portion of the rest of this book is devoted to serving many types of information on the Web.

2.3.2.4 Search Engines

One server application we have not yet covered becomes more important as the amount of information on your server grows. However good you are at organizing your server, it will still become difficult for users to find what they are looking for. At that point, it is desirable to provide them with a way of searching—based on words or phrases—all or part of your server. The software for this purpose is referred to as a search engine. We will explore the features to look for in a search engine, and Section 4.4 provides links to several search engines for Mac Internet servers. In Section 6.4, we discuss how to download, install, and configure Phantom and SearchServer. For now, consider a little history on the subject.

The World Area Information Server (WAIS) was arguably the first network-based, information-gathering resource and was developed by Brewster Kahle at Thinking Machines Corporation as a client-server text searching tool. This text searching capability, used in conjunction with the more powerful browsing tools, is popular at the moment. The key idea in searching arbitrary text reduces the search time for text strings by formatting the text in a way that facilitates searching, in short, indexing the text for quick retrieval of specific words and their location on the information server.

2.3.3 Internet Dining (Clients)

Each of the server activities and tools covered in the previous section has a corresponding client-side tool.

2.3.3.1 File Transfer with FTP

A number of Mac programs allow Mac users to swap files with ftp. Using ftp requires access to both the server computer providing the file or files and the client computer receiving the files. To get files from ftp servers on which you do not have an account, *anonymous ftp* allows you to log in to the remote machine with a login name of "anonymous" and a password of "guest." your e-mail address, or some other password specified by the remote anonymous ftp program. Anonymous ftp is similar to accessing files on an AppleTalk network and using the Chooser to connect to another Mac as a "Guest."

2.3.3.2 E-mail Services

You access a list server—often written as "list server" or "listserv," the latter being taken from the name of a program (L-Soft's LISTSERV®) that provides list services—using your favorite e-mail software. From the client's perspective, a list server is simply another user, albeit one that automatically distributes your messages to it onto a mailing list of subscribers. You also send the list server, among other things, your requests to subscribe to or unsubscribe from mailing lists.

2.3.3.3 Web Browsers

For our purposes, consider a Web browser to be software on the client that can make connections to Web servers and receive information in return. Given this simple definition, we identify two classes of browser: text-oriented and graphical. The former is of interest to Mac users mainly, but not entirely, from a historical perspective, while the latter represents the current generation of Web clients.

Text-oriented Browsers. In the Mac world, text-oriented browsers may seem an anachronism since the Mac has never used a text-based interface. However, the MacLynx browser provides this type of interface, and we discuss why this would be useful for certain Mac users in Section 4.6.1.

Gopher, a now obsolete Internet service, illustrates a text-oriented browser. We mention gopher simply to give you the complete picture of the available tools and to indicate its role in the history of serving the Internet. Gopher opened the eyes of the world to the potential of information serving on the Internet and popularized the idea of transparent network links between documents. All graphical Web browsers can access any remaining Internet gopher servers that have not yet been converted to Web servers. There will be no further discussion of gopher in this book.

Graphical Web Browsers. Graphical Web browsers, which support graphics, sound, video, and application programs, have captured our imagination. The price you pay as a viewer is the time it takes the graphics to download. We will say much more about this as we begin designing Web documents.

NCSA Mosaic, developed at the National Center for Supercomputing Applications (NCSA), was the first popular graphical Web browser and was responsible for shifting the Internet revolution into high gear. Netscape Navigator, from Netscape Communications, Inc., evolved out of Mosaic and grew to be the dominant Web browser in a few months. From a client user's perspective, Netscape was faster because of its caching mechanism—Navigator stores recent files on the client's machine and saves time by using these copies rather than getting the originals over the network—and had a few desirable features missing from Mosaic, such as graphical interfaces for accessing e-mail, maintaining bookmarks, configuring helper applications, and others. On the other hand, Mosaic use persisted since Mosaic had better multilanguage support, Mosaic was free, and source code was available. Hence, Mosaic could be compiled and used on platforms for which Netscape was not available. Netscape, until recently, has been a commercial product and required a license; as a result of the "browser war" with Microsoft's Internet Explorer, Navigator is free and source code is available.

In Section 5.1, we will highlight *all* the important features to look for in a browser and where to go on the Internet to find more information, including who is using what browser.

Through plug-ins and programming languages, graphical browsers can support not only browsing 2-D graphics, but also navigating 3-D "worlds" and running Web-served software on the client. In 3-D worlds, you can zoom into and out of the screen, pick up and move objects, and so on, as if you were actually there. The Virtual Reality Modeling Language (VRML) is the language recognized by these browsers, and what they promise is nothing short of astounding. We do not discuss this technology in detail in this book, but we include pointers to more information in Section 4.6.1.

"Compute-capable" browsers can download pieces of code from the server and execute them on the client. Java (Chapter 12) is the programming language that provides these pieces of code, called *applets*—little applications. Unlike helper applications and plug-ins, which reside on the client and are invoked as needed, applets reside on the server and are downloaded as needed.

2.3.3.4 News

Internet news groups were, along with list servers, one of the first ways for individuals with a common interest to exchange information. They are still often referred to as USENET news groups, since they originated on the USENET network, which connected colleges and universities across the United States. News groups remain a popular way to exchange information; messages are posted to an electronic "bulletin board" for those with similar interests. Today there are thousands of available news groups. Web browsers have special facilities for handling news, but many dedicated news reader applications provide much more versatile interfaces to newsgroups.

2.3.3.5 Chat

"Chatting" is a more recent Internet development, most notable, if you watch too many TV tabloids, for men masquerading on-line as women (or vice versa) and enabling lecherous older men to seduce impressionable younger women. But many legitimate conversations also take place. Celebrities now regularly make appearances in Internet chat rooms, for example. Chat software allows participants to communicate in real time, through text-based conversations.

2.3.4 Internet Cooking

If you are going to cook up an Internet (or intranet) server, you need to create information to serve. For ftp, you can serve files created by any software package. For a list server, simple text editing tools or the list server software itself let you create and edit mailing lists. Our main concern for serving information, then, is creating Web-ready information.

2.3.4.1 Basic Development Tools

HTML Editors. If the information does not already exist, it must be created in a form usable by clients. This refers primarily to HTML, which is understood by Web browsers. Good tools exist for creating and editing HTML even though it can also be edited using a text editor. Some of these tools, and places to go to get a current list of tools, are discussed in Section 4.7.1.

Image Editors. Much Web information also involves the use of images. While many images can be obtained from the Internet—within the bounds set by copyright—you will most likely wish to create images of your own. For creating Web images, Macs quite simply rule. The tools that made Macs the platform of choice for professional designers have all been upgraded to provide varying degrees of support for the Web.

Format Converters. The information that you make available through your Internet information server may already exist in a variety of formats, such as word processing documents or spreadsheets. It will need to be converted to a form that can be interpreted by Internet clients. Section 4.7.3 introduces a variety of conversion programs.

2.3.4.2 Advanced Development Tools

WYSIWYG Tools. While originally the only option for creating Web pages was to buckle down and learn the *HyperText Markup Language (HTML)*, today there are many programs that can create Web-ready HTML files with a "what-you-see-is-what-you-get" interface, in much the same way that word processors virtually eliminated text formatting languages and editors. (If you don't remember the Time Before *WYSIWYG*, consider yourself lucky.) For creating splashy graphical Web pages, even more tools are available for creating Web pages with animations, interactivity, and other multimedia features. Section 4.7.1 covers some advanced Web creation tools.

Programming Tools. The most sophisticated Internet information servers require that you undertake some programming tasks. While these may be performed in a variety of computer languages, the languages Perl and Java are the most commonly used, Perl because it is good at string manipulation and Java because it was developed specifically for Internet use. String manipulation is important in having the server interpret information that is sent from clients (Chapter 11) and Java is important in developing distributed computing (Chapter 12).

2.3.4.3 Site Maintenance

Other tools are available to keep track of the pages and links on your Web site, manage the organization of information, and keep your server performing at its best. Chapter 7 discusses many of these types of tools.

By now you should have a sense of scope for all the issues you need to consider in setting up an Internet information server. Purposely, we have not given you a lot of detail; that comes later. With all the necessary terms and concepts under our belts, we are now ready to progress to the first step in the Global Recipe: planning the server for the intended audience.

CHAPTER 3

Preparing the Kitchen (Planning)

Ingredients

- Intended audience
- Services to support
- Information types to support
- Human resources
- Hardware resources
- Connecting to the Internet

Take a liberal amount of your intended audience and the services you think they are likely to need. You can't be too generous here—you will never anticipate everyone's needs and how they will individually gobble up a good supply of information. Choose server software that can provide for this intended audience and add two other major ingredients: software for reading, writing, and filtering all the anticipated information types, and sufficient resources, both hardware and human. Mix these ingredients together and you have a good plan in the making, with little chance of ending up with anything half-baked!

After reading this chapter you should be able to decide the initial level of support—both human and hardware—to offer via your Internet service, and how your server will be connected to the Internet. Of course, you will add and delete to your list of requirements over time, but you will have started on server implementation through some sound planning. The next chapter goes into more detail about specific items of software.

Planning lets you balance the level of service that you can provide against the resources that need to be expended to establish and maintain the information service.

3.1 Who Is the Intended Audience?

This is the first question you should ask yourself. In our cooking analogy, think of developing an information server in the same way you think about preparing a gourmet meal. There is no point going to the butcher, selecting a choice cut of meat, and marinating it for days if your dinner guests are vegetarians. Likewise, there is no point spending months preparing digitized video for your information server audience if 95 percent of them have neither the bandwidth nor the client software needed to play the video.

A good meal naturally leads from one course to another. You start with just enough to whet the appetite and then proceed through just enough courses to not overwhelm the eater, but to excite all the taste buds. So it should be with an information server. Success depends very much on how you organize the information.

Organization of information is covered in Chapter 8. Beyond the basic organization, you need to be aware of special considerations when dealing with hypertext. We will get to these considerations in Section 9.3. This chapter is devoted to helping you further distinguish the types of information services that exist, which of those you should provide to your intended audience, what information types are associated with those services, and specifically what tools you need to manage and deliver those information types.

The size of the audience using your information server is a function of the subject material presented, the quality and quantity of that material, how that material is organized and then delivered, and any network and hardware limitations. We cannot help you with the quality or subject matter presented on your information server, but we can help you with organization, delivery, and resource needs. Getting these right requires planning.

3.2 What Information Types Will I Encounter?

When you run an information server, you will encounter a wild variety of wonderful information types. Knowing something about these information types is necessary for the information server planning process and is discussed in some detail in this section.

Before we look at the various information types, we need to interject a note about naming conventions and file extensions. Although the Mac OS has never depended on the user to identify a file's type, most other operating systems still need help from the user. Traditionally, other operating systems and their applications have dictated a part of the file name for this purpose. The file extension is the suffix, usually three or four characters, preceded by a "." tacked on to the unique part of the file name. As we shall see, file extensions are associated with specific MIME (Multipurpose Internet Mail Extension) types (Section 3.2.1), and Web browsers depend on the *MIME type* to determine the action to take when receiving a requested file.

To comply with the naming convention of the impoverished masses of non-Mac users: avoid spaces and punctuation (except hyphens, underscores, and the period preceding the extension) in Web file and folder (directory) names. And you should also be aware that Web browsers do distinguish between upper- and lowercase in file and folder names. (However, note that there is no case distinction in *host* names; *www.sdsc.edu* is the same as *www.SDSC.EdU.*)

The good news is that there are only four basic types of information: text (including source code of applications), graphics, sound, and movies (which are a combination of the first three). The bad news is that they come in a variety of formats and that browsers currently only recognize text, GIF, and JPEG files without additional plug-ins or helper applications. These formats each represent some kind of de facto standard, since they are recognized by commonly used software, rather than being defined by a standards organization. The really important software is, of course, that which recognizes one information format and writes another; this type of software is called a *filter*. Filters are vital items in the information server manager's bag of tricks. A typical example is the manager's need to convert some existing word processing document into HTML for Web access. Table 3–1 considers the most common information types.

Table 3-1 Common Information Types

Information Type	Description	Extensions
Text	Any *ASCII* characters.	.txt, .java, .c
HTML	Text with HTML formatting tags.	.html, .htm, .shtml
Graphics	Pixel-based images.	.gif, .jpeg, .tiff, .pict
Movies	A series of images.	.mpeg, .mov, .moo, .qt
Sound	Digitized sound. While all platforms support sound, each has a different native sound format.	.snd, .au, .wav
Binary	Bit-based data representation; may be architecture specific.	.obj, .class, .exe
Compressed/Archived	File or files compressed to smaller size for downloading; each platform has its own preferred formats.	.hqx, .sit (Mac OS) .tar, .Z, .gz (UNIX) .zip, .arc (Windows)
Page Definition Languages	TeX, LaTex.	.tex, .dvi
	PostScript (Adobe).	.ps, .eps
	Rich Text Format (Microsoft).	.rtf
	Portable Document Format (Adobe).	.pdf
Common Gateway Interface script	Instructions for Web server to execute for client. Any programming language, usually Perl.	.cgi, .acgi
Application files	Files produced by particular applications, such as word processors or spreadsheets.	(various)
VRML	Virtual Reality Modeling Language.	.wrl

3.2.1 MIME Types

Having warned you that Web browsers rely on file extensions to take appropriate action, we need to qualify that statement. The first Web browsers did identify the type of a document based on its file extension; however, the Web powers-that-be soon realized that a file extension of a few characters is only helpful if the person or software receiving a file already knows what the extension denotes.

While file extensions remain necessary, Web servers now recognize the type of information it is receiving based on *MIME types*. MIME (Multipurpose Internet Mail Extensions) is a standardized method of assigning types to documents. It was developed originally for use in mail messages so that mail programs could recognize types of embedded documents by their MIME types. The same mechanism has been adopted to assign and detect the format of Web documents.

Current browsers use MIME content/type information to identify the real information being sent. MIME provides a standardized, more extended, and human-readable system of identification independent of the filename and contents. As we shall see during Web server installation, this system of identification is distributed with most Web servers. For a gentle introduction to MIME types, refer to the URL *http://www.cs.wisc.edu/docs/mime.html*. Further information is given in Chapter 8.

As we configure the various clients and servers described in this book, we will encounter MIME types. The basic idea is that when you, as a client, access information on various servers, your client software runs the appropriate application to interpret that information once it is received. For example, a PostScript viewer displays a PostScript file, a video viewer shows a film clip, a molecule viewer views a molecule, and so on. If that application is invoked from the Web browser itself, we refer to it as a *helper application*. Helper applications extend the functionality of a Web browser since they interpret information that could not be interpreted directly by the browser.

Having introduced helper applications, we must also mention *plug-ins*. A helper application appears as a separate window, and beyond the initial loading of the file by the Web browser, there is not necessarily any communication between browser and helper. A plug-in is integrated into the Web browser and appears within the browser window. While not advanced at this point in time, the opportunity exists for a variety of plug-ins to communicate with each other under the control of the browser. The emergence of JavaBeans will facilitate this process (see Chapter 12).

As a general rule it is worth noting that, over time, software has evolved to accommodate automatically a larger variety of MIME types. For example, it may not be necessary to download software to handle a MIME type because the standard Web browser can handle it, or the software to handle the MIME type has become part of the operating system and just needs to be invoked as a helper application. Plug-ins and helper applications are discussed in Section 5.1.

3.2.2 Text Files

What constitutes a *text file* is somewhat arbitrary. However, for reasons of simplicity, let's define it as any file containing just those characters conforming to the *ASCII* character set, as shown in

http://www.w3.org/hypertext/WWW/Protocols/rfc1341/7_1_Text.html.

Here we consider ASCII characters to be those that can be read by humans. This classification, though, is somewhat arbitrary. PostScript files or RTF (Rich Text Format) files (see below) are types of text files, since they are also made up of ASCII characters, but there are not many people who curl up in bed with a PostScript file that has not been suitably interpreted by a printer. In other words, PostScript and RTF files, among others, are a special form of text file. Text files are the most common information format that you will encounter and wish to serve.

Any file that is not an ASCII text file is a *binary file*—any file that produces indecipherable output when you force your Mac to display it as text. Normally, the Mac OS will attempt to open a binary file in the appropriate application. If the Mac OS cannot figure out the file type, it opens a Mac OS Easy Open dialog box as in Figure 3–1, from which you must choose the appropriate application. (This assumes Easy Open is installed and turned on.) Binary files include images, sounds, and movies, as well as compressed files, compiled applications, and application-specific files.

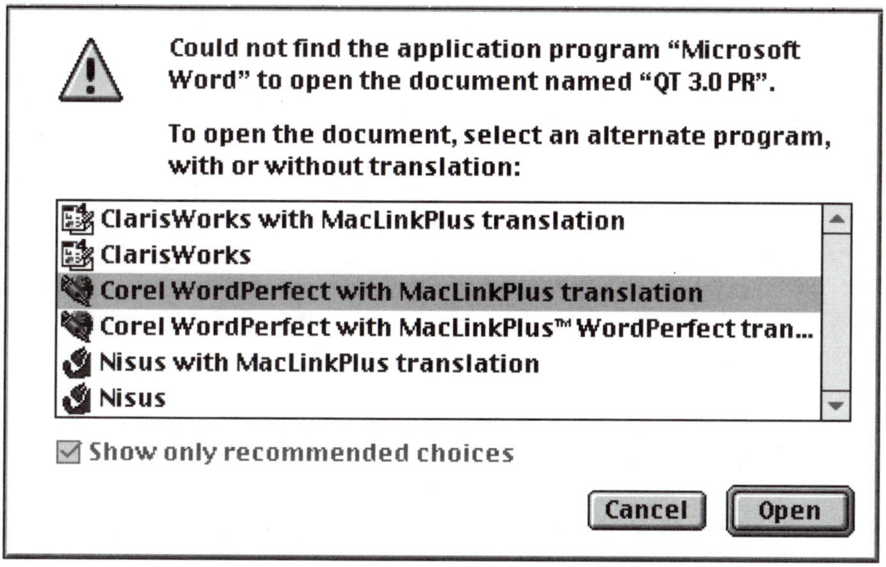

Figure 3-1 Mac OS Easy Open Dialog Box

3.2.3 HyperText Markup Language (HTML)

For serving the Internet, the most important special-purpose text files are HTML files. HTML is the so-called "language of the Web" and the format with which you will likely have the most contact. HTML is used to "tag" standard text, which causes a program (e.g., a Web browser) to present that text in a certain way.

HTML was developed by Tim Berners-Lee and the folks at Conseil Européen pour la Récherche Nucleaire (CERN), now known as the European Laboratory for Particle Physics, and is based on Standard Generalized Markup Language (SGML). SGML has been around for a long time and is used extensively in the publishing industry.

HTML is popular because it is relatively simple to use, although as HTML evolves to support tables, special characters, and so forth., it is by necessity becoming more complex. As HTML editors get better, more of that complexity is hidden from the user (Section 4.7.1). As with all markup languages, you only need to use a subset of its features. The major attraction of HTML is, of course, the links it allows you to create to other documents anywhere in the world. Chapters 9–11 cover HTML in detail.

3.2.4 Graphics

For graphics, both on the Web and elsewhere, it is tough to beat the Mac. In the same way that 80 percent of all computers used for color publishing jobs in the advertising, graphic design, printing, publishing and prepress industries are Macintosh (according to a 1996 study by Griffin Dix Research Associates), more Web pages are created on a Macintosh than any other platform. After all, what is the Web but desktop publishing with the "printing press" built into a browser.

Macintosh graphics and multimedia formats are more standardized, and therefore more flexible. In fact, the operating-system-level integration between 3-D and video formats provided by Apple's QuickTime Media Layer even allows you to cut and paste 3-D data and motion video.

Because graphics have become key to the appeal of a Web site, the Mac OS is the top platform for creating Web sites, used by 64 percent of U.S. Web design firms, according to the October 1996 *WebWeek Magazine*. With a Mac, you have access to the top software for graphics production—Adobe Photoshop and Adobe Illustrator top that long list, not to mention many other programs for creating 2-D and 3-D graphics and animations. With these programs, you can create graphics in just about any of the plethora of graphics formats for any platform; we consider only the most popular on the Web here. Of those listed, GIF and JPEG are viewable with most graphical Web browsers.

GIF (Graphics Interchange Format) files are the most common. This format, with the extension *.gif*, is recognized by all graphical Web browsers, and information providers tend to make their images available as GIFs. This format was developed in 1987 by CompuServe, the well-known on-line service. The major drawback of this format, since it was developed for use with 8-bit color displays, is that it only supports 256 colors, which may be insufficient to provide the richness needed for some images.

There have been extensions to this standard, notably GIF89A, which includes support for more colors. Most current Web browser versions recognize the enhancements offered by GIF89A, such as GIF animations, the simplest way to add movement to a Web page, and transparent images, in which the image's background appears to be the same as the browser's and the image "floats" on the page. You can read more about transparent images and GIF animations at *http://www.yahoo.com/Computers_and_Internet/Internet/-World_Wide_Web/Page_Design_and_Layout/Graphics/-Transparent_Images/*

http://www.yahoo.com/Arts/Visual_Arts/Animation/-Computer_Animation/Animated_GIFs/

JPEG (Joint Photographic Expert Group) format has higher resolution and more colors than GIFs while generally offering higher compression than GIFs. Thus, JPEG can create smaller, high-resolution images for faster downloading on Web pages. On the other hand, JPEG uses a "lossy" compression scheme—the quality of an image can be degraded in color or detail when it is compressed. The format has not been used as commonly as the GIF format, partly because early Web browsers did not support it. MPEG (see below) is derived from JPEG.

PNG (Portable Network Graphics) is an emerging Web graphics format, supported by a recommendation from the World Wide Web Consortium, designed to supplant GIF. GIF has certain limitations on image quality, and since 1995, GIF patent holders have demanded royalties on programs that produce GIF images.

PNG is an extensible, patent-free file format for the storage of indexed-color, grayscale, and truecolor raster images. PNG is a portable, well-compressed format that does not lose image information as JPEG compression can. As a patent-free replacement for GIF, PNG is designed for on-line viewing, has a progressive display option, and supports improved color matching across platforms. For more information on PNG, see

http://www.boutell.com/boutell/png/

http://www.wco.com/~png/

TIFF (Tagged Image File Format) was designed by Microsoft and Aldus Inc. and is the format produced by most scanners. This high-quality format is readable by most image processing applications, such as PhotoShop and Illustrator, but not within most Web browsers. TIFF is commonly used to exchange high-resolution images across platforms.

For further details on these and other graphics formats, see:

http://www.cis.ohio-state.edu/hypertext/faq/usenet/graphics/-fileformats/faq/top.html

http://www.dcs.ed.ac.uk/~mxr/gfx/

The major trade-off in comparing graphics formats is size of the image file versus resolution. We will deal primarily with standard GIF files, since these provide a compromise between quality and size and are suitable for most Web-based applications. Table 3–2 compares the major Web graphics formats.

Table 3-2 Web Graphics Formats

Format	Color Depth	Compression	Recommended Use	Comments
GIF	8-bit (256 colors)	LZW	Simple graphics— logos, clip art	Variations allow transparent images, and animations. First Web standard.
JPEG	24-bit truecolor	4:1 to 20:1	Photographic art	High compression for small images. Compression is "lossy" and unpredictable.
TIFF	24-bit truecolor	LZW	High-resolution images	Not viewable in a Web browser, but useful for cross-platform exchanges.
PNG	1-8 bit palette 1-16 bit grayscale 24-, 48-bit	Lossless, 10-30% smaller than GIF	All GIF uses, some TIFF uses	The latest versions of Adobe PhotoShop and Illustrator produce PNG images. Browsers can display PNG images with plug-ins; built-in support is coming.
FlashPix	24-bit truecolor	Less compact than JPEG	Photograpic art	Emerging competitors to JPEG format. Not yet widely supported either by graphics software or Web browsers.
WSQ	24-bit	Lossy, but better quality than JPEG		WSQ is wavelet scalar quantization.

3.2.5 Sound

The first Macs came complete with 8-bit sound; every Macintosh sold today has 16-bit CD-quality stereo sound capable of handling a sampling rate of 44.1 kilohertz. The Macintosh also has MIDI capability built in, so driving complex sound modules and synthesizers is simple. The QuickTime Musical Instruments extension that comes with QuickTime 2.5 includes 41 instruments (and more can be added), allowing a Macintosh to output sampled MIDI files in multivoiced sound through any speakers. Some of the best sound-manipulation software, such as Opcode's StudioVision Pro and Arboretum Systems' Hyperprism series, are available only for the Macintosh.

Since sound was not an original component of many other systems—today, PCs come with a variety of different add-on sound cards—sound formats are one of the least standardized information types, even on the Mac, and Web browsers typically need a helper application or plug-in to play sound files. Each hardware platform, and sometimes each sound card manufacturer, has a preferred format or several preferred formats. Nevertheless, with appropriate software, it is straightforward to interpret any sound format on a Mac (see Section 5.5).

Some sound types, such as Progressive Networks' RealAudio format, QuickTime audio files, and MPEG Audio Layer 3 provide less platform-dependent alternatives for the Web. Common sound formats are listed in Table 3–3. For a more detailed discussion of sound formats, see

http://www.cs.ruu.nl/wais/html/na-dir/audio-fmts/.html

Table 3-3 Common Sound Formats

Name	File Extension	Description
none	.snd	Macintosh produced.
HCOM	none	Macintosh produced.
QuickTime	.qt, .mov	Movie format with audio.

Table 3-3 Common Sound Formats *(Continued)*

Name	File Extension	Description
IFF/8SVX	.iff	Amiga produced.
	.mod, .nst	Another Amiga format.
WAVE	.wav	Microsoft Windows produced.
	.voc	SoundBlaster produced.
m-law	.au, .snd	NeXT and Sun produced.
AIFF	.aif, .aiff	Silicon Graphics IRIX produced.
RealAudio	.ra	Web format by Progressive Networks.
MP3	.mpeg, .mpg, .mp3	MPEG Audio Layer 3, a movie format with highly compressed audio.

3.2.6 Movies

For capturing and editing digital video, several Macintosh models come ready to go right out of the box with RCA and S-video connections that connect to VCRs and camcorders. With the Avid Cinema card available on some Macintoshes, including some home models, you can "print" to videotape as easily as printing to a laser printer. In fact, the Avid Cinema solution is also available for Macintoshes as a separate PCI card with software that makes video editing simple.

With integrated sound and graphics, Macs excel at producing multimedia movies and animations—not to mention their use for professional movie production. QuickTime was recognized in 1997 as one of *Videography* magazine's Editors Choices and as *Television*

Broadcast Magazine's "Editors' Pick of Show" award for the advancement of the art and science of television broadcast at the National Association of Broadcasters (NAB) trade show.

With movie formats, there are many fewer competing standards. Table 3–4 provides links to more information on movie formats, and we discuss movie players in Section 5.6. The QuickTime software built into the Mac OS provides support for, in addition to sound, digital video. Desktop video can be saved in standard high-quality QuickTime format and in MPEG-1 format that works entirely in software—no separate hardware card is needed.

QuickTime by Apple, along with its sibling QuickTimeVR, is one of two common Web movie formats. QuickTime software comes with the Mac OS and is available for Windows systems. The QuickTime 2.0 plug-in, which offers the same features to both platforms, and the QuickTime 3.0 software are available free from the QuickTime Web site. Your Mac OS installation CD-ROM may come with earlier versions of QuickTime. We show you how to upgrade in Section 5.6.

QuickTime 3.0 supports playback, editing, and integration of QuickTime, MPEG, AVI, OMF, DVCAM, and OpenDML file formats. QuickTime 3.0 also supports industry standard digital audio file formats, including Wave, AIFF, Sound Designer II, AU, and MPEG Layer 2, as well as many common still image, animation, and MIDI formats.

MPEG (Motion Picture Expert Group) is a binary compressed format for video and more common on UNIX systems. As stated above, the latest versions of QuickTime will play MPEG movies. In fact, the International Standards Organization (ISO) has adopted the QuickTime file format as the basis for MPEG-4.

RealPlayer from Progressive Networks is a format designed for streaming video as a companion to Progressive's RealAudio sound format. Prior to the Apple-Microsoft agreement in August 1997, Microsoft had been working with Progressive to incorporate RealPlayer into the Internet Explorer browser. (RealAudio and RealPlayer plug-ins and helper applications are available for the Macintosh.) At the time of writing, it was not clear whether the agreement with Apple had affected this arrangement.

Table 3-4 Movie Formats

Location	Description
http://www.quicktime.apple.com	Apple's QuickTime page.
http://www.yahoo.com/-Computers_and_Internet/Multimedia/Video/MPEG/	Information on MPEG format.
http://www.realaudio.com	RealVideo from Progressive Networks.
http://www.mac-dvr.com/	Mac Digital Video Review newsletter.
http://www.el-dorado.ca.us/~dmnews/	Digital Movie News newsletter.
http://www.det.mun.ca/staff/gporter/mmfaq.htm	A multimedia FAQ.

3.2.7 Compressed Files

Compressed files are useful for conserving disk space and simplifying distribution, since they take less time to transmit over the Internet. Archive files bundle up an entire folder or directory hierarchy into one file for distribution. There are various compression algorithms and software that implements them, and Mac OS, UNIX, and Windows each have their compression and archive software of choice. For example, BinHex Archive (.hqx), MacBinary (.bin), and StuffIt Archive (.sit) files are common Mac OS formats. Windows leans toward .zip and .arc files, and UNIX uses .gzip, .Z, and .tar formats. If you are distributing compressed or archived files, your best bet is to use a format that you know the receiver of the compressed file will have or offer several formats.

For the Mac OS, Aladdin Systems produces the de facto standard software for compressing and uncompressing files. StuffIt Expander is widely distributed freeware—it comes with Netscape Navigator, for example—that uncompresses .hqx, .bin, and .sit files. The commercial version, StuffIt Deluxe, will also compress and uncompress most UNIX and Windows compression formats. Further details are available at *http://www.aladdinsys.com*. If you are serving large files for a variety of platforms, StuffIt Deluxe is a must.

3.2.8 Page Definition Languages

Because of HTML's limited and screen-oriented formatting commands, documents in which the arrangement and styles for text and images must be retained are often distributed in one of several page definition formats. The TeX, Rich Text Format, and PostScript formats use plain text files annotated with printing and display commands. The newer Portable Document Format (PDF) from Adobe Systems can also be displayed with a browser plug-in or helper application.

RTF (Rich Text Format) was developed by Microsoft as an interchange format and, because of the popularity of Microsoft Word for word processing, has become a standard interchange format. It is one of the easiest ways to convert documents written using Word, WordPerfect, and other popular Mac and PC word processing programs into HTML for use on your information server. For details, see

http://www.lib.ox.ac.uk/internet/news/faq/archive/text-faq.html

However, RTF does not work well for complex documents including equations and embedded graphics images.

PostScript was developed by Adobe Systems Inc. as a device-independent text representation and is now recognized by most printers. Although PostScript files comprise only ASCII characters, they generally must be printed to view the contents. Encapsulated PostScript (EPS) is an integral part of the PostScript language that supports the embedding of images. For details see

http://karlsberg.usask.ca/Postscript-FAQ.html.

Portable Document Format (PDF) was developed by Adobe Systems as a more compact format that could also be displayed and navigated easily on screen. The free Adobe Acrobat Reader plug-in and helper application allow you to view and page through longer documents, such as software user manuals, either on- or off-line. See

http://www.adobe.com/acrobat

TeX and LaTeX, two text formatting languages, were developed by Donald Knuth at Stanford University and have a large following, particularly in the physics, computer science, and mathematics communities. If you interact with UNIX users, you will sooner or later encounter TeX and its derivatives, such as LaTeX. One of the reasons for its lingering popularity is its ability to format complex mathematical equations (and because there are so few WYSIWYG word processors for UNIX). The marked-up file is processed by the TeX program producing a DVI (DeVice Independent) file. The DVI file is an intermediate format that can be processed into a variety of other formats including PostScript and HTML. For details see

http://www.cis.ohio-state.edu/hypertext/faq/usenet/de-tex-faq/top.html

3.2.9 VRML

The Virtual Reality Modeling Language (VRML) has become the de facto standard for displaying 3-D "worlds" on the Web. In these worlds, users navigate the world using controls provided by a browser plug-in or helper application. While VRML can be used to create quite complex worlds, the file contents are ASCII text. The worlds may also incorporate GIF or JPEG graphic textures to provide realistic surfaces. A word of warning: The two versions of this standard, VRML 1.0 and the more current VRML 2.0, are incompatible. VRML 1.0 browsers cannot display VRML 2.0 worlds, and vice versa. At the time of writing, the Mac OS lacked a VRML 2.0 browser, although several were in beta release.

3.2.10 Applets and Objects

So far, the MIME types that we have discussed require a client to take well-defined action such as displaying or viewing text and images or starting a particular plug-in or helper application. Several new technologies, however, enable the client to run arbitrary programs from the server. The most common of these Web programming languages is Java, developed by Sun Microsystems' JavaSoft branch and supported by a number of major computer companies, including Apple. With Java, Web sites can embed small programs, called *applets*, that perform complex functions ranging from graphic menus to image processing and spreadsheets. Applets stand to change the dynamics of the client-server relationship dramatically. Most current Web browsers support Java, including Netscape Navigator and Internet Explorer.

Microsoft, noticing the potential of Java and perhaps upset that the technology did not come out of Redmond, Washington, introduced a technology that competes with Java, called ActiveX. Embedded ActiveX programs are called "objects." Many small companies have jumped on the ActiveX bandwagon, putting their faith in Microsoft's admittedly large coattails. Not surprisingly, Microsoft's Internet Explorer browser supports ActiveX objects.

3.2.11 A Word on Standards

This list of file and MIME types should in no way be considered the best or last word on the subject. Web "standards" come and go as software companies introduce new formats that succeed or fail to gain popularity and as older standards are revised to reflect new developments. VRML and QuickTimeVR, for example, still face competition from alternative formats, Microsoft's ActiveX is vying with JavaSoft's Java, and no clear leader has arisen in the battle over streaming audio and video.

If your intended audience is one that demands the latest Web technologies, you will have to be aware of new developments and decide whether to support those MIME types. If your audience is satisfied with fewer bells and whistles, you can probably serve the same information with well-established and stable MIME types.

3.3 What Human Resources Will I Need?

The variety and fickle nature of information types on the Web may have suggested to you that the most important and most expensive resources for serving the Internet are the humans who have to keep your server aimed at a moving target. The hardware nuts and bolts pale by comparison to the human resources required to maintain a server, because nuts and bolts are relatively inexpensive when compared to labor costs. Setting up and maintaining a good server takes people's time.

How do you measure the time required to maintain a server? This is a question that is difficult to answer without knowing how complex a server will be. Here are a couple of observations from our own experience:

- An organization of 10 people serving a minimal amount of information requires 10 hours per week of someone's time to set up and maintain the server in the first year.

- An organization of 20 people with information serving a vital part of their operation requires a *full-time employee* to set up and maintain the server in the first year.

Within these guidelines, there are two relatively independent categories of responsibility: technical support and information supply.

3.3.1 Technical Support

Technical support for an Internet server performs such duties as maintaining the server hardware, troubleshooting, installing and upgrading server software, supporting new MIME types and server tools, guiding the Web site's evolution, monitoring server performance, ensuring server security, as well as interacting with the staff responsible for networking (if this is a separate task) and the staff providing information to be served.

In an example from our immediate experience, SDSC, our (the authors') employer, has approximately 150 employees and admittedly a high-end Web presence, particularly on the technological end. In addition to a full-time Webmaster, SDSC has evolved a "server systems" group of a half-dozen members to ensure a smoothly running Web site. This group also provides operating system support for the server hardware, programming support, and the staff expertise to ensure that information from SDSC's databases, research projects, and other groups can be served on the Internet and the center's intranet as appropriate.

3.3.2 Information Supply

The other responsibility for your human resources is to provide information to serve. A large organization cannot depend on a Webmaster to provide information as well as keep the server running. *It may be one Webmaster managing the server, but the information supply should come from the source, that is, everyone in the organization.*

To continue the SDSC example, both Phil and Dave have been tapped to act as "deputy Webmasters," responsible for maintaining the information in the research and public information sections, respectively, of SDSC's Web site. In addition, Phil manages the Web presence for a number of his own research projects, and Dave supports his group's intranet information and general Web needs. Other staff members manage other SDSC Web sections and the Web pages of individual research projects. These duties are a part of Phil's responsibilities as a senior principal scientist and Dave's duties as magazine editor and science writer.

From these observations and examples you can try to assess your own needs. Determining what human resources are required is not simple, since *a successful information server generally has more than one person providing information as an integral part of their job function.* That cost is hard to determine.

3.3.3 A Note on Mail Aliases

In the same way that you might change the computer that serves your Internet information, through turnover or promotion, the person who is the Webmaster or the ftp archive administrator today may not be the same person next year. Part of your planning process should include establishing *mail aliases* to ensure that the mail always gets to the correct person at any point in time.

Whether you establish a "virtual user" named, for example, *webmaster@sdsc.edu*, or instruct your mail system to direct all mail addressed to Webmaster to be sent to a particular employee, mail aliases allow you to have another person assume Webmaster duties without having to scour your Web site for references to the former Webmaster's e-mail address.

3.4 What Hardware Will I Need?

Hardware refers to the resources, both computer and network, needed to have the information server operate efficiently. This is a difficult issue to address. First, the information server is usually also used for other computing tasks. Second, the demands for information on each server can be quite different. For example, the number of hits made on the server is a function of the popularity of the information—NASA's Mars Pathfinder Web site and dozens of mirror sites fielded millions of hits during the first days of the 1997 Mars landing, while Phil's molecular biology pages get a few thousand hits per week. Then again, the number of hits does not necessarily indicate server load, since the amount of information transferred by a single hit can vary dramatically. Further, a Web forms interface may permit users to perform a database lookup or a complex calculation, both requiring significant hardware resources.

Apple Computer sells Power Macintosh systems designed specifically for running as network servers. You may want to consider these systems for your information server; however, as we show below, an information server is not necessarily a large consumer of hardware resources other than network bandwidth and disk space.

Here we make a general recommendation on what hardware is required initially. Once your server is established you should monitor activity very closely and try to have the resources—both monetary and personnel—available to respond quickly to the need for a new disk drive, more memory, and so forth. We appreciate that this is a poor recommendation, but information server growth is very difficult to predict. Let us consider each of the major potential problem areas separately.

3.4.1 Network Bandwidth

The required bandwidth is a function of the services you are supporting. The rules of thumb are:

- Whatever services you provide require a *dedicated connection*—that is, 24 hours a day, seven days a week.
- For mail and ftp support only, you might get by with a 28.8-kilobaud type connection supporting the SLIP or PPP protocols (see Section 3.5.3).
- For Web access you need at least an Integrated Services Digital Network (ISDN), (128-kilobaud) connection, or better still an Ethernet connection (10 megabits per second). T1, T2, T3, or ATM connections will be required for very high bandwidth.

Section 3.5 discusses the various connection methods in greater detail.

3.4.2 Disk Space

Next on the list of hardware requirements is disk space. Here's a good rule of thumb: You can never have enough disk space. In a multiuser environment, without disk quotas, all available space always gets consumed. What varies is the amount of time it takes to consume that space. Here are some basic rules to follow:

- If possible, keep the information you are serving separate from other data. This may call for separate partitions, if not separate disks.
- If possible, spread the information across various disks connected to separate disk controllers to minimize I/O load.
- If you permit users to write to the server by, for example, uploading files via ftp, you need to monitor disk space usage more carefully than would otherwise be the case.
- Providing index files to facilitate searching can *double* disk space requirements since the index files (depending on the indexer used) can be as large as or larger than the original files.
- Graphics, sound, and audio files are large even in a compressed state—be prepared with extra disk space.
- Security may require that you keep multiple copies of information available for each service you are offering.

These rules become particularly important when we look at examples of interacting with the server through, for example, *CGI scripts* (Section 11.3). Often these scripts write temporary files on the server and will fail if the file system is full, frustrating the user.

3.4.3 Memory Requirements

As a general rule, this would seem a nonissue on most of today's Mac OS platforms since they typically come with a minimum of 16 MB of memory, and often with 64 MB of memory or more. You are unlikely to see *swapping* on a computer dedicated to basic information serving with 16 MB of memory or more, regardless of the information being served. The key words to note in this statement though are "dedicated" and "basic." If you have other memory-intensive applications running—that is, if the server is not dedicated—and the information server process gets swapped out, interactive response will be hampered. Similarly, if you permit memory-intensive applications to be run on the information server, and those applications get run a lot, you will also have problems.

3.4.4 CPU Requirements

What is true for memory is true for Central Processing Unit (CPU) power—other applications on a nondedicated server are more likely to kill you than information-serving applications. The possible exception is a lot of gathering, index generation and searching, which can be CPU, memory and I/O intensive.

3.5 How Do I Connect to the Internet?

So far we have introduced the types of information we can make available from our information server, the services we can provide for disseminating that information, and the human and hardware resources necessary to provide those services. The next step is to make sure you have the prerequisite network infrastructure within your organization or home to provide the desired level of service.

If the computer you will use as the information server is already connected to the Internet and operating satisfactorily, that is, allows you to send and receive mail, and use ftp and the Web, you can skip to Section 3.5.5. If you have yet to get connected to the Internet and are contemplating how best to do this, read on.

There are four networking requirements for serving the Internet:

- A physical network connection
- An Internet Protocol (IP) address
- Appropriate networking software
- A name for your server

An *Internet Service Provider (ISP)* can provide you with all or none of these components. But before you decide what your ISP will provide, you need to understand a little bit more about your options for each one.

3.5.1 Choosing a Connection Method

First you must consider the physical connection to the Internet. Even if an ISP will run your Internet server from its hardware, you still need to consider your connection to the ISP for updating the information on your site. The information in this section will also help you choose an ISP with a sufficiently fast connection to the rest of the Internet.

In simple terms, the physical Internet connection can be characterized in one of two ways: dedicated and nondedicated. As the names suggest, a dedicated connection has a single function: It continuously listens for packets (chunks of information) destined for your information server and broadcasts packets as required.

A *dedicated connection* typically uses a copper cable—such as thin coaxial, thick coaxial, or twisted pair—or optical fiber (FDDI) cable. These media are already found in most large organizations and are starting to appear in some suburban communities. Dedicated connections are generally fast in transmitting data, fast at establishing the connection, and automatic, requiring no human intervention to make the connection. The wire over which the connection runs may belong to and be maintained by the organization, or it may be leased from and maintained by a telephone company or other carrier.

A *nondedicated connection*, on the other hand, is used for purposes in addition to the Internet connection, usually as a voice line. Typically, this is a telephone line attached to a regular telephone exchange. Such nondedicated connections are generally slower and require startup time to establish the connection, for instance, one modem dialing another. The dialing action may be automatic or invoked manually.

The line between dedicated and nondedicated connections has blurred since the widespread adoption of Integrated Services Digital Network (ISDN) lines and cable modems. An ISDN line can multiplex, that is, carry both voice and data at the same time, which for our purposes makes them a dedicated connection. ISDN lines are reasonably fast and connect very fast and without any user intervention. ISDN lines are maintained by the telephone companies, and you pay as you would for a voice line, albeit at a different rate. These rates are regional and expected to rise as the telephone companies realize what a valuable service ISDN provides. Cable modems, provided through cable television companies such as Time Warner and Cox Communications, provide transmission speeds approaching that of an Ethernet connection and offer a very cost-effective solution for dedicated or nondedicated connections

Table 3–5 summarizes the characteristics of each type of connection. A networking expert, though, will tell you that the information in the table is misleading because, for example, you never reach peak speeds, compression changes these numbers, ATM (Asynchronous Transfer Mode) can be run over ISDN, and so on. These are valid criticisms. The goal here is simply to put each service into perspective, so that you can decide which service or services to investigate further.

Table 3-5 Types and Characteristics of Internet Connections

Connection Type	Peak Speed (thousands of bits per second—Kbps)	Type of Connection	Payment Structure
Nondedicated			
Modem	1.2–28.8	Manual	Usage Based
ISDN	56–128	Automatic	Usage Based
Cable Modem	10,000	Manual or Automatic	Flat Fee
Dedicated			
T1	1,500	Automatic	Flat Fee
Ethernet	10,000	Automatic	Flat Fee
T3	45,000	Automatic	Flat Fee
FDDI	100,000	Automatic	Flat Fee
ATM	155,000	Automatic	Flat Fee

So here's a rule of thumb for choosing an ISP: If your ISP is using a nondedicated modem connection for *its* link to the Internet, you may want to consider switching to a larger ISP. *The type of connection to the Internet determines the kind of server you can operate.* If you want users to have continuous access to your server, a dedicated line is a must. Since the majority of Web servers operate through dedicated lines, we will concentrate on this type of infrastructure. However, the principles for serving the Internet apply just as well to a dial-up or nondedicated connection.

Here are some additional rules of thumb for the type of Internet access needed to support different server loads:

- A small business. A few Web hits per hour downloading text and images plus the occasional ftp archive access—ISDN, cable modem.
- A medium-sized business. Thousands of Web hits per hour downloading text, images, sound, video, plus tens to hundreds of downloads from the ftp archive per hour—T1 and above.
- A large business. Hundreds of thousands of Web hits per hour and thousands of ftp downloads—T3 and above.

Obviously, this is just a gentle introduction to getting connected to the Internet. Table 3–6 provides locations of more detailed information.

Table 3-6 Further Reading on Internet Connectivity

Location	Topic
http://www.msic.com/enet_info.html	Ethernet Information.
http://www.macworld.com/pages/august.97/-Feature.3805.html	Building an officewide Ethernet to connect Macs.
http://www.san.rr.com/Around_Town/aboutrr.htm	Road Runner San Diego, a cable modem service of Southwestern Cable and Time Warner.
http://rpcp.mit.edu/~gingold/cable/	Cable modem resources on the Web.
http://www.eff.org/pub/GII_NII/ISDN/	ISDN information, including a tutorial.
http://www.isdn.ocn.com/	Comprehensive site discussing ISDN.
http://www.macworld.com/pages/october.97/-Feature.3915.html	Setting up a Mac ISDN connection.

3.5.2 Getting an IP Address and Domain Name

Once your information server is physically connected to the Internet, it needs a unique address so that clients on the Internet can locate it. The most likely ways you can get assigned an Internet Protocol (IP) address are

1. from the network manager of your organization
2. from an ISP
3. from the Network Information Center (NIC)

The first two options require little work on your part, and the second and third options will cost you money. The third assumes that you or your organization has no form of Internet access already and requires that you register yourself or your organization. Table 3–7 indicates how to register on-line with the NIC for an IP address.

Table 3-7 Where to Register for IP Addresses

Where to Register	Location of Internet Server
http://rs.internic.net/	U.S.
http://www.apnic.net/	Asian Pacific region
http://www.ripe.net/	Europe

These days you are strongly encouraged to work through an ISP rather than apply for addresses directly from the NIC. Either way the result should be an assignment of a group of IP addresses pertinent to the size of your organization. Table 3–8 provides further information on IP addressing.

Table 3-8 Further Reading on IP Addressing

Location	Description
http://www.wcmh.com/uworld/archives/95/tutorial/-001.html	A tutorial on IP addressing.
http://www.shiva.com/prod/tips/-SHIVA13.TIP.html#HDR3	Another perspective on IP addressing.

3.5.2.1 Domain Names

We discussed the format of the IP address in Section 2.2.4—nnn.nnn.nnn.nnn—where the numbers represent, respectively, the network domain, institution, division, and computer. If you get an IP address from your organization's network manager, the first three numbers will be determined by the group of IP addresses assigned to your organization. In addition, your host name will already be partly defined—for example, your-computer-name-here.sdsc.edu.

If you *are* the network manager for your company or organization and you haven't already registered for one, you will also need a domain name. When you register through InterNIC (see Table 3–7) or a large ISP, you also choose and register a unique "domain name" for your company or organization—*bobsleds-r-us.com* or *macrame.org*, for example.

Smaller organizations or individuals, particularly those without dedicated Internet connections, may not want or need to register a full-fledged domain through InterNIC—or perhaps your company's name is taken. Instead, you may just let your ISP dictate your domain name. In this case, your company's URL will be something like *http://www.an-isp-name.net/~your-company,* or perhaps something longer.

Such URLs can be unwieldy and difficult to remember. There are at least two alternatives to traditional domain name registration. V3 Redirection Services, operating out of the Netherlands at *http://come.to*, allows you to create a URL for your company of the form *http://come.to/your-company.* At the time of writing they were offering this service for free, as long as you agree to display their advertising banner on your site.

Another service, DynIP, allows you to create a fixed domain name for your Internet server, even if you have a "floating IP address" given by your ISP each time you connect from a nondedicated line or if the permanent URL assigned by your ISP is long and confusing. DynIP is located at *http://www.dynip.com*, and the Mac DynIP software is available from *http://www.aprs.net/dynip.html*.

3.5.3 Network Software

The Mac OS includes all the networking software you need to communicate with the Internet. Called Open Transport, this software provides the tools for both AppleTalk networking and the Internet's TCP/IP protocol. Open Transport works with Mac OS 7.1 and later versions, and is the only networking option for Mac OS 7.6 and Mac OS 8. (Older Mac OS versions also support Apple "classic networking," but Open Transport is preferred for Internet connectivity.)

Open Transport installs two control panels (and a handful of extensions) in your System Folder. The AppleTalk control panel lets you configure how your Mac is connected to an AppleTalk network, which allows you to share printers and exchange files through Personal File Sharing with other computers on the network.

The TCP/IP control panel allows you to configure your Mac for an Internet connection. Remember that the term "Internet" implies at least support of the TCP/IP protocols. Typically, a dedicated server runs the TCP/IP protocols directly, thereby supporting such standard services as ftp. Additional services, such as http, can be thought of as being layered on top of TCP/IP.

A nondedicated line requiring access to TCP/IP services requires additional protocols and, hence, software. The most common protocols for use on modem lines are *SLIP (Serial Line Internet Protocol)* or *PPP (Point-to-Point Protocol)*. TCP/IP runs on top of either SLIP or PPP.

Mac OS 8 includes Open Transport/PPP software, which installs a third control panel, conveniently named PPP. To use a nondedicated line through a telephone exchange, open the PPP control panel and enter your ISP number and your account information. You must also configure the TCP/IP controls (see the next section).

When you connect to an ISP via SLIP or PPP, a temporary IP address is assigned from a pool of available addresses. Your Internet server, which is going to have clients connecting in this manner, needs to have modems accessible that can accept SLIP and PPP connections and it must be running the SLIP and PPP protocols. Table 3–9 provides pointers to additional information on the PPP and SLIP protocols.

Table 3-9 Further Reading on the PPP and SLIP Protocols

Location	Description
http://www.stokely.com/stokely/-unix.serial.port.resources/ppp.slip.html#ppp.link	Pointers to software supporting PPP and further information.
http://www.cis.ohio-state.edu/htbin/rfc/rfc1661.html	The official definition of PPP.
http://www.cis.ohio-state.edu/htbin/rfc/rfc1055.html	The official definition of SLIP.
http://www.fcr.com	LinkUPPP 1.1, a commercial Mac PPP/SLIP software alternative.
http://www.macworld.com/software_collection/-Software.1089.html	FreePPP, another Mac PPP alternative.

3.5.4 Configuring the Network Software

This topic falls under network administration, which this book does not propose to cover in any detail. For a simple connection, there are really only five things you need to know, and we summarize them here:

- *IP Address*—This is the address of the form nnn.nnn.nnn.nnn (e.g., 128.59.98.1) assigned in one of the ways described above.
- *Subnet Mask*—This number defines how a network segment may be divided further into subnets. The value depends on the size of your network. For D-class networks configured to support 256 hosts (2^8), this is usually set to 255.255.255.0. For C-class networks configured to support 65536 (2^{16}) hosts, this is usually set to 255.255.0.0.
- *Default Router*—This is where to direct network traffic so that it may be sent correctly. Usually a computer will be designated by the network administrator as a default gateway. This may either be on your organization's network or at the ISP.
- *Name Server*—This IP address tells your computer where to start resolving host names to numeric IP addresses. You may want to establish a limited DNS service for local host names and use an ISP's name server for the rest of the Internet.
- *Search domains*—If you provide a partial host name, TCP/IP will look for hosts by concatenating the partial host name with the

search domains listed here. For example, at SDSC, the search domain might be *sdsc.edu*, so a request asking for host *rosebud*, would automatically be converted to *rosebud.sdsc.edu*.

With this information from your ISP or your network manager, configuring your Mac network software involves opening the TCP/IP control panel and entering the values for your IP address, subnet mask, router IP address, name server IP addresses, and the optional search domains (see Figure 3–2). Depending on the level of service you purchase from your ISP, this TCP/IP information may also be provided by your ISP's server each time you connect.

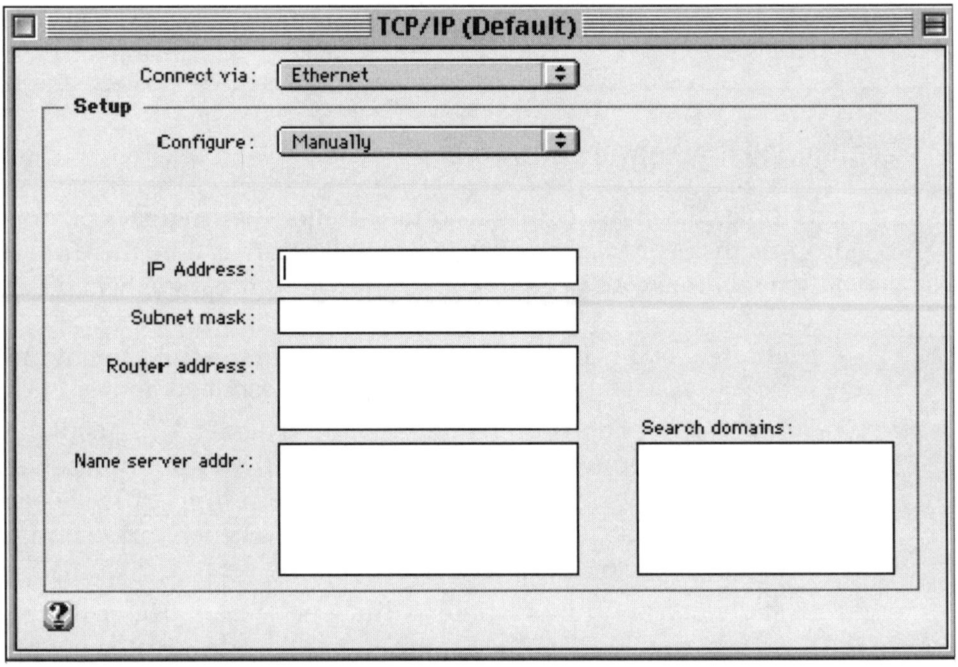

Figure 3-2 TCP/IP Control Panel

3.5.5 Naming the Server

Now that you have an IP address, you need to name your future Internet server. Again, the key here is to plan ahead. While your ftp archive or Web server might be running on one computer this year, next year you might be serving information from another. The reason for the change could relate to efficiency (the popularity of the server required a more powerful computer), reorganization (the original computer was assigned to a new project), and so on. Your goal is to hide this underlying turmoil from users accessing your system, regardless of the information service they are using.

It is traditional practice—if one to two years can be considered long enough to establish a tradition—to provide the following aliases for an information server:

- *www.organization.domain* for the organization's Web site—for example, www.sdsc.edu
- *ftp.organization.domain* for the organization's ftp site—for example, ftp.sdsc.edu
- *listserv@organization.domain* for the organization's list server—for example, listserv@sdsc.edu

These names could refer to the same computer or to different computers. The point is, the computer (and hence IP address) can change without requiring the name to change. Therefore, users of your information server who have added *http://www.sdsc.edu/* to their Web browser hotlists will not be disappointed when they visit the site in the future, since the URL will remain valid even though you have changed the computer.

This approach is also useful for users who do not know which computer in an organization they want to access, even though they know the IP address of the organization. For example, if you know Digital Equipment Corp. has some nifty software on their ftp server, your first guess in trying to locate their ftp archive would be *ftp.digital.com* or *http://www.digital.com*. This scheme can be extended in larger, more diverse organizations. So, *ftp.dept.organization.com,* for example, might be a good guess to locate a departmental ftp server in a large organization.

However, this approach works only if there is one server providing this service in the domain or subdomain. If there were two ftp servers for *sdsc.edu,* they must be consolidated (the best choice) or there should be a designated primary (called ftp) and secondary (called ftp1 or some such name) server.

To establish a generic domain name for an information service, do one of the following

- ▼ If you are not responsible for maintaining the name server database, ask your network administrator to add the alias.
- ▼ If you are responsible for maintaining the name server database, add the alias to the primary name server database file.

3.5.5.1 Virtual Hosts

Although server names of the form www.company.com have become standard for a company's Web server, the growing acceptance of the Web has led to an increased interest in avoiding long and clunky URLs for major subdivisions of a large Web server—for example, *http://-www.your-company.com/projects/aProject*. A new standard is evolving that uses virtual hosts to shorten such a URL to something like *http://-aproject.your-company.com.* Rather than running a separate Web server program, the main Web server intercepts requests for virtual hosts—the short form—and translates them into requests for information as in the long form.

Virtual hosting is available for Mac Internet servers as well. Using features of DNS software such as QuickDNS Pro or the Pardeikes Welcome Plug-in *(http://welcome.comcon.de)* for Web servers such as WebSTAR or Quid Pro Quo, you can create virtual hosts on your Mac. The Welcome plug-in, for example, provides a straightforward interface for defining rules that map virtual hosts to separate folders of information.

3.5.6 Internet Service Providers

As we indicated at the beginning of this section, one way to meet the four requirements for connecting to the Internet is to take advantage of an Internet Service Provider (ISP). ISPs provide services that, at a price, make part or all of this book unnecessary, depending on the level of service they provide. Here are some examples of the types and levels of services they offer:

- A complete package—The ISP provides hardware, software, Internet access, and information serving via ftp, mail servers, and Web pages. You simply provide them with the information and how you want to see that information presented. They format, organize, and present that information at their site.
- A network provider—The ISP provides hardware, software, and Internet access at their site, but you organize and format the information.
- A turnkey system—Hardware, software, services, and maintenance are provided by the ISP as a package for installation at your site. You format, organize, and present the information.
- A consultant service—The ISP helps you set up your server at your site and ensures that it is operational, and it formats and organizes your information. There is the option for ongoing maintenance.
- A basic connection—The ISP provides you with an IP address and a connection to the Internet, otherwise you are on our own.

Unless you have Internet access through your place of work, you will need an ISP to gain access to the Internet. How much you pay defines the level of service you will get. Which ISP you use and the level of service you purchase should be considered carefully.

If you are going to use an ISP, the first step is to get a list of providers in your region. From there, you can examine the services offered by each one. We appreciate that getting this list from the Internet is putting the cart before the horse: How can you determine, from the Internet, details of Internet provision when you do not yet have an Internet connection? One option is to visit a cyber café or a friend who is connected. Table 3–10 provides the locations of lists of ISPs.

Table 3-10 Lists of Internet Service Providers

Location	Lists of ISPs
http://www.celestin.com/pocia/	A list of 1,250 providers (Aug. 1997) in the U.S., Canada, and many other countries.
http://www.thelist.com	Directory of more than 3,000 ISPs (Aug. 1997) in the U.S. and Canada.
http://www.yahoo.com/Business_and_Economy/-Companies/Internet_Services/	Comprehensive list from Yahoo!.
http://www.psi.com/orgservices/demand/	The view from a typical Internet provider.
http://www.bsdi.com/white-papers/-becoming-an-isp-kolstad.html	Becoming a service provider and an overview of the business.
http://web.cnam.fr/Network/Internet-access/-how_to_select.html	How to select an Internet provider.

Remember that if you are using an ISP's hardware, you need to consider not only the type of connection that exists from the ISP's information server to the Internet, but also the connection from your system to the ISP's server.

3.5.6.1 Mac OS 8 Internet Setup Assistant

The basic Mac OS 8 installation includes a software "assistant" that will lead you through the necessary steps to configure your Mac for accessing the Internet, up to and including connecting you to an ISP registration server where you can "shop" for an ISP.

The aptly named Internet Setup Assistant configures your TCP/IP and PPP control panels and lets you choose from three national ISPs. The assistant will also let you create several Internet configurations, which is useful if you, for example, use your Mac for connecting to your workplace through a dial-up connection and also an ISP for home use. However, the Assistant is aimed at client activities rather than configuring your Mac system as a server.

As for registering with an ISP, the registration assistant allows you to choose from a limited number of ISPs. (When Dave dialed in from home, he could have registered with Pacific Bell, Sprint, Concentric, or Netcom—all popular choices, but a far cry from the more than 100 ISPs with local numbers in the 619 area code, according to *http://www.thelist.com*.) Figure 3–3 shows the first screen of an ISP Registration Server.

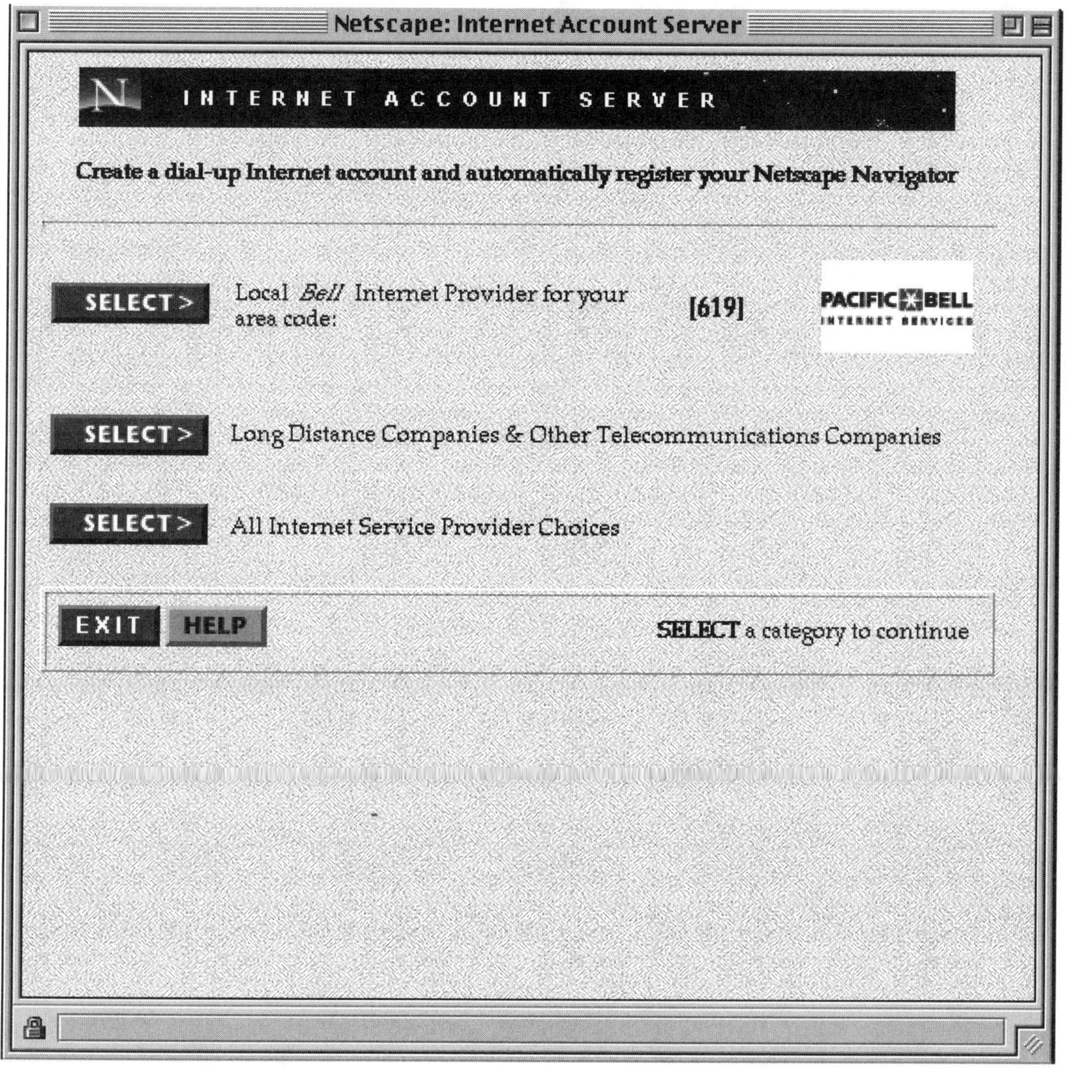

Figure 3-3 ISP Registration Server

▼▼▼

You have now been introduced to all the ingredients you will need to cook up a great information server. More resources are listed in Table 3–11. We can now move on to the basic utensils needed to begin cooking.

Table 3-11 Further Reading on Internet Connectivity

Location	Description
http://www.lanl.gov/general-information	General information about the Internet.
http://www.racal.com/internet.html	Starting point for getting Internet documentation.
http://www-neteng.uchicago.edu/Docs/terms.html	Glossary of Internet-related terms.
http://www-neteng.uchicago.edu/Docs/terms.html	Overview of TCP/IP.
gopher://ss1.racal.com/00/Networking/-TCP%20IP%20Admin.txt	Guide to setting up an Internet connection (free).
http://www.sunquest.com/netsvc/net_eval.html	A randomly selected commercial Internet service consultant.
http://oac3.hsc.uth.tmc.edu/staff/snewton/-tcp-tutorial/sec5.html	A brief tutorial on name serving.
http://titus.is.co.za/dnsrd/	A comprehensive guide to DNS.

• CHAPTER • 4

Choosing Your Appliances (Selecting Software)

Ingredients

- Server software
- Client software
- Development tools
- Support tools
- Web server add-ons

From the global recipe you now have a basic idea of what you will be able to cook using this cookbook. It is now time to get to know your kitchen a little better, a prerequisite to cooking and serving a fine meal.

Now that you have planned out your Internet server—your intended audience, the types of information you might encounter, the human and hardware resources, and your network connectivity—you are ready to select the server software that will meet your needs and fit within your budget.

As stated previously, this book discusses three basic services that you can support on your information server.

- An ftp-based service (file transfer protocol)
- An electronic mail-based service (e-mail)
- A Web-based service

We can no longer talk about an information server in a generic sense. Yes, the server may be a single piece of hardware, but the software, knowledge, and effort required varies when serving e-mail, files via ftp, Web pages, and Java applets. In this and subsequent chapters we begin with the simplest types of service—electronic mail and ftp file serving—and then move on to more complex Web-based information services incorporating sound, video, and downloadable applications.

An excellent on-line resource at which you can dig further into much of the information in this chapter is ComVista's Mac Internet Resource Database at

http://host.comvista.com/Internet.tfm

Once you've chosen to look more closely at some software options using the information in this chapter, Chapters 5–7 cover the ins and outs of installing various packages, including our recommended choices.

A Note on Software Versions. We cannot tell you what version of server software to get for the different types of information you will serve. Whatever we suggest may not be the current version when you read this book. Such is the force of this technology. Instead, we suggest you look at the appropriate README files before downloading any code or executables. A rule of thumb, since we prefer reliability to being on the cutting edge, is not to take beta releases, but to stick to the last full release of the software. Software does not always get better with subsequent releases and nearly always requires more resources to run, often in support of new features of no obvious relevance to what you wish to do. Conversely, if you take a very old, but stable version of the software, it may work now, but not when you or your system administrator upgrades the Mac OS. (All the packages we describe will work under Mac OS 8 for example, but we can't pass any judgment on Rhapsody.) You are then forced to repeat the install using a newer version that works with both the new and the old versions of the operating system and that you decided not to install the first time around—twice the work!

4.1 FTP servers

An ftp server can have various features that might make sense for you. If you want to read more about anonymous ftp see

http://iss.net/iss/anonftp.html

Throughout this book we shall refer to the files that you serve to users via ftp as the *ftp archive*. Features of an ftp server are

Basic

- Most widely available mechanism for transferring files
- Supported on all major platforms
- Relatively secure, because it has been tested over a long period
- Supports ASCII (text) and binary transfers
- Efficient
- Recursive—whole directory (folder) structures can be copied

Advanced

- You can provide instructions and comments when a user accesses the ftp archive and when they access specific directories within the archive.
- The person accessing the archive can be informed of when files were last modified in the archive.
- You can classify groups of users according to the login ID they use to access the ftp archive and from what host or subnet they come from.
- You can restrict how many simultaneous ftp users are allowed to access your system, in total or according to each class that you have defined.

- You can restrict who can upload files to and delete files from your ftp server.
- The server can uncompress and compress files automatically as they are transferred.
- You can log who accesses your ftp server and what they do.
- The server can provide a graceful mechanism for notifying ftp users of an impending shutdown.

The structure of the ftp archive is as simple or as complex as you wish to make it, and it is the only part of your overall file system that an anonymous ftp user is allowed to see. Once you have archived some files and correctly configured the ftp software (Section 5.2), users can access your ftp archive using ftp or a Web browser since all browsers support the ftp protocol.

Ftp also provides a mechanism, beyond electronic mail, for users to send you information that you might wish to make generally available on your server. That is, you can create a writable folder in your ftp archive in which ftp users deposit information. Permitting the uploading of information is discussed in Section 5.2.

Unlike UNIX, there is no generic ftp client or server included with the Mac OS distribution, but Table 4–1 lists some of the available ftp server software available to Mac users. Unless you have special requirements for high-speed transfers or stability, it will be difficult to beat the $10 shareware package NetPresenz (formerly FTPd) from Stairways Software. Note that NetPresenz also provides gopher and Web server capabilities as well.

For servers that demand higher-performance transfers, the ability to connect large numbers of simultaneous users, or a server that can run a long time unattended, you may want to consider one of the commercial packages, Rumpus by Maxum Development or Sonic FTP from Sonic Systems. Maxum—the company from which Apple licensed the technology for its Personal Web Sharing software—also produces Rumpus Pro to handle the traffic and volume of ftp "megasites."

In the same way that NetPresenz also offers Web and gopher serving features, you may also want to examine whether your Web server software provides sufficient ftp serving capabilities.

Table 4-1 Mac OS FTP Servers

Location	FTP Server
http://www.maxum.com/Rumpus/	Rumpus, commercial software by Maxum Development.
http://www.sonicsys.com/sonicftp.html	Sonic FTP, commercial software by Sonic Systems, Inc.
http://www.intercon.com/products/interserverp.html	InterServer Publisher, FTP, gopher, and HTTP commercial software by InterCon Systems.
http://www.stairways.com/netpresenz/	NetPresenz, HTTP, Gopher, and FTP server shareware by Stairways Software.
http://www.wpine.com/other/#FTPcs	FTPcs, FTP client and server commercial software by White Pine Software.

4.2 Mail Services

Electronic mail services, or e-mail services, are vital if you are trying to reach a wide and diverse audience. Many people have e-mail access but nothing else. Examples are users in developing countries and those using the less expensive services offered by Internet Service Providers (ISPs) like CompuServe and America Online. This situation will change as more and more people gain access to more sophisticated services. In the meantime, however, e-mail services are important and easy to offer because

- E-mail services require minimal computing resources, and e-mail clients are available for many platforms.
- Most users know how to use e-mail already, so there is no learning curve.
- E-mail can provide a great deal of information.

- E-mail reaches the widest possible audience. Users located in secure environments, for example, may have no other access to the Internet beyond e-mail.
- E-mail services are the most mature of the information services you could provide. Some people believe, therefore, that e-mail is the most secure service. Of course, breaches, when they occur, affect more people than the other services. The infamous Internet worm which exploited the popular UNIX program sendmail is a case in point. For an excellent discussion of this security breach, written by Charles Schmidt and Tom Darby, see

  http://www.mathcs.carleton.edu/students/darbyt/pages/worm.html

4.2.1 List Servers

Recall that the basic idea of list server software is to distribute all information to all users who choose to subscribe to the list. The same software is used to maintain all of the mailing lists. Typically, each list deals with a different topic. Subscribers to the list

- Receive information about that server by sending a message with keyword(s), for example, a list of responses to Frequently Asked Questions (FAQs) or all postings to the list in the last month.
- Send a message to the list server and have that message broadcast to all subscribers of the list.
- Receive all postings to the list, either one at a time or lumped together in daily or otherwise collected digests.
- May have a list moderator—someone who monitors what is received and selectively edits what is broadcast to all subscribers.
- Have the option to subscribe or unsubscribe to the list.

The major advantage—and potential disadvantage—of a list server is that it requires no action on the subscribers' parts beyond subscription to the list. After subscribing, they see everything posted to the list—and we mean everything! They have no control (beyond unsubscribing or requesting digests) over what they receive. This may be good if they read with interest most of the material posted to the list. On the other hand, it can be obtrusive since they may have to deal with a large amount of unwanted information. Contrast this to the information-upon-demand services like the Web, where consumers go to the information, rather than have it come to them. For a comprehensive discussion of list servers, see

http://www.grfn.org/~topher/listserv.html

http://www.cis.ohiostate.edu/hypertext/faq/usenet/mail/archive-servers/-faq/faq.html

As an information provider, typically you establish the list server, assign new lists, and remove old lists as demand dictates. You may also assign a moderator or moderators to each list. It is good "netiquette" to indicate whether a list is moderated or not to folks when they subscribe. Moderation serves to filter out information that is not appropriate to the list, but it is a form of censorship.

Table 4–2 lists some of the list servers available for the Mac OS. Of the two freeware packages, Macjordomo—named after, but not ported from, the UNIX-based list server software "Majordomo"—was only in beta release at the time of writing. Both AutoShare and Macjordomo offer the essential list serving features for most needs.

Of the commercial packages, CommuniGate offers a modular suite of messaging software, of which the list server is only one module. CommuniGate also has server modules for networking, faxing, paging, printing, and other communication tasks. For small organizations of less than five employees, CommuniGate is free.

LetterRip and ListSTAR, the latter produced by the makers of WebSTAR, are two highly rated, feature-packed list server programs that will work well for organizations with high demands for a list server.

Table 4-2 Mac OS List Servers

Location	List Server
http://www.dnai.com/~meh/autoshare/	AutoShare, freeware by Mikael Hansen.
http://leuca.med.cornell.edu/Macjordomo	Macjordomo, freeware by Michele Fuortes.
http://www.stalker.com/CommuniGate/SERVER/	CommuniGate Server, commercial client and server messaging software by Stalker Software.
http://www.fogcity.com/letterrip.html	LetterRip, commercial software by Fog City Software.
http://www.starnine.com/liststar/	ListSTAR, commercial list server by StarNine Corporation.

As an aside, if all you need are the very basic list server functions—taking an incoming message and sending it to a list of subscribers—some Mac OS e-mail client software can be configured to do this for you. With Eudora Pro or Claris E-mailer, for example, message filters can forward messages automatically or reply with canned responses. If you don't mind a little manual effort to handle requests for subscribing and unsubscribing names from a list, you might get by with the client software you already use.

4.2.2 Other Mail Services

You can also use e-mail to serve information, as described in Section 2.3.1. An information server processes a mail message requesting some information. The request is in a form that can be recognized by software that can return an automatic response. You may want to provide two possible types of response:

- A canned reply—information on a specific product sold by your organization, details of a piece of software you are giving away, or the hypertext framework of this book. In Table 4–2, both AutoShare and ListSTAR offer this capability.
- A file from your ftp site and sent to the user as part of the e-mail reply. Why not just go to the ftp site and get the file directly? As stated earlier, some users will only have e-mail access. If you want them to have access to your ftp archive, you will want your server to have this capability.

In Table 4–3, FireShare provides the ability to distribute files from your ftp site via e-mail. Some of the commercial list server packages also provide this functionality.

The distinction between e-mail services and other forms of service cannot be delineated completely. An example of this is making all messages to a list available through a Web service so users can reference previous discussions. This integration requires a filter to mark up mail messages with HTML so they can be served as Web documents.

Consider also whether to provide a gateway between the Web and your mailing lists. This service simplifies a user's ability to subscribe to various mailing lists and, therefore, may be of value to your user community. Users no longer have to know the names of the lists and can use a Web form that ensures the correct syntax for subscribing to the appropriate list.

Table 4–3 describes other mail-related software for the Mac OS. Many of these, such as the Eudora Internet Mail Server (EIMS) (formerly the Apple Internet Mail Server and before that MailShare) perform basic e-mail tasks such as distributing messages via the Post Office Protocol and the Simple Mail Transfer Protocol to accounts within your organization. EIMS is required by the AutoShare list server discussed above.

Table 4-3 Mac OS Mail Service

Location	Mail Service
http://nspace.cts.com/html/NetLife/NSpace/FireShare/	FireShare, shareware by Jerry Stratton. Allows file exchange via e-mail.
http://www.eudora.com/freeware/	Eudora Internet Mail Server (EIMS), freeware from Eudora.
http://www.opendoor.com/maildoor/	MailDoor Multi-domain Mail Clerk, commercial software from Open Door Networks Inc.
http://www.stalker.com/SIMS/	Stalker Internet Mail Server by Stalker Software.
http://grant.media-gn.nl/r2x/index.html	RingTwice, freeware by Grant Software Solutions.
http://www.sonicsys.com/sonicmail.html	Sonic Mail, commercial software from Sonic Systems.
http://www.spiderisland.com/product/tfv5.html	TeleFinder BBS, commercial Web, BBS, and mail server software by Spider Island Software.
ftp://ftp.comvista.com/pub/net/mail/MailStop1.1.6.sit.hqx	MailStop, freeware from the University of Minnesota.
http://thelorax.starnine.com/scripts/listserver.cgi.hqx	listserver.cgi from StarNine lets users subscribe or unsubscribe to ListSTAR lists via a WebSTAR CGI script.
http://www.starnine.com/mail/mail.html	StarNine Mail, commercial software from StarNine.

4.3 Web Servers

Mac OS Web servers—those servers that support at least the http protocol used by all Web browsers—are numerous, and each is varied in its capability. For the Mac OS, there does appear to be a commercial package of choice. WebSTAR offers a full range of features, but there are various other commercial, shareware, and freeware packages that may suit your needs. However, what is a very capable Web server today is soon obsolete. The best we can do is to answer the question, "What features of an http server are important?"

- *Error logging* that supports CERN/NCSA common log format. Every event performed by the server is logged to a file. The advantage of using the most common log format is that there are already tools written to summarize this information should you need to do that (Section 7.2.3 is devoted to this topic).
- *Support for server-side includes* (Section 10.4). A server-side include is similar to an include statement in a number of programming languages. For example, rather than manually inserting the date the Web page was last modified into the HTML each time you modify the file, you can simply include a function that returns the modification date based on the file modification date retained by the Mac OS. Allowing external commands to be invoked through server-side includes, however, represents a security risk. Many servers support this feature, yet optionally allow you to turn it off. In any but the most secure environments, server-side includes are a must for creating comprehensive and easily managed Web pages.
- *Extensibility.* Each time a new Web technology is developed you don't want to update your Web server software. Servers including WebSTAR and Quid Pro Quo allow you to add plug-ins (similar to client browser plug-ins) with new processing capabilities to your server. The two most common plug-in formats are WebSTAR (or W*API) and MOSAPI (My Open Server Application Programming Interface).
- *Limited file access.* Typical for servers supporting this feature, the Web page administrator explicitly specifies what folders and files are accessible. These files are then cached and made available for serving. Limited file access increases security but requires more effort to maintain.

- *Access prohibited by IP address or domain name*. Only specified remote Internet hosts can access the server. Useful in creating intranets.
- *Actions based on file type*. The server can perform some action on specific types of file, for example CGI scripts. In other words, good support for many MIME types, and extensibility to support for new MIME types.
- *Default directory tree*. A directory (folder) hierarchy is automatically configured for containing files associated with the Web server and the information being served.
- *Available search engines*. Text search engines require close cooperation with the Web server. Search engines generally only support a subset of the available Web servers.
- *Cost*. Not all servers are free. Whether you buy a server should depend on whether you need support services and not on software quality. The free Web servers are generally of high quality.

If you thought that this is a long list of considerations, note that it is only a partial list. Do not be deterred, however; most http servers support a significant number of these options. Table 4–4 provides some links to more information on Web servers, features, and comparisons.

Table 4-4 General Web Server Information

Location	Description
http://www.webcompare.com/	Web server comparison site.
http://www.yahoo.com/Computers_and_Internet/-Software/Internet/World_Wide_Web/Servers/	Links to servers and server information compiled by Yahoo! search engine.
http://www.w3.org/Servers.html	Server discussion from the World Wide Web (W3) Consortium.
http://serverwatch.internet.com/	Web site and newsletter on Web server developments.
http://WWW.Stars.com/Software/Servers/	A current survey of Web servers others have recently installed.

Table 4–5 lists some of the available Web servers for the Mac OS. At the time of writing, according to a 1997 Georgia Tech survey, the commercial software WebSTAR and its shareware sibling MacHTTP dominate the Mac OS Web server market. In fact, that survey found that MacHTTP and WebSTAR were used by nearly 25 percent of respondents, making them the second most popular Web server across *all* platforms. See

http://www.gvu.gatech.edu/user_surveys/survey-1997-04/graphs/-webmaster/Which_Server.html

Table 4-5 Mac OS HTTP Servers

Location	HTTP Server
http://www.starnine.com/webstar/	WebSTAR, commercial software from StarNine.
http://www.apple.com	Personal Web Sharing, commercial software from Apple.
http://www.socialeng.com/	Quid Pro Quo, freeware by Chris Hawk's Social Engineering.
http://www.tenon.com/products/webten/	WebTen, commercial software from Tenon Intersystems. (Mac OS version of the Apache Web server.)
http://www.starnine.com/machttp/	MacHTTP, shareware from StarNine. The original Mas OS Web server.
http://www.stairways.com/netpresenz/	NetPresenz, Web, ftp, and gopher server shareware from Stairways Software.
http://www.sonicsys.com/sonicweb.html	Sonic Web, commercial software from Sonic Systems.
http://www.spiderisland.com/	TeleFinder, commercial software from Spider Island Software.

Table 4-5 Mac OS HTTP Servers *(Continued)*

Location	HTTP Server
http://www.mdg.com/frame/more_download.html	Web Server 4D, commercial Web/database server from MDG Computer Services.
http://www.softarc.com/fcis/fcis.html	First Class, commercial software by SoftArc. Touted as an intranet server.
http://sodium.ch.man.ac.uk/pages/httpd4Mac/home.html	httpd4Mac, freeware by Bill Melotti.
http://www.ai.mit.edu/projects/iiip/doc/cl-http/-home-page.html	MacCommon LISP Server, freeware by John C. Mallery.
http://summary.net/soft/easyserve.html	EasyServe, freeware by Jason Linhart.
http://netwings.com/nest.html	Netwings Internet Server, commercial multiservice server from Netwings.
http://www.webink.com/	Webink and Webink Pro, commercial Web/database servers from Webink.
http://www.clearway.com/pages/-firesite-home.html	FireSite, commercial Web server from Clearway Technologies.
http://www.pictorius.com/	Net Servers, free commercial software from Pictorius.

WebSTAR, with its complete set of features, security, and extensibility via plug-ins—which function much like the more familiar plug-ins that add functionality to Web browsers—is the leading Mac OS Web server and is the standard against which other Mac OS Web servers measure themselves. Other servers such as WebTen insist they are faster than WebSTAR, but for a high-end, large-scale Mac-based Web server, we recommend WebSTAR.

Of the budget alternatives, we recommend Quid Pro Quo, a full-featured freeware package that made a splash with its version 1.0, for most small-scale sites. Another solid choice is the shareware

MacHTTP, distributed by StarNine, and the second most popular Mac OS Web server, according to a Georgia Tech survey. For sheer uniqueness, the MacCommon LISP Server out of MIT can be extended with your own LISP code, which opens up all sorts of possibilities for adding artificial intelligence functions into your server. CL-HTTP can be extended with, for example, computed URLs, constraint-guided Web walking, VRML generation, and dynamic form processing.

4.3.1 Emerging Server Technologies

Internet server technology is evolving rapidly, with the biggest developments in Web-based servers, rather than mail or ftp servers. Even the definition of what constitutes a Web-based server is undergoing change. This change is occurring on two fronts:

- Hardware specific to Internet information serving and retrieval is becoming available.
- Software with a wider range of capabilities is becoming available. For example, consider the integrated Web/database servers Webink and Web Server 4D in Table 4–5.

The term "Web server" will evolve from referring to a combination of generic hardware and specific software to referring to specific hardware and specific software. Vendors are already selling hardware made from basic components but customized for information serving, notably database servers, which optimize such features as text searching and handling many simultaneous network connections.

Further, with languages like Java, the idea of a Web server as a single piece of software handling http requests is disappearing. In Java, it is easy in a few lines of code to open a TCP/IP connection to a server, which can then be used to communicate with a server-side application that does not rely on the http protocol. This lends credence to the idea of a "global computer," since computation and information lookup are easily distributed. We will return to this notion in Chapter 12.

4.4 Search Engines

As your site grows, your audience will appreciate the availability of a search engine or index into your information. This section introduces software that gathers, indexes, and searches all or parts of the information on your Internet server. This is not a discussion of the various search engines, such as Alta Vista, Lycos, or Webcrawler, that you use when you browse the Internet. An informative paper on those can be found at

http://www.indiana.edu/~librcsd/search/

The situation is complicated since gatherers, indexers, and search engines can be mixed and matched.

- Gatherers, also known as "crawlers," are programs that visit Web pages and all the Web pages referred to from those pages until the entire site has been visited.
- Indexers maintain a database about all the pages that it knows about; that information might come from the HTML TITLE tag, the first paragraphs, the META tag, or the entire document.
- A search engine takes user queries and searches through some database for matches to that query. Thus, one way to provide search capability on your Web site is to run a crawler that creates an index and then have a search engine that queries the index.
- These tools can be further contrasted to robots which, for our purposes, follow the detailed definition found in

  http://info.webcrawler.com/mak/projects/robots/faq.html

  A robot actively searches the whole Web by requesting documents and then placing them in an index. While the principle is the same as a gatherer or crawler, a robot generally covers the entire Web, using some heuristics to determine when to stop gathering documents. Here we are being more specific, restricting ourselves to the information at your site and possibly explicitly defined hyperlinks elsewhere.

As you can see from Table 4–6, many search engines for the Mac OS were designed to run specifically with WebSTAR, and most require additional software. We recommend the shareware Search-Server because of the value and because it will run on any CGI-compatible server without additional software. (And it is freeware for users of the Quid Pro Quo Web server.)

Of the commercial products, Phantom from Maxum Development requires no additional software and provides your site with all three components of a complete search tool—gatherer, indexer, and searcher. And because Phantom has a built-in Web server mode, it can run as a stand-alone search engine on a separate machine, which keeps your primary server free to handle additional incoming requests.

Table 4-6 Mac OS Search Tools

Location	Search Tools
http://www.maxum.com/phantom/	Phantom, commercial search engine and crawler from Maxum Development.
http://www.socialeng.com/html/searchserver.html	SearchServer, shareware/freeware search engine from Social Engineering for any CGI-compatible Web server.
http://www.cybertech.apple.com/applesearch/	AppleSearch, freeware from Apple that works with WebSTAR or MacHTTP.
http://www.blueworld.com/macsite/searcher/	MacSite Searcher, commercial software from Blue World Communications. Requires WebSTAR, UserLand's Frontier, and Claris FileMaker Pro.
http://www.dadatypo.com/LTODBS/suites/-webServerScripts/simpleSearch.html	simpleSearch, freeware from dada typographics. Requires WebSTAR and UserLand's Frontier.
http://associate.com/innovative/glen_stewart/-about_warpsearch.html	WarpSearch, shareware by Glen Stewart. Works with any CGI-compatible Web server.
http://www.metasys.co.jp/	Mango, commercial software from Metasys. Requires Tango from Everyware Development.

4.5 Name Server

In addition to your Internet server software and a search engine, we will mention one more piece of software that you may want to consider if you expect much traffic at your Internet server: a name server, or DNS server. Recall from Section 2.2.4 that name serving—also referred to as Domain Name Service (DNS)—is the ability to resolve the IP address in the form, for example, 123.123.123.123 from a name of the form *pauline.sdsc.edu.*

Remember, as you are using the URLs listed in this book to look up information, you are acting as a client. You are resolving the names to locate the various items you need on a variety of servers. Thus, it is important that you understand how names are resolved. In simple terms, the name-to-number mapping is needed since humans work better with names, but computers work better with numbers. All your information serving tools can use the names—most of the URLs in this book are names—and these must be resolved (converted to a number) if the server is to route your request to the destination.

We should emphasize that maintaining a DNS is not a trivial matter. For clients to access your information server they must resolve the names; name resolution may or may not be a function of your information server. Your ISP may provide the DNS service for your site. *However, if you want to register your own domain with InterNIC, you will need both a primary and secondary name service.* Of the DNS servers listed in Table 4–7, QuickDNS Pro and Sonic DNS can serve as primary and secondary server. Keeping the DNS server on your local network also decreases traffic on the link to your ISP, yielding faster responses.

QuickDNS Pro and Sonic DNS also offer the ability to perform load balancing, which distributes network traffic among multiple hosts for a popular Web server or other environments, making it possible for several computers to share the same URL. In other words, *http://www.your-server.com* could be running on two or more computers that each handle some of the incoming requests.

Table 4-7 DNS Servers

Location	Description
http://www.menandmice.com/	QuickDNS Pro and QuickDNS Lite, commercial software from Men & Mice. Works with WebSTAR.
http://cybertech.apple.com/macdns.html	MacDNS, commercial software from Apple.
http://www.sonicsys.com/sonicdns.html	Sonic DNS, commercial software from Sonic Systems.
http://www.gross.net/sw/nonsequitur/	NonSequitur, freeware DNS. In beta release at time of writing.

So far we have only covered the essential server software—the server itself, a search engine, and a name server. Other Web server additions, such as server-side includes, CGI scripting, and database connectivity, will be discussed in Chapters 11–13. And you will likely want some tools for performing such tasks as managing your site remotely, tracking your server's performance, and security, not to mention more mundane computer maintenance tasks such as backups, disk utilities, and virus software. We will discuss most of these tools in Chapter 7.

4.6 Client Software

In addition to server software, you will need to install client software on your Mac so that you can view and test the information you plan to serve. In this section, we cover Web browsers, ftp clients, viewers, and players.

The distinction between a browser, viewer, and player is somewhat arbitrary, but maintaining the distinction may help clarify your needs. In this book, a browser is software to browse a combination of text and graphics, a viewer is software to display and possibly edit a graphics image, and a player plays sound, animation, or video. If a browser calls a viewer or player to display a particular file, the viewer or player is called a helper application.

4.6.1 Web Browsers

If you are going to support Web access to your information server, you need a Web browser, also called the Web client. A browser also offers the simplest way to download the software for your Internet server and to view your own Web documents. In theory you do not need to view your own documents before serving them, but we recommend it. In practice it is foolhardy to serve something you have not viewed yourself. Even when using a What-You-See-Is-What-You-Get (WYSIWIG) HTML Editor, your first attempts at HTML markup will generally be What-You-See-Is-Not-What-You-Want. Different browsers on different platforms with different preference settings will interpret the HTML generated by the editor in slightly different ways.

There are several choices for Mac OS Web browsers. There is a catch-22 here. To select the browser that best suits your needs, you need to access the Web for information and reviews of the latest releases, but to access the Web requires a browser. To solve this dilemma, we suggest you install one of the recommended browsers. If later you find the browser you have chosen is inadequate, refer to *http://www.browserwatch.com/* to help you make another selection.

The Browserwatch Web site has a test page that you can view with the browser you are currently using, see what it looks like, and then see what that same page looks like when viewed with other browsers. Since the HTML specification is constantly evolving, the test indicates how many of the current features of HTML are recognized by a particular browser (very useful). This discussion should be telling you to update your browser regularly.

Table 4–8 lists some of the more popular browsers for the Mac OS. If you have Mac OS 8, the installation CD-ROM includes no fewer than three of them: Netscape Navigator, Microsoft's Internet Explorer, and Apple's CyberDog (based on Apple's discontinued OpenDoc technology). If you purchased Mac OS 8 prior to or shortly after the Apple-Microsoft announcement at MacWorld 97, Netscape Navigator will automatically be installed as your default browser. Part of the agreement with Microsoft will make Internet Explorer the default browser for future Mac OS releases. We are going to avoid this mine field by not recommending a particular browser. They are all fine pieces of software.

Table 4-8 Mac OS Web Browsers

Location	HTML Browsers
http://www.ncsa.uiuc.edu/SDG/Software/MacMosaic/	MacMosaic, freeware from NCSA.
http://www.netscape.com/flash3/comprod/products/-communicator/	Netscape Communicator/Navigator, commercial software from Netscape.
http://www.microsoft.com/ie/mac/	Internet Explorer, free commercial software from Microsoft.
http://www.aolpress.com/press/	AOLPress, freeware from America Online.
http://cyberdog.apple.com/	CyberDog, free software from Apple
http://www.lirmm.fr/~gutkneco/maclynx/	MacLynx, freeware from the Lynx group.

Note that MacLynx is a line-oriented browser. Why even consider a line-oriented browser on a Mac? MacLynx suggests one good reason: For visually impaired Web surfers, MacLynx can take advantage of Apple's SpeechManager software to read the text downloaded from Web pages.

In choosing your browser, you may also want to check out these URLs:

http://www.gvu.gatech.edu/user_surveys/

http://browserwatch.internet.com/stats.html

These sites contain statistics for which browsers were used to select, at random, heavily accessed Web pages. Based on BrowserWatch statistics at the time of writing, Netscape should be your first choice since it has 58 percent of the market share for all platforms. Internet Explorer has 33 percent, while CyberDog, in third place overall, has 2 percent.

4.6.1.1 VRML Browsers

The implications of the Virtual Reality Modeling Language (VRML) are profound, since it brings information across the Internet in much the same way we traditionally get information. Rather than click your way through highlighted text on the screen, VRML lets you "walk" into a virtual library, take a virtual book off the virtual shelf, open it, and read. At the time of writing, the higher-end hardware resources needed to use VRML effectively have so far precluded its wide use. Further, while extensive libraries of scene information are emerging that can be used to make your scenes, you must still do a lot of work to develop the necessary pages. For these reasons, VRML is not covered in depth in this book; however, we do provide you with adequate pointers to information you need to get started (Section 14.4).

Table 4–9 gives locations for available VRML plug-ins for Mac OS browsers. For another source of all things VRML, we recommend you visit the VRML Repository at

http://vrml.sdsc.edu

Table 4-9 VRML Browsers

Location	Description
http://www.livepicture.com/html/viewers.html	RealSpace Viewer, commercial VRML 2.0 plug-in or browser from Live Picture.
http://www.intervista.com/products/worldview/index.html	WorldView, free commercial VRML 2.0 plug-in from InterVista.
http://cosmo.sgi.com/	CosmoPlayer, free VRML 2.0 plug-in from Silicon Graphics.
http://quickdraw3d.apple.com/Viewer.HTML	Whurlwind 3-D Browser and Web Surfer, VRML 1.0 freeware from Apple.
http://www.virtus.com/products_vr.html	WalkThrough Pro, commercial VRML 1.0 browser and world creator by Virtus.

4.6.2 FTP Clients

For downloading files from an ftp archive, you may not actually need software in addition to your Web browser. By pointing to URLs of the form *ftp://ftp.site.com*, just about any browser version will let you download and save files from an anonymous ftp archive. In addition, recent versions of Navigator and Explorer also let you upload, or send files to, an ftp archive with the "Upload File..." menu option. Uploading and downloading files are the two most important functions of an ftp client, so your Web browser may suffice for the basics.

However, it can be useful to have a dedicated ftp client, particularly if you do a lot of ftp downloads and uploads. While a Web browser will allow you to access any ftp archive, regardless of whether that archive resides on a server supporting Web (http) access, an ftp client is still a useful addition to your toolkit. A Web browser will only access anonymous ftp archives; however, an ftp client can access files on any computer running an ftp server provided you know a username and password on that machine. In these days of distributed computing you will likely need such file transfers between computers upon which you have accounts. Table 4–10 lists some Mac OS ftp clients.

Table 4-10 Mac OS FTP Clients

Location	FTP Client
http://www.stairways.com/anarchie/	Anarchie, Archie and ftp shareware by Stairways Software.
http://www.dartmouth.edu/pages/softdev/fetch.html	Fetch, shareware by Jim Matthews. Free to education and nonprofit organizations.
http://www.vicomtech.com/ftp.software.html	Vicom FTP Client, commercial software from Vicom Technologies.
http://www.ncsa.uiuc.edu/SDG/Software/Brochure/MacSoftDesc.html#MacTelnet	NCSA Telnet, freeware from NCSA. Telnet software that supports ftp sessions.

If you use software such as Anarchie, you can search through the world's ftp sites using "Archie." Archie lets you search what amounts to a global table of contents of ftp archives, which makes finding information on ftp servers straightforward. In particular, the Macintosh community has two major FTP sites—Info-Mac and UMich—with collections of Macintosh software and information. Info-Mac is accessible via the Web at *http://www.pht.com/info-mac/* and several mirror sites; the UMich archive is on the Web at *http://www-personal.umich.edu/~sdamask/umich-mirrors/*.

If you plan to make files available via ftp from your Internet server, you should make sure that those files are registered at an Archie server. We shall see how to do this in Section 6.1. For now, it's sufficient to know that such a capability exists. Anarchie communicates with the Archie servers by means of a protocol called *Prospero*.

4.6.3 Viewers and Players

Table 4–11 lists sources of many Mac OS utilities for viewing graphics and playing sounds and movies on the Internet.

Graphics Viewers. The major types of graphics files on the Web, GIF and JPEG, can be viewed directly in most Web browsers with no additional software. However, for developing the information to serve on your Web site, you will want at least some basic graphics utilities to create these image types. GraphicConverter (Section 5.4.1) views more that 80 different graphics formats and can save images in more than 30 formats.

Audio Players. Sound has been integral to Macintosh systems from the beginning. Assuming your intended audience has hardware support for sound, what software do you use to play sound files? The answer depends on the browser being used to access the sound and the format of the sound file. Sound files, unlike most other file types vary depending on the hardware vendor; Macintosh, Windows, Sun, SGI, and other platforms all have their own preferred formats. Chances are that you will need a helper application or a plug-in. There is no shortage of Mac OS sound tools. SoundApp (Section 5.5) can play and convert most sound formats.

Movie Players. Like audio players, movie players can pose challenges with respect to hardware support, format conversion, and the availability of helper applications. Again, this is no problem for the Mac OS. In fact, Mac OS conversion tools provide excellent support for cross-platform environments. Apple's free QuickTime software and Netscape plug-in allow you to view the two most common movie formats—MPEG and QuickTime. The QuickTime software and browser plug-in from Apple (Section 5.6) lets you view both QuickTime and MPEG movies.

Table 4-11 Lists of Mac OS Viewers and Players

Location	Viewers, Editors and Players
http://www.lemkesoft.de/us_contents.html	GraphicConverter, shareware by Thorsten Lemke.
http://www-cs-students.stanford.edu/~franke/SoundApp/	SoundApp, freeware by Norman Franke.
http://www.macworld.com/software/-IndexSoftware.WebGraphics.html	MacWorld archive of Web graphics viewers and converters.
http://www.macworld.com/software/-IndexSoftware.Sounds.html	MacWorld software archive of Sound utilities.
http://www.macdownload.com	Another magazine-provided source of Mac OS utilities.
http://quicktime.apple.com/	Apple's QuickTime software and plug-in.
http://www.wavenet.com/~axgrindr/quimby4.html	Mac Sound Utilities listing.

4.7 Development Tools

In addition to server and client software, you will also need tools to create the information you want to serve. Here we discuss the options for creating Web pages, converting existing information to a Web format, and designing the look and feel of your site.

4.7.1 HTML Editors

As we shall see in Chapter 9, writing HTML is relatively straightforward using a standard text editor or word processor. However, a WYSIWYG HTML editor that works like a word processor and does the coding in the background, while presenting you with a final view of the Web page, definitely speeds up the markup process and simplifies creation and debugging of complex documents. There are a number of approaches for editing HTML:

- You can download a free HTML editor.
- You can buy a commercial HTML editor or purchase a Web browser with editing capabilities.
- You can export from an existing word processing package that produces HTML format. Most current versions of Mac word processors support this option.
- You can use a free or commercial filter to convert an existing format to HTML as described below (Section 4.7.3).

When making a choice it is worth noting these pros and cons of HTML editors:

- Documents produced using an HTML editor nearly always look better than those written directly in HTML, simply because most people do not remember all the syntax necessary to produce a high-quality document.
- Editors are WYSIWIG; anything else involves a two-step process—writing and viewing.
- The evolution of HTML is occurring faster than the editors that write it. Thus, features supported by HTML may not be available using your editor.
- An HTML editor will shorten the development cycle.

- HTML produced by WYSIWYG editors may be difficult or impossible to maintain and edit by hand.
- Tags inserted with one HTML editor may not be editable in a different editor.

Table 4–12 provides the locations of current lists of the many HTML editors available for Mac OS.

Table 4-12 Lists of HTML Editors

Location	Description
http://host.comvista.com/Internet.tfm	Jon Wiederspan's Macintosh Internet Resources Directory.
http://www.macworld.com/software/-IndexSoftware.WebAuthoring.html	MacWorld's software directory.
http://www.yahoo.com/Computers_and_Internet/-Software/Internet/World_Wide_Web/HTML_Editors/-Macintosh/	Yahoo! list of Mac OS HTML editors.

In choosing an HTML editor, cost will undoubtedly play a major role. At the low end, you can learn HTML yourself and use SimpleText to edit the HTML code and view it in your browser. Cost: $0. Another low-cost option, upgrade your word processor to a version that can produce HTML-formatted versions of your documents. This way, you can place images and format text and view the results in a Web browser.

The next level would be to invest in a low-cost, non-WYSIWYG editor. The primary advantage of these editors is a combination of closely controlling the HTML source without typing in the sometimes tedious HTML tags. Among the non-WYSIWYG HTML editors listed in Table 4–13, BBEdit, BBEdit Lite, and PageSpinner have all been rated highly.

Table 4-13 Non-WYSIWYG HTML Editors

Location	HTML Editors
http://www.barebones.com/bbedit.html	BBEdit (commercial) and BBEdit Lite (freeware) from Bare Bones Software. Text editors with HTML extensions.
http://www.algonet.se/~optima/pagespinner.html	PageSpinner, shareware from Optima Systems.
http://www.miracleinc.com/Products/W2Lite/index.html	Web Weaver Lite, commercial software from Miracle Software.
http://www.cris.com/~raydaly/htmljive.html	HTMLjive, freeware by Ray Daly. HTML editor written in JavaScript.
http://www.cs.umd.edu/~keleher/alpha.html	Alpha, shareware by Pete Keleher. Text editor with HTML extensions.

WYSIWYG Web page creators—the most expensive option with the most Web design features—give you precise control over the look of your pages with virtually no HTML coding. Even here, though, features can vary widely. At the very least, the editor will support text formatting, tables, and placement of GIF and JPEG images, as in the Netscape editors. At the high end, the Web site creation tools support frames, pixel-level control of layout, site management, and varying preview capabilities.

These packages generally combine functions—HTML editing, image editing, image mapping, and others—that you might otherwise have to get from a handful of separate shareware or freeware utilities.

Given that some Web browsers offer the ability to edit Web pages as well, the question becomes a matter of the features that other editors provide to justify at least a separate software download or possibly a separate purchase. GoLive CyberStudio, for instance, offers Web site and page spell-checking; multiserver Web site administration; WYSIWYG frames preview; support for ActiveX and WebObjects; visual link checking, table editing, and layout; advanced site management; and JavaScript editing.

Table 4–14 lists some of the available WYSIWYG editors for the Mac OS. While we (well, Dave in particular) really like GoLive CyberStudio, most of these commercial packages provide a great deal of control over the look of your Web pages. As far as cost, CyberStudio falls in the middle of the price range for the programs listed here.

Table 4-14 WYSIWYG Web Page Editors

Location	WYSIWYG Editor
http://www.golive.com/	CyberStudio, commercial software from GoLive.
http://www.adobe.com/prodindex/pagemill/main.html	PageMill and SiteMill, commercial software from Adobe.
http://www.claris.com/products/claris/homepage/-homepage.html	Home Page, commercial software from Claris.
http://www.netobjects.com/	Fusion, commercial software from NetObjects.
http://www.symantec.com/vpagemac/index_product.html	Visual Page, commercial software from Symantec.
http://www.netscape.com/flash1/comprod/products/-communicator/	Communicator or Navigator Gold, commercial software from Netscape.
http://www.microsoft.com/frontpage/	FrontPage, commercial software from Microsoft.
http://www.newsoftinc.com/Products/Mac/PersonalPage/-index.html	Presto! Personal Page, commercial software from NewSoft.
http://www.sq.com/products/hotmetal/hmp-org.htm	HoTMetaL Pro, commercial software from SoftQuad.
http://www.randomnoise.com/	Coda, commercial software from RandomNoise. Creates Java applets.

4.7.2 Image Editors and Map Makers

Even though the WYSIWYG Web editors help you place images on your Web pages, very few of them help you create and edit the images. Unless you plan to stock your Web pages entirely with clip art, you will need some sort of image editor to create your images. Chances are that at least a low-end paint program was included in the software bundle with your Mac. At the opposite end of the spectrum, Adobe PhotoShop and Adobe Illustrator are the recognized leaders in image creation and manipulation. In between are an almost unlimited number of options. Table 4–15 provides you with some places to look for lists of Mac OS image editors.

Table 4-15 Image Editors and Clickable Map Builders

Location	Description
http://www.dcs.gla.ac.uk/~snaddosg/Creations/-ImageMapper/ (also at *http://www.macdownload.com)*	ImageMapper, shareware by Stuart Snaddon. Creates client-side, server-side, and Java highlighted image maps.
http://www.macworld.com/software/-IndexSoftware.WebGraphics.html	MacWorld software for Web Graphics.
http://www.macworld.com/software/-IndexSoftware.GraphicsUtilities.html	More MacWorld software.
http://www.yahoo.com/Computers_and_Internet/-Software/Reviews/Titles/Graphics/	Yahoo! list of graphics software reviews.
http://www.pht.com/info-mac/ *http://hyperarchive.lcs.mit.edu/HyperArchive.html*	Info-Mac archive (and a mirror site).

On the Web, however, images are not always just for show. They also serve as *clickable maps*—navigation tools in which parts of an image are hyperlinked to another Web page (see Section 10.2). In other words, when you mouse-click on a clickable image, that point on the image is mapped to another URL, which is downloaded to your browser. (Clickable maps were originally devised as CGI scripts handled by the Web server, but they proved so useful that the maps were incorporated into the HTML language to be interpreted by the client. We will only be considering these "client-side" image maps.)

Clickable map builders produce the map that relates a point on an image to a URL.

Many of the WYSIWYG Web editors listed in Table 4–14 include the ability to create clickable image maps as part of the package. However, Table 4–15 lists software utilities whose sole purpose is to create clickable maps. (Technically, the map is only a few lines of HTML text, but trust us: This is one bit of HTML you really don't want to create by hand.)

4.7.3 Filters

Filters are programs that translate one file format to another format—or in our discussion here, a non-Web format to a Web-servable format. There are a large number of forever-changing filters available via the Internet. The trick is to not download those filters that you think you might need, but to wait until you need a filter and then download it. This way you get the most capable version when you need it. Table 4–16 provides sites where current lists of available filters formats to and from HTML are maintained.

Table 4-16 Lists of HTML-based Filters

Location	Description
http://www.w3.org/hypertext/WWW/Tools/Filters.html	List of HTML-based filters.
http://www.yahoo.com/Computers_and_Internet/Internet/-World_Wide_Web/HTML_Converters/-Shareware_Freeware/	List of HTML-based filters.
http://host.comvista.com/Internet.tfm	Jon Wiederspan's Mac Internet Resource Directory.

Table 4–17 provides a list of the more common HTML filters. Filters are characterized by whether they filter with word processing documents, computer code, mail files, graphics, or other types of textual information. Note that most current Mac OS word processors provide options for saving documents in HTML format; therefore, you don't need an external filter. Also worth mentioning is Terry Morse's Myrmidon, a Chooser extension that "prints" to HTML instead of a printer, so it will produce an HTML-format file from any application that can print.

Table 4-17 Common HTML Filters

Location	Information Type/Filter
Word Processing	
http://www.sunpack.com/RTF	RTF to HTML, shareware by Chris Hector.
http://www.unimelb.edu.au/~ssilcot/-SilcotsHTMLMacrosReadMe2.5.2.html	SS-Nisus HTML Macros, freeware by Sandra Silcot for Nisus Writer.
Desktop Publishing	
http://www.extensis.com/products/CyberPress/	CyberPress, commercial software from Extensis for Quark XPress.
http://www.astrobyte.com/BeyondPress/	BeyondPress, commercial software from Astrobyte for converting Quark Xpress.
http://www.logic.be/ftpserver/-X0001_Collect_HTML_read_me.html	Collect HTML, commercial software by Kris Coppieters for converting Quark Xpress.
http://www.hexmac.de/	HexWeb, commercial software from HexMac International for converting Quark Xpress.
ftp://mars.aliens.com/pub/Macintosh/HTML_Xport.sit	HTML Xport, shareware by Eric Knudstrup for converting Quark Xpress.

Table 4-17 Common HTML Filters *(Continued)*

Location	Information Type/Filter
http://www.msystems.com/mcohen/websucker.html	PageMaker Websucker, freeware from Multimedia Systems Consulting.
http://www.harlequin.com/webmaker/	WebMaker, commercial software from the Harlequin Group for converting FrameMaker.
Spreadsheets and Databases	
http://staff.westlake.com/jamie/CSV-to-HTML	CSV to HTML, freeware converter by Jamie Flournoy. Converts CSV-format spreadsheets to HTML.
http://www710.gsfc.nasa.gov/704/dgd/xl2html.html	XL2HTML, freeware by Jordan Evans for converting Excel 5.0 spreadsheets.
http://www.cais.net/wrngrp/dbf-to-html.html	Dbf-to-html, shareware from the Warner Group for converting database files.
Miscellaneous	
http://www.tjp.washington.edu/bdm/genealogy/-sparrowhawk.html	Sparrowhawk, shareware by Bradley Mohr. Converts GEDCOM genealogy files.
http://www.med.ufl.edu/medinfo/mtx/	MTX Tool, freeware by Richard Rathe. Converts MTX files to HTML.
http://www.terrymorse.com/	Myrmidon, commercial software by Terry Morse. Uses Chooser extension to print HTML format from any application.

▼▼▼

You have now chosen the essential software you need for getting a basic, fully functional Internet server up and running. In the next chapter, we will fire up the grill in your Internet restaurant.

• CHAPTER • 5

Digging In (Client Software)

Ingredients

- Using Web browsers
- Using ftp
- Using a list server
- Viewers, players, news readers, and chat clients

It is now time to learn how to make appetizers—the first batch of recipes in this book. A good appetizer is both a culinary delight in itself and also prepares the palette for the forthcoming joys of the main course. Here are recipes for a variety of appetizers.

Knowing how to use the basic software clients—including software for e-mail, ftp, and Web browsing—is a prerequisite to installing an information server since you need a client to download server software and test the functioning of the server. The great majority of information about the Internet, both in books and on-line, covers clients. In this chapter we have filtered this vast supply of information, present you with a concise summary of installing and using client software, and point you to the best sources of additional information.

We begin simply with a discussion of how to install and configure a couple of the most popular Web browsers and then install some ftp and list server clients. Your client needs will still not be fully satisfied. Recall from Sections 4.4 to 4.7 that you will need ancillary tools to support external graphics viewers, sound players, and video clips—a subset of these tools are often invoked directly from your Web browser and are referred to as helper applications and plug-ins. We end this chapter with examples of how to install the most popular ancillary software tools.

The order in which tools are installed here and the tools themselves are recommended. We will justify these recommendations as we proceed.

Since you bought this book to learn how to set up an Internet server, chances are that you have some experience with Internet client activities, such as browsing the Web. In this case, you probably have at least a Web browser installed, and you may want to refer to this chapter to install software you do not yet have.

If, on the other hand, you are new to the Internet and need to "bootstrap" yourself on, that's only slightly more difficult. When you install Mac OS 8, you also install the Internet Setup Assistant, which walks you through the steps to getting on-line, including registering with an ISP. The Mac OS 8 installation will also install a Web browser—most likely either Netscape Navigator or Internet Explorer. If you do not have OS 8, your best bet will be to contact an ISP by phone and have them walk you through the steps. They may even provide browser software. You can also purchase Internet software, such as the Apple Internet Connection Kit, which provides browser software and connection instructions.

From this point on, we will assume that you now have some version of a Web browser installed or ready to be installed. Otherwise, we would have to account for too many variables and our discussion would drag on interminably. The next sections will lead you through the steps of installing, configuring, and downloading an upgrade to your Web browser, as well as other necessary client software.

5.1 Web Browsers

In this section, we cover how to install, and if necessary configure, three of the most popular Web browsers—Netscape Navigator, Microsoft Internet Explorer, and CyberDog. Choosing a Web browser was covered in Section 4.6, and we have chosen these three because they either come with the Mac OS 8 installation CD-ROM or are readily available even if you do not have Mac OS 8. They are also the three most popular browsers at the time of writing.

In fact, we recommend you install (at least) both Navigator and Internet Explorer, particularly if you are using high-end Web functions such as JavaScript or Java, since Web pages you develop may appear different in a different browser. You will want to make sure the contents of your Web pages are fully decipherable.

5.1.1 Netscape Navigator

Netscape Navigator™ is currently the most popular of the Web browsers, and we recommend it particularly now that Navigator and Communicator are available for free. (Netscape Navigator is one product from Netscape Communications Inc. As the most popular product, it is frequently and incorrectly referred to as simply Netscape.) At the time of writing, Navigator 4.04 was the latest release, although Navigator 3.01 is shipped with Mac OS 8.

Netscape Communicator 4.0 is a software suite that includes Navigator, as well as tools for creating Web pages, reading e-mail, conferencing, and others. Navigator 4.0 is also available as a standalone. We will only concern ourselves with Navigator. (If you are using any version of Navigator 3 Standard, you may want to consider upgrading to Navigator 4.04, since version 4 requires substantially less memory to run than version 3. However, if you're using Navigator Gold and use the HTML editor, you would need to download the complete Netscape Communicator package.)

5.1.1.1 Software Snapshot

Table 5–1 and Figure 5–1 give a snapshot introduction to Netscape Navigator.

Table 5-1 Netscape Navigator Software Snapshot

Location (via Web)	*http://home.netscape.com/comprod/mirror/index.html*
Location (via ftp)	*ftp://ftp.netscape.com/pub/*
Source Available	Yes.
Questions (after subscribing)	*http://help.netscape.com*
Best Features	Good functionality, current de facto standard, widely used and therefore familiar, includes Java support. Supports network proxies for secure environments.

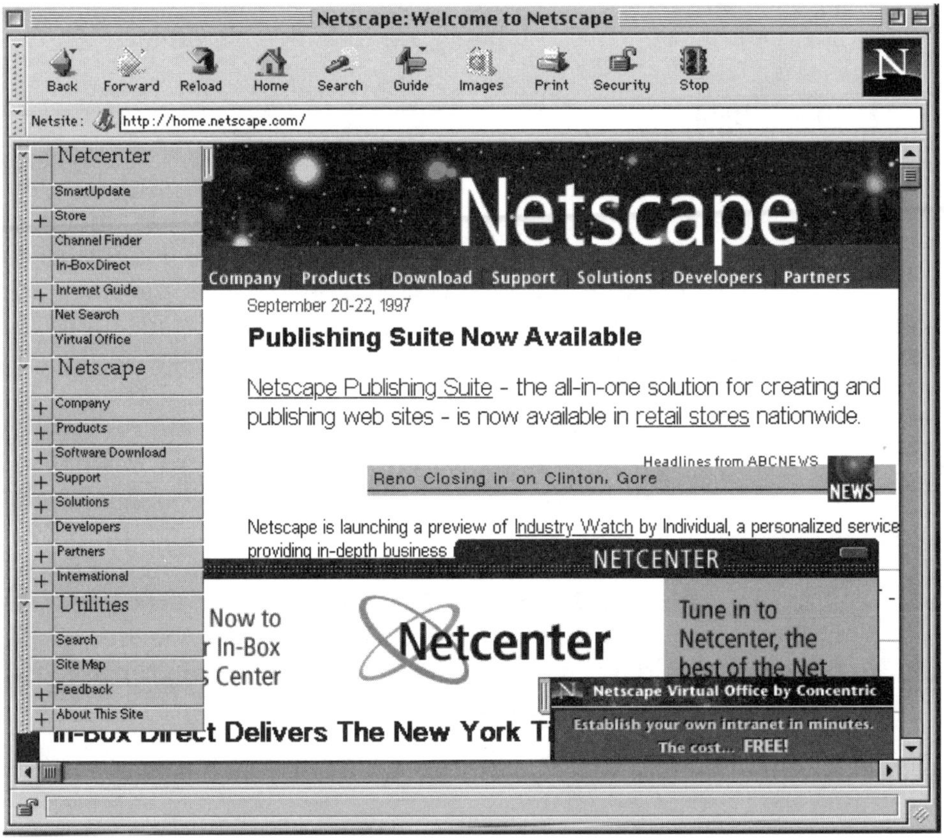

Figure 5-1 Netscape Navigator 4.04 (©1998 Netscape Communications Corp. Used with permission. All Rights Reserved. This electronic file or page may not be reprinted or copied without express permission from Netscape.)

5.1.1.2 Installation—A Template for all Software Installations

This is the only complete example in this book of uncompressing an .hqx file; there is no point repeating it for every piece of software, since the steps are the same.

When you download Mac software from the Internet, most of the time it will be in the form of a Mac BinHex Archive, a compressed file with an .hqx extension. To extract this type of file, you need an additional piece of software such as StuffIt Expander from Aladdin Systems, *http://www.aladdinsys.com*. If you already have a Web browser installed, it probably included StuffIt Expander as a helper application. StuffIt Expander is common Mac OS freeware, so you can also get this from a friend with a Mac.

For the sake of discussion, let's say you're upgrading your Web browser to Navigator 4.04, the latest version available at the time of writing. Here are the steps to downloading and installing Navigator 4.04—and just about any other Mac OS software—from the Web.

1. Point your browser at the Netscape Web site (see Table 5–1 for the appropriate URL).
2. Follow the instructions for downloading; eventually you will get to a link that starts the download. A small window should appear that says "Save <filename>.hqx" and shows the progress.
3. When the download is complete, it should be opened and "unstuffed" automatically by StuffIt Expander. If not, double-click on the .hqx file to open it with StuffIt Expander.
4. StuffIt Expander will produce a folder that contains the software installer (or possibly the software itself).
5. If the folder has a file with "Installer" in the name, double-click on it to begin the installation. For small pieces of software, the program may not have an installer program. In this case, read the "Read Me" file to complete the installation. You may have to restart your Mac after installation.

5.1.1.3 Configuration

Once downloaded, uncompressed, and installed, you can start Navigator 4.04 immediately by double-clicking the program icon. You configure Navigator to suit your needs by selecting Edit: Preferences (choose the Preferences menu item from the Edit pull-down menu).

Unlike the set of four Navigator 3 preferences options under the Options menu, Navigator 4 has one Preferences option under Edit. There are myriad items that can be configured, some of which change the appearance of Web pages, as shown in Figure 5–2.

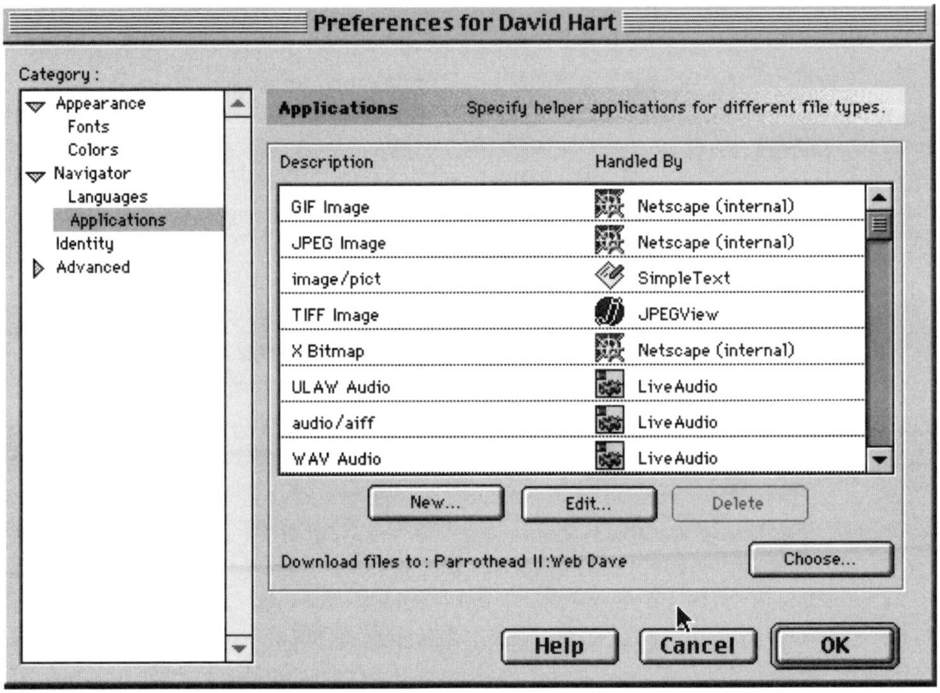

Figure 5-2 Netscape Navigator 4.03 Preferences Dialog

However, there are several important preferences to check: security, the cache, identity, the default home page, and helper applications. We consider each option separately.

Security. Click on the "Advanced" category in the Preferences dialog. Navigator allows to you choose whether to allow Java (see Section 12.3), JavaScript (Section 12.2), and cookies (Section 11.6). Other advanced security options are available by selecting Netscape: Security Info (the Security Info option under the ship's wheel menu). Within the security window, select the Navigator option and select when you want to be warned or advised about sending encrypted or unencrypted information. The defaults are adequate for most sites.

Cache. When a Web page is fetched from a server and displayed on the client, that page is cached, or stored, on the client. Thus, if that page is revisited, it can be retrieved from the cache rather than having to be retrieved again from the network, a much slower operation. In principle, caching is a good idea, but the size of the cache depends on how much disk space you can spare. Most browsers generally default to a 5-megabyte cache; this should suffice for most casual browsing. If you spend a lot of time on-line, you may want to increase your cache size, to 10 megabytes perhaps, but you may end up loading old, cached versions of frequently updated pages.

In the Edit:Preferences dialog, select "Cache." (Click on the triangle next to "Advanced" if you can't see the Cache option.) The defaults are adequate for most situations, although you may want to increase the cache size if you have a large hard drive. You can also empty the disk cache and set the Cache folder to something other than the default.

It is important to remember caching when modifying Web pages. After a page is modified, if you wish to see those changes, that page should be reloaded (View: Reload). Otherwise, Navigator may display the unmodified page from the cache. When developing Web pages, the cache can be set to zero, forcing the page to be reloaded every time. This is useful for frequently viewing your edits.

Identity. When you first start Navigator 4.04, the program walks you through the steps for establishing your network "identity" in the form of your name and e-mail address. Should these change, you can change them in the Preferences dialog, under the "Identity" option. Netscape uses your network identity when accessing ftp sites and secure Web pages.

Default Home Page. This setting controls the page that is loaded when you click the "Home" button from the Navigator toolbar. If you don't change it, it will send you to the Netscape Web site. Choose Edit: Preferences… and select the "Navigator" item. In the Home Page section, you can type in the URL you want to be your home page, click the "Use Current Page" button to make that page your home page, or click "Choose Local File" to start with a file on your computer—perhaps a list of your favorite jumping-off points for Web browsing. On this Preferences dialog, you can also choose whether you want Navigator to load your home page, a blank page, or the last page you visited when you launch the application.

Fonts. It is possible to change the default font for Navigator from the basic 12-point Times. Choose "Fonts" (under Appearance) in the Preferences dialog. Here you can set your default font and your default fixed-width font. For fixed-width font, you should choose a monospaced font such as Courier or Monaco and probably use a slightly smaller point size. You can also tell Navigator to use or ignore the fonts specified by a Web page.

Helper Applications. Recall from Section 2.3.3 that a helper application is a separate application called by a Web browser to handle a particular MIME type. For this to work, the browser must be given appropriate MIME type mappings—which file extensions indicate a particular MIME type and how to deal with files of this type.

Choose "Applications" in the Preferences dialog. Navigator displays the MIME types it understands and how each is handled. For the most part, the defaults cover all of the basics—and then some. Scroll down and look for a file description of "Macintosh BinHex Archive." Double-clicking this entry will open the Edit Type dialog, and you should see that files of this MIME type (which have the "hqx" extension) are handled by StuffIt Expander, meaning that hqx files will be unstuffed automatically.

As you download new helpers or plug-ins, you may want to add new MIME type mappings. Eventually you may also want to modify some of the defaults. For example, look for a file description of "PostScript Document," which may show "Unknown: Prompt user" in the handled-by column. You could select and edit this MIME type mapping (or double-click the entry) to change the action to "Save to disk." This will save you the trouble of having to answer a dialog box every time you want to download a PostScript file. Better still you may specify a PostScript viewer here. As you become more familiar with the types of files you encounter frequently, you can fine-tune these mappings further.

Navigator 4.04 also includes, mixed in with the list of MIME types, some less common Web protocols, such as telnet and tn3270, an IBM 3270 terminal emulator, that need to be handled by separate applications. (Navigator 3.01 listed these separately under Options: General Preferences: Applications, and Internet Explorer calls them Protocol Helpers.) Netscape also includes the application for viewing HTML source in this category. Scroll down to find the "View Source" entry; this entry controls the program in which the View: Page Source command displays the HTML source for a Web page. You can set this to be Communicator (Navigator), SimpleText, your word processor, or your HTML editor.

5.1.1.4 Using Navigator

As shown in Figure 5–1, the primary Netscape Navigator actions are controlled by a set of buttons at the top of the browser window: Back, Forward, Reload, Home, Search, Guide, and so forth. (Search and Guide take you to Netscape's Web site: The Search page has links to major Internet search engines, while the Guide page is a guide to Netscape's Web site.)

Originally, you could say that hyperlinks would appear as underlined text, and clicking on them downloaded a new page. This is still true, but as Figure 5–1 shows, there are many other ways to navigate the Web these days. There are JavaScript menus, image maps, frames, pull-down menus in forms, and other interfaces to help you move around. Some sites even use Java applets as navigation devices even though applets can be much more powerful. As a general rule, click on anything that looks as if it might take you where you need to go. The Back button at the top of the window will always take you back.

5.1.2 Internet Explorer

Internet Explorer™ from Microsoft is the strongest competitor to Netscape Navigator, with the substantial clout of Microsoft behind it. As part of the Microsoft-Apple deal announced in August 1997, Internet Explorer will become the default browser installed with future versions of the Mac OS. At the time of writing, Internet Explorer 4 had just been released. Internet Explorer 3.01 shipped with Mac OS 8.

5.1.2.1 Software Snapshot

Table 5–2 and Figure 5–3 give a snapshot overview of Internet Explorer.

Table 5-2 Internet Explorer Software Snapshot

Location	*http://www.microsoft.com/ie/mac*
Source Available	No
Questions	*http://www.microsoft.com/IESupport/* *giraffe@microsoft.com*
Bugs	*http://www.microsoft.com/support/feedback/*
Best Source of Information	*http://www.microsoft.com/ie*

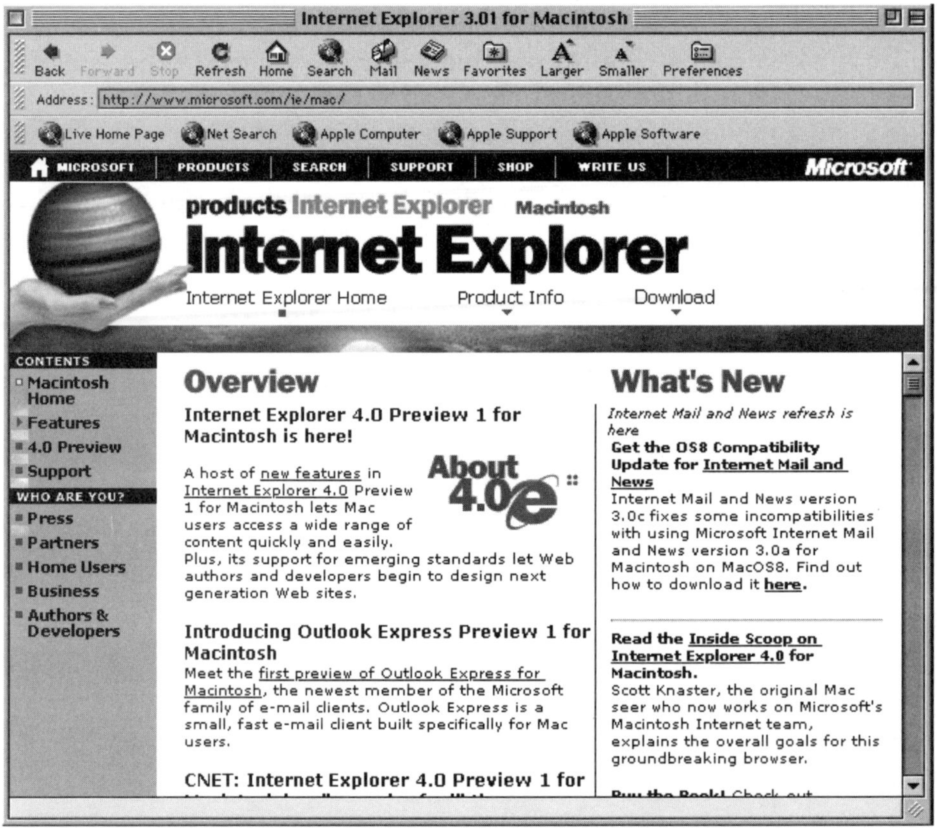

Figure 5-3 Internet Explorer 3.01 (Screen shot reprinted by permission from Microsoft Corporation.)

5.1.2.2 Installation Notes

Internet Explorer has a standard Macintosh install. Once you have downloaded and unstuffed the Internet Explorer .hqx file, or have your Mac OS 8 CD-ROM, you install Internet Explorer by double-clicking on the Installer program.

If you already have Netscape Navigator installed along with a number of plug-ins, the Internet Explorer installation gives you the option of using the Navigator plug-ins folder as the plug-ins for Explorer. (Explorer can use the same plug-ins as Navigator.) You can also select Cancel from this dialog box to create a new folder for Explorer.

The installer also asks whether to make Internet Explorer your default Web browser. And the first time you start Explorer, it will take you to Microsoft's registration page.

5.1.2.3 Configuration

Internet Explorer also has many options to tailor the program to suit your needs, all of which you can control from the Edit: Preferences dialog. Again, many of the options change the look and feel of Web pages. We will again describe how to adjust the security, identity, cache, and helper applications options.

Security. Depending on your personal level of concern about Internet security, you can set a number of security-related options. Under the Web Content set of preferences, you can turn on and off ActiveX and scripting (such as JavaScript) under "Web Content." You can turn Java on and off under "Java." Unless you have a need for stronger than normal security, these are okay to leave on.

Under "Security," you can control the alerts that appear when you enter or leave secure pages. If you want to minimize the number of these alerts, we recommend turning all of these off, except for the first, "When entering a page that is secure." This way, when you shop on the Web, you should get an alert as you enter any page where you are asked for a credit card number or other confidential information.

Under "Cookies," you can also manage—view, delete, or choose to decline—any cookies that Web sites may want to put on your computer. The "Never ask" option is fine for normal security. You can try the "Ask for each cookie" to see how often Web sites try to place cookies on your computer.

Cache. The cache option works the same as for Netscape Navigator. To set the amount of disk cache, change the location of the cache folder, or clear the cache, choose the "Advanced" option.

Identity. To set your network identity, as well as your e-mail account information, scroll down in the Preferences list to the E-mail: General option. Selecting this option brings up a form with blanks for your e-mail address, name, and the servers that receive and send your mail.

Default Home Page. The "Home/Search" option of the Preferences dialog lets you set your home page. Either enter the URL for your preferred home page, click the "Use None" button to start with a blank page, or click "Use Default" to reset your home page to the Microsoft home page. Here you can also set the search engine that is used by the "Search" button on the Explorer toolbar.

Fonts. To change your default font from the standard 12-point Times, choose the "Language/Fonts" option and select the variable-width (proportional) and fixed-width font. To set the font size that is displayed, you must leave the Preferences dialog and choose a size from the View: Text Size menu option.

Helper Applications. The Preferences dialog lists options for setting both File Helpers (under "Receiving Files") and Protocol Helpers (under "Network"). For the most part, you can leave Protocol Helpers alone; the most common Web protocols will be handled by your default browser. For less common protocols, the defaults are set to common tools for handling them.

The File Helpers screen works in much the same way as Navigator, which makes sense since the function is the same. Double-clicking (or selecting and choosing Change...) will allow you to change how a particular MIME type is handled. For the most part, the defaults will work fine. You may want to confirm, however, that file types "BinHex" and "BinHexed StuffIt Archive" are handled as "Post-process with Application" with StuffIt Expander (see Figure 5–4).

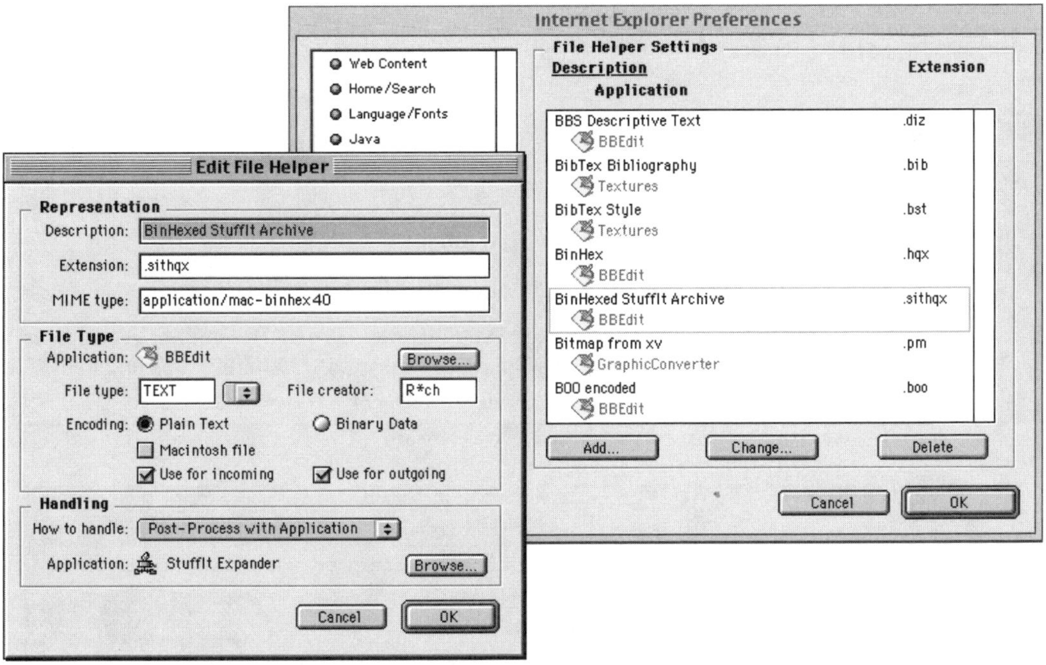

Figure 5-4 Internet Explorer File Helper Preferences

5.1.2.4 Using Internet Explorer

As Figure 5–3 shows, using Internet Explorer has very much the same feel as Netscape Navigator, with the row of buttons across the top of the window providing the key navigation commands. The navigation options that appear within the Web pages themselves should look almost identical in both Navigator and Internet Explorer.

5.1.3 CyberDog

CyberDog 2.0, which ships on the Mac OS 8 CD-ROM, is the third most popular browser overall on all platforms—a distant third with two percent of the market—despite the fact that there will likely be no further versions. CyberDog is based on Apple's OpenDoc technology, which is being maintained but not further developed by Apple. OpenDoc is component technology that allows programs to create documents that incorporate both static information and dynamic text and graphics from the Internet.

While Navigator and Internet Explorer are very similar applications, CyberDog has a different feel to its Web browsing interface.

5.1.3.1 Software Snapshot

Table 5–3 and Figure 5–5 give a snapshot overview of CyberDog.

Table 5-3 CyberDog 2.0 Software Snapshot

Location	*http://cyberdog.apple.com/*
Questions	*http://cyberdog.apple.com/feedback.html*
Bugs	*http://cyberdog.apple.com/br/bug.html*
Features	Integrated Web browser, e-mail, ftp, gopher client. Uses Apple's OpenDoc technology. Different look and feel than Navigator or Internet Explorer.

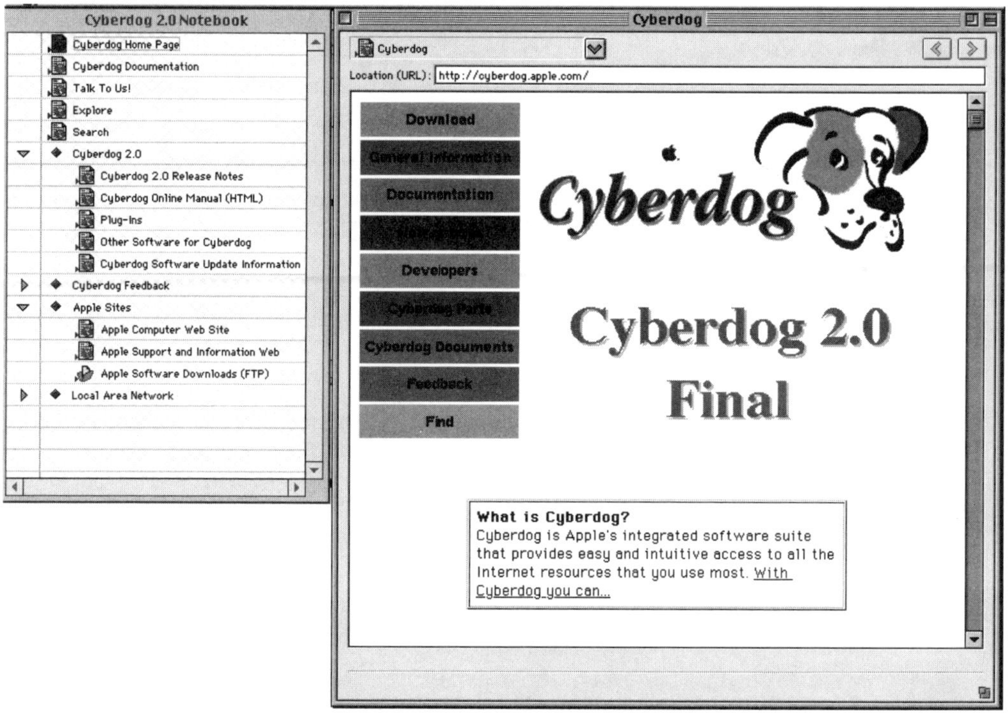

Figure 5-5 CyberDog 2.0

5.1.3.2 Installation

CyberDog 2.0 is distributed with the Mac OS 8 CD-ROM. Double-clicking on the CyberDog Installer will start the mostly unremarkable installation process. In installing CyberDog on Dave's Mac, the Installer required quitting all applications—a common requirement for Mac installations; however, in this case, the installer recognized the "HP Background" system extension (required for background printing to Dave's Hewlett-Packard (HP) DeskJet). This required a visit to the Extensions Manager, turning off the HP Background extension, restarting, and starting the install again.

To use plug-ins—CyberDog can use most Netscape Navigator plug-ins—CyberDog requires an additional piece of software, the CyberDog Plug-in Viewer, that was in Beta 5 release at the time of writing. Start CyberDog, and from the Notebook window, double-click the "Plug-ins" entry (or go to *http://cyberdog.apple.com/plugins.html* with any Web browser). You need to download and unstuff a .hqx file then move one OpenDoc extension and one CyberDog library to the appropriate folders, as described in the accompanying Read Me file.

5.1.3.3 Configuration

The CyberDog preferences are accessed by the Edit: CyberDog Preferences... Menu option.

Cache. In the Preferences dialog, the Cache option lets you set the size of the disk cache or clear the cache.

Security. Under the Cookies option, you can choose to allow cookies to be stored on your computer or to "toss" your cookies. Under the Security option, you can choose whether to be warned when you enter secure Web spaces and forms. And under the Web option, you can decide whether or not to turn Java on. (CyberDog does not support JavaScript, a Netscape technology, which is a disadvantage as more Web sites add JavaScript elements.)

Identity and Helper Applications. Installing and using CyberDog has one aspect that is difficult to figure out through the available menu options and even through the on-line documentation at *http://cyberdog.apple.com*. Your network identity, e-mail settings, and MIME type mappings are set using the Mac OS Internet Config utility, which Mac OS 8 installs in the Internet folder. Once you know where to go, changing a file mapping is similar to the process for Navigator or Internet Explorer. The Helper Applications option allows you to set the programs that will handle ftp, http, nntp (news), e-mail and other protocols. (In effect, you set your default browser here.)

5.1.3.4 Using CyberDog

If you have used Netscape Navigator or Internet Explorer to browse the Web, your first look at the CyberDog interface might cause you to hesitate for a moment. Double-clicking on the CyberDog icon brings up not a browser window, but the CyberDog Notebook. The Notebook can contain not only Web bookmarks but also e-mail addresses, gopher sites, or telnet connections. Only when you click on a Notebook entry (or enter a URL via the CyberDog: Connect to... menu item) will the browser window appear, as in Figure 5–5.

The browser window has many fewer buttons. The left and right arrows in the upper-right-hand corner are the Back and Forward buttons. The down-pointing arrow above the location text box will display a drop-down menu of the sites you have visited to get to the current Web page.

And like Netscape Navigator 3.01 and earlier versions, but unlike the Navigator 4.03 stand-alone application and Internet Explorer, CyberDog has an integrated e-mail interface and news reader.

5.2 Using FTP

As described in Section 4.1, ftp provides the simplest mechanism for gaining access to files on a remote server connected to the Internet. Groups of files can be transferred together, and files can be transferred across slow communication lines typical of modem connections. What follows are the basics of ftp:

1. Start your ftp client (Anarchie or Fetch).
2. Choose File: Open....
3. Log in to the remote ftp server by entering a login name of "anonymous" and a password of your full e-mail address.
4. Select the files you wish to download (or directory you want to upload to) by moving to the appropriate directory.
5. Make sure the modes—ASCII/text for text files, binary for others—are set correctly for the file(s) to be transferred.
6. Click to download or upload the file(s).
7. Close the connection.

Ftp is a useful way for users to upload files to your information server should that be desirable. For anonymous ftp, this requires that you maintain a world-writable directory; we discuss the security implications of maintaining a world-writable directory in Section 7.3.

5.2.1 Fetch

Fetch was developed by Jim Matthews to let Macs at Dartmouth College talk to host computers and use the Internet. A popular ftp client, Fetch puts a Mac-like interface, similar to an "Open File" dialog box, upon what would otherwise be a series of UNIX commands. Fetch does not let you perform Archie (ftp server) searches (see Section 4.6.2). Fetch is shareware available free to educational and charitable organizations or for $25 otherwise. Table 5–4 and Figure 5–6 give a snapshot overview of Fetch.

Table 5-4 Fetch

Location, Questions, and Bugs	*http://www.dartmouth.edu/pages/softdev/fetch.html*
Features	Uses interface similar to Mac "Open file" dialog, uses drag and drop, allows multiple connections. No Archie searching.

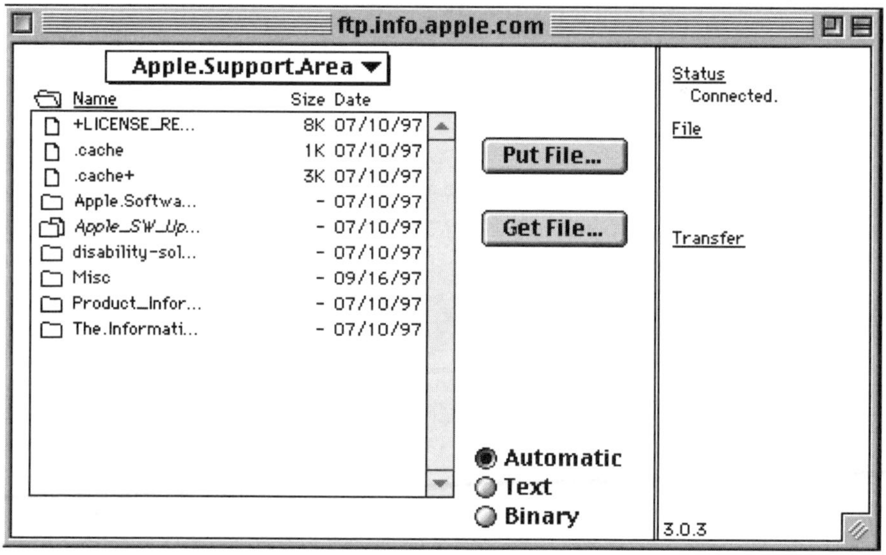

Figure 5-6 Fetch

Go to the Fetch Web page, download and unstuff the .hqx file (less than 1 MB). Double-click the installer. No restart is necessary.

You configure Fetch by selecting the Customize: Preferences... menu option. Under the General tab, you may want to check the "Use Internet Config" option if you have set up your network preferences for a program such as CyberDog. This will also add your e-mail address to the default password box.

Under the Download tab, you can set the default folder where you want Fetch to store downloaded files, as well as the editor you want to use for reading text files. Under Upload, you can specify the default formats for uploading files; Text for text files and Raw Data for others are the recommended settings. We also recommend turning off the options for Fetch to add .hqx, .bin, and .txt extensions automatically to file names—particularly the .txt option, which will add .txt to the end of any .html files you ftp, for example.

5.2.2 Anarchie

Developed by Peter Lewis's Stairways Software, Anarchie also puts a familiar Mac interface on top of the normal ftp command lines; however, Anarchie adopts a Finder-like interface. You browse through ftp sites the same way you would navigate the files and folders on your hard drive. A key feature of Anarchie is its ability to perform Archie searches. Anarchie is a shareware ftp client—the registration fee is $10. Table 5–5 and Figure 5–7 give a snapshot overview of Anarchie.

Table 5-5 Anarchie

Location, Questions, Bugs	*http://www.stairways.com/anarchie/*
Features	Interface similar to Mac OS Finder; will tell you when newer version is available; can perform Archie and Mac Search ftp searches.

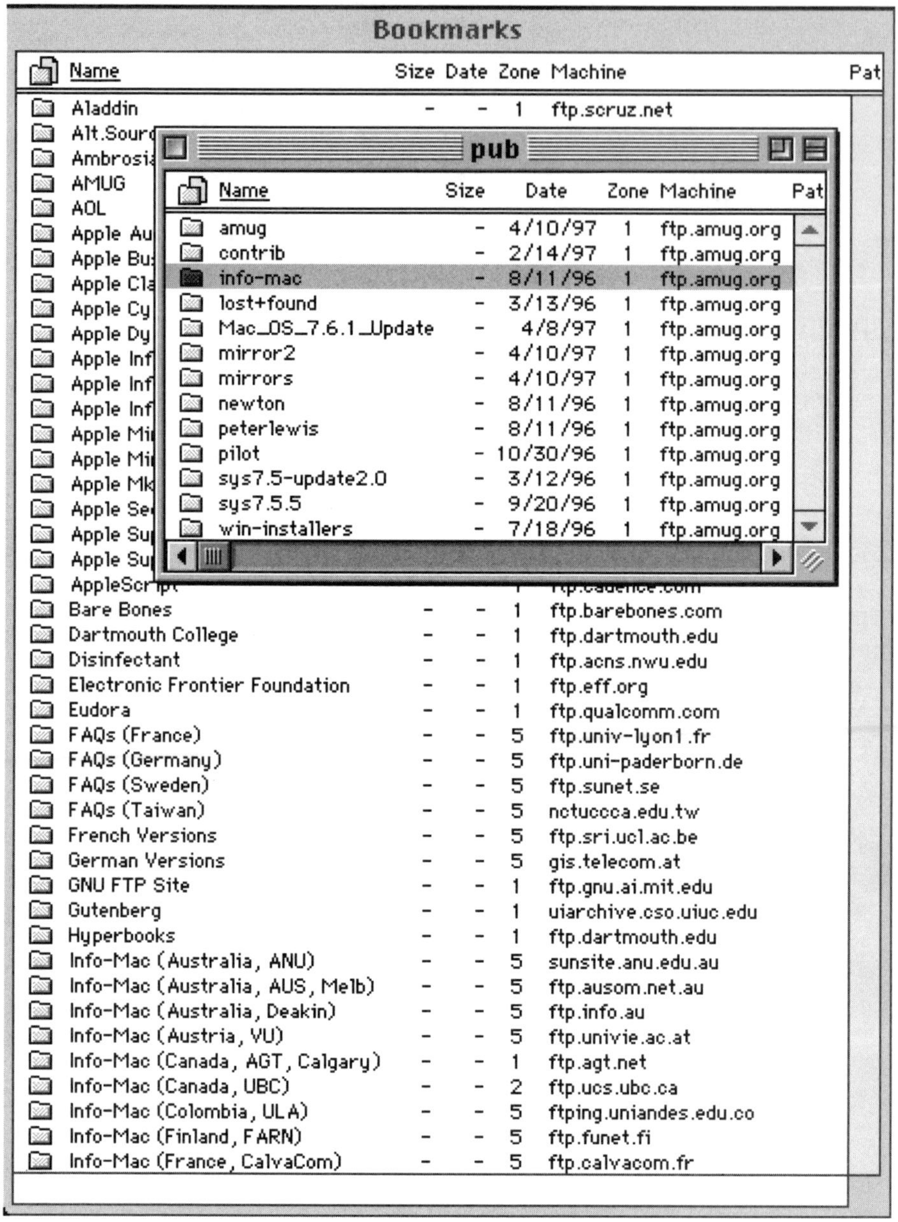

Figure 5-7 Anarchie

Download and unstuff the .hqx file. That's it. Anarchie does not have a separate install program. You can set Anarchie's preferences by choosing the Edit: Preferences… menu item. The defaults are fine for most situations. Anarchie uses Internet Config for its regular configuration.

5.2.3 Downloading—An Example

The basic concept behind ftp is to get a file from a server or send a file to a server, and both Anarchie and Fetch require similar steps to upload or download a file. Table 5–6 gives the steps for each program. Beyond the basics, both programs offer additional ftp functions. Anarchie, for example, offers Archie searches.

Table 5-6 Downloading with Anarchie and Fetch

Anarchie	Fetch
Double-click Anarchie icon.	Double-click Fetch icon. (New Connection… window appears.)
Choose File: List Bookmarks to open bookmarks list (if not already open).	
Double-click bookmark *or* Choose FTP: FTP… and enter server name (and optional path) and select List.	Choose Shortcut from pull-down menu *or* Enter host name and optional directory (user ID and password not needed for anonymous ftp). Click OK.
Browse through folders and files, as in Finder. (Status windows appear as new lists of folders and files are downloaded.)	Browse through folders and files, as in Open File dialog box. (Status information appears in the right side of the Fetch window.)
To download a file: Double-click filename.	To download a file: Double-click filename (or select file and click Get File….
To upload a file: Choose FTP: Put… Choose file to upload from Open File dialog, click Open. (Alternately, drag-and-drop file icon to the ftp server window.)	To upload a file: Click Put File… Select file to upload in Open File dialog, click Open. Choose file format for upload (optionally change file name) and click OK.

If you plan to install an ftp server, we recommend you visit a few of the larger ftp archives. As you browse through their structure, you will want to keep in mind a number of points regarding ftp and ftp-accessible software distributions:

- Many information providers go to considerable trouble to ensure that access to information in their *ftp archives* is straightforward. You should endeavor to do the same.
- If you do not already have access to a Web browser, ftp provides an efficient means of getting one.
- The top level of an ftp directory (folder) tree is usually */pub,* but when you log in the directory is usually */.*
- ASCII files will be transferred successfully in binary mode between your client and the server, albeit at a slower rate. Binary files will *not* be transferred successfully in ASCII mode.

5.3 Using a List Server

Most likely, your first use of a list server was (or will be) based upon instructions received by e-mail or read from the Web. These instructions describe how to subscribe to a specific list. Let us take a step back from that scenario, for a moment, to understand how a list server operates. As we discussed in Section 4.2, the same list server software maintains multiple lists, where each list relates to a specific topic of interest to a community of users.

To learn about the commands that can be sent to a list server, you can send e-mail to a list server with no subject line and a message body that contains the single word, "help." For example, you might send mail to the UNIX list server at SDSC—*listserver@sdsc.edu*. Or for a Macintosh example, Dave requested help from his own list server, *autoshare@hart-mac.sdsc.edu*. What was returned is shown in the following example and provides all the information needed to use the AutoShare list server. The commands generally work for most list servers on any platform; read this help information carefully.

```
Welcome to the list server help!

Available AutoShare list server commands in the body are:

  SUB <list> <name>       subscription to a list
  UNSUB <list>            cancellation of a list
  LIST                    lists maintained by the list server
  REVIEW <list>           the subscribers of a list
  SET <list> <option>     options are
                            CONCEAL and NOCONCEAL
                            DIGEST and NODIGEST
                            MAIL and NOMAIL
                            ACK and NOACK
  INDEX <list>            index of archive files
  GET <list> <file>       gets you an archive file
  WHICH                   shows which lists you are on
  RELEASE                 list server software information
  QUERY <list>            subscription status information
  SEARCH <list> <string> searches the list for the text

'All' may be used for the Unsub, Query, Set, Index, Get,
Review and Search commands to apply the command to all
subscribed lists, e.g. 'query all'.

Several alias commands are available as well:

  SUB:    subscribe
  UNSUB:  unsubscribe, signoff
  LIST:   lists
  REVIEW: rev, recipients, who
  INDEX:  ind
  GET:    send

Addresses for this particular AutoShare list server:

  list server              autoshare@hart-mac.sdsc.edu
  list server Admin        Postmaster@hart-mac.sdsc.edu
  Lists                    <list>@hart-mac.sdsc.edu

Virtually,
The List Server Admin <Postmaster@hart-mac.sdsc.edu>


---
This message has been returned to you by
AutoShare, a Macintosh list server and auto-responder,
a freeware EIMS (AIMS, MailShare) companion application
```

Notice we sent mail to *autoshare,* which happens to be one of several list server packages available for the Macintosh (see Section 4.2.1). Each list server has slightly different commands, but the principle is the same.

You may or may not be able to send mail to Dave's list server at the time of writing. Because SDSC already has an organizationwide e-mail system, it is somewhat confusing to have an independent mail server within the larger domainwide mail service. Many Macintosh users may find themselves in a similar situation. As we show in Section 6.2.3, you can still run a list server from your Macintosh, even if you do not control your organization's mail server.

Once you have made contact with a list server, if you do not know the name of the list you are interested in, the next step is to determine what lists are maintained on that particular server. As indicated by the **HELP** command, the command **INDEX** provides you with details of the available lists. Here is an abbreviated example using SDSC's list server.

```
From list server@sdsc.edu Thu Jan 18 09:07:12 1996
Date: Thu, 18 Jan 1996 09:04:37 -0800
From: Mailing List Processor <list server@sdsc.edu>
To: fred@chem.harvard.edu
Subject: Re: your list server request "index"

Index of mailing lists
admin
afarmers
afsusers
agua_leaders
….
vistech
vrml-behaviors
vrml-modeling
vtc_wg
vtcsupport
webster
websupport
workgang
www_ug
```

The **INDEX** command returns an index of the lists available at this site. This statement is not strictly true, since there are actually more lists at this site, some of which are for internal use only. To see internal lists you would have to be accessing the list server from the same Internet domain—sdsc.edu in this example. As you can see, some of the names are not very meaningful, which suggests this rule of thumb: When you create lists on your list server give them meaningful names.

After obtaining an index of the lists available on the list server, you might again send e-mail to the list server, this time relating to a specific list with one or more of the sample commands in Table 5–7 as the body of the message. Note that list server commands are case insensitive.

Table 5-7 List Server Commands

Command/Description

`sub hpcwire`
or
`subscribe hpcwire`
 	
Description: Add yourself to a list called hpcwire.

`sub immee@podunk.edu sdsc_discuss_applications` **Description:** Add someone else to a list by giving their e-mail address (requires their verification).

`unsub hpcwire`
or
`unsubscribe hpcwire`
 	
Description: Remove yourself from a list called hpcwire.

Table 5-7 List Server Commands *(Continued)*

Command/Description
`unsub wombat@cyberpunk.sdsc.edu sdsc_important`
Description: Remove someone else (wombat) from a list (requires their verification).
`help sdsc_important_workstations`
Description: Find out more about a specific list called sdsc_important_workstations.

To mail submissions to an SDSC mailing list to which you are a subscriber, you would address mail to the desired mailing list with the suffix *@sdsc.edu*. For example, sending a mail message to *sdsc_important@sdsc.edu* would broadcast the contents of your message to everyone subscribing to the *sdsc_important* list, assuming it was unmoderated. If it were a moderated list, the message would be sent to the list moderator, who would then decide whether it should be posted. *It is important to remember that you send list server commands to the list server address, not the mailing list address.* Sending the message "unsub sdsc_important" to sdsc_important@sdsc.edu, for example, is bad. All subscribers to the sdsc_important list would see your request, but the list server software would not.

Using these simple examples as templates you should now be able to subscribe, unsubscribe, and post to a list. If you need more information refer to

http://www.daily.umn.edu/~broeker/guide.html.

And for sources of mailing lists, try

http://www.liszt.com, or

http://www.tile.net/tile/list server/viewlist.html

5.4 Graphics Viewers

Tables 4–11 and 4–15 summarized locations for downloading some of the many popular graphics viewers for the Macintosh. Here we provide further details on two chosen almost at random from the many possibilities. Chances are you already have software on your Mac that can be used to view images in many formats.

5.4.1 GraphicConverter

If you want to view and save images in *any* format, you might want to download GraphicConverter (see Table 5–8 and Figure 5–8). This shareware package by Thorsten Lemke will import more than 80 graphic file formats and export about 35 graphic file formats. GraphicConverter also offers batch file conversion, a slide show feature, and some basic image manipulation tools, such as zoom, rotate, and trim (or crop). Installation is a snap—download and unstuff the .hqx file and double-click the installer.

Table 5-8 GraphicConverter Snapshot

Location	*http://www.lemkesoft.de/us_contents.html*
Questions/Bugs	*http://www.lemkesoft.de/us_gcfaqs.html*
Features	Imports about 88 graphic file formats; exports about 35 graphic file formats; batch conversion; slide show; rotate, zoom, and trim.

Figure 5-8 GraphicConverter

5.4.2 Ghostscript

One of the very few file formats that GraphicConverter cannot open is PostScript, the page definition language by Adobe. (Technically, PostScript is a page definition language, so PostScript files might contain formatted text as well as images.) If you don't want to buy high-end software such as Adobe Illustrator or TechPool's Transverter Pro, you can download Aladdin Ghostscript, software ported to the Mac by Jim Schindall, which lets you interpret and display a PostScript file according to the Adobe document structuring conventions. Ghostscript is a port of UNIX software and retains parts of the UNIX command-line look and feel, although most functions can also be accessed from the menus. If you often encounter PostScript files, Ghostscript is recommended (see Table 5–9).

Table 5-9 Ghostscript Software Snapshot

Location	*http://www.cs.wisc.edu/~ghost/mac/index.html* *ftp://ftp.cs.wisc.edu/pub/ghost/aladdin/gs501/mac/*
Downloads	Download both of these: *ftp://ftp.cs.wisc.edu/ghost/aladdin/gs503/-mac/macgs-503-files.sit.bin* *ftp://ftp.cs.wisc.edu/ghost/aladdin/gs503/-mac/macgs-503-fonts.sit.bin* And one of the following: (Both PowerPC and 68K) *ftp://ftp.cs.wisc.edu/ghost/aladdin/-gs503/mac/macgs-503-fat.sit.bin* (PowerPC only) *ftp://ftp.cs.wisc.edu/ghost/aladdin/gs503/-mac/macgs-503-ppc.sit.bin* (68K only) *ftp://ftp.cs.wisc.edu/ghost/aladdin/gs503/mac/-macgs-503-68k.sit.bin*
Binaries	PowerPC, 68K, and FAT
Documentation	*ftp://ftp.cs.wisc.edu/ghost/aladdin/gs503/mac/-macgsmanual.html*
Questions	*mac-gs@aladdin.com* news: *comp.lang.postscript*

From Ghostscript you can control the display of a PostScript file, for example, the specific page of the file to display, magnification of a portion of the image, and page orientation.

Once you download and unstuff all the Ghostscript components, you can begin to set up the Ghostscript viewer.

- The "files" download will create a folder named "MacGS 503 *f*" that will be the main Ghostscript folder.
- The "fonts" download will create a folder containing a folder named "fonts." Move the "fonts" folder into the "MacGS 503 *f*" folder.
- The application download—there are PowerPC, 68K, and FAT versions—will create a folder containing the Ghostscript application. Move the application into the "MacGS 503 *f*" folder.

You can now start Ghostscript and view PostScript files. The MacGS 503 ƒ folder should also have an "examples" folder with PostScript files to try.

5.5 Sound Player

Macintoshes have all the hardware needed for listening to sounds, but because of the many sound formats out there, you may need software to listen to (or convert) sounds that originated on different platforms. If you are not sure whether you have basic sound software, here is a URL to visit and find out:

http://www-dsed.llnl.gov/documents/tests/au.html

SoundApp by Norman Franke, described in Table 5–10, is a great freeware sound player and converter that can read SoundCap, Studio Session Instruments, SoundEdit, AIFF, AIFF-C, System 7 sound and "snd" resource, QuickTime MooVsoundtracks, Sun Audio .au and NeXT .snd, Windows WAVE, MPEG audio layers I, II and III, Sound Blaster VOC, MODs, ScreamTracker 3 module, Multitracker Module (MTM), MIDI, Amiga IFF/8SVX, Sound Designer I and II, IRCAM, PSION sound, DVI ADPCM, and raw GSM.

SoundApp can convert most of these formats to a Macintosh sound and sound suitcase, AIFF, WAVE, Sun Audio and NeXT, Sound Designer II, QuickTime, and PSION formats. SoundApp also supports generic QuickTime conversion, which allows any QuickTime-recognized format to be converted to a QuickTime movie file.

Table 5-10 SoundApp

Location	*http://www-cs-students.stanford.edu/~franke/SoundApp/* and other Mac archives, such as *http://www.macdownload.com/*
Questions/Bugs	*http://www-cs-students.stanford.edu/~franke/SoundApp/*
Features	Will play and convert most common sound file formats.

5.6 Video Viewer

To play the movies you will most often encounter on the Web, QuickTime offers the best solution for Macs (see Table 5–11). The QuickTime media layer comes with the Mac OS, and you can view movies with either QuickTime-ready SimpleText or with MoviePlayer. There is also a system extension that allows you to view MPEG movies. And for browsing the Web, you should have the QuickTime plug-in that lets Netscape Navigator or Internet Explorer show QuickTime movies in the browser window. This is a no-brainer—go to the QuickTime Web site and download this software.

Table 5-11 QuickTime Snapshot

Location	*http://quicktime.apple.com/sw/qtmac.html*
Help	*http://quicktime.apple.com/sw/qthelp.html*
Features	With latest QuickTime, QT MPEG extension, MoviePlayer, and QuickTime browser plug-in, you can view most movies on the Web. Supported by most digital video software.

All of the information that you need is included with the distribution and not repeated here. Because this software involves system extensions, you will have to restart after installing. There may be some confusion stemming from all the various components, but the installers generally put the pieces in their proper locations:

- The QuickTime installer will put three extensions in your Extensions folder: QuickTime, QuickTime Instruments, QuickTime PowerPlug (for PowerPC models).
- For playing MPEG movies, you need to download the QuickTime MPEG Extension; the installer will put it in your System Folder.
- MoviePlayer is a small application that you can put anywhere you store your utilities or applications. The complete MoviePlayer comes with two MoviePlayer plug-ins that must be in the same folder as MoviePlayer.
- The QuickTime plug-in needs to go in the Plug-ins folder for your Web browser—Netscape Navigator or Internet Explorer.

5.7 News Readers

Although this book will not discuss how to set up an Internet news server, you may want to consider installing a news reader client in order to read and participate in the thousands of on-line news groups, many of which pertain to serving the Internet as well as your special interests. News group participants may be a source of answers that you can't find elsewhere. Furthermore, if you installed Netscape Navigator 4.04 (Section 5.1.1), you no longer have the news reader provided in Navigator 3.01. (The full Communicator 4.04 package, on the other hand, includes the Collabra news reader.)

5.7.1 Newswatcher

Newswatcher is freeware by John Norstad of Northwestern University's Academic Technologies group. The first time you start Newswatcher, it will prompt you for startup information, including your news server host name if it is not already in your Internet Config setup. Table 5–12 gives a snapshot overview of Newswatcher.

Table 5-12 Newswatcher Software Snapshot

Location	*ftp://ftp.acns.nwu.edu/pub/newswatcher/*
Questions/Information	*http://charlotte.acns.nwu.edu/jln/progs.html*
Source available	Yes.
Features	Simple to set up, read news with minimal trouble. Save subscribed groups.

5.8 IRC Chat Client

Internet Relay Chat (IRC) provides a way of communicating in real time with people across the Internet. In some sense, "chatting" is like participating in a live news group, with many conversations devoted to particular topics. To chat, you run a client program that connects to a server on one of the IRC networks and ask to join a particular "channel" or conversation. The conversation between you and the other participants is carried on through the server. On average, there are about 20,000 users and 5,000 channels on the large IRC networks. For more information on IRC, see *http://www.irchelp.org/*

http://www.irchelp.org/irchelp/new2irc.html

5.8.1 IRCle

IRCle is one of several IRC clients available for the Mac. IRCle is $15 shareware by Onno R. Tijdgat of MacResponse. Installation is uneventful; it is possible to join a conversation as soon as you download, unstuff, and start the program. The one downside to IRCle is a rather intimidating preferences dialog. We recommend using the defaults until you become more familiar with IRC. Table 5–13 gives a snapshot overview of IRCle.

Table 5-13 IRCle Snapshot

Location	*http://www.xs4all.nl/~ircle/* *http://www.amug.org/~ircle/*
Questions/Information	*http://www.amug.org/~ircle/general.html* *http://www.amug.org/~ircle/related.html*
Features	Multiwindow interface; easy to start up; stable.

▼▼▼

Once you install the basic client software—Web browser, ftp client, and possibly players for graphics, sound, and movies, a news reader, and chat client—you are ready to handle anything that might come your way or that you might want to serve on the Web. In the next chapter, we install the software that lets you start serving information to the Internet community.

• CHAPTER • 6

Firing Up the Grill (Getting On-line)

Ingredients

- Anonymous ftp
- A list server
- A Web server
- A search engine

We have now come to recipes for the main course. You may serve a simple yet satisfying dish (anonymous ftp), an efficient diet-conscious meal (list server), or a variety of chef's specials (Web servers). The course should have the appropriate side dishes and condiments (search capability).

To this point, everything we have implemented has been to support client activity. We are now at the point where we install the software for server activities. We will start with the simplest installation (ftp) and then establish a list server before proceeding to the most complex activity: a Web server. Chapter 4 discussed the rationale for which of these server types to install and the most common software options for each type of server.

In this chapter, we show you how to install and configure some recommended software options—namely, ftp with NetPresenz, the AutoShare list server, and the NetPresenz, Quid Pro Quo, and WebSTAR Web servers. If you are supporting a Web server you may wish to provide an index of searchable information to help the user locate the item of interest. SearchServer and Phantom provide complete packages for searching, and we discuss how to install and configure both. So let's get started with ftp.

6.1 Anonymous FTP: NetPresenz

If you have decided to support an anonymous ftp server, NetPresenz by Stairways software offers an inexpensive shareware option. In addition to supporting most of the advanced ftp features (as described in Section 4.1), NetPresenz allows your Macintosh to become a Web or Gopher server. It honors the privileges and passwords defined through the Mac OS Users & Groups control panel and supports multiple logins, MacBinary (.bin) and BinHex (.hqx) transfers and much more. It runs either in the background or as a normal application displaying the log file. Table 6–1 gives a snapshot overview of NetPresenz.

Table 6-1 NetPresenz Snapshot

Location	*http://www.stairways.com/netpresenz/* *ftp://ftp.stairways.com/stairways/*
Questions	*http://www.stairways.com/netpresenz/netpresenzfaq.html*
Documentation	*http://www.stairways.com/netpresenz/netpresenzdocs.html*
Requirements	System 7, MacTCP 1.1 or Open Transport 1.1.1, and File Sharing enabled; Open Transport 1.1.2 and System 7.5 or later recommended.

6.1.1 Installation and Configuration

Download and unstuff the 700-KB NetPresenz .bin file; in the resulting folder are two applications and several subfolders, including one for documentation. Following the Quick Start instructions in the Documentation folder will help you get your ftp server up and running in a matter of minutes. We won't repeat them in detail here but will summarize them with our own comments based on our installation.

1. Make sure File Sharing is on. For System 7, check the Sharing Setup control panel; for OS 8, check the File Sharing control panel. Turn off sharing for the hard drive on which you want to maintain your ftp archive, create a folder for your ftp archive, and turn sharing on for this folder—choose File: Sharing… and give "Everyone" access, either Read-only, for download-only ftp access, or Read/Write, if you want users to be able to upload.

   Note: If you already have a publicly accessible folder for sharing files among Macs on your local network, you will probably want to use this folder as your ftp archive as well. Because it uses the Users & Groups setup, NetPresenz cannot choose between two folders to which "Everyone" has access. We had difficulty making both such folders appear when connecting via anonymous ftp.
2. Run the NetPresenz Setup program, which displays a panel with six options (Figure 6–1). Choose FTP Setup from this panel and set the access privileges for you (the Owner), named users (as listed in your Users & Groups list), and Guests (anonymous ftp users).
3. Choose FTP Users and choose the default login directory for the Owner, Users, and Guests. While this will be your ftp archive for anonymous ftp users, you can allow named users to start with any folder to which you have given them permission.

   Note: For some reason, setting the Login Directory does not necessarily mean that users will see the contents of this folder when they first connect. We found that they will instead see a list consisting of only the folder specified by the Login Directory. To switch automatically into the ftp archive folder, add this line to the Login Commands text box:

   cd <ftp-archive-folder>

   where <ftp-archive-folder> is the name of the folder you created in step 1.

4. Choose the Summary option to see if everything is set properly. (Hint: If it says "(you must fix this!)" anywhere, you should fix it.)
5. Double-click the NetPresenz icon and quit NetPresenz Setup.

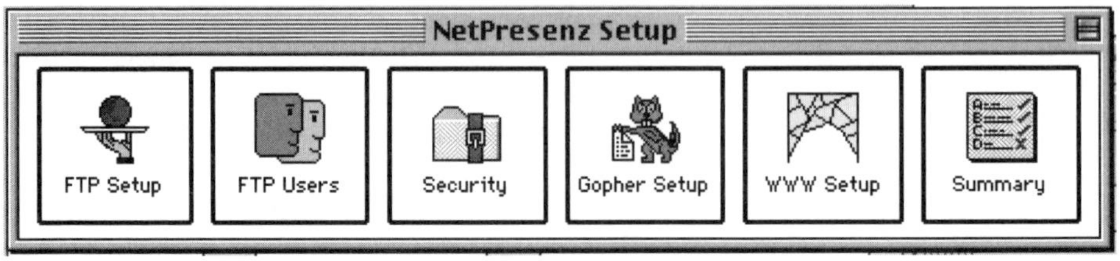

Figure 6-1 NetPresenz Setup

You now have an ftp server running on your Mac. The full documentation goes into more detail. If you are familiar with UNIX ftp servers, you will find that NetPresenz has most (but not all) of the features found in enhanced ftp servers.

- You can provide additional instructions and comments when a user accesses the archive and when they access specific directories within the archive.

  The folder "Startup Messages" in the NetPresenz folder contains files that will be displayed when users log in. The contents of the "Anonymous Startup" file will be returned when a user logs in as either "ftp" or "anonymous"; named users, say "Phil," can get personalized messages from files named, for example, "Phil Startup." Also, you can put a file "!Folder Info" in any shared folder and it will be displayed when a user changes into that directory. (Note that users are not guaranteed to see the text in these files; with the Fetch client, for example, a user may not have the Transcript window open.)
- The person accessing the archive can be made aware of when files were last modified in the archive.
- You can classify groups of users according to their login IDs using the Users & Groups control panel. (However, you cannot classify users based on host or subnet.)
- You can restrict how many users can access your ftp archive simultaneously, up to a maximum of 999.

- You can restrict who can upload files to your server.
- The server can uncompress, compress, and BinHex files automatically as files are transferred.
- The server logs who accesses your server and what they do. The file "NetPresenz Log" is kept in your Preferences folder.

You should also read the Documentation (Part 2) on Security with NetPresenz, more for its common sense advice than for any settings that can be adjusted. Part 2 of the documentation also describes how to restrict ftp access by IP address range; however, since this procedure involves creating a file with ResEdit, it should be undertaken with some care and is not recommended for novice users. (NetPresenz does not allow you to restrict access based on domain names.)

You can now register your ftp site so that it will be indexed by Archie (Section 4.6.2). There is a Web form for doing this at

http://www.bunyip.com/products/archie/register.html

NetPresenz can also function as a Gopher and Web server. Basic Web (or Gopher) setup amounts to choosing Web (or Gopher) Setup from the NetPresenz Setup panel and clicking on the "Web Enabled" (or "Gopher Enabled") checkbox. Since you already have the software installed, we will further discuss using NetPresenz as a Web server in Section 6.3.1.

6.2 E-mail Services

As stated in Section 2.3.2, there are two main types of e-mail services you can provide: a list server and an e-mail information server. An information server, you will recall, can generate "canned replies" and access to your ftp archive via e-mail. In this section, we will install two freeware list servers, AutoShare and Macjordomo. First, however, we will install a mail server, which will allow you to deliver and receive e-mail and which is a prerequisite for AutoShare.

A word of caution: Even though mailing lists are the simplest service to use from the client's perspective, the software for managing mailing lists varies and can be quite complicated to configure. If you have come to expect Mac software to be installed and set up effortlessly, some of the available list server packages will surprise you.

- AutoShare was a bit complicated to start and maintain, but Dave got it working as an SMTP list server running alongside EIMS.
- FireShare and ListSTAR, on the other hand, eluded us, and Dave really doesn't want to talk about it.
- ListSTAR, a major commercial package from StarNine, appeared infinitely customizable for those needing industrial-strength control, but a steep learning curve prevented Dave from getting it to perform the basic mailing list services. The price is also steep.
- LetterRip from FogCity has a much easier setup for a slightly lower price than ListSTAR, and Dave really likes it.
- But Macjordomo, a simple-to-configure freeware package that runs as a POP list server offers an easy way to get a list server up and running.

6.2.1 EIMS/AIMS

Before you can run a list server or e-mail information server, you have to have a basic e-mail server, which allows you to create accounts and send mail from and receive mail for those accounts. The Eudora Internet Mail Server (EIMS)—formerly Apple Internet Mail Server (AIMS) and, before that, MailShare—provides these capabilities. In Internet terms, EIMS functions as both a Post Office Protocol (POP3) and Simple Mail Transfer Protocol (SMTP) server. POP3 receives mail and holds it until the appropriate user asks for it; SMTP delivers outgoing mail.

While this book was being written, Qualcomm announced plans to release EIMS 2.0 as a commercial product (with a list price of $200). However, the company's announcements for EIMS 2.0 indicated that the older EIMS 1.2 would continue to be available as freeware. Table 6–2 provides a snapshot of EIMS.

Table 6-2 EIMS Snapshot

Location	*http://www.eudora.com/freeware*
Documentation	*http://web66.coled.umn.edu/cookbook/mailshare/mailshare.html*
Bugs	*eims-bugs@eudora.com*
Suggestions	*eims-suggest@eudora.com*

The sparse documentation included with EIMS—which will run even on a Macintosh LC with System 7.0—describes the straightforward installation and configuration: download, unstuff, double-click. You can configure the number of simultaneous POP3 and SMTP connections or use the defaults.

Next choose the Server: Account Information option to create accounts for sending and receiving e-mail. As you recall from Section 3.3.3, it is useful to create e-mail aliases for "webmaster@yourhost.com" in the event that the person performing Webmaster duties changes.

1. In the Account Information dialog, click the "Add" button.
2. Type "webmaster" in the User name field, enter a secure password for the webmaster account, and enter "Webmaster" in the Full name field.
3. Click the "Account enabled" checkbox.
4. If your Webmaster will log in as "webmaster" to check mail, click the "Login enabled" box. If your Webmaster prefers to receive mail at another account, you can select "Forward to…" from the Forwarding drop-down menu and enter the Webmaster's preferred account
5. Create other users as appropriate, following the same steps.

6.2.2 AutoShare

AutoShare is freeware by Mikael Hansen that provides list server capabilities along with features such as autoreplies ("canned" replies of text or attached files) and vacation notices. AutoShare extends the capabilities of EIMS or the Stalker Internet Mail Server to handle list server functions, and it uses knowledge of the EIMS file system to retrieve and send out messages. Because AutoShare requires an SMTP mail server on the same Macintosh, you cannot run AutoShare in an environment in which your mail server is, for example, on a UNIX system. To run mailing lists in this environment, you must run a list server client such as Macjordomo (see Section 6.2.3). Table 6–3 provides a snapshot of AutoShare.

Table 6-3 AutoShare Snapshot

Location	*http://www.dnai.com/~meh/autoshare/* *ftp://ftp.dnai.com/users/m/meh/AutoShare/*
QuickStart Documentation	*ftp://ftp.dnai.com/users/m/meh/AutoShare/AutoShare-More/*
Questions, Bugs	*meh@dnai.com*

In addition to setting the AutoShare preferences, installation requires setting up a few folders for AutoShare to store incoming and outgoing documents and messages. Then for each mailing list, you must create a few files for list-specific messages and three e-mail accounts. Although this makes AutoShare more difficult to set up and maintain than a typical Macintosh application, remember that it's free.

Once you have downloaded and unstuffed the latest version of AutoShare and the helpful QuickStart documentation by Jason Snell, follow the steps summarized here (and detailed in the QuickStart instructions).

1. Create a new folder called AutoShare wherever you store your Internet server applications. This will hold the AutoShare application.
2. From the unstuffed "AutoShare 1.x" folder, open the enclosed "AutoShare" folder and then the folder for the version appropriate for your Macintosh (either "PPC" or "68K"). Move the AutoShare application and Process Extenders folder to the AutoShare folder you created in step 1.

3. Open the "Admin" folder (in the same folder as the "PPC" and "68K" folders) and move the AutoShare Admin application to the AutoShare folder created in step 1. Store the FaceSpan extension in the Extensions folder of your System Folder.
4. Place the original "AutoShare 1.x" folder inside the AutoShare folder you created. You can also place the QuickStart documentation in your Autoshare folder.
5. Now you must create the folders AutoShare needs. As an alternative to creating the structure from scratch (detailed in the QuickStart documentation), the "AutoShare 1.x" folder has a "Samples" folder that contains an "Auto" folder preconfigured with the necessary folder structure. Move this "Auto" folder to the root level of your hard drive (as described by the documentation) or store it inside the AutoShare folder you created in step 1 (as Dave did for the sake of keeping his disk organized).
6. Be sure that EIMS is running, and start the "AutoShare" application.
7. Choose the Preferences: Miscellaneous... menu option. Enter the names of the list server administrator and the account to receive bounced mail—these can both be, for example, the Postmaster account that EIMS automatically creates. The defaults for the other preferences should be OK; be sure the Commands option for "Body" is checked.
8. Choose Preferences: Folders... and use the Select buttons to find the matching subfolder within the "Auto" folder from step 5. For example, the Filed Mail folder option should point to the "Filed Mail" folder within the Auto folder. The only exception is the Incoming Mail option. This needs to point to a folder created by EIMS; click the Select button and go to Your Hard Drive:System Folder:Mail Folder:Incoming Mail.
9. Under Preferences: Times..., you can set the schedule for AutoShare to send logs to the administrator and list digests to subscribers. The defaults are set to send these messages daily at midnight.
10. Create an e-mail account with the user name "autoshare" in EIMS. The Full Name can be whatever you like. Click the "Account enabled" checkbox, but turn off the "Login enabled" checkbox. Set Forwarding to "Save as files..." and for the path, you should copy the Filed Mail folder that you set in the AutoShare preferences. (Copy and paste works.) Inside the Auto:Documents folder,

there is a folder called "AutoShare" that must have the same name as this e-mail account. (Note that the documentation says it is possible, but not terribly easy, to call your list server the more common "listserver" name. Dave had mixed results getting AutoShare to do this, however.)

You are now ready to set up mailing lists under AutoShare. In this example, we will set up a list called "bugs." To create other lists, follow the same steps, replacing the list name as appropriate.

1. In the Auto:List Server folder, create a new text file called "bugs"; you can copy the sample file "Fun-l" provided by the AutoShare distribution or create an empty file. This will contain the list of subscribers to the bugs mailing list.
2. In the Auto:Archives folder, create a new, empty folder called "bugs."
3. In the Auto:Documents:AutoShare folder (see step 10 above), you can tailor the messages that users receive when they subscribe or unsubscribe from bugs. By default, AutoShare uses the "Sub" file to reply to a subscribe request. To customize the subscribe reply for a particular list, copy the file "Sub," rename the copy "Sub.bugs," and edit the message you want users to receive when they subscribe to the bugs list. You can similarly customize the unsubscribe message in the "Unsub" file, as well as the other list server messages.
4. Set up accounts in EIMS. First create an account with the user name "bugs"; the Full name is optional. Check "Account enabled" and uncheck "Login enabled." Set Forwarding to "Save as files…" and enter the Filed Mail folder from the AutoShare preferences.

   Next, create two accounts with the user names "bugs.d" and "bugs.m" with "Account enabled" checked and "Login enabled" unchecked. For each, set Forwarding to "Mailing list…" and enter the path to a file within the AutoShare folder named, respectively, bugs.d or bugs.m. For example, the paths might be "Your Hard Drive:Auto:List Server:bugs.d" and "Your Hard Drive:Auto:List Server:bugs.m." You do not have to create these files.

Users should now be able to subscribe and unsubscribe to the bugs mailing list as well as post messages to the list. Note when testing your lists that AutoShare by default does not send messages back to the sender. You must either first set the ACK option—send a mail message to autoshare@your-host with the message "set bugs ACK."

Also by default, lists are set so that only subscribers can post to a list and that anyone can subscribe. You can use the AutoShare Admin application to modify these and other list properties. AutoShare supports subscription, open, moderated, private, and announcement lists. For a moderated list, for example, choose the Configuration: Lists… menu option of AutoShare Admin. Double-click on the list you want to be moderated, and choose the "Moderated" option for List Type. Now, all messages to the list are forwarded to the list owner, and only messages from the owner go to all subscribers.

6.2.3 Macjordomo

If you have to work with a non-Macintosh SMTP server, you can still serve mailing lists from your Macintosh. For example, let's say you are running your Macintosh Internet server within a mixed-platform environment, and the systems/network gurus are running an organizationwide UNIX mail server. The UNIX mail server might intercept mail directed at the EIMS server on your Macintosh, particularly if the UNIX server handles all mail for the domain—for example, *sdsc.edu*—while your EIMS server handles a subdomain, such as *your-host.sdsc.edu*. This is exactly what happened when Dave tested EIMS on his SDSC Macintosh.

One option is to ask the systems/network gurus to perform the necessary incantations that will let you operate a second mail server on a subdomain of the organization network. This was useful for Dave while testing software, but requires that subscribers to your mailing lists adhere strictly to the longer host name. For example, Dave's test mailing lists had to be sent to *listname@hart-mac.sdsc.edu* rather than *listname@sdsc.edu*. The second address would be intercepted by the main SDSC mail server.

Another option for serving mailing lists from a Macintosh is a list server *client*, like Macjordomo. Macjordomo, a freeware package by Michele Fuortes similar in name only to the UNIX package "majordomo," will perform mailing list functions as an e-mail POP client. Instead of networking magic, you will only have to request that your organization's postmaster create regular e-mail accounts for each mailing list you want to manage. Mailing list messages are sent to those e-mail accounts, and Macjordomo works as if it were another e-mail user at your organization, except one that automatically checks its mail and resends the messages to the appropriate lists of subscribers. Table 6–4 gives a snapshot of Macjordomo.

Table 6-4 Macjordomo Snapshot

Location	*http://leuca.med.cornell.edu/Macjordomo*
QuickSetup guide	*http://leuca.med.cornell.edu/Pagine/QuickSetup.html*
Bugs and Suggestions	*mfuortes@med.cornell.edu*

Downloading and unstuffing Macjordomo produces a folder containing an application file and the QuickSetup guide in Microsoft Word format. An HTML version is on the Web page.

- Double-click the Macjordomo application and you are now running a POP list server. There is a limited set of applications preferences for Macjordomo, and the defaults should suffice.
- For managing lists, you need to create an e-mail account in EIMS (or have your site's postmaster create one for you) that accepts subscriber commands. The Macjordomo QuickSetup suggests "macjordomo," of course, but this will likely cause confusion. We recommend using either "listserver" or "majordomo." Check both the Account enabled and Login enabled options and turn off any Forwarding options.

Now you are ready to create mailing lists.

- Switch back to the Macjordomo application, and choose the Lists: Subscription List… menu item.
- Enter the information for the list server account created above. The POP address is of the form "listserver@host.domain.com." Check the "Accept User Commands" checkbox. If you are running the EIMS server, your SMTP server will also likely be "host.domain.com." If you do not control the mail server, you may have different POP and SMTP servers—pop.domain.com and smtp.domain.com, for example. Lastly, enter the e-mail address to which Macjordomo should send problems; this must *not* be the list server account.

- For each mailing list you want to operate, there are two steps. First, create an account in EIMS as you did for the list server account—bugs, to continue the example from above—or have your postmaster create one.
- In Macjordomo, choose the Lists: New List… menu item.

  For the List Name, enter the name you want subscribers to use in commands to the list server, for example "Bugs."

  For the List Address, enter the account you created in the previous step, "bugs@host.domain.com." This is the address to which subscribers send their postings.

  The POP password is the password to the bugs e-mail account above.

  The SMTP server is either your EIMS server or your organization's mail server, in the form *host.domain.com.*

  The "Problems to" account, again, is the list administrator (you, for example) and *not* the list server account.

  The "Reply to" option lets you specify whether responses to a message are distributed to the entire list or to the sender of the message. If you choose List, enter the list address in the "Reply address" box.

  Click the "List is Active" checkbox and then the Save button.

Macjordomo is now ready to start serving the "bugs" mailing list as a basic open discussion list to which anyone can post. You can also add users to the list through Macjordomo by choosing the Lists: Edit List… option and clicking the Users… button. To change the type of list to a subscribers-only posting, a moderated list, or a distribution/announcement list, click the "Advanced…" checkbox in the lower-left corner of the list dialog. This will reveal many more options for managing a list.

You can also customize the messages for each list that Macjordomo sends in response to user commands to the list server account. You can edit the messages once you have created a list, by choosing the Special: Edit List Messages… menu option.

6.3 Web Servers

Now we have come to the part you've been waiting for—installing Web (http) servers on your Macintosh. And we will help you install not one, but three Web servers. NetPresenz, which we installed in Section 6.1, can provide basic Web server capabilities. Quid Pro Quo is a freeware http server that compares favorably with all the Macintosh Web servers available. Finally, WebSTAR is the leading Macintosh Web server, and we will show how to get this package up and serving.

6.3.1 NetPresenz

If you already have NetPresenz installed as your ftp server, here is how to use it as a Web server.

1. Start NetPresenz Setup.
2. Click on "WWW Setup."
3. Click on the "WWW Enabled" checkbox.
4. Click "Choose" and locate the folder from which you want to serve Web pages. In the Finder, locate this folder and choose File: Sharing... to make this folder shared by "Everyone" with read-only access.
5. Start NetPresenz (if it's not already running).

You are now running a Web server. NetPresenz uses the Guest access of AppleShare to define the visible files and folders. The one downside to NetPresenz is that it does not, by default, return a directory listing of a folder (as Apple's Personal Web Sharing and Quid Pro Quo do) if there is no "index.html" file. However, if you enable CGI scripts—by clicking on the "CGI Enabled" checkbox of the WWW Setup dialog—you can use a CGI script to return the directory listing since NetPresenz will look for files such as "index.acgi" or "index.cgi" if it can not find an "index.html" file. An example script that returns the directory listing is included with NetPresenz.

The price you pay for simplicity, however, is limited control over access to your Web site. Because NetPresenz uses the Users & Groups "Guest" access to share Web pages, you cannot limit access to your Web site—or portions of your Web site—by domain, establish password protected areas, or take advantage of other advanced Web features. For this level of functionality, you should install either Quid Pro Quo or WebSTAR.

6.3.2 Quid Pro Quo

Quid Pro Quo 1.0 by Social Engineering made a big splash as a freeware Web server for Macintosh. At the time of writing Quid Pro Quo 2.1 had been released, again as freeware, while Quid Pro Quo Plus and Quid Pro Quo Secure were being sold as commercial products. Quid Pro Quo Secure includes full *Secure Sockets Layer* (SSL) support, which allows you to encrypt the data flowing between clients and your server. (If you are interested in conducting business over the Web, SSL will allow you to protect customers' confidential information.) Quid Pro Quo Plus includes all the features of Quid Pro Quo Secure except SSL.

From the Web page it is not clear how the commercial Quid Pro Quo Plus differs from the freeware Quid Pro Quo, but included with the freeware Quid Pro Quo download is a file that lists the features of the "Plus" commercial version not available in the freeware version: full Open Transport 1.3 multihoming; multiple virtual hosts; support for the HTTP "Host" and "Accept-Language" headers; full documentation and technical support; free upgrades for all minor revisions and special pricing for future major revisions.

However, the freeware version does include advanced server features such as *Java servlets* for extending Quid Pro Quo's built-in features (Section 12.3.7), *server-side includes* for inserting system information or repetitive HTML sections into Web documents (Section 10.4), and a search engine for fast access to all the information on your site (Section 6.4). Table 6–5 gives a snapshot of Quid Pro Quo.

Table 6-5 Quid Pro Quo Snapshot

Location	*http://www.socialeng.com/html/download.html*
Help/Information	*http://www.socialeng.com/html/resources.html* *support@socialeng.com*
Bugs	*bugs@socialeng.com*

Quid Pro Quo is easy to install. Download and unstuff the file from the Social Engineering Web site. This will create an installer application, which you should double-click. Tell the installer where to install your Quid Pro Quo folder. When the installer has finished, you are ready to start serving Web pages. Here are detailed, step-by-step instructions:

- Open the Quid Pro Quo folder and start the Quid Pro Quo application.
- The first time you run Quid Pro Quo, it will walk you through a series of configuration questions. If you do not know how to answer a question, we and Quid Pro Quo recommend using the default option.

  The most important option is choosing the folder from which you will serve your Web pages. This folder can be, but does not have to be, the same folder from which you are serving your ftp archive with NetPresenz. Unlike NetPresenz, you do not have to have File Sharing enabled for this folder.
- Start making some Web pages because you're now running a Web server.
- As a recommended option, make an alias for Quid Pro Quo and put it in the System Folder's Startup Items folder so that your Web server will start up automatically when you restart your Mac.

As you become more familiar with Quid Pro Quo and begin serving more Web pages, you can create "realms" within your Web site and restrict access to those realms based on IP addresses or with password protection. You can also extend the capabilities of Quid Pro Quo with support for Java servlets (Section 12.3.7), WebSTAR and MOSAPI plug-ins, CGI applications (Section 11.3), and scripting through Frontier and AppleScript (Section 11.4).

The one negative aspect of the freeware Quid Pro Quo is the absence of documentation, which is included only with the commercial versions. However, the interface is simple enough that most users should be able to configure most Quid Pro Quo options without it. Many advanced features are also demonstrated on sample pages within the "Examples" folder. (If you happened to download the original Quid Pro Quo 1.0, you did get a manual. Much of the interface is similar, so you may want to keep the older manual, but obviously you should use the outdated reference with care.)

6.3.3 WebSTAR

WebSTAR by StarNine is the leading commercial Web server for the Macintosh, and for the highest performance Macintosh Web servers, WebSTAR is the software of choice. WebSTAR can handle millions of connections per day and can sustain Web hits from a fully utilized T1 connection. Besides being easy to set up and use, it also includes high-end features such as the ability to administer essential server functions from any Web browser on the Internet, Java servlets, dynamic caching, server-side includes, and others. The one element missing from the basic WebSTAR package is the Secure Sockets Layer (SSL), for encrypting data flowing between clients and your server. WebSTAR/SSL is available at additional cost. Table 6–6 gives a snapshot of Web STAR.

Table 6-6 WebSTAR Snapshot

Location	*http://www.starnine.com/webstar/*
Questions	*http://www.starnine.com/support/qa/webstar/* *http://www.starnine.com/support/mailinglists/mailinglist.html*
Further Information	*http://www.starnine.com/webstar/webstar.html*

You can download a 30-day trial from the StarNine Web site. After filling out the form, you will be sent a trial key by e-mail and allowed to download WebSTAR. You then must unstuff the file, run the installation program, and restart your Macintosh. Now you are ready to run a WebSTAR server.

- Double-click the WebSTAR application.
- Once WebSTAR is launched, launch the WebSTAR Admin application.
- In the "Pick a server" dialog box, select your WebSTAR server and click OK.
- Choose Realms from the Configure menu. WebSTAR Admin displays the Realms window.

- WebSTAR should be preconfigured with a Realm named "PI_ADMIN" and a Match string of "PI_ADMIN." (You need these to be able to administer your server software.) If not, you should create a new Realm named PI_ADMIN (or Administration) and a Match string of "PI_ADMIN." Click Add and then click Update. You are now running your Web server.

As your first act as a Webmaster, you will probably want to change the StarNine-provided home page, called Default.html. While you can change the default file, WebSTAR will always serve Web pages starting from the WebSTAR folder. However, to access other sections of your folder hierarchy, you can place aliases to those folders within the WebSTAR folder.

From the bare-bones default setup, you can move on to configure more advanced features of WebSTAR. The electronic documentation walks you through the steps to password-protect certain areas of your Web site, restrict access to particular IP addresses or ranges of IP addresses, support Java servlets (Section 12.3.7), extend the server with WebSTAR and MOSAPI plug-ins, run CGI applications (Section 11.3), and add scripting through Frontier and AppleScript (Section 11.4). With the WebSTAR Admin application, you can perform all of these configuration tasks from another computer.

6.4 Search Tools

As described in Section 4.4, search tools comprise software that gathers, indexes, and searches all or parts of the information on your Internet server.

Most search tools perform some or all of these functions. Gatherers, also known as "crawlers," visit Web pages and all the Web pages referred to from those pages until the entire site has been visited. Indexers maintain a database about all the pages that it knows about; that information might come from the HTML TITLE tag, the first paragraphs, the META tag, or the entire document. A search engine takes user queries and searches through some database for matches to that query.

Thus, one way to provide search capability on your Web site is to run a crawler that creates an index and then have a search engine that queries the index. Two packages that do just that are Phantom and Search Server.

6.4.1 Phantom

Most search engines are developed to be CGI add-ons to your Web server. Phantom, commercial software from Maxum Development, can function as a CGI server plug-in but also runs as a stand-alone Web search engine. Phantom is a combined Web crawler and search engine that allows you to create automatically an index of your Web site's content. Once scanned, users of the Web site can perform searches using simple queries. Phantom also provides site management capabilities such as server mirroring and archiving, broken link detection, automatic updates, and more.

In fact, Phantom allows you to create indexes and perform searches of any number of Web sites from a single Phantom server. You can therefore use Phantom to provide search capability for other related sites. Pages found by Phantom's crawler are indexed into a relational database engine for searching, including context and location of related pages.

Phantom is administered via a Web interface, allows you to schedule automatic updates and backups of search indexes, indexes META keywords—through the HTML <META> tag that was added to assist search engines (see Appendix B)—and provides basic Boolean and begins-with searching options. Phantom's advanced search options include phonetic searches (if you are unsure of a word's spelling), related page, and date searching options. Results are presented in a relevance-ranked order. Table 6–7 gives a snapshot of Phantom.

Table 6-7 Phantom Snapshot

Location	*http://www.maxum.com/Phantom/*
User's Guide	*http://www.maxum.com/Phantom/UsersGuide/Homepage.html*
Help and FAQs	*http://www.maxum.com/Pt_FAQ/FAQList.html* *http://www.maxum.com/misc/lists/maillists.html*

You can download a 30-day demo of Phantom from the Maxum Web site. Once you download, unstuff, and install the Phantom software, you are ready to establish a search engine. Although Phantom will run as either a stand-alone application or a CGI plug-in, the documentation recommends running Phantom as a stand-alone server to begin with. (This feature also lets you run your search engine on a separate Macintosh from your Web server.) The Getting Started guide will walk you through the setup; the steps are summarized here.

- Double-click the Phantom application.
- Phantom is administered entirely through a Web interface, so you must use your Web browser to view the URL

  http://your.host.name:8080/Phantom.acgi$admin

- Choose New Session from the options at the left of the Web page. A session is roughly equivalent to a Web site to be indexed and searched.
- Enter the Session name and the root URL to be indexed, and click Create Session. You may want to change some of the other options available, but the defaults will suffice.

  An important option is the "Disallow crawl on these paths" session field. Phantom does not index the URLs you list here, which gives you a way to restrict the depth of the crawl.

- On the page that Phantom creates, click on Run (to the right of the new session name) to begin indexing. Phantom defaults to a setting that requires it to wait a minimum of 30 seconds between page downloads. While this is set as a courtesy for indexing sites you don't control, you may want to change Phantom's Preferences: Robot options for indexing your own site. Otherwise, the site crawling process does proceed at a crawl.

  For the curious, you can monitor Phantom's progress in the activity log of your Web server.

- To create search indices of other sites, select New Session and enter another session name and URL. You can also Edit Session preferences and set Phantom to reindex a particular site at regular intervals.

Note that because Phantom is administered through a Web interface, you can configure the search engine from any Web-connected computer. (If you try to enter the administration page from another computer, however, Phantom prompts you for a user name and password.)

Once the Phantom crawler has finished indexing a site, you can use Phantom to search the pages. To link to the Phantom search server from a Web page, create a link to *http://your.host.name:8080/*

(The port number of 8080 is the Phantom default and is changeable.) This will give you the default Phantom search page and provide you with the option of searching selected sessions from all of those available. To prepare a custom search page for a particular session, see the "Customizing Search and Results Page" in the electronic documentation. Here is a simple example of how to customize a Phantom search page and the corresponding results page.

- Use your Web browser to view the source from Phantom's default search page. To tell Phantom to search only a particular session, you must find the HTML tag that allows the user to select a session to be searched. This is a line of the form

  ```
  <input type=checkbox name=".Session1" value=1>
  ```

- Change this line to "<input type=hidden name=".Session1" value=1>". This will tell Phantom which session to search without giving the user a choice. Phantom has other optional parameters that you may or may not want to let the user specify for a search.
- Add the line

  ```
  <input type=hidden name=".CustomHF" value=customHF>
  ```

  to the HTML for the search form. This tells Phantom to use custom headers and footers when displaying the Results page.
- Load the Phantom administration Web page

  http://your.host.name:8080/Phantom.acgi$admin

  and click on the session for which you want to define a custom results page. This loads the Session Details page.
- Click on Header.
- Enter the URL for your custom search page. The buttons on the custom results page will now link to this page.
- Type in the HTML-formatted text to appear at the top of your results page for this session.
- Click on the Save Changes button.
- Click on the Footer link and repeat the previous three steps for the custom footer.

Here is an example of a customized Phantom search page that will let a user search the second session defined by the Webmaster after providing search terms and specifying whether to find all or at least one of the search terms and whether to look only in the URL, title, or header of the page. With this page, Phantom will display at most 25 hits and use the defaults for the other parameters—including Detailed/Short descriptions, Phonetic/Literal searches, and Begins with/Contains searches.

```
<html>
<head>
<title>Your Site: Search Page</title>
</head>
<body>
<center>
<h1>Search This Site</h1>
</center>
<hr>
<form action="http://your.host.name:8080/Phantom.acgi$search"
method="post">
<input type=hidden name=".Session2" value=2>
<input type=hidden name=".CustomHF" value=customHF>
Enter some key words to search by:
<input name=".searchText" size=40>
<p>
Find pages with <select name=".andOr">
<option selected>all <option>any </select> of these words.
<input type=hidden name=".maxHits" value=25>
<hr>
<center>
Search for key words found only in:
<input type=checkbox name=".URL" value=URL>URLs
<input type=checkbox name=".Title" value=Title>Titles
<input type=checkbox name=".Header" value=Header>Headers
<hr>
<input type=submit value="Search">
</form>
</body>
</html>
```

6.4.2 SearchServer

While Phantom is the only Mac OS-based search engine with stand-alone server capabilities, its high-end features come with a fairly steep price tag for entry-level search capability. As a shareware option, you can try the SearchServer from Social Engineering, the creators of the Quid Pro Quo Web server. (In fact, for users of Quid Pro Quo, Search-Server is freeware.) SearchServer does not run as a stand-alone server, but as a CGI application with your existing Web server. In addition, you can only index your own server; unlike indexing remote sites with Phantom, indexing local files on your server is a much faster process. Table 6–8 gives a snapshot of SearchServer.

Table 6-8 SearchServer Snapshot

Location	*http://www.socialeng.com/html/searchserver.html*
Information	*info@socialeng.com*
Bugs	*bugs@socialeng.com*

After downloading, unstuffing, and running the SearchServer installer, there are a few additional installation steps that must be done by hand. These steps, and instructions for indexing Web collections and creating custom search pages, are detailed in the Search-Server documentation. The documentation is included as a PDF file.

- Launch the SearchServer application.
- Check that your Web server allows CGI scripts to run, and whether it only allows CGIs to run from the cgi-bin directory.
- Place an alias to the SearchServer application in your topmost Web folder (or in the cgi-bin directory, if CGIs must run there), and rename the alias *search.acgi*.

Now that the SearchServer is installed, you must have it create indexes of your site for it to search. You can index your entire Web hierarchy or selected subhierarchies. This is a two-phase process. First, you must create an index for each searchable portion, or collection, of your Web server.

- ▼ Choose the Edit:Collections... menu item. To create a new collection, click the New... button.
- ▼ Enter a name for the collection, the topmost folder you want to be indexed, and the relative URL path from your top-level Web folder to the "root" folder for this collection. You can also set how often SearchServer will update the index. SearchServer will index the specified topmost folder and all its subfolders; you cannot limit the depth of the search.
- ▼ To create the index the first time, you can choose the File:Index Now menu option.
- ▼ Next, you create custom HTML search and results pages for each collection. A search page must have at least two required parameters: the collection name and the query. Optional fields include the page summary, the match score, the maximum results, query by example, and the results template. While optional, the template option is required for custom results pages.

Here is a bare-bones sample search page, which searches a collection called "Dave's Mac." Only the query string can be entered by the client.

```
<html>
<head>
<title>Dave's Mac Search Server</title>
</head>
<body bgcolor="white">

<form action="/search.acgi" enctype=x-www-form-encoded
method=get>

<h2>Search Server for Dave's Mac</h2>

<b>Search for:</b>
<input name="qry" type="text" size="30">
<input type=hidden name="coll" value="Dave's Mac">

<input type=hidden name="summary" value="yes">
<input type=hidden name="qrybyeg" value="yes">
<input type=hidden name="tmpl" value="results.html">
<input type=hidden name="score" value="star">
<p>
<input name="name" type="submit" value="Search">
</form>
</body>
</html>
```

The "tmpl" input specifies the custom results page. Creating results pages requires adding the tag <search_results> to the HTML for your custom results page. A bare-bones results template is shown below.

```
<html>
<head>
<title>Search Server Results</title>
</head>
<body bgcolor="black" text="white">
<h2>Dave's Mac Search Results</h2>
<search_results>
<hr>
<a href="search.html">Search Again</a>
</body>
</html>
```

While easy to install and maintain, SearchServer was still in beta release at the time of writing.

6.5 Testing Your Internet Kitchen

While you probably have been testing your software as you've installed it, here's a short checklist for making sure everything is working so far. You need to check that your Internet connection, ftp server, list server, and Web server are on-line.

Internet Connection. The easiest way to test that your Internet connection is working is to launch your Web browser and try to view a Web site, say *http://www.apple.com.* If you cannot view the site, you need to go back and check that your networking software, Open Transport, and the TCP/IP control panel are installed and configured correctly.

To test incoming connections, you need to know your IP address (from the TCP/IP control panel) and your host name, which must be properly listed in a domain name server, probably through your organization's network administrator or your ISP. (You can also run your DNS server on a Macintosh, but setting up a DNS is beyond the scope of this book. The leading DNS for the Mac is the commercial QuickDNS Pro from Iceland-based Men & Mice software, *http://www.menandmice.com*.)

You might also download MacTCP Watcher from Stairways Software (the makers of NetPresenz, Anarchie, and Internet Config). MacTCP Watcher examines your TCP setup—for both MacTCP and OpenTransport—and will let you "ping" Internet IP addresses, including your own, to test that the address's network software is responding. MacTCP Watcher is $10 shareware available from *http://-www.stairways.com/mtcpw/.*

FTP Server. With either your Web browser or ftp client (such as Fetch or Anarchie) you will want to check that you can connect to your ftp server via an anonymous login. If you are permitting uploads to your server or have established password-protected areas that provide full access, you will want to check that you have set up these permissions correctly.

Mail Server and List Server. You can test your mail server by creating test accounts, sending mail to them, and logging in under these alter egos to receive the mail. To check your list server, you will want to have several test accounts—what good is a list server without a list?—to test the subscribing, unsubscribing, and message-forwarding functions of the list server.

Web Server. Once you have a Web server running, it would be a good idea to have Web pages to serve. Most Web server packages provide a default page, or at least on-line documentation that you can use to test that your Web server is accepting connections. Use your Web browser and look for your server at *http://your.host.name.* If the page loads, you're on the Web. You may also want to test that you know how to set up areas protected by passwords and with access restricted by IP address. You will also need to have a few pages serving to test your search engine.

6.6 Example Server Recipes

Finally, we now distill all the information in Chapters 4–6 into a few example recipes for Internet servers. Your ingredients may vary, but you should achieve equally satisfactory results.

6.6.1 The (Nearly) Free Mac OS 8 Web Server Cookbook Recipe

In writing this chapter, Dave installed and tested all of the software described in this chapter. However, since some of the commercial programs were only available as 30-day demonstration copies—WebSTAR and Phantom, for example—the final Internet server that remained on Dave's well-connected Macintosh at SDSC included a selection of well-regarded freeware and shareware.

Mac OS. For reference, Dave's Power Macintosh 9600/200 is running Mac OS 8 and Open Transport 1.1.2. During the course of writing, Dave generally updated any other software utilities to the latest release. It is connected to SDSC's local Ethernet, and SDSC's Internet link is a partial T3 connection. In addition to the software below, Dave continued to use his Macintosh for day-to-day work, occasionally with more than a dozen applications running at any one time, including such large applications as Quark XPress. (Where possible, Dave also installed the software on his Power Computing PowerCenter Pro 180, although it did not have a full-time connection or IP address.)

FTP Server. For $10, NetPresenz 4.1 offers a package that is simple to configure yet it supports all basic and most advanced ftp functions.

SMTP Mail Server and List Server. Dave used the freeware Eudora Internet Mail Server (EIMS) 1.2, to set up e-mail accounts for a handful of test users, a list server using the free AutoShare add-on, and a sample mailing list with several dozen real users exchanging vital Internet humor messages. However, because Dave's Mac lives within the sdsc.edu domain, to keep the e-mail addresses simpler for the mailing lists, he switched to a client list server.

POP List Server. Macjordomo, while still officially in beta release (1.0b10) at the time of writing, offered a simple and free alternative to the AutoShare SMTP list server. While he enjoyed having his own personal mail server, using a POP list server freed him from the tasks of managing e-mail accounts and allowed his lists to have shorter addresses—*humor@sdsc.edu* versus *humor@hart-mac.sdsc.edu.*

Web Server. It is tough to beat Social Engineering's freeware version of Quid Pro Quo 2.0 as a low-cost Web server option. While short on documentation and a few essentials for some commercial applications—such as secure forms—Quid Pro Quo is a powerful, easy-to-use, and extensible Web server.

Search Engine. The Quid Pro Quo Search Server 1.0b1, again from Social Engineering, offered a simple option for adding search capabilities via a plug-in to the Quid Pro Quo Web server. Although still in beta release, the SearchServer is freeware for users of Quid Pro Quo (even the freeware version), $25 shareware to anyone else, making it a cost-effective search tool.

That is it—four (or five) pieces of software. While there may be high-end features missing from any given component, you will likely find that this low-budget software selection will provide more than enough functionality to get your Macintosh Internet server up and running. And, not counting the download time, it might take you as little as 30 minutes to get everything installed. As you become more familiar with your specific needs, you may then want to investigate the capabilities of the industrial-strength commercial software.

6.6.2 The Van Hacking Challenge

As another example of a Web server recipe, you might want to visit one of the Macintosh Web hacking challenges, in which a Macintosh Internet server was established and advertised as available to hackers as a dare. In most cases, the sites offered a reward of $10,000. Eventually one of the challenge sites was breached—the Crack-a-Mac challenge at *http://hacke.infinit.se/*—when it added such advanced functionality as remote administration with SiteEdit Pro, multiple domains with ClearlyHome, and interactive connections to databases with Lasso and FileMaker. (The hackable loophole was introduced by the Lasso software, which was patched within 24 hours of the successful hack.)

However, a simpler site, such as that described in the previous section, would likely withstand most aggressive attacks. An example of such a site is the Van Hacking Challenge at *http://www.vanhacking.com/index.html,* sponsored by VirTech Communications. You can visit their site for a lengthier description of why and how they made certain choices, but here is a summary.

Macintosh. They were on a budget, so they dusted off an older Power Macintosh 7200/120 with 48 MB of memory, eventually upgraded to 65 MB, and built-in Ethernet. They did not add any firewall software to filter packets at the network level. They used an unspecified version of Mac OS 7.x and Open Transport 1.1.2 with the "OTTCPSlowLinkTuneup2" software patch.

Web Server. The server was a recycled copy of an older version of WebSTAR, WebSTAR 1.3.2, which had originally come as part of the Apple Internet Server Software 2.0 bundle. Because there are noticeable performance improvements in WebSTAR 2.0, they added RushHour 1.1—a now-discontinued Web graphics accelerator from Maxum Development. WebSTAR 2.0 has this accelerator feature built in

Remote Administration. The developers used Farallon's Timbuktu Pro 3.0.2 (see Section 7.2). Timbuktu Pro allows a Webmaster to manage a server from remote locations.

Automatic Reboot. To protect against common attacks—the so-called Ping of Death and SYN_Flood attacks—that can crash a Web server although not breach it, they installed Maxum Development's PageSentry and Sophisticated Circuit's PowerKey Pro, which can monitor a server and reboot after crashing automatically, without human intervention (see Section 7.2.2).

Given this setup, the Van Hacking challengers officially put their server on the line June 1, 1997, with a prize of $10,000 Canadian. The challenge was to change a line on a password-protected Web "challenge page." During its eight weeks on-line, the site log shows that it withstood approximately 127,456 serious crack attempts on the server.

In the summary posted on the site, the site owners noted that most attacks were by hackers trying to exploit common weaknesses of UNIX and Windows NT. UNIX attacks included ftp attempts to download the challenge page and telnet attempts to link to the server, many searches for the UNIX-style ".rhosts" files, "sendmail" attacks, attempts at triggering CGI scripts remotely, and accessing files using UNIX-style pathnames—none of which work on Macintoshes.

The staff at VirTech Communications concluded: "We have also learned a great deal about Macintosh, UNIX, and Windows NT servers, and the strategies that hackers will employ to try and compromise their security. We know that the Macintosh is in no way susceptible to the typical security problems that UNIX and Windows NT servers face, and that, in all attempts made to penetrate our Macintosh, aided by the friendly and upstanding server software collection, our server is impenetrable."

▼▼▼

At this point you should have a fully functional information server for serving files via ftp, providing a service as a list server, and be ready to serve Web pages. You also have the means to index and provide a search service for this information. Congratulations! Let us now move on to what you need to do to keep your information server healthy and well-maintained.

• CHAPTER • 7

Keeping a Clean and Healthy Kitchen (Staying On-line)

Ingredients

- System and site maintenance
- Security
- Server log files and their formats
- Tools to manage log files
- Handling errors found in log files

That terrible moment has arrived—washing-up time. An unfitting end to a wonderful meal. You can defer the chore, but sooner or later you have to deal with it. The longer you have waited, the more unpleasant it will be. You can wash up by hand or use a dishwasher.

It is now time to consider the mundane, yet important task of server maintenance for each type of information server covered in this book—ftp servers, list servers, and Web servers. Now that you have given yourself or your organization an Internet presence, you will likely want to make your information available continuously. This chapter discusses some of the basic steps for making sure your Macintosh server stays clean and healthy.

First, we introduce you to Macintosh system maintenance, such as performing regular backups and protecting your system against virus infection. Then we turn to software and procedures specific to managing an Internet server, including how to analyze log files and monitor usage on your server. Finally, we discuss how best to make your Macintosh server a secure one.

It is important to note here that your server is the face your organization presents to the world, and mundane tasks that you might postpone on a stand-alone Macintosh take on a new urgency. If your server goes down, so does your world presence.

7.1 Basic System Maintenance

System maintenance for a Macintosh computer is not a complex undertaking. The most difficult part is *adhering* to a maintenance schedule that you establish. As with your personal health, the best medicine for a computer system is preventive maintenance—stopping problems before they occur. While you may not fend off everything that might go wrong, recovering from a mishap will be much easier.

7.1.1 Backup, Backup, Backup

Our first recommendation should go without saying, but we'll say it anyway. Back up your data on a regular basis—as often as the data on your server changes, which is probably every day. With daily backups of the latest information on your server, you will be able to recover from the worst possible system disasters. Even if the hard drive crashes and the motherboard melts down on your server system, you can recover by restoring your server on a new computer. With daily backups, the worst situation is to lose the changes made in the last 24 hours.

If you are part of a large organization, this chore may already be handled for you by the systems administration group. If you must do this yourself, the leading backup software for the Macintosh is Dantz Development's Retrospect. This highly rated package—among other reviews, *PC Week* recommended Retrospect for mixed-platform environments—can back up a network of Macintosh and Windows 95/NT systems. See *http://www.dantz.com.*

You might also consider whether you want to provide another sort of backup—for your electrical power. If you live in an area with frequent power outages or if the availability of your data is of utmost concern, you may want to look into an Uninterruptible Power Supply (UPS), which will keep your server running when the lights go out. A number of UPS vendors are listed at

http://www.yahoo.com/Business_and_Economy/Companies/Computers/-Hardware/Components/Power_Supplies/

7.1.2 A Maintenance Routine

Beyond keeping a regular backup, there are a number of Mac specific "tuneups" you should perform on a regular basis throughout the year. In the December 1997 *MacWorld*, John Rizzo describes a schedule for tasks ranging from rebuilding the desktop (monthly) to updating driver software (annually). Table 7–1 summarizes Rizzo's suggestions. For the complete why's and how's of Rizzo's advice, including recommended software utilities, see

http://www.macworld.com/pages/december.97/Feature.4068.html

Table 7-1 Macintosh Maintenance Routine

Schedule	Tasks
Daily	Back up data
Monthly	Rebuild desktop Repair invisible files
Quarterly	Optimize hard disk Free up disk space
Biannually	Scan for bad blocks
Annually	Update system software Upgrade driver software

7.2 Server Management

In addition to maintaining your Macintosh itself, you will also want to ensure that your server software and your site are occasionally cleaned up, updated, and generally still working. First, we discuss some software tools that help you check that the pages on your site aren't "broken," for example, links that no longer point to valid pages, or you might have an old version of a page on your server while a more recent version sits on the Macintosh on which you develop and test your site. Then we talk about a few tools that make sure your server software itself is actually running and restart your server if necessary. Finally, in this section, we introduce you to the log files stored by your server software, which give you regular updates about who is accessing your site, how frequently, and for what information.

7.2.1 Site Management Software

The most noticeable error on any Web page is not necessarily a page with incorrect information, but a link within your site that returns an "Error: Page not found" or similar response. To avoid this problem, you could plan to visit every link in your Web site regularly to make sure you haven't broken any links in the latest round of updates, but this could rapidly consume huge amounts of time if you're serving hundreds of pages.

A better solution will probably be to take advantage of software tools that automatically check a Web site for broken links or missing pages. Some of these tools we have already discussed. Many Web site creation tools, such as GoLive CyberStudio or NetObjects Fusion (Section 4.7.1), let you verify that links within your pages point to valid locations. This will then let you fix bad links or add appropriate pages. Some search engines, such as Phantom (Section 6.4.1), will also report back any broken links as it crawls and indexes your Web site.

One other situation that will likely arise is that your server is not the same machine on which you develop or test updates and additions to your Web site. Once new components are working, you want to transfer the latest version to your Web server. Several tools for the Mac OS provide the ability to transfer files between remote systems and synchronize files between the server and the development machine. While these features are useful to anyone who works with a computer at the office and on the road, they also can prove invaluable in making sure your production Web site doesn't return a page-not-found error. Table 7–2 lists a few of these tools, most of which can also be used to establish mirrors of your Web site (see Section 8.2.1).

Table 7-2 File Synchronization Tools

Location	Description
http://www.netopia.com/software/tb2/mac/	Timbuktu Pro from Netopia is one of the leading remote operation software tools for the Macintosh.
http://www.Qdea.com/sync.html *http://www.Qdea.com/syncpro.html*	Synchronize! and Synchronize Pro! from Qdea provide file synchronization, mirroring, and backup services between remote Macintoshes.
http://pacific-coast.com/St_Pages/PCSPages/Datasheets/-Site_Editdata.html *http://pacific-coast.com/St_Pages/PCSPages/Datasheets/-Site_EditProdata.html*	SiteEdit and SiteEdit Pro from Pacific Coast software add remote file administration to your server.

7.2.2 Crash Recovery Tools

If a server crash means that someone in your office (maybe you) has to come in evenings or weekends at a moment's notice to restart a balky system, you may want to invest in a software monitor that watches your Macintosh for a system crash or an application that "quits unexpectedly," to use the cryptic message returned by the Mac OS. These monitors use various tricks to make sure your server stays running. The PowerKey Pro will even let you restart your Macintosh by sending it a signal via the ringing of your telephone. Table 7–3 lists a few of these tools.

Table 7-3 Crash Recovery Tools

Location	Description
http://www.vl-brabant.be/mac/	AutoBoot and Keep it Up. Belgian shareware that restarts your Macintosh after a system crash and that restarts an application that quits unexpectedly or accidentally.
http://www.maxum.com/PageSentry/	PageSentry by Maxum Development. Uses real HTTP, FTP, SMTP, DNS, and Telnet client services to test the server for crashes.
http://www.sophisticated.com/products/powerkey.html	PowerKey Pro by Sophisticated Circuits. An "intelligent" power strip with the ability to restart a machine or a crashed application.

7.2.3 Monitoring Usage with Event Logs

Each type of server—list server, ftp, and Web—logs all accesses to the server and any warnings or errors relating to server operation. These log files are both your friend and your enemy. They are your friend since they let you analyze problems and monitor usage. The latter may be important for justifying the resources spent in developing the server and for planning how to expand the server. The log files are your enemy because you cannot ignore them. On heavily loaded servers these log files grow until they consume all available disk space. For example, a Web server receiving one million hits per month can produce approximately 300 MB worth of log files each month.

Monitoring the usage of each type of information server is a two-step process. First, you divide the log files into manageable components based on a given time period. Typically, once per week or once per month, depending on amount of usage, you will rename the current log files and create, if necessary, a new file for new logging. (We say "if necessary," since most servers will create the file automatically the first time they need to write something if it does not already exist.) Next, with the log files in manageable chunks, you summarize the information using a program appropriate to the information type.

We begin with a discussion of which log files get created for each server and their formats. We then look at tools available for analyzing these log files to summarize usage and conclude with errors and warnings contained in these files and how you should respond to these messages.

As before, we introduce server types in order of increasing complexity—ftp server, list server, and finally, Web server.

7.2.3.1 FTP Server

The location and format of the ftp log file depends on the ftp software running on your server. As an example of a specific location and format, consider NetPresenz (Section 6.1). As stated in the NetPresenz documentation, a file named "NetPresenz Log" is kept in the NetPresenz Preferences folder that records who logged in or out and when, as well as what files they put or get. We summarize this format using the following typical session from the file.

```
9:56 AM    10/16/97    132.249.33.126     charlesr@sdsc.edu 3
    log in       Guest
9:57 AM     10/16/97   132.249.33.126     charlesr@sdsc.edu 3
    put file     cylinder.tiff
public_folder:cylinder.tiff
9:58 AM    10/16/97    132.249.33.126     charlesr@sdsc.edu 3
    put file     mountain.tiff
public_folder:mountain.tiff
9:58 AM    10/16/97    132.249.33.126     charlesr@sdsc.edu 3
    log out      Guest
```

These are four records with fields delimited by tabs, where:

- *9:56 AM 10/16/97* is the date and time the record was entered.
- *132.249.33.126* is the remote client initiating the transfer
- *charlesr@sdsc.edu* is the user initiating the request.
- *3* is the session number, numbered from the time NetPresenz last started up. (On busy ftp servers with multiple, simultaneous client accesses, this will let you reconstruct individual sessions.)
- *log in*, *put file*, and *log out* are the commands received.

- *Guest* is the authentication level; *cylinder.tiff* and *mountain.tiff* are the files uploaded.
- public_folder:cylinder.tiff and public_folder:mountain.tiff are the locations of the files on the server.

Several of the Web usage analysis tools below, particularly the freeware Analog software and the commercial Funnel Web, can also analyze NetPresenz log files. We will not discuss them further here. See Table 7–4 for more information on these tools.

There is also the shareware utility FTPd2MacHTTP by Rees Griffiths that converts NetPresenz log files to MacHTTP/WebSTAR format. With this utility you can use any of the Web tools below to analyze your NetPresenz activity. See

http://www.bio.mq.edu.au/FTPd_LOG/FTPd2MacHTTP.html

(Note, however, that this Web page, while still serving, was 18 months old at the time of writing.)

7.2.3.2 List Server

Again, as with ftp, the format of the log file depends on the list server you use. Taking AutoShare (Section 6.2.2) as an example, the log file is automatically mailed to the AutoShare administrator at a time and frequency set by the administrator. The list server owner can choose from four logging options in the Miscellaneous Preferences dialog box:

- Off—no logging will be done
- Always—only important messages will be logged
- Brief—a single line will appear in the log for each transaction
- Tech—every transaction will have detailed information

The following is a typical log report from Dave's AutoShare list server, using the "Always" option.

```
===== AutoShare Log Report, Fri, 19 Dec 1997 08:52:23 =====

Thu, 18 Dec 1997 00:00:07 New log starting up

Thu, 18 Dec 1997 00:00:28 Copying Log.humor
Thu, 18 Dec 1997 00:00:30 Copying Log.Generic

√ Thu, 18 Dec 1997 00:00:37 humor.m@hart-mac.sdsc.edu
Postmaster@hart-mac.sdsc.edu AutoShare Report

Thu, 18 Dec 1997 15:35:58 AutoShare shutting down

Thu, 18 Dec 1997 15:44:49 AutoShare starting up

AutoShare version is 1.4.2
Next log in 08:15:11
Next digest in 08:15:11

Fri, 19 Dec 1997 08:52:21 AutoShare starting up

AutoShare version is 1.4.2
Next log in -8:-52:-21
Next digest in -8:-52:-21

List contributions:                       2
List server requests:                     0
Auto-response requests:                   0
Remote administration requests:           0
Mail-back entries created:                0
Mail-back entries released:               0
Hard bounces:                             0
Soft bounces:                             0
Unresolved bounces:                       0
Test bounces:                             0

Transactions:                             2
```

There are no third-party analysis tools for AutoShare log files, at least as far as Dave could determine. The administrator is therefore responsible for examining the log regularly and watching for anomalies.

7.2.3.3 Web Server

Like ftp servers and list servers, not all Web servers use the same log file format by default. However, most popular Web servers, including WebSTAR and Quid Pro Quo, can produce a widely recognized format called the *common log file format*. A record in this format appears as

```
hercules.sdsc.edu - - [12/Mar/1996:18:54:15 -0800] "GET /
moose/moose.html HTTP/1.0" 200 2238
```

- *hercules.sdsc.edu* is the client requesting the page from the server.
- *[12/Mar/1996:18:54:15 -0800]* is the date and time the request was made, noting that the time zone (U.S. Pacific Standard Time) is 8 hours behind Greenwich Mean Time.
- *"GET /moose/moose.html HTTP/1.0"* is the request made to get the file using version 1.0 of the HTTP protocol where the file is *DocumentRoot/moose/moose.html*
- 200 is the return status for the request (i.e., normal completion).
- 2238 is the number of bytes transferred.

Server-specific log file formats are generally extensions to and variations on the common log format "theme." For Quid Pro Quo, as an example, the default file is "Server Log" (located in the Quid Pro Quo folder) in which information is recorded in Quid Pro Quo log format. A Quid Pro Quo–format log file record can be customized to include some or all of the following information: date, time, from user, URL, hostname, user, result, method, path, search arguments, bytes transferred, referrer, transfer time, user agent, service, cookie, host, result code, and language.

7.2.3.4 Web Usage Analysis Tools

Table 7–4 lists several programs available for performing regular analyses of your server's Web log files. They all produce similar reports, and you might want to compare several to see which combination of ease-of-use, graphical reporting, and cost fits your needs. However, not all of these programs will analyze NetPresenz log files, so if you need to analyze the usage of your ftp archive, you will want to consider that factor as well.

Table 7-4 Programs for Summarizing Web Server Log Files

Location	Description
http://summary.net/soft/analog.html	Analog (freeware) provides multiple report options, but shows its UNIX roots in its interface. Recognizes NetPresenz log format.
http://www.royalsoftware.com/descriptions/-FunnelWeb.html	Funnel Web, a commercial package from Royal Software. Recognizes NetPresenz log format.
http://www.kitchen-sink.com/serverstat/	ServerStat, commercial package from Kitchen Sink Software. They also distribute a free promotional version.
http://sodium.ch.man.ac.uk/pages/wwwstat4mac.html	WWWStat4Mac, shareware from Redpoint Software.
http://www.maximized.com/products/flashstats/	FlashStats, commercial package from Maximized Software.
http://uplate.xpressway.com/sitestatpro/	Site Stat, commercial package from Uplate Software. They also produce a less expensive Site Stat Lite.

We will now show how to install and make use of the information provided from one of these packages, the promotional (free) version of ServerStat. Table 7–5 provides the software snapshot.

Table 7-5 ServerStat Freeware Snapshot

Location	*http://www.kitchen-sink.com/serverstat/promo.html*
Documentation	Included with the downloaded archive.
Bugs, Suggestions	*support@kitchen-sink.com*

Once you have downloaded and unstuffed the ServerStat .hqx archive, the program is installed and ready to go. The first time you start ServerStat, it will prompt you with a dialog box that asks for your name and company.

To compile a default report requires giving ServerStat some basic information from the main ServerStat window (Figure 7–1).

Figure 7-1 Main ServerStat Window

1. Click the Log File… button and locate the Log file to be processed.
2. Click the Output File… button and tell ServerStat where to save the resulting statistics file.
3. Click the Settings button to customize other settings. For our example, we set the log file type to Common Log Format. The default is WebSTAR format.
4. Press the Start button.

With some experimentation, Dave was even able to use ServerStat to analyze the Quid Pro Quo log format. Alter step 3 above as follows:

3(a) Click the Settings button. Choose MacHTTP from the Log Type menu.

3(b) Click the Log Format… button. In the window that opens, order the tokens as Date, Time, Result, Hostname, URL, Bytes sent, From, Agent, Method, Path args, Search args, referrer, Transfer time, User. (This order is indicated in the Quid Pro Quo log file.)

(Dave's main difficulty in analyzing the Quid Pro Quo log was not the fault of ServerStat. Quid Pro Quo stores its log as a preferences file type, which can only be read by Quid Pro Quo. Dave resorted to using the free ResEdit utility from Apple to change the file type to "TEXT" and creator to "ttxt" for SimpleText. Go to *http://swupdates.info.apple.com/* and look under Macintosh:Utilities for the latest version of ResEdit.)

Figure 7–2 illustrates the beginning of the file stats.html produced by ServerStat when viewed through a Web browser.

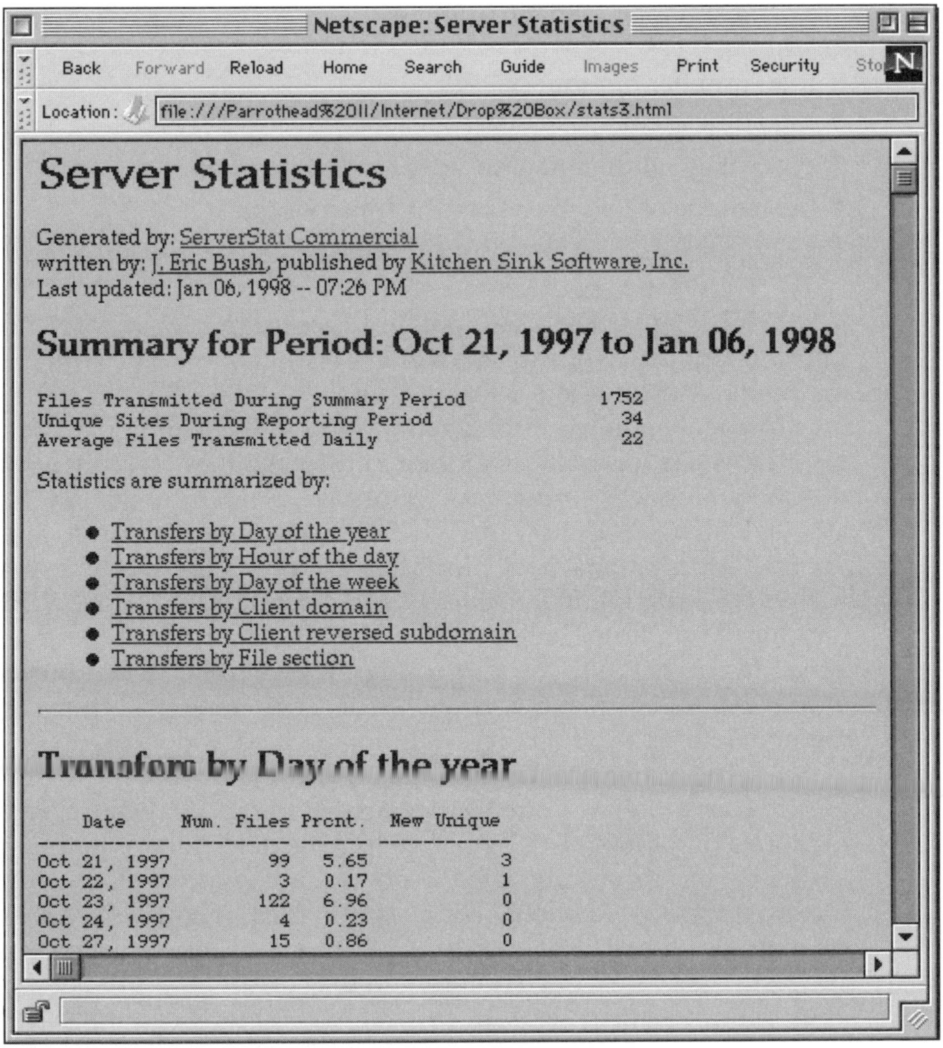

Figure 7-2 Output from ServerStatistics

The following items are summarized by ServerStat:

- total transmission statistics
- daily transmission statistics
- hourly transmission statistics
- transmissions by domain
- transmissions of each Web page

Transmission statistics include

- total number of requests
- total bytes sent
- percentage of the total requests for the time period
- percentage of total bytes for the time period
- percentage of total requests and total bytes per domain and file

While ServerStat does not produce graphical reports of this information, many of the commercial Web analysis tools do, including Funnel Web and Site Stat.

In addition to the information found in the common log format, most browsers log additional data in their log files, notably information about agents (browsers), errors, and referrers for each Web access. Unlike UNIX servers, which may maintain separate log files for this information, most Macintosh servers store this information within the main log file, using extended formats (as described above for Quid Pro Quo). Thus, in addition to the statistics that ServerStat generates by default, you can configure ServerStat to produce summaries based on agent, archive, error, error referrers, from, access method, referer, subdirectory, subdomain, user, and weekday.

Agent summaries, for example, will tell you what browsers people are using to view your Web pages—Netscape Navigator, Internet Explorer, or others. This could help you determine whether your audience can view advanced Web technologies, or Navigator- or Explorer-specific features. Error summaries might tell you what missing files users are regularly requesting. Common mistakes might suggest you create a page pointing to the correct new URL, or modify your default error page with helpful tips. Referrer summaries indicate from which URL a request was made. This tells you which sites are pointing to your site and, just as importantly, which sites are *not* pointing to your site but should be.

7.3 Security

Because the Mac OS does not have a command-line interface and does not include a lot of the high-level Internet software that is common on UNIX platforms—ftp, sendmail, and others—a Macintosh connected to the Internet as a client machine is virtually uncrackable. However, when you add servers to provide Web, ftp, and list server capabilities, you have provided the opportunity for security breaches.

7.3.1 Security Tips

The scope of this book does not allow us to cover Macintosh Internet security in great detail. Here are a few general rules of thumb.

- Macintosh servers, if the software is configured properly, are generally less susceptible to common Internet attacks. Read the security sections of the documentation that accompanies the software.
- As with your own physical well-being, the best security protection is preventive—don't leave any simple security holes open.
- Security risks increase as you add greater functionality and interactivity to your server; you must decide where the risk exceeds the benefits of added features.

The NetPresenz documentation offers some common sense advice about securing your Macintosh server, which we borrow from here. Following these tips will help you avoid leaving out giant welcome mats to would-be intruders.

- Disable guest logins unless you need them. However, you need guest logins enabled for anonymous ftp, Gopher, or WWW access in NetPresenz. On the other hand, Web servers such as Quid Pro Quo and WebSTAR and Maxum's Rumpus ftp server do not need to use Mac OS File Sharing. These packages also avoid the performance overhead of having File Sharing turned on.
- If you want a few people to have access, consider giving them a single account with a shared password. No matter how many people

learn the password, it will always be fewer than the number of people who could log in as guests.

- Only share a small portion of your file system as your ftp archive or Web site. You, as the owner, can still get remote access to it.
- Verify that access privileges are set correctly. This applies not only to Mac OS File Sharing, but also to any other security privileges within a server application.
- Perhaps the most important piece of advice is: Keep your machine locked up. At many large organizations and universities, the most common security risk is computer theft. Make sure your server is in a secured room with access restricted to those employees responsible for its maintenance.
- Running a close second to a secure physical location, one of the most often overlooked security measures is: Keep your password secure. Anyone with your user name, machine address, and password could delete every file on your hard disk. Don't give your password out and don't use an obvious password, such as your user name, real name, birthday, or initials; your husband's, wife's, girlfriend's, boyfriend's, dog's, frog's, or machine's name; your car license plate, make, or model; your student, social security, driver's license, or tax file number; any of the above backwards; or any word from a dictionary (especially an electronic dictionary).

  Good passwords can be found by making up nonsense words, using letters from a common saying, and by including nonalphanumeric characters. For example, "Two peas in a pod" becomes a password of "2piap."
- Check the log file regularly for invalid login attempts to your ftp or Web server.
- If you have doubts about any piece of software, don't run it. The creators have done their best to make it secure, but if that is not good enough for the level of security you need, don't use it.

7.3.2 Security Tools

In addition to the plain vanilla Web server software such as Quid Pro Quo and WebSTAR, additional software tools are available to supplement the security of your site by providing such functionality as password-restricted access on a per page basis and protection against unauthorized CGI scripts. Table 7–6 lists some of the available tools if you decide you need security measures above and beyond those provided by your Web server software.

Table 7-6 Security Tools

Location	Description
http://www.purity.com/websentinel/	WebSentinel commercial software to supplement your server's security.
http://arpp.carleton.ca/cgi/cgibolt.html	CGI-Bolt shareware to prevent unauthorized CGI scripts from running.
http://www.maxum.com/WebLock/	WebLock from Maxum Development lets you set page protection with Users & Groups sharing privileges.
http://host.comvista.com/Internet.tfm	Check Jon Wiederspan's Macintosh Internet Resources Directory for additional tools.

7.3.3 Further Information

For further information on Internet security, you may want to visit the sources listed in Table 7–7. These sources cover topics ranging from security recommendations for particular pieces of software, to the Secure Sockets Layer for encrypted transactions, to the security risks of Java and Web "cookies."

Table 7-7 Security Information

Location	Description
http://www.chi.maxum.com/Security/	Security tips for Maxum tools.
http://www-ns.rutgers.edu/www-security/archives/-index.html	WWW Security newsgroup archive.
http://www.w3.org/Security/Faq/	The W3C security FAQ.
http://hacke.infinit.se/	The Crack-a-Mac challenge page (with other security links).

Table 7-7 Security Information *(Continued)*

Location	Description
http://www.netscape.com/assist/security/ssl/index.html	Netscape's Secure Sockets Layer page.
http://www.cookiecentral.com/	Cookie Central Web site.
http://www-ns.rutgers.edu/www-security/reference.html	WWW security references from the Internet Engineering Task Force's Web Transaction Security group.
http://www.yahoo.com/Computers_and_Internet/-Security_and_Encryption/Organizations/	A listing of Internet security organizations.
http://pantheon.yale.edu/~dff/java.html *http://www.cyber.com/mirror/mladue/HostileApplets.html*	Links to Java security resources.

▼▼▼

That's it. These are the basics for building an Internet information server. If you have enjoyed the experience of putting the server together, fear not, the experience is not over. The technology is changing so fast that there will be lots of new and useful software to install in the future. You can go on implementing software as long as you like, thanks to a world of generous programmers. Check out this book's associated Web site for the latest.

CHAPTER 8

An Orderly Menu (Information Layout)

Good cooking requires efficiency. Delicate dishes will easily be overcooked while you hunt around for the right dish or pan, so be sure to organize your kitchen.

By now you should have a basic understanding of the Internet services you can provide, the tools you need to install to make these services available to a community of information seekers, and how to get connected to the Internet. In short, you are almost ready to begin supplying information.

First, however, you need to focus on the content and organization of the information you wish to serve. An ad hoc approach now will cost you dearly in the future. It takes a great deal of time to reorganize a large amount of poorly organized information, and it could disrupt the services you are providing.

This chapter makes you consider how to map your virtual information world—organized by content—onto the physical world of disks, the Macintosh file system, folders, and files. Your goals should include

- Making it easy to find a specific file of information or program when you need to modify or reference it.
- Maximizing maintainability, which in turn implies
  - Easing the burden of moving information to new file systems and disks.
  - Minimizing the number of copies of redundant information.
  - Facilitating file backup and recovery.
  - Providing a suitable growth path as the amount of information grows.
- Maximizing access efficiency.
- Making it straightforward to navigate your complete information hierarchy should that be desirable for indexing or other purposes.
- Facilitating the maintenance of your information by *mirror sites*, should that be desirable.

Do not confuse this topic on the general principles of information layout with the specific topic of hypertext document organization. What is discussed here applies to all types of information. Organizing hypertext documents is discussed in Section 9.5.2 as part of the general discussion of hypertext navigation.

8.1 Types of Information to Organize

One way to organize the types and locations of information that will be found on your server is by service type. The types of information will remain similar regardless of platform.

Mail Services

- Incoming mail for each user receiving mail
- Mail messages converted to HTML for Web access
- Outgoing canned replies
- Log files

FTP Services

- Generic ftp folders—public, incoming, outgoing, and so on
- Text, images, and compressed tar files organized by subject areas
- Log files

Web Services

- HTML documents
- Images
- Video clips
- Sound files
- Configuration files
- Log files
- CGI scripts and other programs executed or downloaded through the information server

The above is not necessarily a recommendation for how to separate your information, merely a way to think about the information types you will be faced with and how they might be arranged. On UNIX systems, for example, most service types map to a fairly standardized directory structure that has evolved over time. On the Macintosh server, the default location may vary. Each software package from Chapters 5–7 will create some specially named folders and configuration files, but most data folders and their relative placement on your hard drive are up to you as the server administrator.

The preceding simple classification is complicated by various subcategories of information. For example, you can think of subcategories of images associated with Web documents rather than grouping them as a single category. One subcategory is images used by many documents, for example, horizontal bars, arrows, and other basic icons seen in HTML documents. Another subcategory is images used in a specific group of Web documents, for example, a logo for a particular product. Finally, there are those images that will likely only appear on a single Web page. Organizing these subcategories of images should aim to minimize redundancy and make it easy to reference these images (if needed) as you add new pages.

There may be some constraints imposed by either the Mac OS or the software you are installing on how you organize your information. The Mac OS, for example, dictates where it wants Extensions and Control Panels to be stored. These constraints can sometimes be overridden, but doing so may not be advisable.

Do not change the default (that is, the recommended) folder and file layout of software you are installing, unless there is a compelling reason to do so. Making changes can lead to a more significant installation and maintenance effort.

8.2 Folder Hierarchy

How you organize your information will be based on the types of information you support and the complexity of that information. However, it is worth describing one possible scenario since it highlights the issues to consider.

Let's assume you are going to be maintaining a list server, a Web server, and an ftp server. Access to your ftp files is going to be via anonymous ftp and the Web. Other sites will mirror parts of your ftp archive and some Web documents. One possible folder hierarchy you might employ is shown in Figure 8–1.

Note that Macintosh folders are equivalent to UNIX and Windows directories, and common Web usage refers to the information layout as a "directory hierarchy." We will use the terms somewhat interchangeably. In general, we will use *folders* when discussing information layout from the Macintosh perspective, and *directories* when discussing it from the Web perspective.

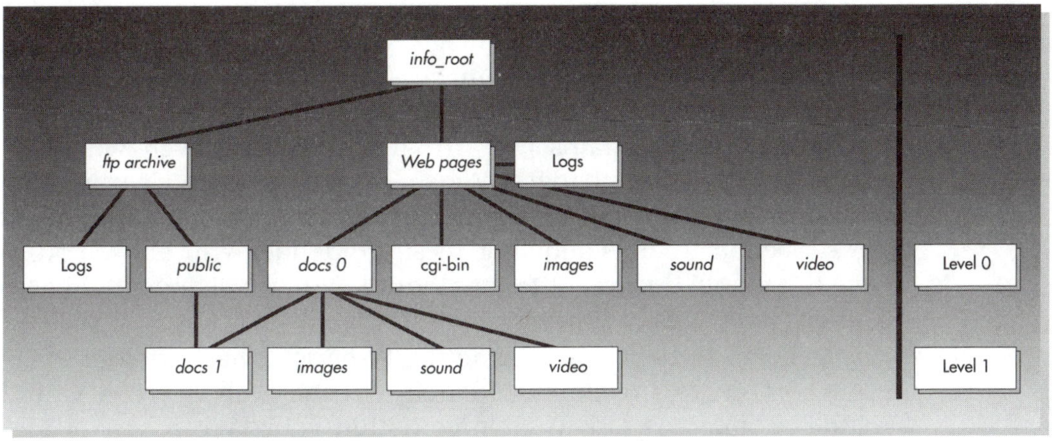

Figure 8-1 Example of a Directory Structure to Support an Information Hierarchy

The directory names shown in nonitalic font are physical folders defined by the Mac OS or the application software—they may or may not have the same names as in the figure—whereas those in italics are what we call "virtual directories." A virtual directory is a placeholder for an actual folder whose name is assigned by you and exists in the hierarchy relative to another actual folder. That is, a virtual directory's location is determined relative to a physical folder, but on your hard drive it may be either a physical folder or an *alias* to a physical folder elsewhere on the hard drive.

So in Figure 8–1, *info_root* might be, for example, your Mac server's hard drive. You should also note how few of these elements have predefined names—and even *cgi-bin* is simply a convention carried over from UNIX servers. When setting up your folder structure, you may want to emulate these UNIX conventions so that others can more easily navigate your site or in case you want to establish a mirror site on a different platform. Folders linked into multiple parts of the hierarchy, such as *docs1*, exist as a physical folder in one hierarchy and as an alias in the others.

This server is arranged with information at different levels based on how general it is. A recommended practice is to organize your information from most general to most specific. At Level 0 of the hierarchy is a set of Web pages *(docs0)* and any associated information used by those pages or any pages lower in the hierarchy. Typically, the home page—the single document that introduces the information hierarchy—is placed here, as well as any images and

CGI scripts used by the home page or any of the pages below it. Thus, as we discussed earlier, images of icons used by many pages should be placed in the Level 0 images folder and be referenced by all documents lower in the tree by way of a relative path name. The relative path name maintains the virtual relationship even when the physical relationship changes. We shall see this more clearly when we discuss hypertext documents and embedding images in hypertext pages (Section 9.3.6). Following these guidelines will allow you to move the whole document tree without having to change references to other Web pages or images.

At Level 1, the *ftp archive* and the *Web pages* share a folder structure *(docs1)* in this example hierarchy. In the Mac OS, you would include an alias to your ftp archive within your Web pages, or vice versa. This might be useful for a couple of reasons. First, if you have users who access your information server by ftp only, and others who access it via the Web, you can maintain a single file, for example a README file, rather than have one accessible via the Web and one accessible to ftp-only users. Second, if your server is successful, there may be sites that wish to mirror all or parts of your Web-accessible information hierarchy. Many mirror programs mirror ftp-based directory hierarchies, since anonymous ftp is the method they use to gain access to the site they are mirroring and compare their local copy of the files with the remote copy (Section 8.2.1).

At the lower levels in our example information hierarchy, we take files posted to the list server, convert them to HTML, and make them available via the Web. Section 4.7.3 highlighted filters for doing this conversion. An example using the MHonArc software for UNIX can be seen at

http://www.sdsc.edu/pb/wpdb/

8.2.1 A Note on Mirroring

Mirroring implies maintaining a current copy of the information on another information server. This could be used within an organization to provide a redundant copy of information. In the event that one system failed, the information would still be available from the other. Alternatively, mirroring could be on a global scale. In a perfect Internet world, global mirroring would not be necessary as all links would be instantaneous. However, in reality, links are often slow. Consider how slow the transatlantic link can be. It is useful for European sites to get information from a site in Europe even though the source of information is a U.S. site. Conversely, if the source of information is in Europe, it is useful for U.S. users of that information to get it from a mirror site in the United States. The European mirror means there is one transfer to the European site and subsequently many continental accesses, which are fast, rather than frustrated attempts at many transatlantic downloads, which are slow.

A common method for setting up a mirror is to have file transfer via anonymous ftp. For the Mac OS, there are other options. Mirroring functions are included within applications that also perform other duties. Table 8–1 lists several applications that can be used to provide mirror sites of Macintosh servers.

Table 8-1 Mac OS Mirror Software

Location	Description
http://www.maxum.com/Phantom	Phantom from Maxum Development is a Web crawler, indexer, and search engine with mirroring capabilities. See Section 6.4.1.
http://www.Qdea.com/syncpro.html *http://www.Qdea.com/sync.html*	Synchronize! and Synchronize Pro! from Qdea synchronize files and folders across multiple Macs and perform backups, as well as mirroring.
http://www.netopia.com/software/tb2/mac/	Timbuktu Pro from Netopia offers remote access between Macs and between platforms, file synchronization, as well as mirroring functions.

The mirror software functions as follows. The information server needs to do nothing apart from making the information available on the Web. The client or mirror site at predetermined times, usually based on how rapidly the information on the server changes, connects to the server, checks its mirror—its directory structure and file contents (based on modification date)—against the server, and downloads from the server the files and directories it does not have, or that have been updated since it last received files. The software optionally also deletes the files on the client that are now missing on the server.

8.3 File Naming

Consistent file naming is an important aspect of information layout for three reasons:

1. It helps you recognize the information content of files.
2. It helps other people recognize the contents of your files.
3. It helps applications recognize the correct files upon which to act and, subsequently, how to act.

For Macintosh Internet servers, reasons 2 and 3 also probably imply a change in your file naming habits. First, you should limit your use of punctuation marks and spaces in your file names, particularly if you intend for them to be shared across platforms. Second, you must use appropriate file extensions for files you intend to serve. Mac OS files include information about which applications can act upon them and indicate some of this information to you in icons. However, users on other platforms may not be provided with such visual cues and most other operating systems and Web browsers will not know how to act on a files without the proper file extensions.

This brings us back to MIME types, which were introduced in Section 3.2.1. Recall that a MIME type is a specification of particular types of files that are universally recognized by programmers and, hence, applications. Thus, *image/gif* is a registered MIME type for a graphics image in GIF format. This GIF file has associated with it an extension of .gif. The MIME specification registers the type of file and the file extension that is used by convention. Hence, Web browsers and Web servers understand the mapping of a file with an extension of .gif to the GIF MIME type and respond accordingly.

Building on our initial discussion of MIME types, Table 8–2 provides useful pointers to further information on MIME types and file extensions.

Table 8-2 Further Reading on MIME Types

Location	Types of Information
http://www.cs.wisc.edu/docs/mime.html	Good introduction
http://www.w3.org/hypertext/WWW/Protocols/rfc1341/-0_TableOfContents.html	Hypertext MIME specification
http://www.cis.ohio-state.edu/text/faq/usenet/-mail/mime-faq/top.html	MIME FAQ
http://www.ncsa.uiuc.edu/SDG/Software/XMosaic/-extension-map.html	Filetype-to-file-extension mapping used by the XMosaic Web browser

The last entry in this table provides an example of the MIME types and associated file extensions recognized by the XMosaic Web browser. Table 8–3 lists common file extensions that we suggest you adopt to be consistent. We met many of these file extensions in Chapter 3.

Table 8-3 Common File Extensions and MIME Specifications

File Extension	MIME Specification
.mime	message/rfc822
.ps	application/postscript
.html	text/html
.c	text/plain
.cc	text/plain
.c++	text/plain
.h	text/plain
.text, .txt	text/plain
.tex	text/plain
.pl	text/plain
.nd, .au	audio/basic

Table 8-3 Common File Extensions and MIME Specifications *(Continued)*

File Extension	MIME Specification
.aiff, .aifc	audio/x-aiff
.tar	application/octet-stream
.uu	application/octet-stream
.saveme	application/octet-stream
.dump	application/octet-stream
.bin	application/octet-stream
.gif	image/gif
.tif, .tiff	image/x-tiff
.jpg, .jpeg	image/jpeg
.mpg, .mpeg	video/mpeg
.hdf	application/x-hdf
.cdf	application/x-netcdf
.nc	application/x-netcdf
.dvi	application/x-dvi
.xwd	image/x-xwd
.rgb	image/x-rgb
.rtf	application/x-rtf
.pdf	application/x-pdf
.src, .wsrc	application/x-wais-source

Those MIME types marked as *x-*, for example, *application/x-wais-source*, are not yet official but are in common use.

▼▼▼

You should now have some idea of how to organize your information. We are now ready to begin cooking up the information to be served from your Macintosh.

• CHAPTER • 9

Web Recipes (Basic Web Documents)

Ingredients

- Existing on-line information
- New information for a new medium
- A plan for how this information should appear
- The tools to make this plan a reality

This is your main course—the pièce de résistance. Everything else was just a prelude to this moment. This is where you take existing information, any new information, and knead it and cook it just long enough to serve an Internet meal entrée that will be both lasting and satisfying.

While this book covers three modes of serving information—ftp, list serving, and Web serving—only Web serving requires significant attention to editing. Sure, you should put a README file in an ftp archive to assist clients in understanding its contents, but that is about the extent of the editing needed for ftp. List servers require a similar amount of editing, mainly for each list's help and information files. For the most part, your list server is simply a conduit for accepting mail and redistributing it to a list of recipients. As a list moderator, you could be creative in editing broadcasts to the list, but this serves little purpose.

On the other hand, the editing of Web documents is crucial. Editing has a strong influence on how information content is perceived, navigated and absorbed by the audience. Presentation affects impact whether it is for a school project by ten-year-olds, or a Fortune 500 company advertising its products. This chapter is devoted to the basics of Web page creating, editing, and publishing.

9.1 "Authoring" and Publishing

To begin our discussion of creating Web documents, we want to draw your attention to the distinct phases of preparing these documents. As promised in Section 2.2.6, Dave has a few strong thoughts on what has, by default, become the first step in the production of Web "content," specifically the "authoring" process.

On the one hand, "authoring" is a useful term because "writing," "designing," and "coding" by themselves do not cover all the aspects of Web page creation. On the other hand, lumping the writing, designing, and coding tasks into a single term suggests that Web sites can be or should be created by one person in one step. Maybe they can be, but *should* they be?

Only for the Web have these multiple tasks become so intertwined in common parlance. In print media and publications, writers, photographers, artists, designers, and editors all work together to "author" the end product. In television and film, writers, directors, camera persons, set designers, actors, and others combine to produce the evening news or a Hollywood film. And professionally created Web sites are also produced by a team of writers, designers, and Web programmers.

The point here is that the term "authoring" is all well and good as long as you remember that "authoring" Web pages comprises several steps:

- Deciding on the information content
- Determining which portions of the information should be expressed as text, as graphic elements, or as interactive Web elements (scripts, forms, etc.)
- Writing the text
- Designing or creating the graphic elements, including audio and video
- Editing the text, graphics, and interactive elements
- Designing a page combining the text, graphics, and interactive elements
- Coding—and testing—the HTML, scripts, and other elements for the Web

That is for a single Web page (or set of pages). Then there is the whole matter of creating an entire Web site, which adds the issues of organizing information, mapping the site for simple navigation, specifying sitewide standards for design and text, and others.

We will go out on a limb and say with 99 percent certainty that you—in fact, no single person within your organization—is an expert at all of these aspects of Web page and site creation.

Web technology is making writers, designers, editors, and programmers out of all of us. Before the arrival of the PC, and hence of widespread word processing, the various steps were more distinct—you wrote something on paper, and if you were lucky enough, a secretary or office assistant performed the editorial role by controlling the look and feel of the document. Graphic design was limited to a very few publications and the domain of graphic designers. Word processors have turned all of us into editors as well as writers. The Web has added designer and programmer to our résumés.

In creating for the Internet, what you write may immediately be made available to a potentially huge audience. We would suggest that lack of peer review for your creative efforts makes it essential that you do a good job, right from the start.

Editors will not disappear, but there will be a new type of editor who controls content and form in this new medium. If you work at a large organization that is using the Web extensively, you may well have an Internet editor already, even though he or she goes by some other name.

Good books have good content and are well organized. Good information servers are exactly the same. It is the implication of "organization" that has changed. Books are a sequential medium with a well-established form, and usually a single theme—the plot of a novel, the explanation of words in a dictionary, the steps in setting up an information server, and so on. Hypertext is less structured and can present multiple themes, that is, the same Web page can be used to make many different points. Global hypertext has taken us away from the sequential organization with which we are familiar and has plunged us into the world of random access.

We will give you some examples of what we think represent good organization in this new world disorder, and we will use these as templates for learning HyperText Markup Language (HTML), often referred to as the "language of the Web." We have based these selected templates on Web pages we have visited (in a virtual way of course) and found useful. That is, pages that have enabled us to achieve what we set out to do when we started looking for information on a specific topic.

Developments of the electronic creating-editing-publishing continuum using hypertext and beyond are just beginning. A book is a very static medium. If you exclude pop-up books for kids, about all you can do to interact with a book is turn the pages. Web publishing brings the full world of interactive multimedia to bear. Creating specifically for the Web is a different experience from traditional writing. Good writing skills are still critical but are now accompanied by skills at using different media to get the message across.

We are getting ahead of ourselves here. What we are attempting to do is excite you to the possibilities of a new global medium with many new opportunities, but first we must cover the basics.

9.2 Hypertext and Text Markup

Hypertext is not a new concept. Ted Nelson first coined the phrase back in 1965. It is beyond the scope of this cookbook to delve into the history of hypertext, but if you are interested, refer to the references in Table 9–1. One of the first commercial uses of hypertext was in the HyperCard products, initially for the Macintosh computer, and then for

PCs running DOS, and finally Windows. Some wonderful applications—*hypercard stacks*—have been built using these products. However, it is the global HyperCard stack—the Web—that has really popularized the use of hypertext.

Table 9-1 Background Information on Hypertext

Location	Description
http://www.w3.org/Markup	The W3 Consortium page on HTML.
http://www.isg.sfu.ca/~duchier/misc/vbush/	"As We May Think," an article by Vannevar Bush, in which the hypertext concept was first suggested.
http://www.picosof.com/850	Home page of Xanadu, the company resulting from Ted Nelson's ideas.

The World Wide Web would not have proliferated if it were not easy to edit and publish for this new medium. Web page creation is not restricted to the computer savvy—anyone who wants to spend a few minutes can add commands to a text file to create a *Web page* or perhaps a *home page*.

A home page is the top of the information hierarchy on a particular theme. This is a physical idea in a virtual world, since the moment you link your page to the Web, there is no top, and for that matter no bottom. What's there is a complex pattern of cross links, hence the name, "Web." To help orient yourself in this virtual maze, it helps to think of specific points that are referred to as "home pages." For example, a particular organization has a home page, which is the top-level entry point for getting information on that organization. Likewise, an individual in the organization may have a home page, which is the top-level page for getting information on that individual. The individual's page exists somewhere in the company's hierarchy, where it is no longer the home page with respect to the organization. Hence, what constitutes a home page depends on how we are viewing the information, from the perspective of someone interested in the company or someone interested in the individual.

9.2.1 Text Markup

Creating hypertext requires *marking up* your text information—inserting additional text that has nothing to do with the information content but, when read by a Web browser, causes a particular appearance or behavior. For example, the Web browser may display a region of text in boldface, provide a link to another home page, or display an image.

Text markup, like hypertext, is not a new idea. It has been used in text processing for many years. You take your basic text, include (or embed) a set of commands that describe how to format that text, pass that file to a program, and have that program either display or print the formatted text based on the embedded commands. Markup for text processing was popularized by such markup formats as Digital Standard Runoff (DSR), nroff, troff, TeX, and LaTeX. While these enjoyed some popularity on UNIX platforms over the years, none have become a standard, partly because they were overtaken by word processing programs on personal computers that are simpler to use (but not necessarily as powerful).

Yet another markup language is the *Standard Generalized Markup Language (SGML)*, which was, until recently, used mainly by the publishing industry. SGML is a well-developed language for describing the most complex documents. The Web's HyperText Markup Language (HTML) is a subset of SGML and, as such, does not have all the formatting features required for more complex documents. However, with each new release of HTML, more features described in SGML are included. (See also Section 14.3.)

The programs that process HTML and display the formatted text and graphics are the client Web browsers discussed in Chapter 5. Web browsers assume many formatting features that are not explicitly specified in HTML. Further, these browsers are forgiving of poor HTML syntax—if the Web browser does not recognize the syntax, it simply ignores it.

Using HTML, you can produce simple Web documents in a few minutes if you understand and remember a few markup commands, or *tags*. If you invest more time, you can produce more sophisticated Web documents with the advanced capabilities of HTML. Even if you use an HTML editor (Section 4.6), it is useful to have some knowledge of HTML. While the editors hide the details of HTML, the current sophistication of these editors means that some manual "tweaking" of the page will probably be required to get the exact effect you desire.

As we mentioned, HTML is evolving. If you are interested in this topic, refer to

http://www.w3.org/MarkUp/

Everything in the printed version of this book should be compatible with at least HTML 3.0. The Web server

http://www.sdsc.edu/Cookbook/Mac

will keep you updated on new HTML developments.

9.3 HTML—The Basics

Much excellent material has been written about HTML and is available on the Internet and in published books. We have provided pointers to what we have found most useful. We have subdivided these pointers into three types (Table 9–2):

(a) General information and detailed indexes of HTML-related information.

(b) Specifics of writing HTML.

(c) Pointers to publishers and book lists either devoted to, or containing large sections on, HTML.

What we do in this book is give you our own concise lesson in getting started with HTML. We begin with a discussion of the more crucial tags that make up the markup language.

Table 9-2 Sources of Information on HTML

Location	Description
General Information	
http://www.yahoo.com/Computers_and_Internet/-Software/Data_Formats/HTML/	Extensive index of HTML-related information.
http://www.gov.nb.ca/hotlist/htmldocs.htm	Well-organized site with various levels of information content.
http://www.w3.org/MarkUp/	Information on the HTML standard, including past history and current developments.
Writing HTML	
http://snowwhite.it.brighton.ac.uk/~mas/mas/courses/-html/html.html	A nicely laid out guide to writing HTML.
http://www.ncsa.uiuc.edu/General/Internet/WWW/-HTMLPrimer.html	The de facto standard primer on HTML.
http://www.nashville.net/~carl/htmlguide/	Great page on the lesser-known features of HTML.
Books on HTML	
http://www.mcp.com	Macmillan Computer Publishing Web site.
http://www.diskovery.com/Diskovery/EPG/-Indices/Books/ByPublisher/	List of publishers of HTML-related books.
http://www.davison.net/books/www.top.html	A comprehensive list from a distributor.

9.3.1 HTML Tags

An HTML tag tells the Web browser or other software reading the Web document, "Hey wake up and format me." (This is not strictly true. Initially, the MIME type—as manifest by the .html or .htm file extension—says, "Ignore white space, line breaks, and so forth, and just obey the tags.") HTML tags are distinguished from regular text by being contained in angle brackets as follows: <A_TAG>. Most tags also have terminators which are introduced by a slash: </A_TAG>. Terminators are not always obligatory, but they are considered good coding practice. Some tags—such as the tag that forces an end of line,
 (break)—do not have a terminator; there is nothing to delimit in this instance.

Consider an example of using an HTML tag:

```
<B>This text will appear in boldface.</B> This will
appear in the standard font.
```

The <B> and </B> turn boldface on and off using a boldface version of the font currently selected.

Appendix B summarizes a large variety of tags and serves as your reference guide. On the server you will find a list of tags for the currently accepted version of HTML. Once you have mastered the principles behind HTML, the reference guide should be all you need, since it serves to jog your memory as to what tags are available. How to use them will have become obvious. Here are a few principles behind using HTML tags.

- Certain tags have additional variables associated with them; these variables are referred to as *attributes* and modify the behavior of the tag. Attributes are tabulated in Appendix B along with their associated tags and are covered in some detail in this and subsequent chapters.
- The characters comprising a tag are not case sensitive, that is, lowercase, uppercase, and a mixture are all valid.
- Not all tags are understood by all browsers. If a browser does not understand a tag, it will ignore it rather than misinterpret it.

9.3.2 Basic Page Structure

Page layout using HTML is straightforward. A basic page includes four tags, properly arranged (and their terminators). First, the document is delimited by <HTML> ... </HTML> tags. Next, the <HEAD> ... </HEAD> tags delimit the header of the document, which is not displayed and annotates the document for you and for anyone displaying the HTML source code of your document.

Within the header, the <TITLE> ... </TITLE> tags define what appears in the title bar of most Web browsers and what appears in the list of URLs that you have visited. Similarly, it is the title that is added to your Web browser's hotlist of frequently accessed URLs. Thus, the title string is an important way for people to recognize your page, and you should think carefully about its content. The text string should be a short and concise description of what is on the page.

Finally, the <BODY> ... </BODY> tags delimit the bulk of the document. The following example illustrates the bare minimum markup for an HTML document.

```
<HTML>
<HEAD>
<TITLE>This text appears in the bookmark.</TITLE>
</HEAD>
<BODY>
This is the body of the document.
...
</BODY>
</HTML>
```

9.3.3 Basic Elements

If you add no other tags to the body of your document, something sensible will usually result when viewed with a Web browser. Even without any HTML tags at all, provided the file has an .html or .htm file extension, the contents of that file will likely appear in the browser. By default, the browser will ignore any white space, blank lines, indents, paragraph breaks, and so forth., and autowrap the text. That is, carriage returns at the end of lines will be ignored and lines will be wrapped to fit the width of the browser. You can see this effect just by adjusting the width of your Web browser window.

You will certainly want a little more control over the look and layout of your document. Now, we will introduce the HTML tags that define basic structural elements of a document: paragraph, line break, preformatted text, headers, and lists. Table 9–3 gives the tags for each of these elements.

Table 9-3 Basic HTML Elements

Tags	Description
<P> ... </P>	Paragraph. (The </P> is optional.) The paragraph style leaves a blank line between paragraphs and the first line is not indented.
 	Line break.
<PRE> ... </PRE> <XMP> ... </XMP>	Preformatted text. White space and carriage returns are displayed exactly as typed. The <PRE> ... </PRE> present the text exactly as it appears on the page, but *will* interpret hyperlinks. <XMP> ... </XMP> ignore hyperlinks.
<H1> ... </H1> <H6> ... </H6>	Headers. HTML defines six header levels, H1 through H6. How each is displayed depends on the browser.
<UL> ... </UL> <OL> ... </OL>	Unordered (bullet) list. Ordered (numbered) list.
<LI> ... </LI>	List item.

With HTML headers, text at each level is emphasized according to its header level, and header levels can be nested. The following example of using header levels in a table of contents illustrates these features.

```
<H1>Chapter 1</H1>
    <H2>Section 1.0 Introduction </H2>
          <H3>Phase I</H3>
          <H3>Phase II</H3>
    <H2>Section 2.0 The Guts</H2>

<H1>Chapter 2</H1>
```

You can take this type of hierarchy one step further with the use of lists. This is not, strictly speaking, a page layout feature, but it takes us to the point where we can format a nice looking page. Lists are groups of items where each item is identified by a bullet (unordered list) or number (ordered list). Some browsers also support roman numerals and letters to identify lists. We will revisit this detail when we discuss the more advanced features of HTML in Chapter 10. Here is an example of using unordered and ordered lists. As you see, unordered and ordered lists can be nested.

```
<UL>
<LI> First list item
<LI> Second list item
    <UL>
    <LI> Part 1 of second item
    <LI> Part 2 of second item
    </UL>
<LI> Third list item
</UL>

Here is an ordered list:<BR>

<OL>
<LI>Numbered item 1
<LI>Numbered item 2
    <OL>
    <LI> Part 1 of second item
    <LI> Part 2 of second item
    </OL>
<LI>Numbered item 3
</OL>
```

9.3.4 Character Formatting and Special Characters

In addition to formatting sections of your document, you may also want to format text on a word-by-word or character-by-character basis. This is straightforward and is illustrated with a few simple examples.

Consider a bibliographic reference as it might appear on Phil's home page.

```
<UL>
<LI> A. Smith and P.E.Bourne <I>The Journal</I>,
<B>The volume number</B>, 1995, The alpha subunit at
2.2 &Aring;
...
</UL>
```

Note first, single characters or groups of characters may be surrounded by tags to force specific formatting of the characters between the tags. In the above example, <B> ...</B> forces boldface and <I> ... </I> forces italics. A number of other character formatting features of this type are possible and are tabulated in Appendix B under Text Layout. The best way to learn them is to just start using them with Appendix B as a guide. We will be meeting more of these character formatting options as we progress to writing more complex Web pages.

Note second, the character formatting denoted by "Å" which will appear in most browsers as Å (Ångstrom). This is an example of a special character. Think of the character as special, either because it is not to be found on the standard keyboard, or if it is found on the keyboard, it has a special HTML function. The "<" (less than) and ">" (greater than) characters are examples of the latter since they are found on the keyboard, yet are used to delimit a tag. (Characters that have a role in specifying HTML syntax are referred to as *metacharacters*.)

What if you wish to use a metacharacter literally, that is, display an HTML metacharacter in your Web page? You use the same kind of special notation we used for Ångstrom—precede the entity description of the character by an ampersand (&) and follow it by a semicolon (;). In our example above, "Aring" is referred to as an entity and is interpreted in a special way by the Web browser. Similarly, less than (<) is represented as "<" and greater than (>) as ">". The extent to which these special characters are supported is browser dependent.

There is an alternative form of special character representation referred to as *character decimal reference.* This representation uses a decimal code to represent the special character, which is preceded by an ampersand (&) and a hashmark (#) and followed by a semicolon (;). So less than (<) appears as < and greater than (>) as >. For a complete list of special characters using the character decimal reference notation refer to sources in Table 9–4.

Table 9-4 Special Character Listings

Location	Description
http://www.bbsinc.com/iso8859.html	The current character set and its interpretation derived from a number of sources.
http://www.w3.org/pub/WWW/MarkUp/html-spec/-html-spec_9.html#SEC9.7	Alternative source of the above.

With a basic understanding of character representation we are now ready to move on to a more complex example which introduces a few new tags and one form of interrelationship between your Web pages.

9.3.5 HTML Anchors

An anchor is an example of a tag and represents the brilliance and simplicity of global hypertext. An anchor is used to reference other points in the same document, other documents on your server, or a document (or point in a document) any place in the world that the author (or editor) of that document wants you to access.

Here is the syntax for a simple anchor:

```
<a href = "http://www.sdsc.edu/">SDSC</a>'s home page
```

What appears in the Web document is

```
SDSC's home page
```

Clicking on "SDSC" will take you to the URL *http://-www.sdsc.edu/*, SDSC's home page. The <a ...> introduces the anchor and </a> terminates it. The hypertext reference "href = *URL*" is an attribute of the anchor tag and specifies the link to any piece of information on the Web.

When you build HTML documents to serve from your own server, it pays to visit the sites you intend to point to, cut the URLs from the Web browser's URL locator text box, and paste them directly into your document. This serves two purposes: First, you know the URL is still active, and second, you are less likely to make typing errors when entering the URL. The context in which you reference the URL is completely up to you as author and editor. This is the heart of how the Web operates. Once a document is served up on the Web, others can use it in any way they see fit (within the limits of copyright law). For example, one person could reference SDSC's home page as one in a list of national computing centers and another as part of a list of architecturally magnificent buildings around La Jolla, California—although you know that is unlikely if you have seen our building.

Variations on this simple anchor permit you to visit not only other documents referenced by URLs, but also points in the current document and in other local documents. Here is an example:

```
<a href="#introduction">Introduction</a>
....
<a name="introduction">Introduction</a>
```

This is referred to as a *relative anchor* because the type (e.g., http) and server (e.g., www.sdsc.edu) are not given; that is, it is an anchor relative to the current document. The "#" (hash mark) indicates that a pointer to the named part of the document follows. Thus, in the current document there is a corresponding *name* anchor, called "introduction." Using relative anchors is useful in large documents. You will see this a lot on the Web and examples are given in this book. For example, a hyperlink called Introduction would appear at the head of a document as part of a table of contents. Clicking on it would take you to the part of the document containing the name anchor.

Finally, then, you could have the following anchor:

```
<a href="http://www.sdsc.edu/index.html#introduction">
SDSC</a>'s home page introduction
```

The link takes you to a particular point in SDSC's home page denoted by the named anchor "introduction."

Another type of anchor supported by most (but not all) Web browsers tells the browser to send a mail message to the recipient specified in the HREF.

```
<A HREF="MAILTO:bourne@sdsc.edu">bourne@sdsc.edu</A>
```

Clicking on the text associated with the hyperlink, in this instance Phil's electronic mail address, bourne@sdsc.edu, tells the browser that the user wants to send mail to the "MAILTO:" address. The browser will invoke its built-in e-mail component, if it has one, or invoke the user's e-mail program with a blank message addressed to the MAILTO: address. For example, Netscape Communicator 4.0 and older versions of Navigator include integrated e-mail components; however, the Navigator 4.0 stand-alone has no such component and can be configured to invoke an e-mail client such as Eudora Pro.

9.3.6 Images

Another great feature of the Web is the presence of images. From the reader's perspective, this makes material more visually pleasing and, hopefully, more informative. Images can also guide the reader to the information they are seeking (see Section 10.2 on clickable maps). From the author/editor perspective, it is trivial to include images as long as they are in a format that can be read by browsers. This implies GIF or JPEG formats unless a *helper application* is present. (Section 4.6.3 covers conversion between various graphics formats.) Here we concentrate on how to display a graphic image as part of a Web page, assuming it is already in the correct format.

The following examples illustrate the simplest form of image inclusion:

```
<IMG SRC="mygraphic.gif">
<IMG SRC="http://www.sdsc.edu/Projects/Cookbook/Cover.gif">
```

The first example is relative and includes an image contained in a file called "mygraphic.gif" that resides in the same directory as the referencing Web page. The second example is fully qualified and includes an image located somewhere on the Web in a document—the <IMG ...> tag (image) introduces an image and the SRC (source) attribute of that tag indicates where to find the image. It is not good netiquette to include hypertext links from other people's images for selection in your Web documents for several reasons. First, such an action places a demand on their server that you have no right to make, not to mention placing high bandwidth demands on the network and causing a delay in serving the page. Second, you do not have the right to use someone else's material without permission. (This problem is not restricted to images.) If you want to use someone else's image, you should contact the owner of the image and request permission to download that image and serve it locally (see below). Finally, if the image on the remote site moves or is deleted, the image on your page is "dead."

The above example says nothing about the characteristics of the image presented—for example, size or relative position of the image on the page, both of which can be specified. By default, the image will appear within the running text as if it were a (possibly large) character, presented at the size stored in the GIF file or shrunk just enough to fit the browser window. An image displayed using the default IMG tag is referred to as an *in-line image* since it appears within a line of text.

There are some wonderful sources of images on the Web that you are invited to download and use in your own pages—a further example of enabling technology. You can, of course, grab many of the images that you see in Web documents. As stated above, you should give suitable acknowledgment and respect any copyright associated with the page. Assuming it is permissible to grab an image seen in a Web page, proceed as follows.

1. With Netscape Navigator or Microsoft Internet Explorer, click and hold the mouse button on the image you wish to save on your Macintosh.
2. A menu will appear with several image-related options.
3. Choose "Save this Image As…."
4. In the dialog box, locate the folder where you would like to store the saved image and click "Save."

If you have enough screen real estate to see your desktop behind your Web browser windows, you might also try clicking and holding on the image, then dragging the image to your desktop or a folder. The image will be saved automatically.

When including images in your own documents, the IMG tag can be supplemented with a number of additional attributes. The ALT (alternative) attribute should always be used, for it is this attribute that provides an alternative display for text-only browsers and for all browsers when image display is turned off—a likely situation when display is via a slow network connection.

Here is an example using the ALT attribute:

```
<IMG ALT= "Cookbook Cover"
SRC="http://www.sdsc.edu/Projects/Cookbook/Cover.gif">
```

In text-only Web browsers, the words "Cookbook Cover" will appear instead of the image. This preserves the reader's ability to comprehend the page when an image cannot be displayed.

The last display features of an in-line image that we need to consider in this introduction are (1) the alignment of text and the image, and (2) changing the characteristics (such as size and border) of the image. Both of these features are seen in Figure 9–1.

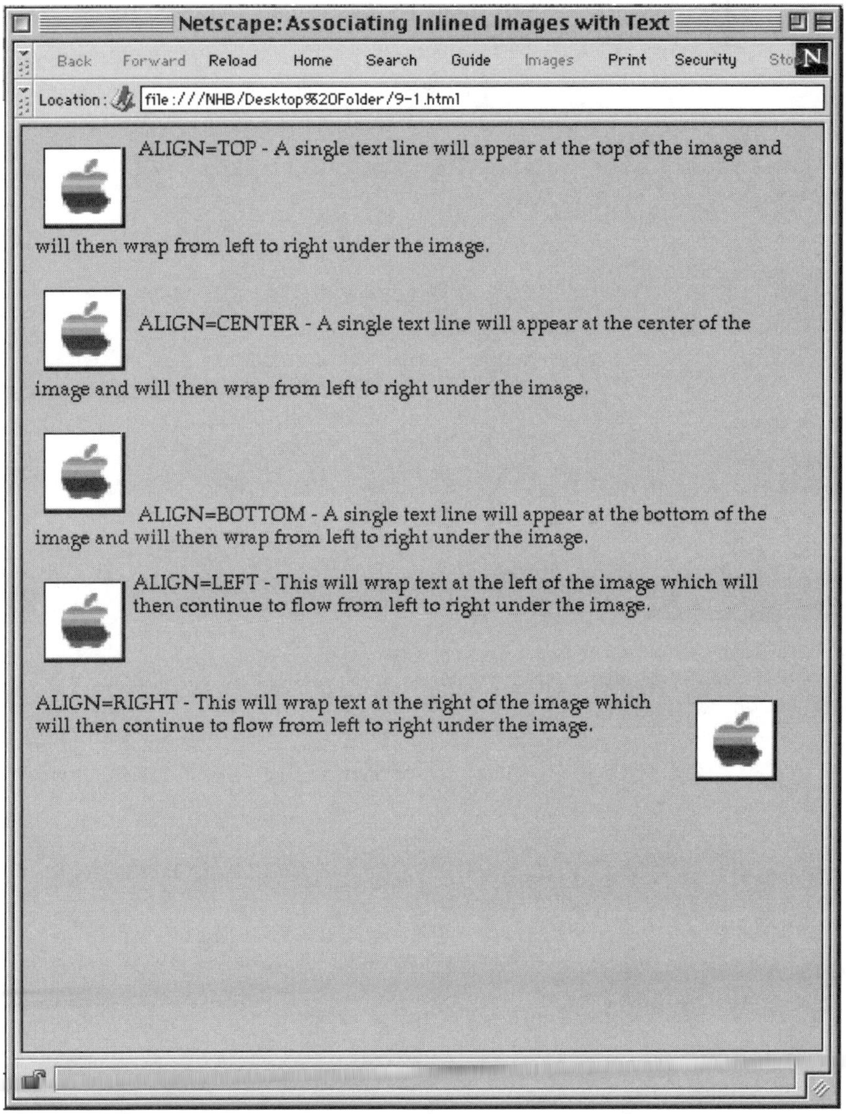

Figure 9-1 Image Alignment in HTML

Here is the HTML used to create this Web page.

```
<HTML>
<HEAD>
<TITLE>Associating Inlined Images with Text</TITLE>
</HEAD>
<BODY>

<P><IMG SRC="email3.gif" HSPACE=5 VSPACE=5 BORDER=0
HEIGHT=50 WIDTH=50 ALIGN=TOP >
ALIGN=TOP - A single text line will appear at the top
of the image and will then wrap from left to right under
the image.

<P><IMG SRC="email3.gif" HSPACE=5 VSPACE=5 BORDER=0
HEIGHT=50 WIDTH=50 ALIGN=CENTER >
ALIGN=CENTER - A single text line will appear at the
center of the image and will then wrap from left to
right under the image.

<P><IMG SRC="email3.gif" HSPACE=5 VSPACE=5 BORDER=0
HEIGHT=50 WIDTH=50 ALIGN=BOTTOM >
ALIGN=BOTTOM - A single text line will appear at the
bottom of the image and will then wrap from left to
right under the image.

<P><IMG SRC="email3.gif" HSPACE=5 VSPACE=5 BORDER=0
HEIGHT=50 WIDTH=50 ALIGN=LEFT >
ALIGN=LEFT - This will wrap text at the left of the
image which will then continue to flow from left to
right under the image.

ß<P><IMG SRC="email3.gif" HSPACE=5 VSPACE=5 BORDER=0
HEIGHT=50 WIDTH=50 ALIGN=RIGHT >
ALIGN=RIGHT - This will wrap text at the right of the
image which will then continue to flow from left to
right under the image.

</BODY>
</HTML>
```

Note the following attributes of the <IMG> tag:

- The attribute ALIGN aligns the image within the text as described on the page.
- The attributes HSPACE and VSPACE define horizontal and vertical space (in pixels) to be left around the image.
- The attribute BORDER defines a border (in pixels) to be placed around the image. The border will be the default text color. A value of 0 indicates no border, which we recommend, since a border around images such as linked navigation icons can be unsightly.
- The attributes HEIGHT and WIDTH specify the height and width of the image in pixels. In enlarging or shrinking the image, these values should be set to the same relative value so as to maintain the aspect ratio of the image.

9.3.7 HTML Templates

A directed approach to learning about the possibilities of HTML is to look at templates that others have prepared for different types of pages and use those as a starting point. Table 9–5 provides some places to go for templates.

Table 9-5 Sources of Web Page Templates

Location	Description
http://home.netscape.com/assist/net_sites/starter/samples/-templates/	Netscape's contribution—15 or so useful starting points.
http://www.inform.umd.edu:8080/EdRes/Faculty_Resources_and_Support/template	Templates for course material.

Another way to learn good techniques of Web page writing is from reading the HTML source of pages you stumble across while surfing the Net. The pages you like can be turned into templates for your own pages. This is easy and is made even easier by the capabilities of Web browsers. As with most Web pages, you have access to the source through the "View Source" option available in all Web browsers. Any time you see a nifty Web page, you can view the source

HTML and see exactly how it was done. What is even better, you can download and save that source—or use the composer functions in the newest versions of the Netscape and Microsoft browsers—and use it as a template for your own information. If you do this, be sure to not violate any copyrights and give credit where credit is due.

9.3.8 Debugging HTML

In contrast to debugging a high-level compiled programming language like C or C++, debugging HTML is easy. You can generally see what the problem is with the HTML just by viewing the page with a Web browser. The page does not have to be served by your http server to be viewed. Provided you have read access to the file, it can be loaded with the "Open file" (or similarly named) option available with all Web browsers. Remember to reload the file (and perhaps empty the disk caches) after making changes otherwise you will not see the changes. It is the unchanged, cached file that will be viewed again (see the Web browser configuration sections in Section 5.1).

Let us make this point quite clear. Browsers use various caching schemes, but the basic idea is the same. Once a page is downloaded to the client, it remains there for a period of time, since the likelihood that file will be revisited is high. It is faster to retrieve the page from the client than go back to the server to get it. A problem arises when the page has been changed (by you or someone else). Without a reload (a function available on all browsers), those edits will not be seen since you are viewing the previously unedited, cached version. Setting your browser cache to 0 will also help you avoid this problem.

Some HTML editors (see below) also have a debugging capability. That is, when you load an existing page into the editor, some problems in the HTML syntax may be highlighted.

9.3.9 HTML Editors

The number and capabilities of HTML editors are changing rapidly, as is the official HTML standard and the de facto HTML standard imposed by some Web browsers. A question to ask yourself at any time is, does the HTML editor support the advanced features that I wish to use? Currently, this implies tables, forms, and frames (see Chapters 10 and 11). Section 4.7.1 discusses HTML editors and provides sources of lists of available HTML editors.

9.4 Design Basics

The "design" of a Web page—its "look and feel"—is created in a process that, when done well, merges techniques and skills from both graphic design and computer interface design. While the terms "look" and "feel," as applied to Web pages, are often clumped together, for our purposes, we will consider "look" to imply how a Web page is presented (graphic design) and "feel" as the organization of the page and its relationship to the organization of other pages (interface design). Look affects how easy it is to read a page, and feel affects how easy it is to navigate and, hence, find the correct piece of information. As you will have ascertained from reading the chapters in this book devoted to feel (such as Chapter 8), we regard feel to be more important than look. This section discusses a couple of useful items related to look.

9.4.1 Colors

With basic HTML tags and attributes, you can control the color of the background, text, links, visited links, and activated links. With more advanced HTML tags, you can control the color of individual letters, phrases, or sections of text, as well as tables or table cells (Section 10.1). The goal in changing colors from the browser defaults—light gray background, black text, blue links, and purple visited links—is to create an attractive and distinctive page that is easy to read. The tricks are to find colors that not only make the text easy to read, but also go well together and appear the same across many browsers and platforms.

Be aware that what appears as a suitable color scheme on one display type may be unreadable on another display type! For example, we have seen a page look fine on a color monitor, but unreadable on an active matrix display using the 256-color palette found on many laptop computers. As a rule, try out your Web pages on as many display types and as many Web browsers as possible to make sure they are readable before releasing them to the world (see Section 9.3.8 on debugging HTML).

The term "Web-safe palette" is used to describe the set of 216 colors that display consistently across most platforms, from high-end graphics systems that can display millions of colors to 256-color displays on laptops. If you stick with these colors, you can be sure that your page colors will look the same across platforms. (But other elements of the design may change!) Table 9–6 lists some sites that help you choose color schemes for your Web pages.

Table 9-6 Web-safe Color Schemes

Location	Description
http://www.hidaho.com/colorcenter	A JavaScript application that lets you try out text and background color combinations. Choose colors from a palette or specify colors in hexadecimal, decimal, or percentage form.
http://www.imagitek.com/bcs.html	A basic form that lets you enter hexadecimal colors and preview the look of the page's color scheme.
http://pages.prodigy.com/bombadil/colors.htm	Links to color choosing tools.
http://www.yahoo.com/Computers_and_Internet/Internet/-World_Wide_Web/Page_Design_and_Layout/-Color_Information	Dozens of sites to help you choose your Web colors.

Colors in HTML are specified by a six-digit hexadecimal (base 16) value. If you do not know or cannot remember your hexadecimal numbering, the sixteen digits are 0–9 and A–F, with A=10, B=11 … F=15. The color format is then six digits 0–F in the format "#rrggbb," where rr, gg, and bb are the hexadecimal values for the red, green, and blue primary colors, respectively. The 216 Web-safe colors are those defined by mixing and matching 00, 33, 66, 99, CC, and FF as the red, green, and blue values. (6 x 6 x 6 = 216.) Systems may "round" other values to the nearest system-defined color, which may alter the effect you are looking for. Table 9–7 provides a quick lookup for the extremes of color you might wish to use and some idea of the effect of mixing primary colors.

Table 9-7 Hexidecimal RGB Color Specifications

Hex Value	Color
#000000	White
#FFFFFF	Black
#FF0000	Red
#00FF00	Green
#FFFF00	Yellow
#FF00FF	Magenta
#00FFFF	Cyan
#00000FF	Blue

Because RGB hexadecimal numbers are not always easy to remember, Internet Explorer and Netscape Navigator both support named colors. Initially, Explorer recognized 16 named colors, but Netscape soon upped the ante, supporting several hundred named colors, from "aliceblue" to "lavenderblush" to "yellowgreen." However, very few of the named colors come from the 216 Web-safe colors. Table 9–8 lists sites with named colors and their corresponding hexadecimal codes.

Table 9-8 HTML Named Colors

Location	Description
http://www.cyberspace.com/~tgmoore/colors.htm	Text list of browser safe hex colors and color names.
http://www.users.kih.net/~jcoldiron/color.html	Buttons let you click on a named color and see it displayed as the background color.
http://www.autek.com/pub_html/colors.html	More than 470 named colors and codes. Slow to download, since each color sample is an image.

9.4.1.1 Color Attributes

To change the color of the page background, use the BGCOLOR attribute of the <BODY> tag. It has the form

```
<BODY BGCOLOR="#rrggbb">
...
</BODY>
```

Once you have colored the background it may also be desirable to color the default text itself and the text representing the various classes of hyperlinks to provide the correct contrast. This is also done with attributes to the <BODY> tag. The attributes are given in Table 9–9.

Table 9-9 Text-based Attributes of the HTML <BODY> Tag

<BODY> Attribute	Description
TEXT	Basic text
VLINK	Visited link
ALINK	Active link
LINK	All other links

Here is a simple example taken from the Netscape documentation that creates an interesting contrast.

```
<HTML>
<HEAD>
<TITLE>Color Control Example</TITLE>
</HEAD>

<BODY BGCOLOR="#000000" TEXT="#F0F0F0"
      LINK="#FFFF00" VLINK="#22AA22"
      ALINK="#0077FF">

This is an example document.  Text is light-gray on
black, and <A HREF="nowhere.html">anchors</A> are
yellow at first, flashing blue-green when activated,
and pale green if already visited.
</BODY>
</HTML>
```

9.4.2 Images

Instead of color, the background of a Web page can be filled with an image using the BACKGROUND attribute to the <BODY> tag to specify the image file. For example:

```
<BODY BACKGROUND="images/bg.gif">
...
</BODY>
```

This will fill the background with the image contained in the GIF file bg.gif. If the background image is smaller than the Web browser display window, the image will automatically tile to fill the available background. This is yet another image for the client to download and should be kept simple (that is, small). Background images should also be very light, as if they are fading away; otherwise, text becomes difficult if not impossible to read.

It is appropriate here to introduce the idea of a transparent background. By modifying the background of an image to match that of the browser background, the image appears to float on the Web page and provides a pleasing look. Good instructions on creating images with transparent backgrounds can be found from the sources in Table 9–10. Table 9–11 indicates some good sites for obtaining background images.

Table 9-10 Information on Transparent Background Images

Location	Description
http://members.aol.com/htmlguru/transparent_images.html	Step-by-step guide, including sources of image editing tools.
http://www.magi.com/~kk/tbi2.html	Another step-by-step guide, but using Lview Pro on the PC.
http://www.icce.rug.nl/misc/examples.html	Examples of opaque versus transparent backgrounds.

Table 9-11 Sources of Background Images

Location	Description
http://the-tech.mit.edu/KPT/bgs.html	Thumbnail sketches of a variety of backgrounds and how to make transparent backgrounds.
http://cameo.softwarelabs.com/gini/	A large collection of images, including a large number of backgrounds.

9.4.2.1 Clip Art

In a previous example, we used the following image:

```
<IMG ALIGN="MIDDLE" SRC="images/hrblue.gif">
```

Like the horizontal rule (<HR>), this defines a separator, but in this case a thick blue line contained in a file in GIF format. Such clip art images are used very frequently in Web pages. Table 9–12 provides sources of clip art images as well as catalogs of other useful images.

Table 9-12 Sources of Clip Art and Other Images

Location	Description
http://cameo.softwarelabs.com/gini/	Over 1,500 buttons, bars, and other common icons.
http://cameo.softwarelabs.com/hotlist/hotlist.htm	Pointers to a very large collection of images.
http://wuarchive.wustl.edu/multimedia/images/gif/	A comprehensive album of images with a searchable catalog.
http://home.netscape.com/assist/net_sites/starter/samples/	Images from Netscape.
http://www.stars.com/Vlib/Providers/-Images_and_Icons.html	A variety of images and icons.

9.4.3 Some Guidelines

Here is a list of guidelines that we and others have found useful in writing Web pages. If you forget all the items on this list just remember the following. The best way to write good pages is

- take note of the features of Web pages you have visited and like;
- solicit and listen to feedback from readers on the pages you have written; and
- strive for maximum information transfer in minimum time.

Try out your Web pages on as many display types and as many Web browsers as possible to make sure they are readable before releasing them to the world (see Section 9.3.8 on debugging HTML).

Navigation

- Make the <TITLE> ... </TITLE> as short and informative as possible, since this is what users maintain in their hotlists. When they visit their hotlists in the future, they should recall from the title what the entry for your page contained.
- Avoid the phrase "click here." Browsing does not necessarily require a mouse and so the term may be meaningless. More importantly, the phrase is redundant, bears no useful information and only draws attention away from the description of where you might go, since you have to read back to and figure out why to "click here."
- Make the URL reference as informative and as locational as possible. We believe people like a sense of knowing where they are on the Web. We always have the location preference turned on if the browser supports it to see where in the world we are. It also raises one's tolerance level for waiting for pages to download when they are coming from far-off places (or places known to have slow network links). Here is an example of what we mean:

  Excellence in scientific computing is part of the mandate of the <A HREF="http://www.sdsc.edu/">San Diego Supercomputer Center</A>, which is located in <A HREF="http://www.lajolla.com/">La Jolla</A> California.

- Use links judiciously by first considering the various views that you want a visitor to have of the information. Avoid linking in such a way that navigation becomes circular and leaves large chunks of information unseen. This is especially irritating when waiting for pages to download using slow connections.
- Make the home page (the top of the document tree) self-explanatory, yet concise, and have links to all the obvious places. Have links back to the home page from pages lower in the hierarchy.
- Use conventional publishing techniques as a guide—an index, table of contents, list of figures, and so forth, remain very effective navigation tools for hypertext.
- In long pages, use named links and anchors to navigate backward and forward to appropriate points in the page. For example, named links supplement scrolling by immediately taking you backward or forward to appropriate sections in the document.
- Break your documents into appropriate chunks and have a reference anchor for each chunk. Granularity is also a consideration when printing (see below).
- Provide links to related sources of information, but be judicious.
- Cater to text-only access: Use the ALT attribute with images, and avoid navigation only by images.
- Cater to slow data links between client and server.
- Specify the size in kilobytes of files and images to be downloaded.
- Have a small version of the image (a thumbnail), which itself is a reference to a larger image, as was described earlier.
- Avoid Web pages that are longer than 10–15 screens of text.

Page Layout

- Experiment with the appearance of your pages by using a Web browser to view them using various page lengths and widths. The autowrap feature of HTML is satisfactory for most features, but for titles and other special blocks of text, a forced break tag (<BR>) should often be used.
- Draw the readers attention by putting important information upfront—do not waffle at the beginning—and using bullets, appropriate separators, and eye-catching icons (with text substitutes of course).

- Avoid using headers <H1> through <H7> for anything other than headings, notably to display text of different sizes. This destroys the logical structure of the document for which headers were intended to preserve. This will come back to haunt you in large documents where the header levels are useful markers and likely to be used later, for example, in developing a tool that automatically generates a table of contents for a fast growing document. Use <EM> ... </EM> and <STRONG> ... </STRONG> to emphasize text and keep an eye out for what emerges as standard HTML to emphasize text.
- Do not use esoteric icons, but instead, use those icons readers will recognize.

Printing

- Since printing only prints the current Web page, make each page a self-contained body of information.

Images

- Use MIME types that you consider generic and then inform the "reader" of what is required to view the image.
- Limit colors—the use of extensive color maps increases the size of the file dramatically and makes downloading to the client Web browser slow.
- Use thumbnail sketches of images as discussed previously.

Table 9–13 contains some useful sources of style guides.

Table 9-13 HTML Source Guides

Location	Description
http://www.w3.org/hypertext/WWW/Provider/Style/-Overview.html	The style guide from CERN.
http://www.cl.cam.ac.uk/users/gdr11/style-guide.html	Useful extensions to the CERN Guide.
http://info.med.yale.edu/caim/StyleManual_Top.HTML	Another useful style guide that considers performance issues.

9.5 Putting It all Together

With this simple understanding of anchors, in-line images, and page layout you are ready to build your first page. By putting together the basic HTML tags and our basic introduction to Web design, we will create example pages for a personal Web site and a group's Web presence.

9.5.1 A Personal Home Page

As an example, we will take Phil's personal home page, which could be used as a template for your own home page. Here is an annotated outline from which we will build the final page. Note that we have used the comment tag, <!-- *comment string* --> to annotate the page. Comments may extend over multiple lines and will not appear when the file is opened in a Web browser.

```
<HTML>
<HEAD>

<!-- This page is used as a sample page in the book,
Mac OS 8 Web Server Cookbook published by
Prentice Hall -->

<TITLE>
Phil Bourne's Personal Page
</TITLE>
</HEAD>
<BODY>
<!-- The ALT attribute displays the text specified
in a text only browser, or when images are turned
off. -- >
<H1><IMG ALIGN="MIDDLE" ALT="[Phils Face]"
     SRC="images/photo.gif">Phil Bourne</H1>

<HR>         <! -- "HR" is a horizontal rule -- >
<H2>Synopsis</H2>
```

```
Hi, I am a computational biologist at the
<A HREF="http://www.sdsc.edu/">San Diego
Supercomputer Center</A>. My professional interests
revolve out of making the most of biological data.
This implies data representation, databases, query
languages and the Web as a research tool. When not
thinking about this I am playing squash, walking,
driving fast or writing on computing trends.

<H2>For More Information</H2>

<UL>
<LI><A HREF="#contact_info">Contact Information</A>
<LI><A HREF="#res_projects">Research Projects</A>
<LI><A HREF="#other_projects">Other Projects</A>
<LI><A HREF="#papers">Recent Publications</A>
<!-- Second level nesting of lists -- >
<UL>
<LI><A HREF="#journal_papers">Scientific Journal
    Papers (1994-)</A>
<LI><A HREF="#comp_papers">Magazine Articles
    (1994-)</A>
</UL>
<LI><A HREF="#grants">Current Grants</A>
<LI><A HREF="#committees">Current Committees </A>
<LI><A HREF="#collabs">Current Collaborators</A>
<LI><A HREF="#education">Education</A>
<LI><A HREF="#profession">Work History</A>
</UL>
<!-- First level 3 header -- >
<A NAME="contact_info"><H3>Contact
Information</H3></A>
Philip E. Bourne <BR>
San Diego Supercomputer Center <BR>
PO Box 85608 <BR>
San Diego CA 92186-9784 <BR>
<P>
Voice:  (619) 534-8301 <BR>
Fax:    (619) 534-5117 <BR>
<!-- See the NOTE below -- >
<A REF =
"MAILTO:bourne@sdsc.edu">bourne@sdsc.edu</A> <BR>
<HR>
```

```
<A NAME="res_projects"><H3>Research Projects</H3></A>
...
<HR>
<A NAME="other_projects"><H3>Other Projects</H3></A>
I am currently involved in one non research related
project:
<H4><A HREF =
"http://www.sdsc.edu/Projects/pb/Cookbook/Cookbook.html”>
A Cookbook for Serving the Internet</A></H4>
...
<HR>
<A NAME="papers"><H3>Recent Publications</H3></A>
...
<HR>
<A NAME="journal_papers"><H4>Scientific Journal Papers
(1994-)</H4></A>
...
<HR>
<A NAME="comp_papers"><H4>Magazine Articles (1994)
</H4></A>
...
<HR>
<A NAME="grants"><H3>Current Grants</H3></A>
...
<HR>
<A NAME="committees"><H3>Current Committees</H3> </A>
...
<HR>
<A NAME="collabs"><H3>Current Collaborators</H3></A>
...
<HR>
<A NAME="education"><H3>Education</H3></A>
...
<HR>
<A NAME="profession"><H3>Professional Background
</H3></A>
<HR>
</BODY>
</HTML>
```

When interpreted by a Netscape browser, the result is shown in Figure 9–2.

Figure 9-2 Example of an Individual's Home Page

Figure 9–2 is a simple, yet effective, layout for your home page. It could be more sophisticated but is functional in the current form. For example, a closing address (for example, a copyright notice) could be formatted using the <ADDRESS> … </ADDRESS> HTML tag. Refinements like this come later. A major attraction of HTML is basic information with only a slight learning curve.

Associating a face with this personal profile seems like a good idea. It is best, however, to include what is referred to as a thumbnail image—a small image of low quality that is quickly downloaded. The thumbnail image can then be made a hyperlink to a larger image. Should the readers of the Web page be interested in the image, they can click on it and wait while the larger image is downloaded. An example of the HTML used in a thumbnail sketch is shown below.

```
<H1><A HREF="./images/big_face.gif"><IMG ALIGN="MIDDLE"
ALT="[Phils Face]" SRC="./images/photo.gif"></A>
Phil Bourne</H1>
```

Thus, clicking on photo.gif (the thumbnail sketch) will display the GIF file big_face.gif (the more detailed image).

The synopsis at the top of the above Web page (Figure 9–2) provides enough information for the reader to decide whether it is worth reading further, or to move on. The remainder of the information is organized like a table of contents, where each item in the list is a hyperlink to another named part of the document. In this way the reader can easily move to the section of interest. Since Phil's profile is in one document organized sequentially, the reader can also simply scroll through it, reading it as if it were a printed resume. The reader can also print the whole profile.

This is an important point. Web browsers do not currently follow links when printing but simply print the complete HTML file. In organizing your pages you need to think of the logical blocks of text that will likely be printed. Each block should be a single Web page represented by a single file.

9.5.2 Structuring Web Documents

By now you should sense that writing and serving Web pages are straightforward. As we stated earlier, that is part of the appeal. Where skill is required, it is in conveying the information.

A key feature of conveying information is planning how to organize the information. First you need to understand your intended audience. How are they going to want to view this information? How will they likely discover the components that they are interested in? Once you have contemplated the answers to these questions, you need to relate those answers to the following practical questions.

- What are the logical chunks of information I should be serving?
- How should those chunks be referenced: as separate HTML files or by named anchors within one or a smaller group of HTML files?
- What hyperlinks (i.e., relationships) should I establish between those chunks of information? In other words, what are the various views that people seeking the information are going to want, and therefore, what pathways should I set up for them to follow?

There is a whole discipline emerging, complete with its own jargon, that deals with the notion of authoring and editing hypermedia. Here we will keep it simple. Let us explore the practical considerations with respect to the three major questions above. First by analyzing the example we already have and then by applying those principles to a more complex example.

The layout of information used for Phil's personal home page is represented by Figure 9–3. This is about as simple as it gets. Phil's professional life is broken down into a few discrete categories—education, professional, publications, and committees—each represented by a square box (the logical chunks of information). If the scope of what someone is interested in is Phil's resume, then this structure works well by keeping the contents in a single file, structured the way most written resumes are structured. You can scroll through the whole document as if you were reading the resume. Also, by printing the page, you print the whole resume, which is what most people would want to do (point 2 above).

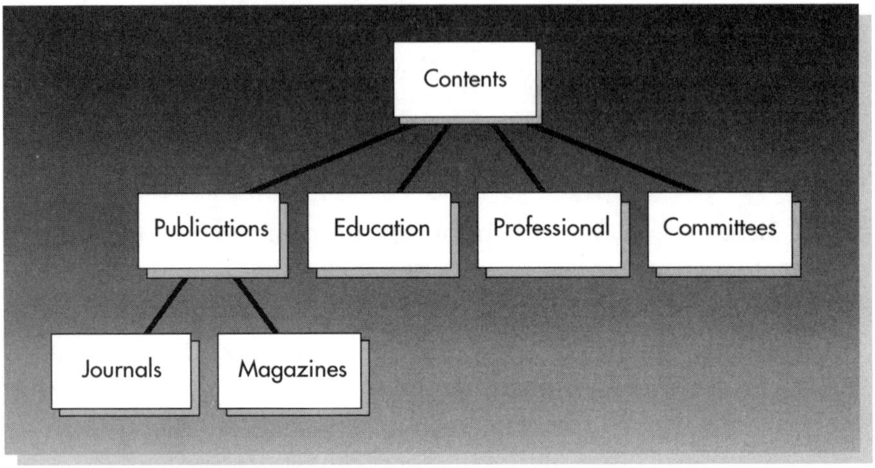

Figure 9-3 Simple Information Layout

The relationships (represented by the lines) between chunks of information are equally straightforward: a single root (contents) from which the user can navigate down one level, and then, in the case of publications, down to a second level. There are no cross-pointers to other chunks of information at this level. All navigation is by going back to the contents. This structure is adequate, and facilitates navigation when the information content is of this complexity. We have included reference points in the form of name anchors for each chunk of information (for example, <A NAME="papers"><H3>Recent Publications</H3></A>). These reference points are not used by this document, but they could be referenced by other documents, as we shall see subsequently (point 3 above).

9.5.3 A Group's Home Page

Let us take this notion of organization between chunks of information to the next logical step with a more complex body of information. In this instance we have information that covers a group of related areas and requires a set of relationships at the second level. This idea of levels has no absolute meaning; it simply provides a point of reference. One person's notion of the first level may be someone else's notion of the tenth. Assigning levels is simply a way of referencing the hierarchy from one viewpoint. Someone interested in a summary of Phil's research group would view this information as the first level and any software they have developed as the second level (Figure 9–4).

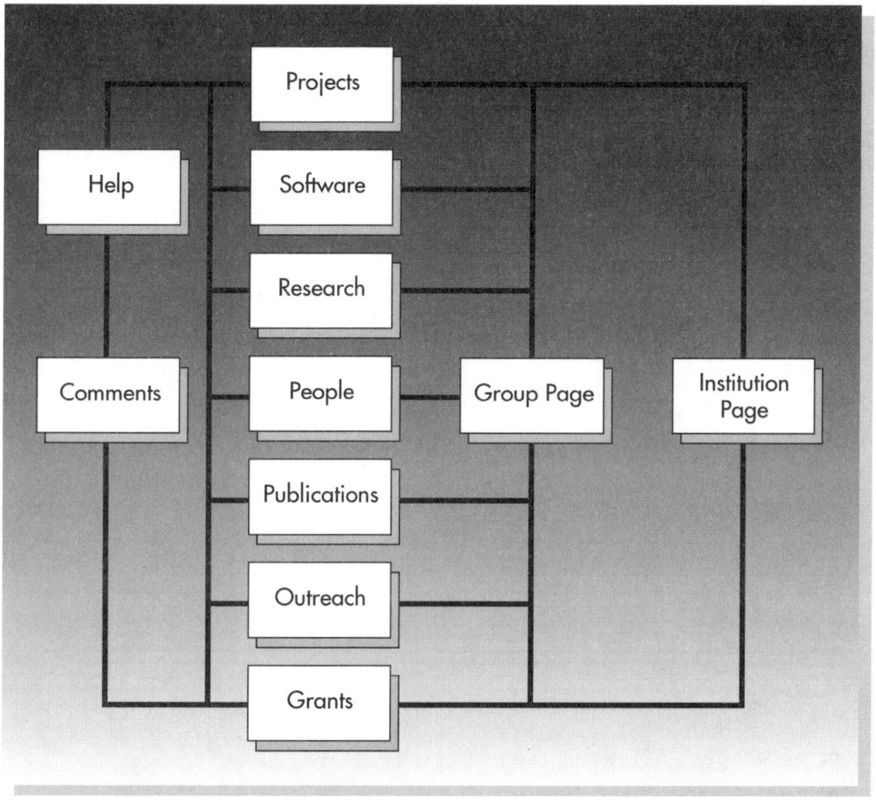

Figure 9-4 More Complex Information Layout

The important idea here is that we can now navigate directly between items at the second level. This implies more links. Having more links implies that it is more difficult to maintain and to navigate these Web pages. More links may confuse the reader, such that they navigate around in circles becoming increasingly frustrated and in the end see only a subset of the information in which they are interested. It is important to think through a complex information scheme before you implement it.

What we have done to support the layout given in Figure 9–4 is to create a template that will appear at the top of each chunk of information (represented by the boxes) and that provides the appropriate navigation facilities. This template follows, and the corresponding page is shown in Figure 9–5.

```
<HTML>
<HEAD>
<!-- A template for Web page navigation
     This is the Top Level Page -->
<TITLE>Title Goes Here  </TITLE>
</HEAD>
<!-- This introduces a background image. -->

<BODY BACKGROUND="./images/bg.gif">
<CENTER>
<H1>Top Level</H1>

<!-- Use a horizontal blue line as separator -->
<IMG ALIGN="MIDDLE" SRC="images/hrblue.gif">
<P>
<!-- Here is the navigation which appears at the top of
each page. On the databases page the URL for the
database page would be replaced with a URL pointing back
to the top level, and so on for the other pages. -->

<A HREF="./Databases.html"> Databases</A> |
<A HREF="./Software.html"> Software</A> |
<A HREF="./Research.html"> Research</A> |
<A HREF="./People.html">   People</A>   |
<A HREF="./Pubs.html"> Publications</A> |
<A HREF="./Grants.html">   Grants</A>   |
<A HREF="./Comments.html"> Comments</A> |
<A HREF="./Help.html">     Help</A>  <BR>
<A HREF="./Search.html">   Text Search</A> |
<A HREF="http://www.sdsc.edu/"> SDSC Home Page</A>
<BR>
<IMG ALIGN="MIDDLE" SRC="images/hrblue.gif">
</CENTER>

<H2>Synopsis</H2>

A summary of the page contents goes here.

<H2>Content</H2>

The content of the page goes here.

</BODY>
</HTML>
```

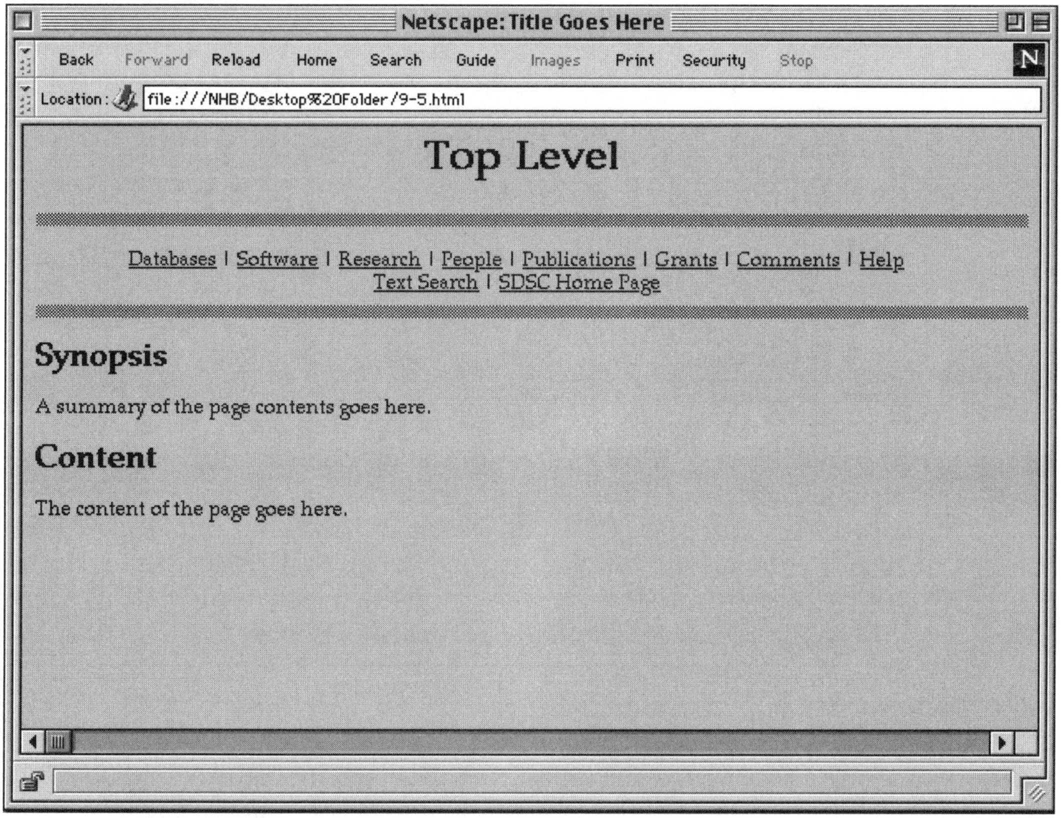

Figure 9-5 Web Page for a More Complex Information Layout

What we have created is a compact, yet easily navigable, set of pages in which it is easy to move between a variety of topics or back to the top level. When creating, for example, the database page, you could change the URL pointing to the database page in the above example to a URL pointing back to the top level. However, you would not want to call it top level, since it is only the top level from a single perspective. A term like "Group Page" would be more appropriate.

```
<!-- On the databases page the following: -->
<A HREF="./Databases.html"> Databases</A> |
<!-- would be replaced by: -->
<A HREF="./Group.html">Group Page</A>   |
```

So far, so good. However, there is a maintenance issue in what we have done here. Suppose we decide to add a new topic, for example, "Education," to indicate classes and other student-related activities that are performed by our group. We now have to go back and add that option to every page that has this menu! Not a big deal for the small number of pages here, but what if we have a complex structure with hundreds of pages? We can avoid this maintenance headache with what is termed a *server-side include*. In practical terms, this means we define the menu once as a separate page and tell the server to include that menu page with special tags in each page. Then as the page is served to a Web client, the server inserts the menu. Let us make that quite clear—the inclusion is not done at the time we create the page, but when the page is served to a Web client. When we want to add a new item to the menu, we need only add it once to the include page, and it will appear on every page that includes that menu. Server-side includes are discussed in more detail in Section 10.4. It should be apparent here, however, that server-side includes are useful for including the same volatile information, that is, information that changes frequently, in a variety of pages.

9.6 Publishing Your Web Pages

Writing pages should be done off-line, in a separate folder or set of folders, organized as you want them to be on your server. You then view the results by opening the file (rather than the URL) from the Web browser. Once you are satisfied with the pages and ready to publish, you can move the enclosing folder to somewhere in the server document hierarchy. If you have used appropriate relative file references in your URLs, then all pages should be found and served after they are moved. Keeping Web documents out of the server hierarchy until you are ready prevents readers from stumbling across them or having them indexed by Web robots.

If your goal is to make your pages widely known, you need to do more than simply make them accessible on your server. The Web robots used by the various search engines will eventually find and index your pages, but you may wish to expedite this process in various ways.

Here are some specific suggestions, including specific Web pages to visit for more information (see Table 9–14).

- Notify Webmasters of heavily used sites relevant to your material and request a link be made.
- Notify relevant newsgroups of your pages.
- Submit your URLs to maintainers of individual search engines, but be aware that the number and popularity of these search engines are constantly changing.
- Use a free service. This entails your filling in a Web form that is then translated into the many formats required to register with each of multiple sites, search engines, bulletin boards, comprehensive lists, for example, the Virtual Tourist, NCSA's What's New, Yahoo!, and WWW Virtual Subject Library.
- Use a commercial service, which operates like a free service, but for a fee and with guaranteed coverage.

Be advised, however, no service can guarantee visitors to your site. For specialty subjects in particular, you may do better to put in the effort of locating Web sites, news groups, and search engines relevant to your subject than indiscriminately adding your URL to hundreds of small, general, or less-popular search engines.

Table 9-14 Further Reading on Getting Your Web Pages Known

Location	Description
http://www.webcom.com/html/publicize.html	A comprehensive discussion of the various options for getting your pages known.
http://www.yahoo.com/Computers_and_Internet/Internet/-World_Wide_Web/Announcement_Services/	As above.

▼ ▼ ▼

You should by now have grasped the basics of writing HTML. We'll now move on to the more advanced features of HTML namely, tables, clickable maps, frames (Chapter 10), and forms. Forms, which let users submit data to the server, open up a new world of client-server interaction, which we'll explore in Chapter 11.

CHAPTER 10

Gourmet Web Recipes (Advanced Web Documents)

Ingredients

- Tables
- Server- and client-based clickable maps
- Frames
- Server-side includes

We have learned how to prepare a simple main course; now for the culinary delights. The difference between a good meal and a great meal is the subtle use of spices and sauces and, of course, presentation.

If you spend more than a couple of minutes surfing the Web, you will come across what we term "advanced" Web documents. Sometimes these documents are highly informative and easily navigable. Other times they serve no useful purpose and take longer to download than would a simple document with the same information content. Use the features of advanced Web documents judiciously in your own pages.

We begin with the simplest advanced feature for use in Web documents, namely *tables*. Tables can be used not only for data that are tabular in nature, but also to format text and graphics in a way not possible otherwise. An example would be to present a page in multiple columns, as found in a newspaper or magazine format. A different type of advanced feature is a *clickable map*, which acts as a visual navigation aid. A more advanced and newer feature for page formatting is *frames*. Frames divide the Web browser window into arbitrary, separately addressable subwindows (a frame set), and a different URL is used to fill each frame.

Maintaining Web documents is an important consideration. Server-side includes provide a way to include the same volatile (that is, fast-changing) information on a number of Web pages. Finally, not all the information you may wish to provide can be handled by a Web browser, in which case a helper or plug-in application is required. A helper application is called from the Web browser but executes as a separate application in a separate window. A plug-in application executes within the browser window.

10.1 Tables

If you are presenting numeric data or information that, in printed form, would best be presented in a table, then it is also best presented in a Web page as a table. Tables can also be used to address shortcomings in HTML for controlling the location of text on a page. Having text in multiple columns is an example.

At the time this is being written, not all Web browsers recognize all the HTML tags and attributes associated with tables, for example the table cell background color or background image. The literal translation of a table by a browser that does not support tables is often unreadable.

Tables are easy to construct, once you understand the following.

- A table consists of a number of rows (horizontal divisions).
- A table consists of a number of columns (vertical divisions).
- A table consists of a number of cells, where each cell is, by default, one vertical and horizontal division.
- By default, cell size scales automatically, based on content.
- A cell can span more than one horizontal or vertical division (or both).
- There are normal (data) cells and cells that contain header information.
- A table optionally can have a border. The border can have a number of specific characteristics.
- The alignment of information in a cell—either text or images—may be explicitly defined. By default, header cells have their information centered, and normal cells have their information left-justified.
- Cell size defaults to just large enough to contain the contents of the cell and is usually acceptable. More control over cell size can be exerted if necessary.

10.1.1 A Simple Example

Here is a simple table that introduces the basic HTML tags used in table construction. This table is shown in Figure 10–1. From this example, you should note

- A table is delimited by the <TABLE> ... </TABLE> HTML tags with an optional BORDER attribute. The width of the border (in pixels) may be specified.
- The HTML tags <CAPTION> ... </CAPTION> define a caption for the table, which appears centered above the table.
- The HTML tags <TR> ... </TR> (table row) define a table row.
- The HTML tags <TD> .. </TD> (table data) define a cell in a row.
- The HTML tags <TH> ... </TH> (table header) define the heading for a column.

```
<TABLE BORDER>
  <CAPTION>A Very Simple Table</CAPTION>
  <TR><TH>Header for Column 1</TH>
      <TH>Header for Column 2</TH>
  </TR>
  <TR><TD>Cell(1,1)</TD><TD>Cell(1,2)</TD></TR>
  <TR><TD>Cell(2,1)</TD><TD>Cell(2,2)</TD></TR>
</TABLE>
```

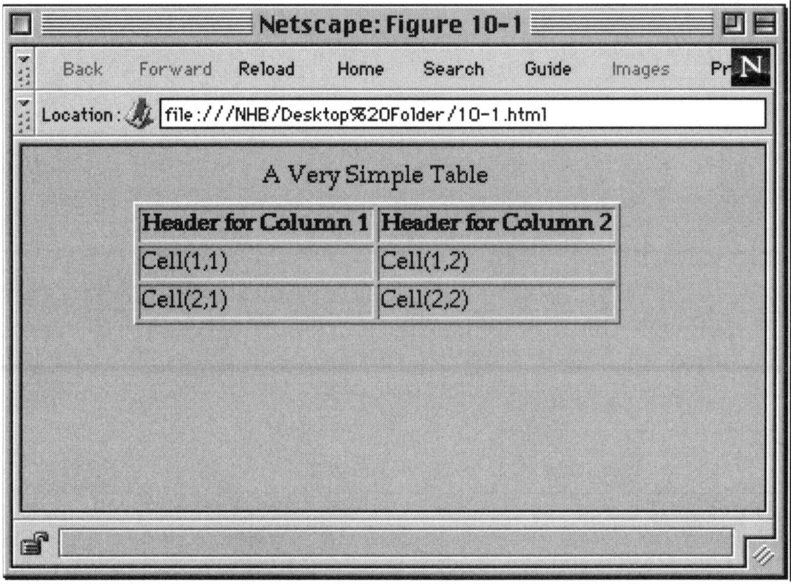

Figure 10-1 Very Simple Table

10.1.2 A More Complex Example

Here is an example of a table where some cells span more than one row and column. The table is shown in Figure 10–2. Here you should notice

- ROWSPAN and COLSPAN are attributes of <TH> or <TD> that cause the cell to cover multiple rows and columns, respectively.
- The trailing </TH> or </TD> is subsumed by a new <TH> or <TD>, respectively, and could be omitted, but good coding practice suggests they be used.

- The ALIGN=LEFT/CENTER/RIGHT attribute of <TH> or <TD> will align text or images in a cell.
- The
 HTML tag is use to force a break in a text line; this, in turn, affects the default size of each cell. The NOWRAP attribute (not shown) can be used with <TD> and <TH> tags to exert some control over the size of cells.

```
<TABLE BORDER>
  <CAPTION>A Table with Cell Spanning</CAPTION>
  <TR><TH ROWSPAN=2><TH COLSPAN=2>Average
      <TH ROWSPAN=2>other<BR>category<TH>Misc
  <TR><TH>height<TH>weight
  <TR><TH ALIGN=LEFT>males<TD>1.9<TD>0.003
  <TR><TH ALIGN=LEFT ROWSPAN=2>females<TD>1.7
      <TD>0.002
</TABLE>
```

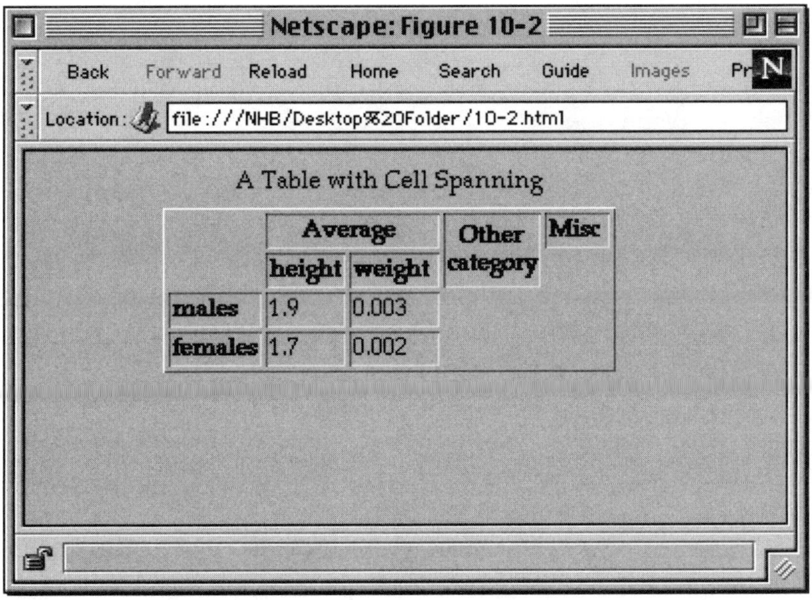

Figure 10-2 Table with Cells That Span Rows and Columns

10.1.3 Further Information

As a rule, browsers are much more finicky when translating the HTML for displaying tables and require much greater attention to correct format. For example, omitting a </TABLE> terminator may cause the browser not to display the table at all. Table 10–1 indicates good sources for a more extensive discussion of tables.

Table 10-1 Sources of Information on HTML Tables

Location	Description
http://webreference.com/html3andns/table.html	The HTML 3.0 specification for tables.
http://www.w3.org/hypertext/WWW/MarkUp/html3/-tables.html	A full description of how to write tables in HTML.
http://www.utirc.utoronto.ca/HTMLdocs/NewHTML/-tables-5.html	Another good source, including a discussion of tables within tables.

Here are some of the additional features that you will find in the above Web pages.

- The CELLPADDING and CELLSPACING attributes can be used with <TH> and <TD> to define the white space around a cell with a border, and the width of the border between cells, respectively.
- The WIDTH attribute can be used with the <TABLE> tag to define the absolute width of tables.
- The <THEAD>, <TBODY>, and <TFOOT> tags can be used to group rows for border rendering, and so forth.
- The COLS = n and ROWS = m attributes of the <TABLE> tag can be used to set the absolute number of columns and rows, respectively, in a table.
- In newer browsers, the BGCOLOR attribute can be used with the <TD> and <TH> tags to set a background color for a particular table cell.

The HTML standard for describing tables is in a state of flux. There are many good working examples found in the tutorials below which introduce the current capabilities. Study them and use them as templates for your own tables. Note that HTML is upwardly compatible. That is, while there may be new features, features used today will continue to function.

Table 10–2 lists some available on-line tutorials for writing HTML tables. A summary of the more common table-based HTML tags and their attributes is given in Appendix B.

Table 10-2 On-line Tutorials for Writing HTML Tables

Location	Description
http://www.newbies-netguide.com/web_pa~1/table2.html	Approximately 20 useful examples of tables.
http://raptor.rit.edu/Nick/tlesson2.htm	A few simple examples, including an orphan cell.
http://www.ozemail.com.au/~dkgsoft/html3/tables.html	Includes nested tables.
http://math-www.uni-paderborn.de/HTML/Dictionaries/-HTML-Dictionary/netscape/tables.html	Another good example of nested tables.
http://home.netscape.com/assist/net_sites/-table_sample.html	A sampler from Netscape Inc.

10.2 Clickable Maps

A clickable map is a visual navigation tool that can be used to great effect. Before you go crazy with clickable maps, however, remember they are based on images that take time to download, and they are of no use to someone who is using a text-only browser. If you want some good examples of what can be achieved with clickable maps, refer to the pointers given in Table 10–3.

Table 10-3 Good Examples of Using Clickable Maps

Location	Description
http://www.caltech.edu/map	Views and directory of the Caltech campus.
http://www.sgi.com/	Silicon Graphics Inc. home page.
http://home.netscape.com/comprod/products/navigator/-version_2.0/frames/eye/index.html	Page on the human eye.
http://www.parc.xerox.com/	Xerox Parc home page.
http://www.duke.edu/~mccann/clickexa.htm *http://www.cris.com/~automata/mapsites.shtml*	Pointers to collections of clickable maps.

Tools for helping you make clickable maps are described in Section 4.7.2. Initially, clickable maps required the server to process the user's clicks (server-side maps), but as maps became more popular, the map definition was included within the HTML file itself and the clicks were interpreted by the user's browser (client-side maps). Client-side maps are now much more common because they have the following advantages.

- They may be used with local files, unlike server-side maps that must use the http protocol.
- There is no need to have a server transaction to resolve a map reference. Clicking on the map can be resolved on the client without reference back to the server, thereby improving performance.
- There is visual feedback. When the user moves the cursor over a region of the map, there is an indication of the URL that they will visit should they click on that region. This does not happen with server-side image maps since that information is on the server only.

Whether you are using a tool or making the clickable map manually, it pays to understand the basic principles. Here is the basic recipe for making a clickable map.

1. Select a GIF image that readers will click on.
2. Define the regions of the image that will map to the various URLs. Regions can be circles, rectangles, and a variety of other polygons. (Using image map software, you will "draw" these regions on the image.)
3. Create the HTML document that will contain the in-line image of the clickable map.
4. Insert the <MAP> tag enclosing the <AREA> tags with coordinate references to URL mapping information in the HTML file. This will be the output of the image map software.
5. Distinguish the in-lined image in the HTML document as a clickable map by having the USEMAP attribute point to the named <MAP>.
6. Create the HTML documents defined in the image map if they do not already exist. That is, make sure there are Web pages to go to when clicking on different parts of the map.
7. Check each link in the map to make sure they work as expected.

Figure 10–3 is an example using a map of the United States; when you click on various regions, you get a list of job vacancies in that region. The job vacancy information is actually solicited through a Web form, and we will see how to do that in the next chapter. For now, worry about how to display information when a region of the map is selected.

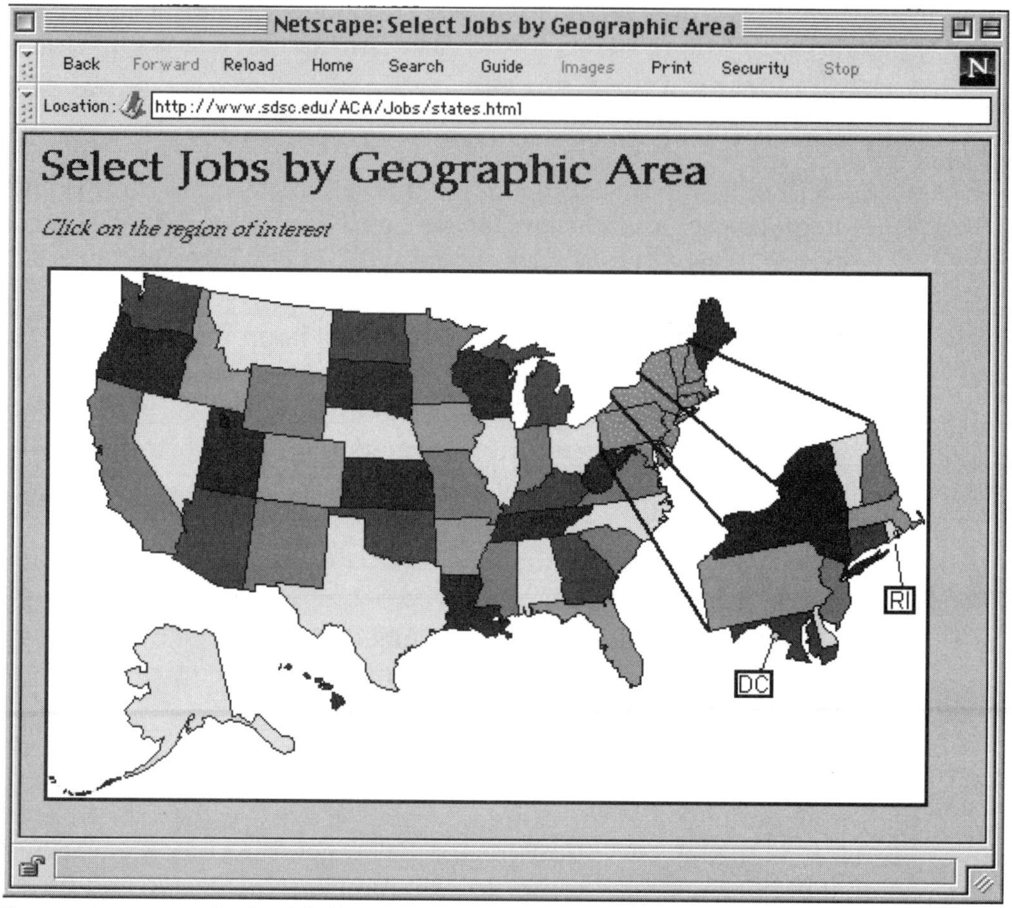

Figure 10-3 Example of a Clickable Map

1. The GIF file shown in Figure 10–3 can be found at

   http://www.sdsc.edu/Xtal/images/states.gif

2. Use ImageMapper (Section 4.7.2) to divide the map into three rectangles for west, central, and east (Figure 10–4) and generate the map. ImageMapper will generate both server-side and client-side maps. For this we generated the client-side map. The following client-side HTML is produced.

```
<MAP NAME="theMap">
    <AREA SHAPE="rect" COORDS="0, 0, 120, 300"
          HREF="pacific.html">
    <AREA SHAPE="rect" COORDS="120, 0, 275, 300"
          HREF="central.html">
    <AREA SHAPE="rect" COORDS="275, 0, 500, 300"
          HREF="east.html">
</MAP>

...

<IMG SRC="image_map.gif" WIDTH=301 HEIGHT=476
    USEMAP="#theMap" BORDER="2" ALT="ImageMap -
    turn on images!!!">
...
```

3. Either copy the MAP and IMG HTML source into your Web document or insert the rest of your HTML source into the file generated by ImageMapper to produce the final document.
4. Create the files pacific.html, central.html, and east.html, which get served when the reader clicks on the appropriate region of the map.
5. Test to see whether all this works!

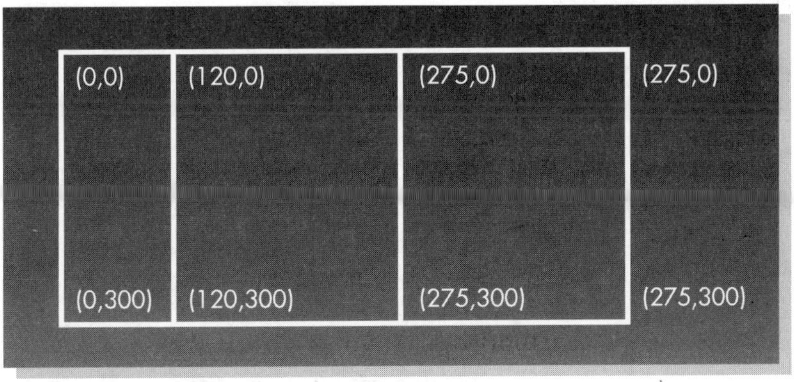

Figure 10-4 Coordinates for a Clickable Map

```
<HTML>
<HEAD>
<TITLE>Select Jobs by Geographic Area</TITLE>

<MAP NAME="theMap">
    <AREA SHAPE="rect" COORDS="0, 0, 120, 300"
          HREF="pacific.html">
    <AREA SHAPE="rect" COORDS="120, 0, 275, 300
          HREF="central.html">
    <AREA SHAPE="rect" COORDS="275, 0, 500, 300"
          HREF="east.html">
</MAP>
</HEAD>

<BODY>
<P ALIGN=center>
<H1>Select Jobs by Geographic Area</H1>
<I>Click on the region of interest</I>

<P ALIGN=center>
<IMG SRC="image_map.gif" WIDTH=301 HEIGHT=476
    USEMAP="#theMap" BORDER="2" ALT="ImageMap -
    turn on images!!!">
</BODY>
</HTML>
```

10.2.1 Further Information

If you are concerned that a significant percentage of your target audience is using browsers that do not support client-side image maps, you may want to provide your image maps as both client- and server-side maps. Older browsers will ignore the tags that support client-side maps, while newer browsers will ignore those that specify a server-side map.

Additional information on setting up server-side image maps can be found at the locations given in Table 10–4. There are two standard formats for server-side maps—those originated by NCSA and CERN Web servers. Table 10–5 has pointers to further information on client-side clickable maps.

Table 10-4 Tutorials on Server-Side Clickable Maps

Location	Description
http://hoohoo.ncsa.uiuc.edu/docs/tutorials/-imagemapping.html	Tutorial for NCSA's httpd server.
http://www.w3.org/pub/WWW/Daemon/User/CGI/-HTImageDoc.html	Tutorial for the CERN server.

Table 10-5 Tutorials on Client-Side Clickable Maps

Location	Description
http://www.iwaynet.net/~rtyler/htmltutorial/-imagemaps.html	A concise introduction on which the material given in this book is based.
http://www.dallas.net/~jwill/html/appenda.html	A more detailed description, including itself as a good example.
http://www.hway.net/ihip/cside.html	Another concise description, including pointers to what browsers support client-side clickable maps.
http://www.yahoo.com/Computers_and_Internet/Internet/-World_Wide_Web/Imagemaps/	Links to tutorials and software at Yahoo!.

10.3 Frames

Defining a frame set in an HTML document divides the browser window into two or more independently accessible regions of arbitrary layout. Each region is referred to as a frame and is filled by a separate Web page. Hyperlinks in framed documents can then not only update and control the contents of their own frames, but also the contents of other frames and windows as well. This capability adds a new dimension to hypertext browsing, since there can be a number of interoperable Web pages in the same browser window.

For example, a table of contents can be displayed in one frame while a specific section of the document is displayed in another frame. Selecting a section from the table of contents will update the frame containing the document section to display the new section. Alternatively, a database query of some kind could be present in one frame and the results of that query present in another frame, since it is often useful to see the query and the result at the same time.

At the time of writing, frames are a part of the emerging HTML 4.0 standard, having been introduced by Netscape Communications Inc. and supported by Netscape's browsers. So compelling is this development, and so large is Netscape's share of the browser market, that few people care that it has not been part of the standard, and HTML authors are using frames enthusiastically.

Possible disadvantages of frames are

1. the inability to print a browser window, but only the contents of the active frame, that is, the frame that has the input focus based on a mouse click;
2. the failure of text-based Web browsers to recognize frames; and
3. the inability to immediately determine the URL of the frame alone.

10.3.1 Layout and Content Documents

Frames introduce the concept of *layout documents* and *content documents*. A layout document, as the name suggests, defines the layout of the frames (the frame set) and the initial content document of each frame. The content document is the kind of HTML document we have been considering thus far. A layout document includes an explicit or implicit reference to a content document for each of its frames. Browsers that do not support frames will not recognize layout documents, and if read will, by default, present a blank screen (however, see the use of the <NOFRAME> ... </NOFRAME> tags in Section 10.3.2), whereas content documents will appear as they always have.

Here is a very simple layout document with the result shown in Figure 10–5. Note:

- There is no text displayed in the layout document, but rather hyperlinks to two content files (fig1.htm and part2.htm).
- The content files are displayed in two columns and each has a name reference ("left" and "right" in this example). The names become important when we wish to create interrelationships between frames, for example, clicking on a link in one frame to update the other frame.
- The frames are introduced with the <FRAMESET> ... </FRAMESET> tags, which replace the HTML <BODY> ... </BODY> tags of content documents.

▼ The COLS=*,* attribute of the <FRAMESET> tag will be explained subsequently.

```
<HTML>
<HEAD>
<TITLE>A very Simple Layout Document</TITLE>
</HEAD>
<FRAMESET COLS=*,*>
    <FRAME SRC=fig1.htm   NAME=left>
    <FRAME SRC=part2.htm  NAME=right>
</FRAMESET>
</HTML>
```

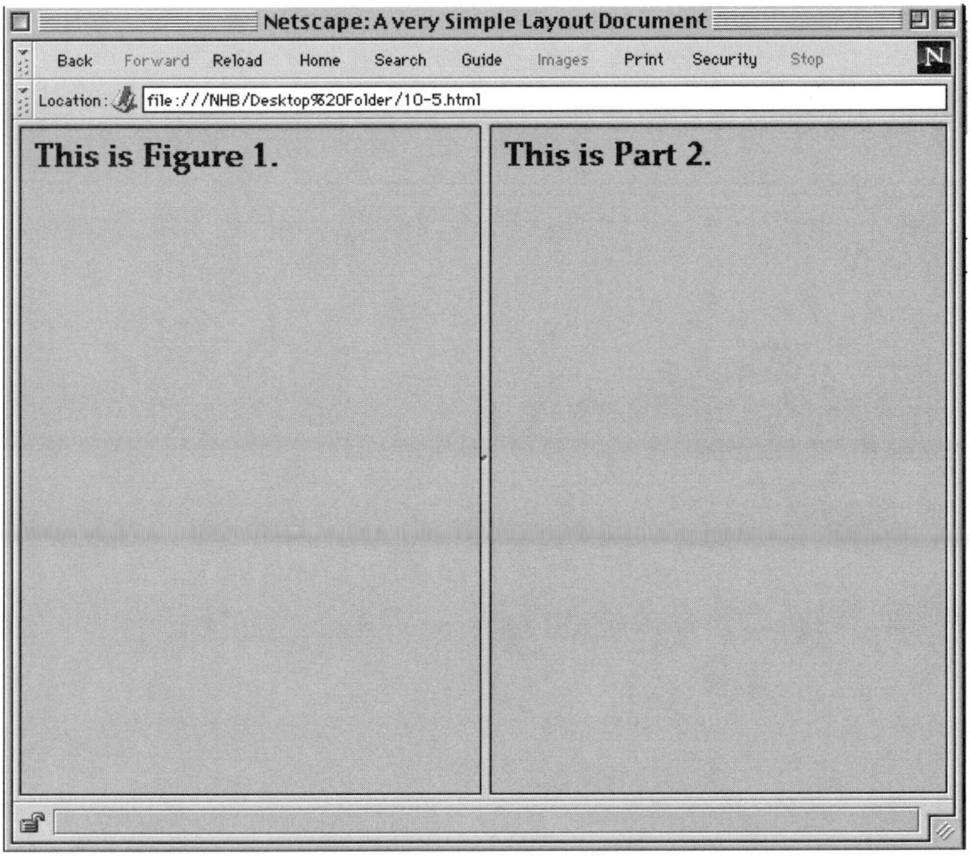

Figure 10-5 Simple Frame Environment

It is possible to nest frames either directly or indirectly. Here is an example of direct nesting with the result in Figure 10–6.

```
<HTML>
<HEAD>
<TITLE>An Example of Direct Nesting</TITLE>
</HEAD>
<FRAMESET COLS=*,*>
    <FRAME SRC=fig1.htm   NAME=left>
    <FRAMESET ROWS=*,*>
          <FRAME SRC=part2.htm  NAME=right_top>
          <FRAME SRC=part3.htm  NAME=right_bottom>
          </FRAMESET>
</FRAMESET>
</HTML>
```

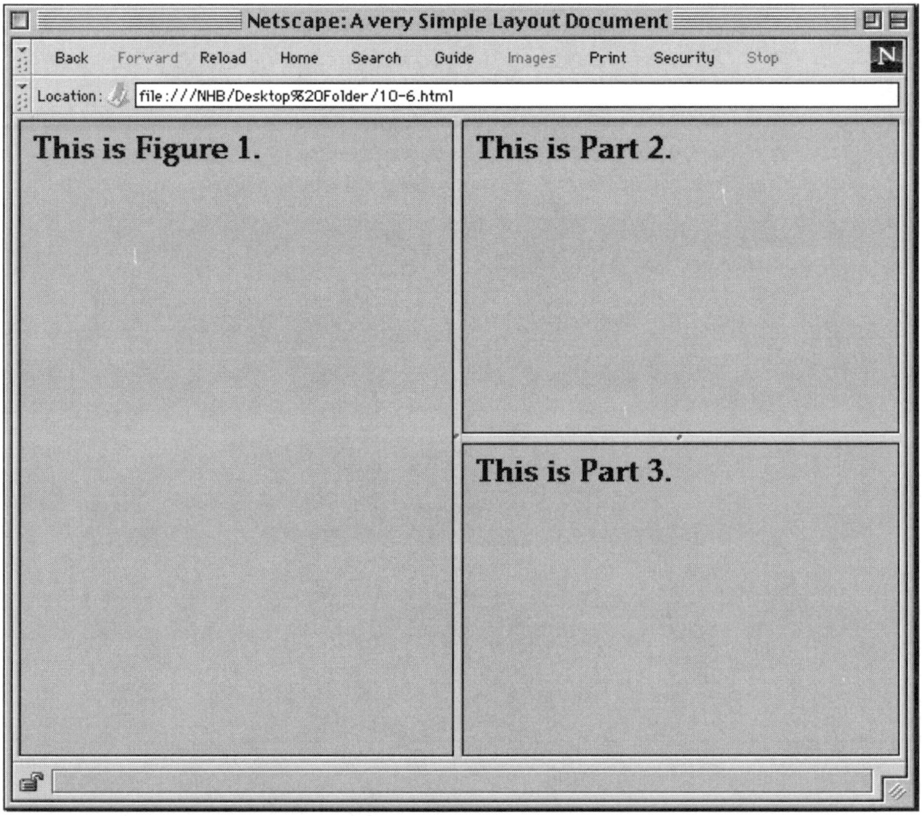

Figure 10-6 Direct-Nested Frames

A possible disadvantage of this approach is that since the addressing is done at the frame level, you loose the ability to jointly address both the frames in the right column. For example, by clicking on an item in the left-hand frame, you may wish to update both right-hand frames. Indirect addressing solves this problem by making the SRC of a frame actually a layout rather than a content file.

```
<HTML>
<HEAD>
<TITLE>An Example of Indirect Nesting</TITLE>
</HEAD>
<FRAMESET COLS=*,*>
    <FRAME SRC=fig1.htm   NAME=left>
          <FRAMESET ROWS=*,*>
          <FRAME SRC=part2-3.htm  NAME=right>
          </FRAMESET>
</FRAMESET>
</HTML>
```

And the file part2-3.htm looks like

```
<HTML>
<HEAD>
<TITLE>A Layout as Part of Indirect Nesting</TITLE>
</HEAD>
    <FRAMESET ROWS=*,*>
    <FRAME SRC=part2.htm NAME=right_top>
    <FRAME src=part3.htm NAME=right_bottom>
    </FRAMESET>
</HTML>
```

10.3.2 Frame Size and Location

A question you should be asking yourself at this point is, how do I control the size and characteristics of a frame? To answer this question you need to understand the COLS and ROWS attributes of the <FRAMESET> ... </FRAMESET> tags. In our examples so far we have used:

```
<FRAMESET COLS = *,*> and <FRAMESET ROWS = *,*>
```

The "*,*" value autosizes the frames in a useful way. The window will be divided equally into two frames (Figure 10–3) with identical size and characteristics. If we use "COLS= *,*" it will be two equal columns and if we use "ROWS = *,*" it will be two equal rows. In Figure 10–4, we nested the frames so that the right-hand column was, by default, further subdivided into two frames of equal size.

To specify the dimensions of each frame, you can give them in pixels (absolute measure) or percentages (relative measure). Whether you use percentages or pixels (or both) depends on what you wish to take place when the reader resizes the Web browser window. Percentages are useful when you wish to expand or contract frames equally relative to each other; pixels are useful if you want a frame to remain a fixed width (or height). An absolute or relative value is given as "horizontal, vertical." Consider an example with this frame layout that produces the Web page shown in Figure 10–7:

```
<HTML>
<HEAD>
<TITLE>A Common and Useful Type of Frame Layout</TITLE>
</HEAD>
<FRAMESET ROWS="70,*">
   <FRAME SRC="./header.htm"  MARGINHEIGHT=0
       MARGINWIDTH=0 NAME="header" SCROLLING="no"
       NORESIZE>
   <FRAMESET COLS="373,*">
       <FRAME SRC="./image.htm"  MARGINHEIGHT=0
           MARGINWIDTH=0 NAME="image" SCROLLING="no"
           NORESIZE>
      <FRAME SRC="./info.htm"  NAME="information">
   </FRAMESET>
</FRAMESET>

<NOFRAME>
This page requires a frames capable browser.
</NOFRAME>
</HTML>
```

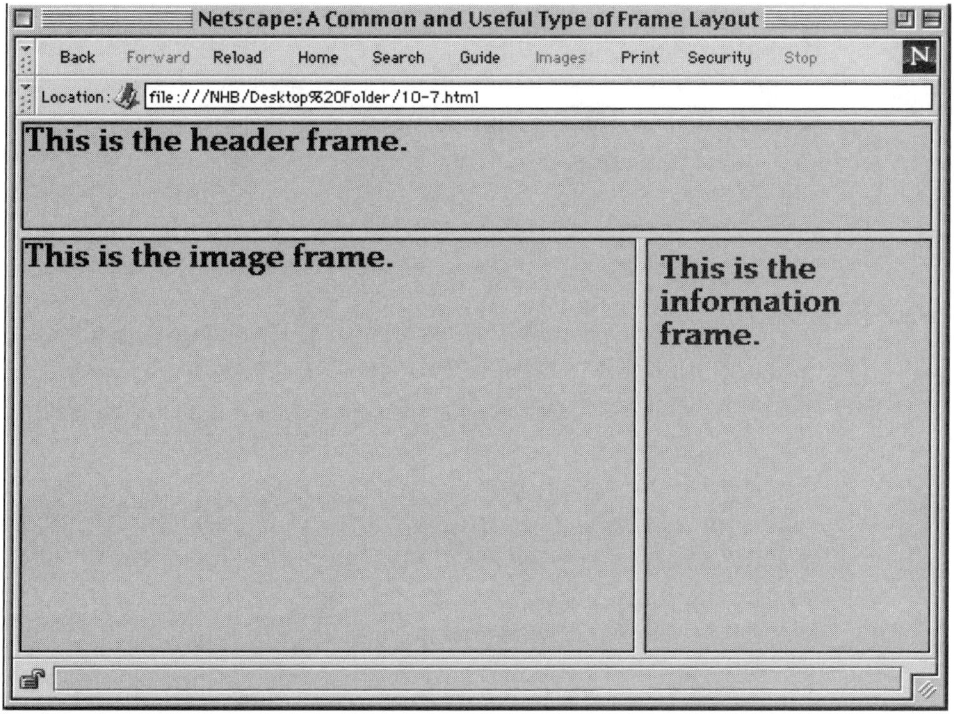

Figure 10-7 Frame Sizing

Note the following:

- The window is divided into two rows, with the second row divided into two columns (defined by the FRAMESET nesting).
- At the top we have a header frame, which is the width of the browser window and is 70 pixels long (ROWS=70,*). There is no margin reserved around this frame (defined by the MARGINHEIGHT and MARGINWIDTH attributes of the <FRAME> tag). The frame will not have scroll bars (SCROLLING="no") and cannot be resized (NORESIZE). If the window is resized below 70 pixels in height, the contents will simply be truncated and a scroll bar will not appear. This is an ideal frame environment for a banner (header message) that is not going to change, regardless of the contents of the other frames.

- Under this header frame are two columns for the image frame and the information frame. The image frame is fixed at a width of 373 pixels (COLS="373,*"), whereas the information frame will take up the remains of the browser window width.
- Pixel and percentages could be mixed (not shown here), for example, COLS="373,*,40%" would create three columns where the first is 373 pixels wide, the last is 40 percent of the overall window width and the middle column takes up the remainder (if there is any). The question then arises as to what happens when 373 pixels is greater than 60 percent of the window width. The answer is, try it and find out; a good habit to adopt for all Web pages prior to making them available on the Internet.
- The <NOFRAME> ... </NOFRAME> tags delimit what will happen if a Web browser that does not support frames is used to display the HTML, assuming it can at least recognize the <NOFRAME> ... </NOFRAME> tags. In the example above, a simple message is displayed to tell the user they need a frames capable browser to view the page.

10.3.3 Frame Relationships

Let us go back to our original two-frame Web page and explore the interrelationships that you can create between frames. In Figure 10–5, imagine having a table of contents in the left frame and an article selected in the right frame. When we select an article from the table of contents, how does the browser know to update only the right frame and display the article?

Without frames, clicking on a hyperlink in, for example, a table of contents, will refresh the whole Web browser window with the new URL. Now we are faced with updating only part of the browser window defined by the NAME attribute of the <FRAME> tag. To address this, name requires an extension to the HTML hyperlink syntax—the concept of a hyperlink "target."

```
<A HREF=documentURL TARGET=targetname>Hyperlink Text</A>
```

In our example, updating the "right" frame would require a hyperlink that explicitly targets that named frame. This is an example of an explicit target:

```
<A HREF="./part2.htm" TARGET=right>Radiation
Carcinogenesis</A>
```

It is also possible to use implicit (predefined) frame names having a specific relationship to the frame containing the hyperlink. Here are some examples of implicit frame names, which begin with a leading underscore (_).

- _self—Directs the browser to update the frame in which the link is located. This is the default target if no target is specified.
- _parent—Directs the browser to update the parent frame if the frame containing the hyperlink is a child frame, otherwise has the same effect as _self. Parent and child are defined by the nesting relationship between frames.
- _top—Directs the browser to update the entire window, regardless of the current frame layout.
- _blank—Creates a completely new browser window.

The last predefined frame is noteworthy, since it does not reference a frame in the existing window, but creates a new browser window and displays the contents of the hyperlink. This example displays the contents of part2.htm in a new browser window:

```
<HTML>
<HEAD>
<TITLE>An Example of Generating a New Window</TITLE>
</HEAD>
<A HREF = "./part2.htm" TARGET = _blank>part 2 </A>
</HTML>
```

Opening new browsers in this way should be used judiciously. It is not always obvious to the user that this has happened, since browser windows may lay one on top of the other, and each new browser window expends a significant amount of client resources, notably memory.

10.3.4 Further Information

The best way to learn how frames are used is to view the source of the layout files and their associated content files for examples that use frames well. Some good examples can be found in Table 10–6. If you need further information on using frames, some good sources are given in Table 10–7.

Table 10-6 Examples Using HTML Frames

Location	Description
http://home.netscape.com/comprod/products/navigator/-version_2.0/frames/eye/index.html	A tutorial on vision.
http://www.spunwebs.com/sites2c/fotoalbum.html	The Ava Gardner Photograph Collection.
http://www.netscape.com/comprod/products/navigator/-version_2.0/frames/frame_users.html	A large list of sites that use frames supplied by Netscape Inc.

Table 10-7 On-line Tutorials for HTML Frames

Location	Description
http://home1.gte.net/gerow/frames/	A crash course in frames.
http://www.spunwebs.com/sites2c/frmtutor.html	A step-by-step introduction.
http://www.hotwired.com/webmonkey/html/96/31/-index4a.html	Basic and advanced frames techniques.

10.4 Server-Side Includes

Simply stated, the main use of server-side includes is any situation where you have the same information that you wish displayed on multiple Web pages. Server-side includes are particularly useful when that same information is going to change frequently. Thus, server-side includes save you the labor of editing each page to make the same changes. You keep that information in a separate file, make the change to that one file, and have the multiple pages include (read) that file when they are served by the Web server. (If you are familiar with the use of #include statements in one or more programming languages, the idea is the same.) An example of where you might use a server-side include was given in Section 9.5.3 where we defined a menu bar as a navigation tool. By keeping the menu bar in a separate file we can update it, adding or deleting options, and immediately see those change on all the Web pages that include the menu bar.

There are negative aspects to using server-side includes, notably, performance and security. Performance is an issue since you are not just sending some HTML to a client but building that HTML on the fly, or as we shall see, actually executing commands on the server. Security is an issue since the client has access to these server commands.

While the principle is the same, invoking server-side includes differs from one Web server to another. The description given here is for Social Engineering's Quid Pro Quo Web server. You need to understand the syntax of this command since most HTML editors are currently incapable of adding it for you.

10.4.1 The Include Command

We begin our discussion by examining how to include a file. Quid Pro Quo 2.0 installs with server-side includes enabled and configured such that files with the ".shtml" extension are parsed for server-side include commands.

Therefore, to begin experimenting with server-side includes, you simply create the HTML file with the proper commands. For starters, the <!--#INCLUDE ...> tag introduces the HTML syntax to invoke a server-side include (hence the name). Attributes may be FILE (as shown in the following example), which includes a file specification relative to the original document, or VIRTUAL, which specifies a file relative to the document root.

```
<HTML>
<HEAD>
<TITLE>An example of a Server Side Include</TITLE>
</HEAD>
<BODY>
<!-- Include a menu bar -->
<!--#INCLUDE FILE="./includes/menubar.shtml" -->
</BODY>
</HTML>
```

An important point to note is what happens when you "view source" for a Web page that uses a server-side include. What you see is the page *after* the include. There is no indication that the contents came from a separate file that was included with a server-side include.

To *disable* server-side includes, choose the Control: Server Settings… menu option, and click on the Suffic Mappings icon. For the .shtml mapping, change the Action to "Text" instead of "SSI." Conversely, you could also create other suffix mappings, such as .shtm, that tell Quid Pro Quo to invoke server-side includes.

10.4.2 Other Server-Side Includes

Notice that we said earlier that the "main use" of server-side includes is for including the same information on multiple Web pages. There are other uses; the <!--#INCLUDE …> HTML tag is only one of a number of commands that can be used to invoke server-side actions—and other SSI commands. All involve the server performing some action and including the results of that action in the Web page sent to the client.

Table 10–8 has the complete list of commands for the Quid Pro Quo server. The list will vary slightly from Web server to Web server. What follows are examples of how you might use each of these server-side commands.

Table 10-8 Server-Side Commands for the Quid Pro Quo Web Server

Command	Description
CONFIG	Describe how to format the output of other SSI commands.
ECHO	Insert the value of one or more variables.
FLASTMOD	Insert the date of the last modification to the file.
FSIZE	Insert the size of the file.
INCLUDE	Insert the text of a document.
EXEC	Insert the output of a CGI script.
SHOW, HIDE	You can use these commands to dynamically change the text of an HTML page based on the user's browser type, the date and time, or a random number.

In our first example, the modification date of the file is determined from the file header itself. You do not have to be bothered with remembering to change this date each time you modify an HTML document. Including the date of modification is a powerful way of informing the reader of how current, or alternatively how seminal, the information on the Web page is. The LAST_MODIFIED variable is just one of several variables that can be used with the ECHO command. Table 10–9 lists all the variables that can be used with the ECHO command. ECHO and its associated variables are supported by most Web servers.

```
<HTML>
<HEAD>
<TITLE>An example of a Server Side Include</TITLE>
</HEAD>
<BODY>
...
<!-- Include the local time -->
<I>Last Modified by Phil Bourne on
<!--#ECHO VAR="LAST_MODIFIED"--></I>
</BODY>
</HTML>
```

Table 10-9 Variables Associated with the ECHO Command

Variable	Description
SERVER_SOFTWARE	Always "Quid Pro Quo."
SERVER_NAME	Domain name of the server.
SERVER_PROTOCOL	Always "HTTP/1.0."
SERVER_PORT	The TCP port used by the server. Usually 80.
REQUEST_METHOD	The HTTP command used to download the file.
REMOTE_HOST	The domain name of the client, or if none, the IP address.
REMOTE_ADDR	The IP address of the client.
AUTH_TYPE	The security type used to access the current realm.
REMOTE_USER	The user's name if the user's browser preferences are configured with one, otherwise blank.
CONTENT_LENGTH	Length of the data that the user is posting. Usually blank.
DOCUMENT_NAME	The current filename.
DOCUMENT_URI	The virtual path to the file.
DATE_LOCAL	The current date and time in the local time zone.
DATE_GMT	Current Greenwich Mean Time.
LAST_MODIFIED	The date the current file was last modified.
PAGE_COUNT	The number of hits that the current page has received.
TOTAL_HITS	The total number of hits served by Quid Pro Quo.
REFERRER	The URL of the page that referred the user to this page. May be blank.

The next example causes a specific CGI script to execute on the server. Quid Pro Quo's server-side includes allow you to include the output of any CGI in your web page. You can even include the output of multiple CGIs in the same page, or call the same CGI more than once with different parameters. (However, unlike some UNIX Web servers, you can not execute arbitrary programs on the server with server-side includes in Quid Pro Quo.)

```
<HTML>
<HEAD>
<TITLE>An example of a Server Side Include</TITLE>
</HEAD>
<BODY>
...
<!-- Use of EXEC to return the results of a CGI script
     that returns a random URL. The $ indicates a file
     argument to the script. -->
<A HREF="<!--#exec virtual="/cgi-
   bin/randomurl.acgi$/cgi.rurl"-->">
This is a link created by a direct call to the URL
   Randomizer CGI.</A>
</BODY>
</HTML>
```

When invoking a CGI script in Quid Pro Quo, the results of that invocation are returned, and, as we shall see in Chapter 11, this is usually in the form of HTML that gets displayed by the Web browser.

10.4.3 Further Information

Table 10–10 has pointers to on-line tutorials for learning about server-side includes.

Table 10-10 On-line Tutorials for Using Server-Side Includes (SSIs)

Location	Description
http://www.internetter.com/ssi/index.shtml	Tutorial for SSIs that work with most servers.
http://www.carleton.ca/~dmcfet/html/ssi.html	Basics of server-side includes, applicable to most Web servers.
http://zippy.sonoma.edu/~kendrick/nbs/unix/www/ssi/	General SSI information (with source code specific to UNIX machines).

10.5 "Active" Pages and HTML Extensions

While server-side includes (SSIs) provide the ability to insert dynamic information such as date and time stamps or repetitive information such as menu options on your Web pages, they have a limited vocabulary of half a dozen commands and about 20 variables. Furthermore, while most SSI commands are supported by most server software, some commands and variables are server dependent. If you write pages that depend heavily on SSIs and then upgrade your server application to a different program, you may have a difficult time translating or removing invalid SSI commands throughout your site.

If you like the idea of dynamic "active" pages but don't think that SSIs have enough power to support your needs, you might want to consider some of the various Web server plug-ins that support even more commands within your HTML files. These plug-ins extend the power of your server by preprocessing files that have the new variables and sending the user a dynamically created HTML file. Table 10–11 lists some of these active page server plug-ins.

Table 10-11 Active Page Tools

Location	Description
http://www.digitalcomet.com/cometpage/products/-cometsite/	CometSite commercial software from Digital Comet adds 75 different commands to HTML pages.
http://www.maxum.com/NetCloak/	NetCloak commercial software from Maxum Development adds 30 new commands.
http://www.ice.com/htpl.htpl	HTPL (HTML Preprocessing Language) freeware from Tim Endres and ICE Engineering.
http://www.morphtech.com/	DynaMorph commercial software from MorphTech.
http://www.spiderlink.it/OpenWorld/	OpenWorld freeware from Marco Bambini.

As an example of these plug-ins, Dave installed OpenWorld with his Quid Pro Quo server. This was chosen mainly because it was one of two freeware options. OpenWorld offers a set of about 60 server parameters and several new tags that you can include in your HTML files. (HTPL is a more complex line-oriented language with if-then conditions and other programming language constructs to customize the HTML the client sees.)

Installing OpenWorld was straightforward after downloading and unstuffing the .hqx archive.

- Quit your server application.
- Copy the OpenWorld plug-in file into the server folder's "Plug-ins" folder.
- Restart the server.

Once installed, the server will filter all files with the .ow extension through the OpenWorld plug-in. Figure 10–8 shows the beginning of an example OpenWorld page. You can also tell your server to filter all .html files through OpenWorld by changing the server settings for the .html extension. In Quid Pro Quo, choose Server Settings... from the Control menu and select the Suffix Mappings option. Edit the .html (and .htm) lines to be processed by OpenWorld.

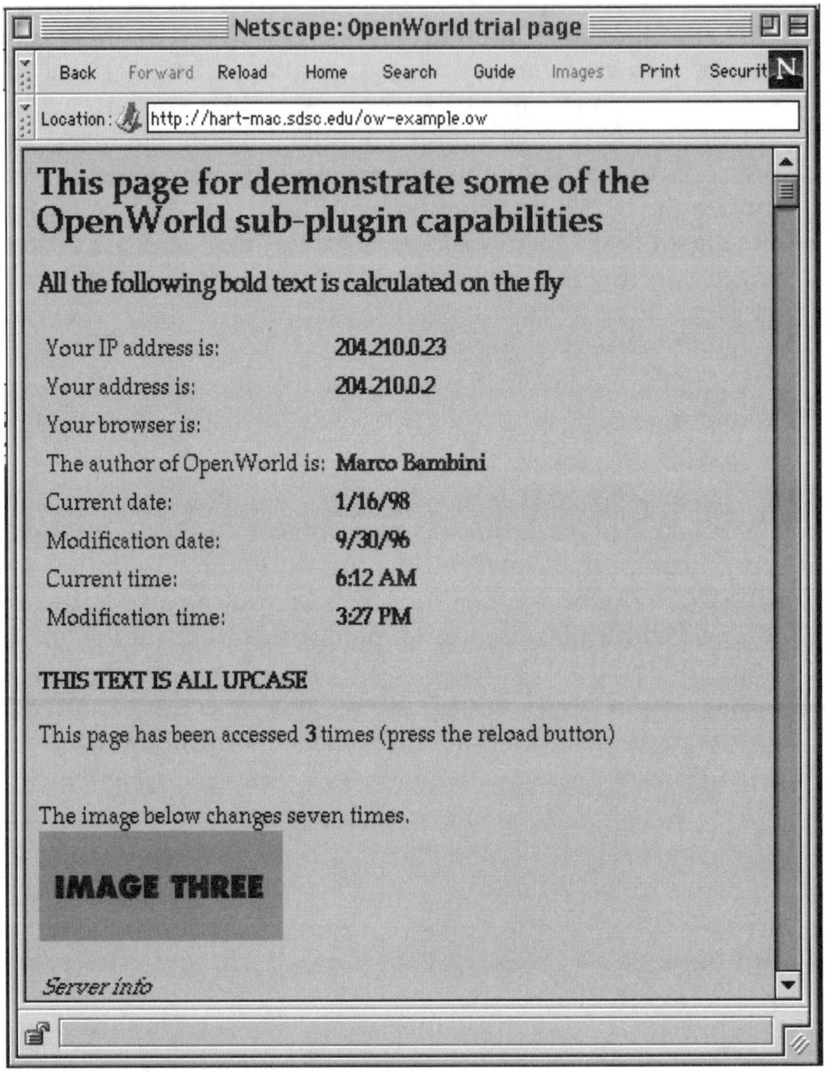

Figure 10-8 OpenWorld Server Preprocessor Output

▼▼▼

At this point you should be able to provide a comprehensive and useful set of Web pages that can be browsed. We can now move on to the next step beyond the browsing of information, which is to allow the user to interact with your Web server. In the next chapter we explore how the client user can solicit specific responses from your server by way of a Web form.

• CHAPTER • 11

Forms (Web Input Processing)

Ingredients

- A Web form through which the user can provide input
- The Common Gateway Interface (CGI) for processing that input on the server
- Returning output to the user

Many people are satisfied after the main course and rarely eat desserts. For others, no meal is complete without a dessert. Here we learn how to make your basic dessert.

11.1 Interactive Web Pages

Thus far, our discussion of serving information via the Web has been "passive"—simple requests for information that the client user reads and subsequently navigates by way of a hypertext link to more information on the same or other servers. There is another very powerful aspect of Web technology that you will likely need to support—input from the client and an appropriate response to that input by the server. We like to think that, from a user's perspective, this makes your information server an "active" as opposed to "passive" provider of information.

On an active server, the same information is not necessarily served to everyone. What gets served is in response to input from the user. For example, you may use the server to collect information from Web users and see a simple customized acknowledgment based on their input. Alternatively, the Web user could provide input to a program that gets executed on the server and the results of that program would be returned to the Web client browser for display. Finally, the user might upload information to the server and see that information immediately made available to a worldwide audience. These are some examples of the role of an active server that we will show you in this chapter. There are many other ways in which an active server could be used, but the principles are the same.

The support of input processing, that is, an active server, can be thought of as a four-step process.

1. Provide a Web page that collects user input—a Web form.
2. Pass that input through a *Common Gateway Interface* (CGI) for processing.
3. Process the input with a program (called a *CGI program* or *CGI script*) that produces some form of output.
4. Return the results to the user as HTML, graphics, or plain text, that can be displayed by the client browser.

11.1.1 Overcoming Stateless Interaction

One final consideration that arises when creating Web forms and processing input is the notion of "state." Under normal circumstances, a Web server receives a request from clients and processes those requests by returning streams of HTML to the client browsers. The server does not "remember" which client requested which piece of information. When a client makes a second request, the server does not recognize that client as one that made a previous request. This is what we mean when we say the Web is "stateless." This works fine for requesting most Web pages where the client simply displays the served information.

On the other hand, consider the implications of this stateless behavior when, for example, you are querying a database through a Web server. You pass the query to the server and results are returned. No problem here, but what if you wish to use those results in a subsequent query? With stateless interactions, all the needed information must be passed *back* to the server for the second query, since the server retains no results from the first query. This is inefficient in terms of the network bandwidth required, the load on the server, and the management of the information sent back and forth with each incremental request.

It is more desirable to have the server store the results of the query and pass to the client only the subset of information needed to decide whether a second query is needed. If needed, the subsequent query would ideally be performed on the data already stored on the server. So how do you associate a set of query results with a particular client for subsequent access?

There are various tricks for making this association. All use the same basic idea—provide each client with a unique identifier so that it may be identified repeatedly by the server. On the first query, the results are stored on the server with a certain identifier. That identifier is then passed back to the client. A subsequent query passes back both the new query information and the identifier so the server can recognize and use the correct information already on the server.

There is a security issue here, however. There is little to stop another client from gaining access to this information on the server if that client acquires the token. Nevertheless, this method works well if the security of the information being sent to the server is not a major concern.

Meanwhile, let's start with the basic idea of a client identifier. A good example (Table 11–1) has been developed by Rob Hooft and Michael Scharf from the European Molecular Biology Laboratory (EMBL).

Table 11-1 Example of Overcoming Stateless Web Interaction

Location	Description
http://biotech.embl-heidelberg.de:8400/	Original site.
http://biotech.embl-ebi.ac.uk:8400/	U.K. mirror.
http://biotech.pdb.bnl.gov:8400/	U.S. mirror.

They developed this application because the program on the server takes too long to compute to be executed interactively through a Web browser. The basic idea is that you upload your data to the server, have computations performed on those data and view the results later. An alternative, not implemented, would be to have the server e-mail you the results—a better option when security is an issue. Here are the basic steps, from the user's perspective, which you can adopt in developing similar applications.

1a. Download the designated Perl program from the server using the "Save As..." feature of your client browser.

Execute the program on your client, providing the name of a file containing the data that will be uploaded to the server for processing. This represents a security risk and you should carefully examine this program before executing it on your client.

b. Alternately, upload your data file to the server using the capabilities of your Web browser.

2. Processing begins on the server to create a local HTML file. This file contains an identifier (which happens to be derived from the server's process ID that created the file) and which is the key to accessing your results on the server.

3. Later, by accessing the local HTML file with your Web browser, you can follow a link to your output on the server, review the material and, optionally, download the results. The output remains on the server for a designated period of time.

Beyond the client-side security risk mentioned in step 1a (and avoided by step 1b), there are server-side security issues associated with this application. Precautions are taken to allow access to the original input data and the output generated by only the user that submitted it. That is, the person accessing the data must know the identifier and connect from the same Internet host. However, the process is not foolproof. Sensitive data should not be uploaded to a server in this way.

A less elegant version of this procedure would be to upload a file to an ftp location on the server, either via ftp or using a capability supported by some Web browsers. Then, from a Web form downloaded from the server, indicate to a CGI script the name of the file you uploaded. The script would provide you with a reference number that you could later use to locate your output on the Web server.

None of these approaches are as secure (for your server and the client) as using a client-side "cookie," the basics of which are described in Section 11.6.

Now that we've introduced the issues of stateless interaction, this chapter discusses the four steps for supporting an active server. We will give you the basic principles, followed by some examples that you can adapt to your own needs. The sophistication of the interaction between client and server, including how it handles the stateless nature of the Web, depends on step 3—the capabilities of the program processing the input from the Web form. But first, let's start with step 1—the form.

11.2 Forms

If you have ever written code for a graphical user interface, you will appreciate the simplicity of writing a Web form in HTML. You may also appreciate that this same interface will run unchanged on a PC or UNIX computer. While simple to write, the HTML form is limited in what can be represented, in comparison to an interface generated with a graphical user interface language. However, like other features of HTML (for example, tables and frames) the syntax to describe forms is evolving, and better interfaces for passing information to server programs will be produced. As we shall see in Chapter 12, Java and JavaScript provide more detailed, computer-independent graphical user interfaces, but require more programming effort.

Here is your recipe for building a Web form. You may need to know this since, at this time, some free HTML editors do not produce forms. However, most WYSYWIG editors, such as GoLive CyberStudio, and some shareware packages, such as PageSpinner, do support forms.

1. A form is defined using the same basic HTML constructs that we saw in Chapters 9 and 10.
2. A form is delineated by <FORM> ... </FORM> tags and associated attributes.
3. Tags and associated attributes are used within a form to collect input. Each of these input collection types associates the input with a variable name that will be used for processing on the Web server.
4. The contents of a form can be cleared (reset) with a reset button.
5. A form can be submitted to the server for processing from either
   - a submit button
   - a text box
   - a clickable image

We will see examples of all these features. For the impatient, a summary of the syntax for creating a Web form is given in Appendix B.

11.2.1 A Simple Example

Here is a simple form to get us started. This is the form from which Phil solicits comments from readers of the page that was shown in Section 9.5.3.

```
<HTML>
<!-- A simple form to solicit input from "readers" -->
<HEAD>
<TITLE>Reader's Comments Form</TITLE>
</HEAD>
<BODY BACKGROUND="./images/bg.gif">
<CENTER>
<H2>Reader's Comments Form</H2>

<FORM METHOD = POST ACTION="comments.cgi">

<!-- Solicit input in the form of a table -->
<!-- The table provides better control over text box
placement. -->
```

```
<TABLE CELLPADDING = 5>
<TR ALIGN = LEFT VALIGN = TOP>
    <TD><B> Name:</B></TD>

    <!-- Associate input in this field with the vari-
able called "name" -->
    <TD><INPUT NAME = "name"></TD>
</TR>
<TR ALIGN = LEFT VALIGN = TOP>
   <!-- Associate input in this field with a variable
called "email" -->
    <TD><B> E-mail Address:</B></TD>
    <TD><INPUT NAME = "email"></TD>
</TR>
<TR ALIGN = LEFT VALIGN = TOP>
    <TD><B> Phone Number:</B></TD>
    <TD><INPUT NAME = "phone"></TD>
</TR>
<TR ALIGN = LEFT VALIGN = TOP>
    <TD><B> Comments:</B></TD>

    <!-- Associate anything entered in this text box
to a variable called "comments" -->
    <!-- Define a text area of 7 rows and 60 columns
in which to enter comments -->
    <TD><TEXTAREA NAME = "comments" ROWS = 7
          COLS = 60></TEXTAREA></TD>
</TR>
</TABLE>

<!-- Define the buttons to either submit the form for
processing or clear the form -->
<INPUT TYPE="submit" VALUE = "Submit Comments">
<INPUT TYPE="reset" VALUE = "Reset Form">

</CENTER>
</BODY>
</HTML>
```

Figure 11–1 illustrates this page when viewed through a Netscape Web browser.

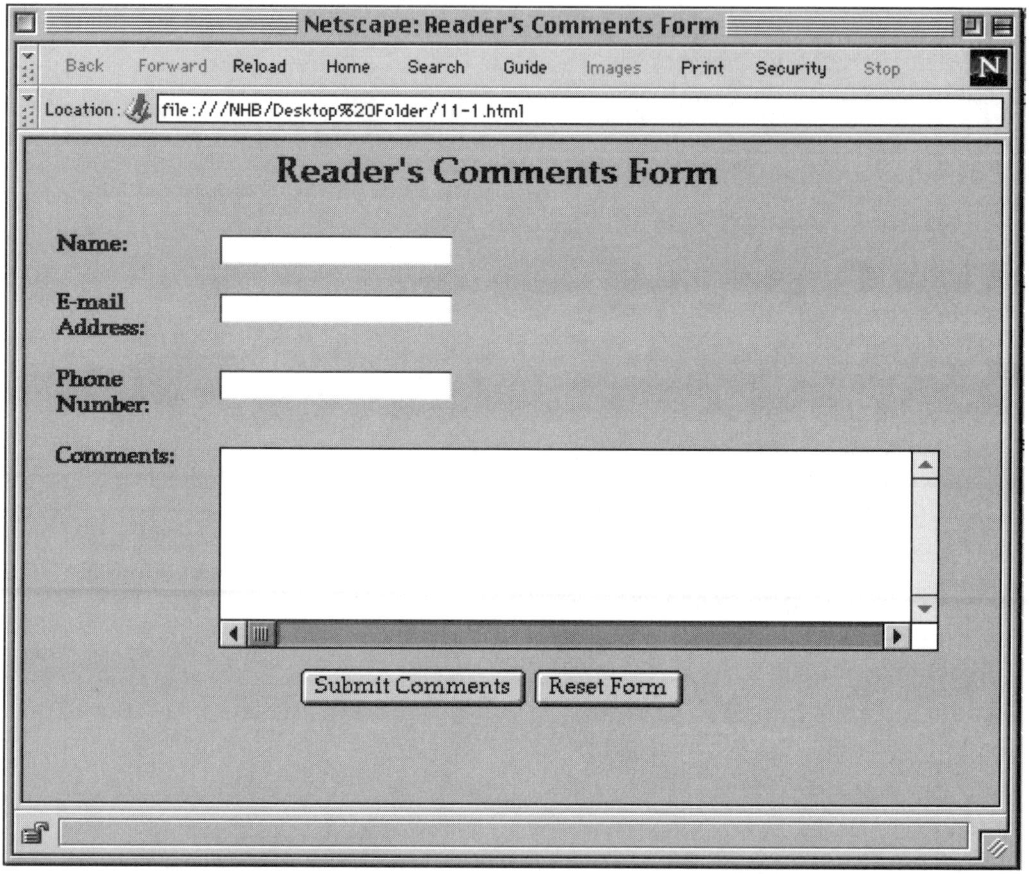

Figure 11-1 Simple Web Form—The Comments Page

To make this example more interesting, we embedded this form in a table to reinforce what we learned about tables in Section 10.1 and to illustrate the use of tables as a formatting feature as well as a data representation feature. The <TD> ... </TD> (table data) tags are used here to define a table cell, not to contain plain text, but to contain a form input fields from which, as we will see below, information will subsequently be passed to a processing program on the server. Embedding the various forms options in a table gives you greater flexibility over the exact placement of forms features. The result is to left-justify and vertically align the names of the forms fields (Name, E-mail Address, Phone Number, Comments) as the first column and the text entry fields as the second column.

11.2.2 The <FORM> Tag

The most crucial question regarding Web forms is, "What happens when I submit the form?" This is where the first unexplained line in our form comes in. We refer to

```
<FORM METHOD=POST ACTION="comments.cgi">
```

There are three components to the <FORM ... > tag:

- <FORM ...> introduces the form and has an associated </FORM> to indicate the end of the form;
- The < ... METHOD=POST ... > attribute defines how the form will be processed by the server; and
- The <... ACTION="comments.cgi"> attribute defines a URL that is a program on the Web server to process the form.

The file extension .cgi is the clue to the role of comments.cgi and stands for common gateway interface (CGI). We will show you how the CGI works and then we will come back to some examples on designing more complicated forms.

11.2.3 Input Collection Types

There are six common input collection types available in an HTML form:

- text box, which allows a single line of text,
- buttons of two types:
  - radio buttons, for selecting only one of a number of options,
  - checkbox buttons, for selecting one or more of a number of options;
- text area, which allows multiline text input;
- pop-up menus from which a single option is selected; and
- scrollable lists, from which one or more options are selected.

The <INPUT> tag is used to define text boxes, radio buttons, and checkboxes for user input. For example,

```
<TD><INPUT NAME = "name"></TD>
...
<TD><INPUT NAME = "email"></TD>
...
<TD><INPUT NAME = "phone"></TD>
```

all define cells in the table through the use of the <TD> ... </TD> (table data) tags. Without the TYPE attribute, the INPUT tag defines a text box with a default size (since no SIZE attribute is specified) of 20 characters. Hence, the table cell is set to a width of 20 characters. If more than 20 characters are entered, the text will scroll from right to left as defined by the text box. The full text string is retained, but only 20 characters are seen on the screen at any one time. Whatever the user types in that text box is associated with a variable name defined by the NAME attribute.

In a similar fashion, but not shown in our example, you can define radio buttons and checkboxes with the INPUT tag. A set of radio buttons lets the user select one of several options, as in the following example.

```
<INPUT TYPE="radio" NAME="radio1" VALUE="A"> Choice A<BR>
<INPUT TYPE="radio" NAME="radio1" VALUE="B"> Choice B<BR>
<INPUT TYPE="radio" NAME="radio1" VALUE="C"> Choice C
```

To allow the user to choose one or more of the available options, you use the CHECKBOX type, as in the following example.

```
<INPUT TYPE="checkbox" NAME="check1" VALUE="A"> Choice A<BR>
<INPUT TYPE="checkbox" NAME="check1" VALUE="B"> Choice B<BR>
<INPUT TYPE="checkbox" NAME="check1" VALUE="C"> Choice C
```

In our example, we also define a TEXTAREA of seven rows, with each row having 60 columns. This is to contain the comments made by the reader. Comments are passed to the server having been associated with the variable name “comments.”

```
<TEXTAREA NAME = "comments" ROWS = 7 COLS = 60></TEXTAREA>
```

The user of the form is not limited to making a comment of seven lines with a maximum of 60 characters per line. The 420 characters are simply the part of an arbitrarily long comment that will be seen on the form at any one time. Vertical and horizontal scroll bars will automatically be added if the user enters text beyond seven lines or 60 characters per line, respectively.

Finally, pop-up menus and selection lists are defined with the <SELECT> ... </SELECT> tag. The basic <SELECT> format creates a pop-up menu from which the user can choose one option:

```
<SELECT NAME="popup1">
<OPTION>Choice A
<OPTION>Choice B
<OPTION>Choice C
</SELECT>
```

Adding the MULTIPLE attribute to the <SELECT> tag changes the pop-up menu into a list from which more than one option can be selected.

11.2.4 Submit and Reset

At the bottom of the example form, the user is given the option to either submit the form for processing or clear it and start again:

```
<INPUT TYPE="submit" VALUE = "Submit Comments">
<INPUT TYPE="reset" VALUE = "Reset Form">
```

The TYPE attributes to the <INPUT ... > HTML tag define the type of input and the VALUE attributes define what text appears in the button. Since we are all human and prone to screw up, it makes sense to always include a TYPE="reset" button since this resets the form with empty or (as we shall see) default values.

11.2.5 Further Information

Appendix B has a summary of HTML forms syntax, and Table 11–2 contains pointers to on-line tutorials covering Web forms.

Table 11-2 Tutorials for Writing Web Forms

Location	Description
http://robot0.ge.uiuc.edu/~carlosp/cs317/cft.html	Interactive forms tutorial.
http://www.webcom.com/~webcom/html/tutor/forms/	Good tutorial from the folks at Web Communications.
http://www.w3.org/hypertext/WWW/MarkUp/html3/-forms.html	Forms syntax supported in the HTML 3.0 specification.

11.3 The Common Gateway Interface (CGI)

The Common Gateway Interface (CGI) executes a program, using as input values passed from client to server. Typically, this will generate some output (text and graphics), which is passed back to the client for display. The CGI, therefore, takes care of steps 2 through 4 for Web input processing.

The CGI is a feature of the Web server distinct from Web forms. Forms happen to be the most convenient way of getting information from the Web client to a CGI program using the http protocol. Chapter 12 introduces other methods of client-server exchange.

How does a Web server know that a request is a script or program to be executed and not just some HTML to be served? The file type .cgi provides the distinction—files with this extension are referred to as *CGI scripts* or CGI programs. Whether execution of the CGI script on the server is permitted depends on how you configured the Web server. For the Macintosh, there are two common scenarios:

1. Most commonly, any file with an extension of .cgi located below DocumentRoot in the folder hierarchy can be executed.
2. Alternatively, Mac Web servers such as WebSTAR and Quid Pro Quo allow you to restrict CGI scripts to a folder named DocumentRoot:cgi-bin. This is an optional restriction carried over from UNIX

servers for security purposes; this makes it more difficult for hackers to upload and run arbitrary programs on your server.

CGI scripts can be debugged in one of two ways. Either you can run them stand-alone by passing the script the argument it would normally get from the Web form, or you can run the application through the client Web browser since, like standard output, standard error is passed back to the client through the CGI. (This depends on the particular Web server and how that server is configured.) Here is a detailed sequence of events for what happens when a CGI script or program is invoked.

- When you hit the "Submit" button on a Web form, a text string containing all input to the form is passed to the URL specified by the ACTION attribute of the FORM tag.
- Specifically, the text string is attached to the URL to form a single string. The text string and URL are separated by a question mark (?).
- The format of this text string depends on the METHOD attribute of the FORM tag. Currently, one of two METHOD attributes may be specified, POST or GET.
- The GET method operates like any request for a URL from the server, except the URL has added variables for the script. GET passes a text string to the CGI, whereupon the server equates it with the server variable QUERY_STRING and the REQUEST_METHOD variable is set to GET.
- The QUERY_STRING defined by the GET method is of limited size (256 characters in most implementations) and is not suitable for large amounts of input. For example, our reader's comment form including name, e-mail address, and comment, would easily exceed 256 characters.
- The POST method opens up a separate channel of communication. The POST option solves the text string size limit since it processes the whole input stream as standard input and there is, therefore, no limitation on its size. In using the POST option the server variable REQUEST_METHOD is set to POST and QUERY_STRING is set to null. Further, the variable CONTENT_LENGTH defines the length, in bytes, of the query string.

- Regardless of whether the POST or GET method is used, the information will have a well-characterized format in which all the variables being passed to the CGI script are attached to the URL. As a Web client user, you will most likely have seen these strings in the "Location" field of your Web browser. The particulars of the typical formats that you may have seen are described below.
- When the text string gets to the server, what happens next is a function of your program.

For a standard CGI, the server will run the script and wait for an answer. When the CGI returns an answer, the server displays the results. Because the waiting can slow down your server, server software such as WebSTAR and Quid Pro Quo have been extended to handle asynchronous CGIs, usually indicated by the .acgi extension (although scripts with a .cgi extension can also run asynchronously). With ACGIs, the server can run a script, continue serving without waiting, and display the results when the script ends. For the purposes of our discussion, ACGI scripts are just a type of CGI script.

Here are the three formats for the text string passed to the CGI program or script. What gets passed depends on whether you are using the GET or POST methods and whether you are using named parameters (that is, name-value pairs), as we did in the one form example we have seen so far.

Keyword List (escaped) GET method, unnamed parameter	HREF="/cgi-bin/script_name?John%20Smith"
Keyword List (delimited) GET method, unnamed parameter	HREF="/cgi-bin/script_name?John+Smith+Jr"
Named Parameter List POST method, named parameter	HREF="/cgi-bin/script_name?first_name=John &last_name=Smith&title=Assistant%20Professor"

Keyword List (escaped). The text string is of the form: HREF="/cgi-bin/script_name?John%20Smith" The ? separates the script name (the program used to process the input stream) from the variable information. Thus, this example passes the words "John Smith" to *script_name* on the server for processing. Then *script_name* could, for example, trigger a database lookup for the name John Smith. Spaces, tabs, carriage returns, and so forth, are examples of special characters and if they are to be taken as literal text they must be represented correctly when passed to the CGI script or program. That is, they must be marked to indicate their special meaning. This marking is achieved using the percent (%) followed by the two-digit hexidecimal code for each character. For example, %20 represents a single space. A complete conversion table for hexidecimal, decimal, and ASCII can be found at

http://www.bbsinc.com/iso8859.html

Keyword List (delimited). Variables are delimited by the "+" (plus) character and is the old style delimiter commonly seen in the "Location" text box of a Web browser when doing a word search.

Named Parameter List. The named parameter list *is used by all forms and is by far the most common way of getting information to the server.* We will be using this exclusively in subsequent examples. Again, the question mark (?) is used to separate the URL describing the CGI script to be executed from the arguments to be passed to that script. The rest are name=value pairs each separated by an ampersand (&). Again, special characters such as white space are marked.

Code already exists in a variety of programming languages for decoding the various text strings passed to the CGI, so there is no need to rewrite these. Examples you can use are given in Section 11.4.

11.3.1 Further Information

Table 11–3 lists sites for tutorials on CGI programming, prewritten scripts in Perl as well as AppleScript, and sources for various parsers.

Table 11-3 Tutorials on CGI Programming

Location	Description
http://www.comp.it.bton.ac.uk/mas/mas/courses/html/-html3.html	Good CGI tutorial.
http://agora.leeds.ac.uk/nik/Cgi/start.html	Another CGI tutorial.
http://www.lu.se/info/Editor/HyperCgi.html	A few CGI programs for Mac servers.
http://www.yahoo.com/Computers/World_Wide_Web/-CGI___Common_Gateway_Interface/	Yahoo! listing associated with CGI.
http://www.best.com/~vincek/hp/hp.html	Tutorial, including interfaces to databases.
http://www.awpa.asn.au/cgi/	Good introduction to CGI programming and pointers to other places.

11.4 Common CGI Languages

CGI scripts can be written in any language with which you are familiar, once you have written (or obtained from elsewhere) the appropriate code to parse an input stream from a Web form. Macintosh servers also commonly use the AppleScript and Frontier scripting languages for CGI programs. We begin with a brief discussion of AppleScript, because it is the easiest to start with—most of the necessary software is already part of the Mac OS. Next we cover UserLand Frontier. Frontier is also a scripting language and hence not as difficult to program, but Frontier CGIs tend to run faster than AppleScript CGIs. Finally, we introduce Perl, a full-fledged programming language and the language of many CGI programs available on the Web.

A new development that affects your use of CGI scripts is the idea of Java servlets. While technically these server-side processing extensions don't use the CGI interface, they can perform most common CGI tasks as well as many tasks beyond the realm of CGI. We discuss servlets briefly in Section 12.3.7.

11.4.1 AppleScript

AppleScript created by Apple Computer, is used by the Mac OS to control the actions of "scriptable applications"—those with AppleScript support—and to transfer information between applications, computers, or networks. Based on the syntax and structure of spoken language, AppleScript has many of the same elements and components—verbs, nouns, adjectives, and prepositions—that languages have. With AppleScript you can customize your Mac OS environment and define new commands, as well as write CGI programs for your Web server, which, as far as AppleScript is concerned, is just another scriptable application.

The basic AppleScript software is included with your Mac OS. In the Extensions folder of your System folder, there are three extensions: the AppleScript Extension, AppleScriptLib, and ObjectSupportLib. Also in the Extensions folder is the Scripting Additions folder. Scripting additions, also known as OSAX—the Mac file type for scripting additions—are add-on modules to the AppleScript system. They provide special resources or commands to the AppleScript environment, such as those needed to write CGIs or parse the input from posting a form.

Finally, the Script Editor application is found in the AppleScript folder in the Apple Extras folder on your startup drive. This application is used to read, write, and record AppleScript scripts. Table 11–4 lists some sources of information on using AppleScript for CGI scripting.

To give you a feel for what AppleScript looks like, here is a script by Joshua Baer for creating a new message in Claris Emailer Lite and queuing it for delivery. This script and others are available at the sites given in Table 11–4.

```
-- summary: creates outgoing message, saves it to out box
-- freeFormName: recipients Real Name (string)
-- emailAddress: a valid SMTP address (string)
-- theSubject: the subject of your message (string)
-- theBody: the body of your message (string)

on createEmailerMessage(freeFormName, emailAddress, ¬
theSubject, theBody)
   tell application "Claris Emailer Lite 1.1v4"
         create mail subject theSubject ¬
               body theBody ¬
               recipients {name:freeFormName, ¬
address:emailAddress, type:1} ¬
               with save
   end tell
end createEmailerMessage
```

Table 11-4 AppleScript and the CGI

Location	Description
http://applescript.apple.com/	Apple's AppleScript site.
http://devworld.apple.com/dev/techsupport/insidemac/-AppleScriptLang/AppleScriptLang-2.html	Apple's AppleScript Language Guide (also available as a book).
http://www.comvista.com/lessons/START_HERE.html	A Macintosh/AppleScript CGI tutorial.
http://edb518ea.edb.utexas.edu/scripts/cgix/cgix.html	A selection of AppleScript CGI programs.
http://www.scriptweb.com/	A good overview Macintosh scripting, including AppleScript and Frontier.
http://www.scriptweb.com/osaxen/	Scripting additions for writing AppleScript applications and CGIs.
http://cgi.skyweyr.com/scriptweb/applescript.html	Joshua Baer's AppleScript pages, with example scripts and a glossary.
http://oasis.bellevue.k12.wa.us/cheeseb/	The AppleScript Sourcebook by Bill Cheeseman.
http://www.latenightsw.com/scripting.html	A source of AppleScript info, including a list of scriptable applications.

This simple script highlights some similarities and differences between AppleScript and traditional programming languages.

- The function createEmailerMessage is declared with the "on" keyword, rather than the typical "function" keyword. The function is explicitly ended with the "end createEmailerMessage" line.
- The "tell" block is used to send information to, in this case, an application. No other information is needed. When checking the script syntax in the Script Editor, you are prompted to locate the application on your hard drive with the standard Mac OS Open File dialog box. The script remembers this location.
- There are no end of line delimiters, such as semicolons; carriage returns delimit the end of a line. The "¬" indicates that a line is continued on the next line.
- There is no explicit typing, but AppleScript has 14 value classes (types) as well as automatic and explicit coercions.

A more detailed example of using AppleScript to write a CGI script is given in Section 11.5.1.

11.4.2 UserLand Frontier

Initially just a scripting language for the Macintosh created by Dave Winer and Doug Baron, UserLand Software's Frontier in version 5 has evolved into a full-fledged Web content management system. (UserLand integrated its Web-site management software, Clay Basket, into the Frontier suite.) Frontier builds an object-oriented Web site framework around an object database, an integrated scripting language with a large set of verbs, a multithreaded run-time environment, and a built-in outliner, or editor.

Frontier implements Web site management by storing all the pages of the site internally in a database and publishing the actual HTML for your site. The "root," as this database is called, stores not only text, but also objects of various types including tables, images, menus, constants, and other page elements.

For example, a Frontier script can process a raw text file into HTML by using object database information such as link data, macro expansions, page templates, or graphics. After proofreading in a scriptable Web browser such as Netscape Navigator, you can publish the file on your Web site via ftp with a single command.

For writing CGI programs, the key component of Frontier is its scripting language, UserTalk. UserTalk has more than 600 built-in system management verbs for retrieving system status information and folder contents, operating on files, starting applications, and sending information between scriptable applications.

Comparisons by *MacWeek* and *MacTech* (see Table 11–5) found scripts written in Frontier's UserTalk language to be 8 to 50 times as fast as a comparable AppleScript. For writing CGIs, speed is only one advantage of Frontier; another is Frontier's multithreading. Unlike single-threaded AppleScript, multithreaded CGIs under Frontier allow multiple clients to access a CGI simultaneously. Further, similarities between UserTalk and AppleScript mean that only minor changes are needed to port AppleScript CGIs to UserTalk.

The one disadvantage to Frontier is its somewhat steep learning curve. As freeware, Frontier comes with limited documentation and tech support outside of the mailing lists and archived FAQs. Because Frontier is not only a scripting language, but also a Web site management tool, Web server maintainers must learn new concepts about using the object database as well as the scripting language.

To install Frontier, download and unstuff the archive from the UserLand Web site given in Table 11–5, open the folder, and launch the UserLand Frontier application.

Table 11-5 Frontier Scripting Sources

Location	Description
http://www.scripting.com/frontier5/	UserLand Software's Frontier, freeware scripting.
http://www.mactech.com/articles/mactech/Vol.12/12.01/-AS-vs-Frontier/text.html	A *MacTech* article comparing AppleScript and Frontier for CGI scripting.
http://www.scripting.com/lists/	A list of about a dozen Frontier mailing lists.
http://www.circumtech.com/frontier/	Frontier information at Daniel Berlinger's Circumstance Technology Web site.
http://www.siteparc.fr/fgranger/fbfaq/-Frontier_beg_FAQ-10.html	A list of Frontier Web resources from François Granger's Frontier FAQ.

Table 11-5 Frontier Scripting Sources *(Continued)*

Location	Description
http://www.macweek.com/mw_1028/rev_frontier.html	A *MacWeek* review of Frontier 4.0.
http://www.cat.uc.edu/dave/frontier/	The Frontier Outpost.
http://garnet.berkeley.edu/~aron/bookmarks/frontier.html	A list of Frontier-related links.
http://www.scripting.com/frontier5/tutorials/scripting/ *http://www.acmetech.com/diana/Frontier/FContents.html*	Two tutorials of Frontier scripting.
http://www.scripting.com/frontier/netScripting/-MasonHale.html *http://www.bact.wisc.edu/FrontierCGIShop/siteOutline*	Tutorials for writing Frontier CGI programs.

To give you some idea of what scripting in Frontier is like, here is a sample script that changes the name of any file in a folder that ends in .htm to end in .html. The script and others are available at the UserLand site:

http://www.scripting.com/samples

```
«This script changes the extension of .htm files to .html.
local (folder, f)
if file.getfolderdialog ("Choose a folder to convert", @folder)
    fileloop (f in folder, infinity)
        local (name = file.filefrompath (f))
        if string.lower (name) endswith ".htm"
            if name [sizeof (name)] == 'M'
                file.rename (f, name + "L")
            else
                file.rename (f, name + "l")
```

In addition to some of Frontier's general similarities to AppleScript, there are some other points to note.

- The indented, nested structure of the code is enforced by Frontier's Outliner. There are no "end" statements as in AppleScript; the outline format makes them unnecessary.
- This script shows how Frontier can call predefined dialog boxes, in this case, to have the user select a folder.
- Frontier lets you perform repetitive operations on groups of files with the built-in verb "fileloop."
- The constructs "string.lower" and "file.rename" suggest the object-oriented nature of Frontier and its object database.

A more detailed example of using Frontier to write a CGI script and setting up your Web server to understand Frontier CGIs is given in Section 11.5.2.

11.4.3 Perl

Most existing programs for processing Web forms input are written in Perl, an interpreted programming language. The major reasons why you might consider using Perl on your Mac Web server are

- Perl is an interpreted, not a compiled language, which facilitates portability and ease of use.
- Many Perl scripts have already been written, and you might find one that performs a task similar to the one you require.
- Perl is available free for a wide variety of platforms, including the Macintosh.
- Perl is a very good language for string manipulation.

This last point is important, since it is a text string that gets passed to the CGI program from the Web form. Given the popularity and advantages of Perl, we have given several Perl CGI program examples in Section 11.5. Table 11–6 has pointers to on-line sources of information on Perl, and Table 11–7 has pointers to free libraries of useful routines for Perl CGI programming.

Table 11-6 Information on Perl

Location	Description
http://www.perl.com/CPAN-local/ports/mac/-MacPerlFAQ.html	How to download and install Perl for the Macintosh.
http://www.charm.net/~web/Vlib/Providers/Perl.html	Collection of useful links to Perl resources, including libraries.
http://www.perl.com/	Definitive source of Perl information.
http://www.perl.com/perl/info/software.html	Source of Perl software.
http://www.seas.upenn.edu/~mengwong/perlhtml.html	Index of Perl archives.

Table 11-7 Perl Libraries for CGI Programming

Location	Description
http://mors.gsfc.nasa.gov/MacPerl.html	List of MacPerl-related links and scripts, including Mac ports of libwww-perl and other useful libraries.
ftp://sunsite.cnlab-switch.ch/software/platform/MacOS/-perl/scripts/	A collection of MacPerl CGI scripts.
http://www.oac.uci.edu/indiv/ehood/perlWWW/dev/	Summaries and locations of the more popular Perl libraries.
http://www.ics.uci.edu/pub/websoft/libwww-perl/archive/	libwww-perl mailing list archives—a good source for current happenings with Perl- and Web-related libraries.

11.5 Forms by Example

It is beyond the scope of this book to teach you AppleScript, Frontier, or MacPerl. However, by closely following the annotated examples below, you could modify the scripts used in these examples for your own use. We start with examples for AppleScript (Section 11.5.1) and Frontier (Section 11.5.2), then provide an example in MacPerl (Section 11.5.3). Another Perl example can be found in Section 13.4.2. The code for all these examples is available from the book's Web site.

11.5.1 AppleScript: An E-mail Submission

In this example, we describe a form and CGI script that parses input from a form and sends the input to a designated recipient by e-mail. Dave has found this basic functionality useful for such purposes as submitting registration information for a conference, allowing clients to submit requests for printed documents, and subscribing to list servers. We also include this example to show an AppleScript CGI program.

For this basic functionality, you don't need to reinvent the wheel. Table 11–8 lists several CGI scripts for performing variations on this basic task.

Table 11-8 E-mail Submission of Form Input

Location	Description
http://www.lib.ncsu.edu/staff/morgan/email-cgi.html	An AppleScript CGI for sending form input via e-mail.
http://www.nmd.com/staff/sjohnson/cgi/forms/	A CGI script written in C for the same task.
http://www.netdreams.com/Net.Dreams/5th/flexmail/-index.shtml	Flexmail, an inexpensive form-to-e-mail utility that works as a WebSTAR plug-in.

Here are the steps to install the "email.cgi" script on Dave's Quid Pro Quo 2.0 server.

1. Download and unstuff the .hqx file. The email-cgi folder will have a compiled AppleScript application, the AppleScript text, and an instructions file, email-cgi.html. Put the email.cgi file in any folder from which you plan to call the script (or in the cgi-bin folder if you plan to restrict it to that folder).
2. Download and unstuff two extra AppleScript pieces: Parse CGI (*ftp://ftp.lib.ncsu.edu/pub/software/mac/parse-cgi-osax.hqx*) and MondoMail (*http://www.acmetech.com/files/mondo/MondoMail.hqx*). All these programs are free, and the URLs are given in the instructions.
3. Parse CGI is a AppleScript extension. Put it in the System Folder:Extensions:Scripting Additions folder.

4. Double-click email.cgi. It should ask you for the location of MondoMail. Select the MondoMail application using the dialog box. Quit email.cgi.
5. Create an input form, such as the one given below. Several named fields are required by the script:

   to_address = "To:" address (in user@host.domain format)

   from_address = "From:" address (in user@host.domain format)

   subject = "Subject:" line for e-mail message

   mailer = SMTP host that MondoMail sends message through
6. Put the HTML form in the same folder as the email.cgi file within your Web hierarchy.
7. Start the MondoMail application by double-clicking it.
8. Test.

```
<HTML><HEAD>
<TITLE>Section 11.4.5: Sample Form</TITLE>
</HEAD>
<BODY BGCOLOR="#FFFFFF">

<H2>Registration Form</H2>
<P>
The information entered is mailed to the recipient indicated
 by a hidden field.
<FORM METHOD="POST" ACTION="email.cgi">

<INPUT TYPE="hidden" NAME="to_address"
VALUE="dhart@sdsc.edu"><BR>
<INPUT TYPE="hidden" NAME="mailer"
VALUE="smtp.sdsc.edu"><BR>
<INPUT TYPE="hidden" NAME="subject"
VALUE="Form registration"><P>

Name: <INPUT TYPE="text" NAME="user_name" SIZE="20"
MAXLENGTH="40"><BR>
E-mail: <INPUT TYPE="text" NAME="from_address" SIZE="20"
MAXLENGTH="40"><BR>
Address: <INPUT TYPE="text" NAME="mailing_address" SIZE="20"
MAXLENGTH="40"><BR>
City, State ZIP: <INPUT TYPE="text" NAME="citystatezip"
```

```
SIZE="20" MAXLENGTH="40"><BR>
Phone: <INPUT TYPE="text" NAME="phone" SIZE="20"
MAXLENGTH="20">
<HR>
<CENTER>
<INPUT TYPE="Submit" NAME="Submit Registration">
<INPUT NAME="Clear" TYPE=Reset>
</CENTER>

</FORM>
</BODY>
</HTML>
```

The email.cgi script will parse the form input and send the contents of all the fields in the form to the recipient in the to_address field. It will also display the posted information to the user as confirmation. To change the format of the confirmation page, it is straightforward to edit the script with Apple's ScriptEditor, using the existing format to get you started.

11.5.2 Frontier: Soliciting Feedback

Using Frontier as your CGI scripting language involves first configuring the software of your Web server, as well as writing the scripts you want. Setting up your Web server so that it can accept and process requests with Frontier CGI scripts is a straightforward process. However, to be honest, Dave did not get this right on the first try. Some trial and error was required in order to get his Quid Pro Quo server to process Frontier CGIs. He never did figure out why it took so much effort. While these steps apply to a Quid Pro Quo server, the same steps should work with minor adjustments for a WebSTAR server.

1. Make an alias of the UserLand Frontier application and put it in the document root of your Web folder hierarchy. (For WebSTAR servers this will be the WebSTAR folder. Quid Pro Quo allows you to specify another folder as the document root.)
2. Rename this alias "Frontier.acgi." This name is somewhat arbitrary. "Frontier.fcgi" should work as well, but Frontier.acgi worked for Dave. Now Frontier is ready to go.

3. Switch to Quid Pro Quo and select the Server Settings option from the Config menu.
4. Choose the "Actions" option and push the New Action button.
5. Type "Frontier" in the Action field and type ":Frontier.acgi" in the Location field. The ":" indicates a relative path to the file starting from the document root folder. Replace "Frontier.acgi" with whatever filename you decided to use in step 2. Click the OK button to save the changes.
6. Once again, choose the Server Settings option from the Config menu.
7. Choose the "Suffixes" option and push the New Mapping button. This dialog lets you tell Quid Pro Quo how to handle different types of files.
8. Enter a suffix of ".fcgi" (the conventional, but not obligatory, extension for Frontier CGI scripts), "*" for both type and creator, and "text/html" for MIME type. Choose the "Frontier" option from the pop-up list of Actions. Click the OK button to save the changes.
9. Restart Quid Pro Quo and Frontier.

Now you should be ready to run a Frontier CGI script. As an example, let's start with the form shown in Figure 11–1. We need to make one small change to Phil's original form to send the posting to a Frontier CGI. Change the <FORM> tag to

```
<FORM METHOD=POST ACTION="comments.fcgi">
```

Next we need to create the UserTalk script so the form can pass information to it. Remember, what gets passed to the CGI script is a string similar to

```
http://hart-mac.sdsc.edu/forms/comments.fcgi?name=
Phil&email=bourne@sdsc.edu&phone=xxx-yyy-zzzz&
Comments=comments%20go%20here
```

Using Frontier as your CGI scripting language has the advantage that the parsing of the escaped character sequence is handled automatically. Frontier turns the form fields and values into a table called "argTable," which we'll see in the following script.

The trick to running a Frontier CGI script is that no file ending in .fcgi will be in the document folder, despite what the <FORM> tag suggests. (If it's not exactly a trick, it's a new way of doing things for those who haven't used Frontier before.) Instead, scripts must be added to and stored in the *Frontier.root* object database.

- After starting the Frontier 5 application—the most recent at the time of writing—select the Frontier.root option from the Window menu to display the Frontier.root window if it's not already displayed.
- Double-click the "user" table entry, then the "webserver" subtable entry, and finally the "cgis" subtable entry. In Frontier-speak, you are looking for the user.webserver.cgis table. Double-clicking the triangles or the Kind column will expand to show the table items in each case. Double-click the Value column to open the user.webserver.cgis table in its own window.
- To run a Frontier CGI with the action "comments.fcgi" in the <FORM> tag, you must create a new script called "comments" in the user.webserver.cgis table. Select the New Script option from the Table menu. You will be asked to give it a name; enter "comments" without the .fcgi. This will add a new entry to the table and open a script editing window with the line "on comments ()" already entered. Enter the following comments script in this window. When you're done, choose Save Database from the File menu.
- Now, calls to "comments.fcgi" will be processed by Frontier with the comments script.

What follows is an annotated version of the Frontier UserTalk script, comments.fcgi, used to process this input stream. This is a very simple read-write exercise, which Dave modified from an example in the on-line tutorial by Mason Hale. We are simply writing, in a specific format, the comments we have solicited to a file for later use and displaying an acknowledgment to the user. Familiarity with any programming language should make it possible to follow this script, even if you are not familiar with UserTalk syntax.

```
on comments (params)
   local
      html = webServer.httpHeader ()
      dataFile = file.getSystemDisk () + "Comments"
      i
      entry
      field
      order = {"Name","E-mail", "Phone", "Comments"}
      req = {"Name", "E-mail", "Phone", "Comments"}
   on add (s)
      html = html + s + cr
   with params^
      if defined (argTable)
         entry = clock.now () + tab
         «Start HTML return page.
         add ("<HTML><HEAD>")
         add ("<TITLE>Thank You!</TITLE>")
         add ("</HEAD><BODY BGCOLOR=white>")
         add ("<H2>Thank you for your comments.</H2>")
         add ("<P>")
         add (entry)
         « Create data file, if necessary.
         if not file.exists (dataFile)
            file.new (dataFile)
            file.setType (dataFile, 'TEXT')
         file.writeLine (dataFile, "##################")
         file.writeLine (dataFile, entry)
         « Add each field to record and to result page.
         for i = 1 to sizeOf (order)
            if (defined (argTable.[order[i]]) and (argTable.[order[i]] != nil))
               field = string (argTable.[order[i]])
               entry = order[i] + ": " + field
               add ("<P>")
               add (entry)
               file.writeLine (dataFile, entry)
            else
               if req contains (order[i])
                  return (webserver.errorMessage (order[i] + " is required.", params))
         « Finish return page
         add ("</BODY></HTML>")
      else
         html = webServer.errorMessage ("No Data", params)
   return (html)
```

The comment that appears in the file Comments (at the top level of your hard drive) after the execution of this script is

```
####################################
2/10/98; 8:13:47 PM
Name: Phil
E-mail: bourne@sdsc.edu
Phone: (xxx) yyy-zzzz
Comments: My Comments
```

and the page displayed in the Web browser of the person submitting the form is shown in Figure 11–2.

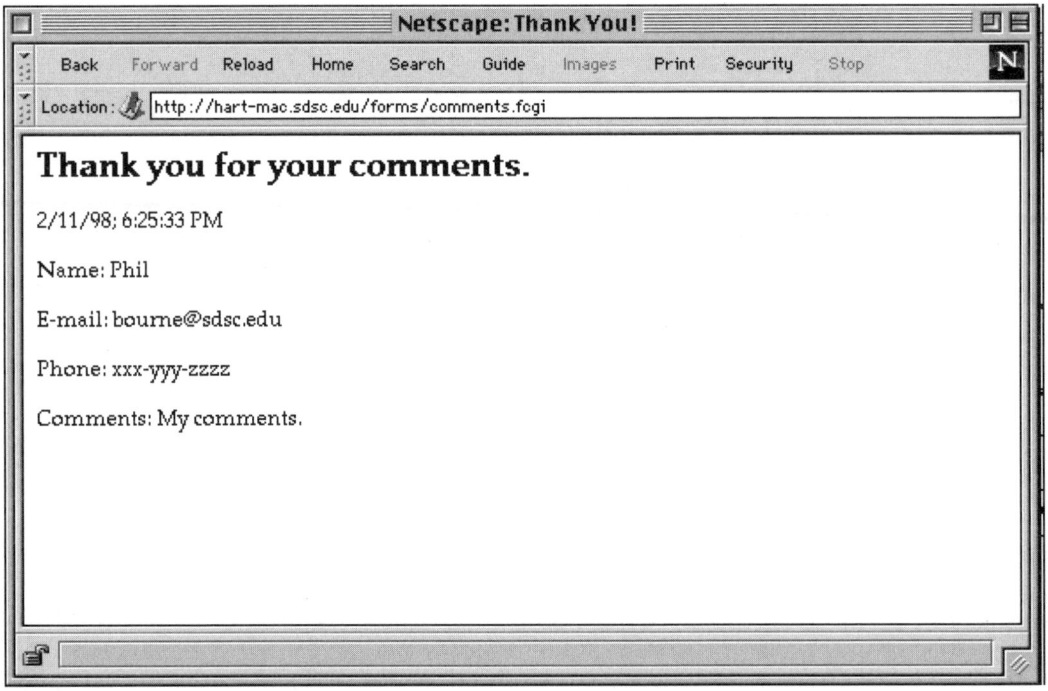

Figure 11-2 Simple Page Generated by a CGI Script

11.5.3 Perl: An Automated Archive

A major problem with any information server responsible for maintaining volatile—frequently changing—information is keeping that information current. In many cases the only hope is to off-load the update tasks to client users. We call this type of resource, which is fully automated and updated by the user, a *self-sustaining archive*. The negative features of such an archive are (a) no opportunity to moderate the contents, and (b) difficulty in validating the data being placed in the archive. However, for certain forms of information for which accuracy and appropriateness are not critical, it works very well.

Another feature of this example is the notion of multiple views—making the same information accessible in different ways. This example of a page that lists job openings provides two views:

(a) by level of position—faculty, post doc., industrial, or other, and

(b) by location in the United States—western, central, or eastern.

The example (in its original UNIX form) can be found at

http://www.sdsc.edu/Xtal/ACA/Jobs/jobs.html

It works as follows.

1. Employers post details of vacant positions via a Web form.
2. Using information provided on the form, the position is posted to different Web pages based on U.S. location and level of position. (Accessing jobs via a map of the U.S. was shown in Section 10.2 during the discussion of clickable maps.)
3. Information is also posted to an ftp archive, so that it is accessible to those readers without Web access (not shown in this example).
4. Jobs are automatically removed from the list after six months (not shown, since this is not part of the Web form processing, but a later step using a separate Perl script).

Here is the annotated HTML Web form used to submit job information. Read it carefully. The top half of the Web form is shown in Figure 11–3.

```
<HTML>
<HEAD>
<!-- http://www.sdsc.edu/Xtal/ACA/Jobs/adv.html -->
<TITLE>Post a Position Available</TITLE>
</HEAD>

<BODY BGCOLOR=#FFFFFF>
<P ALIGN=center>
<!-- Opening images with specific sizes and positions -->
     <IMG ALT="[SDSC Logo]" SRC="http://www.sdsc.edu/images/sdsc_logo.gif"
          WIDTH=522 HEIGHT=35 VSPACE=5 ALIGN=MIDDLE><BR>
     <IMG SRC="http://www.sdsc.edu/Xtal/images/aca_logo.gif"
           ALT="American Crystallographic Association" ALIGN=MIDDLE><BR>
<P ALIGN=center>

<I>Supported jointly by the American Crystallography Association <BR>
and the San Diego Supercomputer Center</I>

<!-- Begin form -->
    <FORM METHOD="POST"
     ACTION="postjob.cgi">

<HR>
<H2>Complete This Form To Post A Position</H2>
<STRONG>
  Caution - please carefully check over the information you have
provided before submitting the form, as all job submissions will be
automatically posted to the job lists.
</STRONG>
<HR>

<!-- Pop-up lists for type of position and location in US -->
Type of Position
     <SELECT NAME="type">
     <OPTION> Post Doc
     <OPTION> Faculty
     <OPTION> Industrial
     <OPTION> Other
     </SELECT>

     <SELECT NAME="area">
     <OPTION> Eastern US
     <OPTION> Central US
     <OPTION> Western US
     <OPTION> International
     </SELECT>
```

```
Geographical Area
<P>

<!-- Series of text boxes of set size -->
      <INPUT SIZE=50 NAME="title" > Title of Position <p>
      <INPUT SIZE=50 NAME="institution"> Institution <p>
      <INPUT SIZE=50 NAME="location"> Institutional Location <p>
      <INPUT SIZE=50 NAME="dept"> Institutional Dept. <p>
      <INPUT SIZE=50 NAME="site"> URL to which a candidate may refer
           (if known)
<P>
      <INPUT SIZE=20 NAME="start"> Start date <p>
      <INPUT SIZE=20 NAME="end"> Duration (if applicable) <p>

Job Description
<P>
<!-- Text area of specific size to contain job description -->
    <TEXTAREA NAME = "details" ROWS=10 COLS=60>
    </TEXTAREA>

<P>
  <INPUT SIZE=50 NAME="contact_name"> Person to Contact <p>
  <INPUT SIZE=50 NAME="contact_address"> Contact's Surface Mail
Address<P>
  <INPUT SIZE=50 NAME="contact_email"> Contact's Email Address<P>
  <INPUT SIZE=50 NAME="contact_phone"> Contact's Phone Number<P>
  <INPUT SIZE=50 NAME="contact_fax"> Contact's Fax Number<P>
  <INPUT SIZE=50 NAME="requirements"> What is to be submitted
        (CV, 3 references, etc.) <P>

Any other details (affirmative action, etc.) <P>
   <TEXTAREA NAME = "other_details" ROWS=5 COLS=40>
   </TEXTAREA>

<P>
<!-- Submit and clear buttons
<INPUT TYPE="submit" VALUE="Submit Position">
<INPUT TYPE="reset"   VALUE="Reset Form">
<HR>

If you submit a position and later wish to change it or have it
disappear from the list please contact the
    <A HREF = "MAILTO:toscano@sdsc.edu">Job List Editor</a>.
<HR>
</BODY>
</HTML>
```

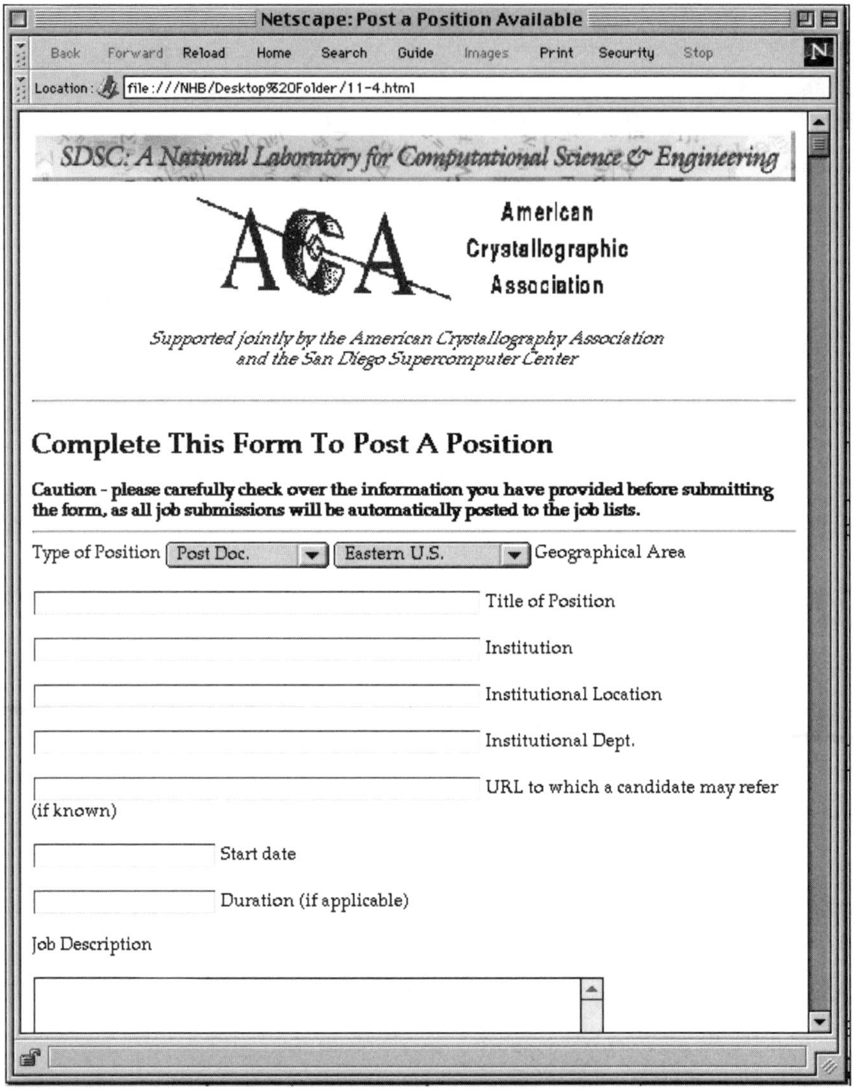

Figure 11-3 Another Web Form—The Self-sustaining Archive

Here is the annotated version of the MacPerl script used to process the input to the Web form. This provides the same functionality as the original UNIX version but has been modified by Dave to use the CGI.pm and Mac Files.pm packages. In order for the script to work properly, you must also create eight empty archive files that contain at least the necessary tags that the script uses to find the different sections. (You can also include additional HTML formatting and headers, which the script leaves alone.)

The files pd.html, faculty.html, industry.html, and other.html must have, in the following order, the tags:

```
<!start shortlist>
<!start listings>
<!end listings>
```

The files east.html, central.html, pacific.html, and international.html must have, in the following order, the tags:

```
<!end Post Doc>
<!end Faculty>
<!end Industrial>
<!end Other>
<!end list>
```

```
#!perl
# Adapted from code written by Rich Toscano.
$url = "jobs.html";  ## the calling URL.

# import, read, parse.
use CGI qw/:all/;
use Time::localtime;
use Carp;
use Mac::Files;

# Modifies the appropriate job category file based on job type.
# Allowable job types are Post Doc, Faculty, Industrial, and Other.
# Begin by defining the appropriate file to modify by equating it with
"oldfilename"
if (param('type') =~ /Post Doc/) {
    $oldfilename = "pd.html";
}
elsif (param('type') =~ /Faculty/) {
    $oldfilename = "faculty.html";
}
elsif (param('type') =~ /Industrial/) {
    $oldfilename = "industry.html";
}
elsif (param('type') =~ /Other/) {
    $oldfilename = "other.html";
}
else {
    die;
}
```

```
# Define a new file - this way if there is a screw up
# we can recover the previously intact file!
$newfilename = $oldfilename.".tmp";

# Get the date and time in an appropriate format.
$date = localtime->mday()."/".localtime->mon()."/".localtime->year();
$anchor = time();

# Open the existing and new file.
open (READ, "$oldfilename") || croak "Can't open file $oldfilename: $!\n";
open (WRITE, ">>$newfilename") || croak "Can't open file $newfilename: $!\n";

while ($line=<READ>)
{
# If the "<!start shortlist>" string is found make a new entry immediately
# following it in the new file. Thus, this is a flag indicating where in the
# file to place the update. We retain inverse chronological order, i.e., the
# user sees the newest entries first when scrolling through the file.

 if ($line =~ /^<!start shortlist>/) {
            print WRITE "$line\n";
            print WRITE li(a({-href=>"\#$anchor"}, param('title'),
                  param('institution'), param('location'), "[$date]"));
         next
    }

# If the "<!end listings>" string is found write summary information.
# Thus, this is a flag after which summary information is written.
    if ($line =~ /^<!end listings>/) {
          print WRITE "$line\n";
          print WRITE p, hr, i("Last posting:", $date);
          print WRITE "Problems?  Send mail to
<A HREF=\"mailto:bourne\@sdsc.edu\">bourne\@sdsc.edu</A>.\n";
          last;
    }

# If the "<!start listings>" string is found enter the full job description,
# formatting it based on the variables collected from the Web form.

    elsif ($line =~ /^<!start listings>/) {
          print WRITE $line;
          print WRITE hr, h3("<A NAME=\"$anchor\"></A>", param('title')), "\n";
          print WRITE h3(param('institution'));
          if (param('dept') ne '') {
          print WRITE "<B>Department: </B>", param('dept'), br;}
          if (param('location') ne ''){
          print WRITE "<B>Location: </B>", param('location'), br;}
          if (param('site') ne ''){
          print WRITE "<B>URL: </B>", a({-href=>param('site')}, param('site')),
br;}
```

```
 if (param('start') ne ''){
        print WRITE "<B>Start Date: </B>", param('start'), br;}
        if (param('end') ne ''){
        print WRITE "<B>Duration: </B>", param('end'), br;}
        if (param('details') ne ''){
        print WRITE "<B>Description: </B>", param('details'), br;}
        if (param('other_details') ne ''){
        print WRITE "<B>Other details: </B>", param('other_details'), br;}
        if (param('requirements') ne ''){
        print WRITE "<B>Please submit: </B>", param('requirements'), br;}
        if (param('contact_name') ne ''){
        print WRITE "<B>Person to contact: </B>",param('contact_name'), br;}
        if (param('contact_address') ne ''){
        print WRITE "<B>Surface mail address: </B>",param('contact_address'),
br;}
        if (param('contact_email') ne ''){
        print WRITE "<B>Email address: </B>", param('contact_email'), br;}
        if (param('contact_phone') ne ''){
        print WRITE "<B>Phone number: </B>", param('contact_phone'), br;}
        if (param('contact_fax') ne ''){
        print WRITE "<B>Fax number: </B>", param('contact_fax'), br;}
        print WRITE "<B>Job Posted: </B> $date<br>\n";
        print WRITE "<B>Job ID Number: </B> $anchor<br>\n";
        next;
    }
# Finally if nothing else write an existing line from OLDFILE to NEWFILE.
    else {
         print WRITE "$line\n";
    }

}

close READ;
close WRITE;

FSpExchangeFiles($newfilename, $oldfilename);

# This section makes a pointer to the job listing in the appropriate
# location file which is accessed via the clickable map.
# Define the appropriate file to update.
if (param('area') =~ /Eastern US/) {
        $oldlfilename = "east.html";
}
elsif (param('area') =~ /Central US/) {
        $oldlfilename = "central.html";
}
elsif (param('area') =~ /Western US/) {
        $oldlfilename = "pacific.html";
}
else {
        $oldlfilename = "international.html";
}
```

```
$newlfilename = $oldlfilename.".tmp";

# Open the original file and a new file.
open (OLDFILE, "$oldlfilename") || die "Can't open job file $oldlfilename:
$!\n";
open (NEWFILE, ">$newlfilename") || die "Can't open job file $newlfilename:
$!\n";

# Append an entry with the appropriate URL to the listing when the
# flag "<!end TYPE>" is found.
$marker = "<!end ".param('type').">";
while ($line=<OLDFILE>)
{
    If ($line =~ /^$marker/) {
          print NEWFILE li(a({-href=>"$oldfilename\#$anchor"},
param('location')));
          print NEWFILE "$line\n";
          next
          }

 # Reestablish the flag after the last member of the list.
    elsif ($line =~ /^<!end list>/) {
          print NEWFILE "$line\n";
          last;

 # Otherwise just copy the line to the newfile.
    else {
          print NEWFILE "$line\n";
          }
}
# Include some ending information
print NEWFILE "<p><I>Last modified: $date</I><P>";
print NEWFILE "Problems?  Send mail to
<A HREF=\"mailto:bourne\@sdsc.edu\">bourne\@sdsc.edu</A>.\n";

close OLDFILE;
close NEWFILE;

FSpExchangeFiles($newlfilename, $oldlfilename);

# Print out a message which is sent back to the employee.

print header, start_html("Job Posting Results"),
   h1("Job Posting Results"),
   hr,
   p, "Your job was successfully posted to our ",
   a({-href=>"$oldfilename"}, param('type'), " job list. "),
   "For further assistance, send mail to the",
   a({-href=>"mailto:bourne\@sdsc.edu"}, "Job List Editor. "),
   "If you would like a job removed from the listings, please make sure to
include the ",
   b("Job ID Number."),
   end_html;
```

Figure 11–4 illustrates the result of posting an industrial type position. A brief summary, including position title, location of position, and date posted, for each available job appears at the top of the Web page. The summary links to a name anchor in the same file. Thus, it is easy to find details of a specific posting in a large list of available positions.

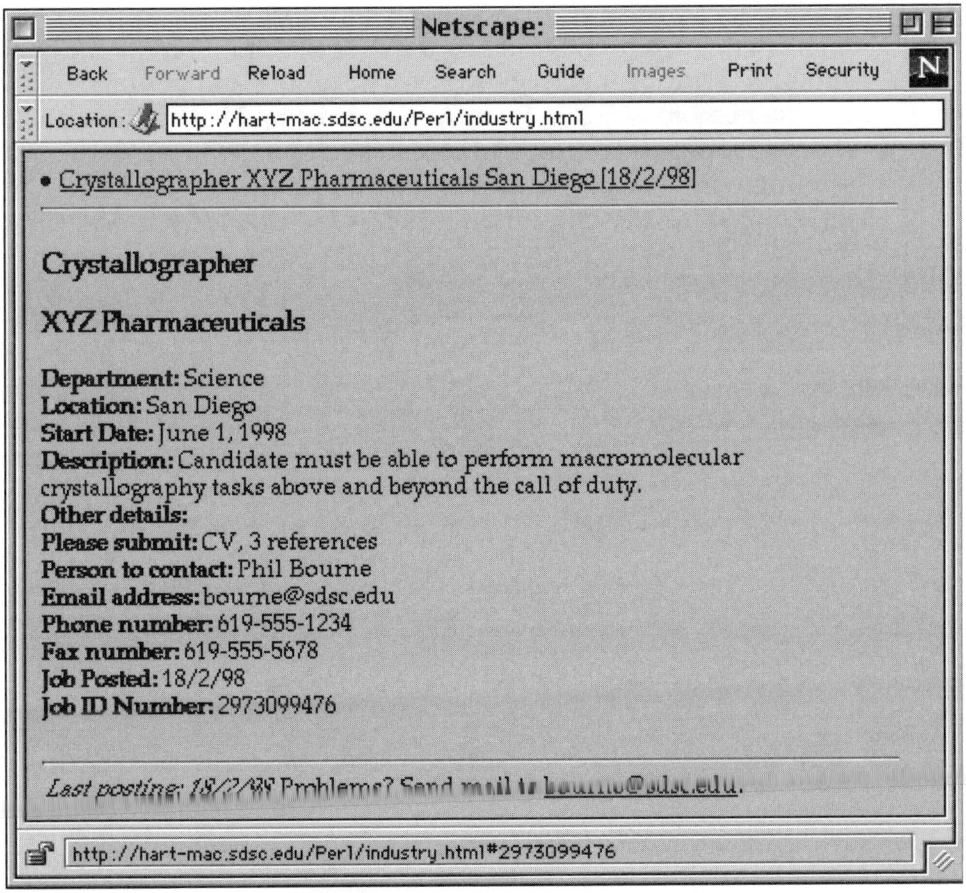

Figure 11-4 Web Page from the Self-sustaining Archive

11.5.4 "Canned" CGIs and Forms Tools

You may need your Web site to provide the interactivity and processing that forms and CGI scripts provide, but you may not have the staff time to devote to writing and developing custom scripts to handle your transactions. If you aren't a programmer, you may not want to spend days or weeks learning to write Perl or AppleScript code for the few tasks you want your Web site to perform. You may not have to.

There are a number of software tools that automate the creation and processing of forms, giving you flexibility and interactivity without the need to write code, as well as existing CGI scripts and applications for performing common form-processing tasks besides sending e-mail with the form contents. Table 11–9 lists a few forms tools and some existing forms-related CGI scripts for the Macintosh.

Table 11-9 Canned CGIs and Forms Tools

Location	Description
Custom Forms	
http://www.maxum.com/NetForms/	NetForms by Maxum Development supports the creation and processing of forms without writing code.
http://mac.nombas.com/ppc/sewse/index.html	ScriptEase: WebServer Edition by Nombas, Inc., simplifies the programming required to process custom forms.
Canned CGIs for Forms	
http://webcrossing.com/	WebCrossing, a CGI application to provide Web-based discussion boards and forums.
http://interaction.in-progress.com	Interaction lets you create and manage dynamic, social Web sites with threaded discussions, chats, and shopping.
http://www.netdreams.com/Net.Dreams/5th/upload/-index.shtml	Upload by NetDreams allows you to create forms through which users can send files to your server.
http://weyl.zib-berlin.de/HTMLs_English/-lutz_programs.html#mailfile	CGI that allows clients to request files be sent to them via e-mail.
http://www.pliner.com/formsaver	CGI to take form information and save as a tab-delimited file.
http://www.lu.se/info/Editor/HyperCgi.html	Another CGI to take form contents and save to a tab-delimited file.

11.6 Cookies

Cookies provide a means to overcome the limitations of the Web's stateless interaction. Netscape Communications, the originator of cookies, defines them this way:

> Cookies are a general mechanism which server-side connections (such as CGI scripts) can use to both store and retrieve information on the client side of the connection. The addition of a simple, persistent, client-side state significantly extends the capabilities of Web-based client/server applications.

When a server returns an HTTP object to a client, the server may also send a piece of state information, a cookie, that the client will store. When the client makes a future request of that same server, the client transmits the current value of the cookie from the client back to the server.

Cookies fall in a gray area of the client-server interaction. They are a request from the server to the client—instead of a request from client to server, as in a normal client-server relationship—to store information provided by the client that the server can access during later client requests.

You can look at the cookies stored on your Macintosh. If you use Internet Explorer, choose the Edit:Preferences… menu item. From the left side of the preferences dialog, select the Cookies option under Receiving Files. This will display the cookies that Internet Explorer has permitted to be written. For Netscape Navigator, it is slightly more difficult. In the HardDrive:System Folder:Preferences:Netscape *f* folder, there should be a file called MagicCookie. (You can also use Find File to search for MagicCookie.) Dragging the MagicCookie file onto your Netscape window will show you exactly what information has been stored on your computer.

Obviously, letting Web servers write information to your computer presents some security and privacy issues. As far as security goes, cookies are constrained both in what they can store and which servers can read them. A browser will not give up cookie data to any server except the one that set the cookie; otherwise, if your browser tossed its cookies to every site you visited, this would be a security risk and would make cookies worthless.

As for what they can store, according to Netscape, cookies are limited to

- 300 cookies total in the cookie file.
- 4 kilobytes per cookie, for the sum of both the cookie's name and value.
- 20 cookies per server or domain. Completely specified hosts and domains are treated as separate entities and have a 20-cookie limitation for each, not combined.

Even though security should not be a major concern, privacy might be. Unless you provide additional information, a Web site's cookie can only indicate that you, or more specifically your browser, visited that site (or pages on that site) and when. When you make choices or enter data into forms or dialog boxes, the site might also store that in the cookie, since this information distinguishes you from other visitors. Depending on your perspective, you might have qualms about your privacy—even though the information is being stored on *your (client) computer.* As a general rule, then, you should not provide information—or, as an Internet server, ask for information—that could compromise your (or your clients') privacy.

Cookies, in a nutshell, provide a powerful way to develop applications for Web-based environments. Shopping applications can store information about currently selected items, for-fee services can send back registration information and free the client from retyping a user ID on next connection, and sites can store client preferences on the client, effectively enabling a site to customize its appearance or behavior for every repeat visitor.

A Web server has three methods of sending these cookies to a client and later retrieving them: CGI scripts, JavaScript embedded in an HTML page, or Java applets. Table 11–10 has some general information on cookies, as well as writing and reading cookies with CGI scripts. In the next chapter, we will go into more detail and give some examples of managing cookies with JavaScript (Section 12.2.4).

Table 11-10 Information on Cookies

Location	Description
http://home.netscape.com/newsref/std/cookie_spec.html	Netscape's specification for persistent client-state HTTP cookies.
http://www.cookiecentral.com/ *http://www.cookiecentral.com/cgidemo.htm*	Cookie Central, including CGI cookie demos.
http://www.illuminatus.com/cookie.fcgi *http://www.illuminatus.com/cookie_pages/code.html*	Andy's HTTP Cookie Notes and CGI cookie source code in AppleScript, Frontier, and MacPerl.
http://www.yahoo.com/Computers_and_Internet/Internet/-World_Wide_Web/HTTP/Protocol_Specification/Persistent_Cookies/	Yahoo! section on persistent cookies.
http://www.yahoo.com/Computers_and_Internet/Internet/-World_Wide_Web/HTTP/Protocol_Specification/-Persistent_Cookies/Security_Issues/	Some links to articles on the privacy issues raised by cookies.

▼▼▼

You should now be able to create your own Web form, and—if you are already familiar with Perl, AppleScript, or Frontier—have input to that form processed by a CGI script you have written. The examples in this chapter can serve as templates for developing your own Web forms interface. If you are not already familiar with one of the common CGI scripting languages, you should at least be able to process Web forms data by modifying the templates we have given or by downloading and customizing existing scripts. (The scripts from this chapter are available from the book's Web site.)

• CHAPTER • 12

Cooking with Java and JavaScript (The Global Computer)

Ingredients

- JavaScript
- Java

For some diners, no meal is complete without a good cup of coffee. Coffee can be instant or ground and percolated slowly. The more effort that goes into the making, the better the taste.

12.1 Computing via the Internet

What we have learned to do so far is to serve information in the form of text, graphics, and, to a lesser extent, sound and video, and to accept and process information submitted via Web forms from client users. The information is processed by a CGI script or program on the server and a response is sent to the client Web browser as new Web pages.

We now move on to the next logical step in the development of your information server. This step could be described as permitting users to compute via the Internet. The basic idea is that the user downloads a piece of code from your server and runs it locally on the client or invokes it on the server from the client, or both, as part of a dialog between server and client. There are many possible applications of this technology. For some of the latest examples of what can be done refer to

http://www.developer.com/directories/pages/dir.java.html.

These examples show you, the information provider, a wealth of new capabilities to enhance the information you deliver. Here are some examples of these capabilities.

- In-line sounds that play in real time whenever a user loads a page. That is, the sound does not have to be invoked separately. An example is music that plays in the background on a page as it is being read.
- Cartoon-style animation, once downloaded, is displayed in real time, since it does not depend on continuous downloading to view each consecutive frame.
- Objects rendered or moved in real time on a Web page. For example, the mouse can be used to direct the rotation of an object. (This is also the domain of VRML, but used here to describe Java-based capabilities.)
- Web pages made more interactive. In other words, a dialog maintained between the user and the server, bypassing the stateless nature of a Web interaction. An example would be an iterative database query—the output from one query is used as input to the next.

While these capabilities are impressive, they are just the beginning. Future developments will only be limited by our imaginations, programming skills, and network bandwidth—witness the current developments in collaboration via the Internet. *Network computing*, as we have called it, has the potential to completely change the way we compute. In this book there are many examples of downloading applications, configuring them, and executing them. In the future, when you choose to run an application, it will be fetched from an Internet server, configured without your even knowing it, and run. This will happen *each time you invoke the application*. You will always be running the latest and greatest version of software since the software is stored at a remote site that has the expertise and resources to develop and maintain that application.

The current tools that make this new type of computing feasible are the Java programming language from Sun Microsystems Inc., and JavaScript from Netscape Communications. It is beyond the scope of this book to teach you how to program in Java and JavaScript. It is within the scope, however, to provide you with an overview of the capabilities of Java and JavaScript, give you very simple examples of how to use these tools, and point you to additional information. After reading this chapter you should be able to state one of the following:

- Yes, I will develop applications in Java or JavaScript.
- No, my server does not need to provide Java or JavaScript capability.
- I do not need Java or JavaScript today but will revisit using these tools at a later date.

12.2 JavaScript

Since JavaScript is simpler than Java, we begin with it. Developed originally by Netscape Communications, JavaScript is less functional but easier to program than Java. JavaScript was originally called LiveScript and designed to let Web pages take advantage of Navigator capabilities beyond those provided by basic HTML. It was renamed JavaScript about the time that Java appeared on the scene by virtue of Netscape's licensing the "Java" name from Sun. JavaScript code is embedded in HTML documents and interpreted by the viewer's Web browser. JavaScript requires versions of Netscape Navigator 2.0 or later, and its popularity resulted in Microsoft including (some) JavaScript support in versions of Internet Explorer 3.0 and later. Table 12–1 contains pointers to additional information on JavaScript, and following are a few simple examples of how JavaScript is incorporated into Web pages.

Table 12-1 Sources of Additional Information on JavaScript

Location	Description
http://www.yahoo.com/Computers_and_Internet/-Programming_Languages/JavaScript/	The Yahoo! starting point for information on JavaScript.
http://www.htmlgoodies.com/javagoodies/	Excellent staring point for tutorials and example scripts.
http://home.netscape.com/sv/eng/mozilla/3.0/handbook/-javascript/	Netscape's introduction to JavaScript basics.
http://www.javascripts.com	JavaScripts.com, access to scripts. Requires registration.

12.2.1 Hello World

Our first example is about as simple as it gets with JavaScript.

```
<HTML>
<HEAD>
<SCRIPT LANGUAGE="JavaScript">
<!--
// Non-JavaScript supporting browsers skip the following line
document.write("Hello World.")
// -->
</SCRIPT>
</HEAD>
<BODY>
That's all, folks.
</BODY>
</HTML>
```

What users see in their Web browsers is the following:

Hello World. That's all, folks.

This covers the basics of how HTML and JavaScript work together:

- The <SCRIPT> ... </SCRIPT> HTML tags delimit JavaScript code within an HTML document.
- The LANGUAGE attribute to the <SCRIPT> tag defines the language of the embedded code—a promise of more languages in the future.
- The comment delimiters, <!-- ... -->, prevent Web browsers that are unable to recognize JavaScript from displaying the code in the browser window.
- The statement

  ```
  document.write("Hello World.")
  ```

  declares the document object with the write method and assumes to write to an HTML document defined within <BODY> ... </BODY> tags. There are assumed attributes of the document object that can be explicitly overwritten. The use of objects and methods is made clearer in the discussion of Java in the next section.
- The HTML code wraps around the JavaScript.

Let us now look at a couple of examples that introduce features of the JavaScript language.

12.2.2 Declaring Functions

The next short example shows how to declare a function and then use that function. In this script, note that a function, square(*i*), has been declared, which is subsequently called with a specific value of *i* (2 in this example).

```
<HTML>
<HEAD>
<SCRIPT LANGUAGE="JavaScript">
<!--  for non-supporting browsers
  function square(i) {
    document.write("The call passed ", i ," to the
    function.<BR>")
    return i * i
  }
  document.write("The function returned ",
          square(2),".")
// end hiding contents from old browsers  -->
</SCRIPT>
</HEAD>
<BODY>
<BR>
All done.
</BODY>
</HTML>
```

The result seen in the Web browser is

The call passed 2 to the function.
The function returned 4.
All done.

12.2.3 Controlling the Browser

Now let us look at an example that works with features of the browser itself by popping up a separate alert window. These simple examples should give you a feel for what you might do with JavaScript.

```
<HTML>
<HEAD>
<SCRIPT LANGUAGE="JavaScript">
<!--  for non-supporting browsers
  function helloworld() {
          alert("Hello World!")
                          }
// end hiding contents from old browsers  -->
</SCRIPT>
</HEAD>
<BODY>
<FORM>
<INPUT TYPE="BUTTON" VALUE="Press Me"
ONCLICK="helloworld()">
</FORM>
</BODY>
</HTML>
```

Note the following new features:

- Again we defined a function—helloworld(), but this time that function calls another built-in function available as part of the JavaScript libraries called alert(), which takes a single text string argument and pops up an alert window with the text string and a dismiss button.
- The ONCLICK attribute of the <INPUT> tag defines what happens when a button (specified with the TYPE attribute) is pressed. In this case it invokes the helloworld() function.

12.2.4 Baking with JavaScript: Cookies

Section 11.6 described the basics of why you might want to use cookies. Here we provide the basic JavaScript framework for managing cookies. At minimum, you need to have a function to write or update a cookie and a function to get information from a cookie. Table 12–2 has some sources of JavaScript code for cookies.

Table 12-2 JavaScript Cookies

Location	Description
http://home.netscape.com/sv/eng/mozilla/3.0/handbook/-javascript/advtopic.htm#1013101	Netscape's JavaScript handbook section on cookies.
http://www.cookiecentral.com/demomain.htm	Cookie Central's JavaScript demos.
http://www.ozemail.com.au/~dcrombie/cookie.html	Duncan Crombie's JavaScript Cookies page.
http://www.sna.com/mmatteo/Java/jscookies.html	Marc Matteo's Cookies with JavaScript page.
http://www.hidaho.com/cookies/cookie.txt	Sample JavaScript for cookies from hIdaho Design.

As an example of creating and using a cookie with JavaScript, we borrow with permission the example from Marc Matteo, which records and displays how many times a user visits the Web page that creates the cookie.

```
<html>
<head>
<title>A Cookie Counter</title>
<!-- Basic JavaScript cookie code. By Marc Matteo,
http://www.sna.com/mmatteo/ -->

<script>
cookie_name = "Counter_Cookie";

// Updates the Counter_Cookie.
// Called as the client leaves the page.

function doCookie() {
      if(document.cookie) {
      index = document.cookie.indexOf(cookie_name);
      } else {
              index = -1;
      }
      if (index == -1) {
              document.cookie=cookie_name+"=1; expires=Tuesday,
```

```
01-Apr-1999 08:00:00 GMT";
      } else {
            countbegin = (document.cookie.indexOf("=", index) + 1);
            countend = document.cookie.indexOf(";", index);
            if (countend == -1) {
                   countend = document.cookie.length;
            }
            count = eval(document.cookie.substring(countbegin,
count end)) + 1;
            document.cookie=cookie_name+"="+count+"; expires=Tuesday,
01-Apr-1999 08:00:00 GMT";
     }
}


// Gets the count that the client sent when requesting this document.
// Returns string for displaying the number of times client has
visited.

function gettimes() {
    if(document.cookie) {
        index = document.cookie.indexOf(cookie_name);
        if (index != -1) {
            countbegin = (document.cookie.indexOf("=", index) + 1);
            countend = document.cookie.indexOf(";", index);
                if (countend == -1) {
                    countend = document.cookie.length;
                }
            count = document.cookie.substring(countbegin, countend);
            if (count == 1) {
                return (count+" time");
            } else {
                return (count+" times");
            }
        }
    }
    return ("0 times");
}
</script>
</head>

<body onUnload="doCookie()">
<!-- When page is loaded, client browser increments Cookie_Counter. -->
<h3>Here is the counter:</h3>
```

```
<center>
<!-- This script section simply calls the gettimes function to extract
the count
        from the cookie. -->
<script>
    document.write("<b>You have been to my site "+gettimes()+" be-
fore.</b>");
</script>
</center>

<p>
If you re-load this page, the counter above will update. The count is
kept in a cookie being stored in your browser.

</body>
</html>
```

This example gives you a feel for some longer JavaScript functions. In particular, note the references to "document.cookie," which contains the string value of the cookie that the client sent along with the request for this page. Use string methods such as substring, indexOf, and lastIndexOf to determine the content of the cookie.

12.3 Java

Java is a programming language akin to C, Fortran, Basic, Perl, and so on. In many ways Java combines the best features of all of these languages while remaining lightweight, that is, not overburdened with esoteric syntax. A powerful feature is the ability to invoke Java programs from a Web page; however, that is about as far as the similarity with JavaScript goes. Table 12–3 compares the Java programming language and the JavaScript scripting language.

Table 12-3 Comparison of Java and JavaScript

Java	JavaScript
Compiled on server.	Interpreted on client.
Complex but powerful.	Simple but limited.
Run-time support by several Web browsers.	Run-time support limited.
Full-blown object-oriented language.	Uses built-in extensible objects, but no classes or hierarchies.
Strong typing.	Weak typing.

Make no mistake, Java is a programming language and requires programming skills to use it effectively. It is much more complex than using HTML, and about as complex as C++. Moreover, like C++, Java is an object-oriented language and not a structured language like C or Fortran. If you are not familiar with the techniques of object-oriented programming using languages like C++, Smalltalk, and Objective C, there will be an additional learning curve. Do not be deterred, however. First, if you are not familiar with object-oriented programming, Java is a good language in which to get your feet wet, particularly since there is a flood of free Internet-accessible documentation, tutorials and general help. Second, JavaScript is an intermediate approach between HTML and Java, so you can begin with JavaScript and make the further transition to Java as your needs become more complex. Given the increasing capabilities and availability of JavaScript, you may be able to bypass Java altogether.

It is beyond the scope of this book to teach you the principles of object-oriented programming. However, to understand what Java has to offer we will touch on some of the basic principles. Additional sources of information on the capabilities and shortcomings of Java can be found in Table 12–4.

Table 12-4 Sources of Additional Information on Java

Location	Description
http://java.sun.com/doc/language_environment/	A white paper by the Java developers summarizing the features and motivation behind the Java language.
http://www.rain.org/~da5e/macjava.html	The MacJava Web site.
http://soli.inav.net/~panther/jmac/	JMAC Macintosh Java news source.
http://www.connect.hawaii.com/connect-bin/-review.index?Java	Reviews of recent books on Java.
http://java.sun.com/doc/tutorial.html	Java tutorial from Sun Microsystems Inc.
http://sunsite.unc.edu/javafaq/javatutorial.html	Another very good tutorial.
http://www.yahoo.com/Computers_and_Internet/-Programming_Languages/Java/-Guides__Tutorials_and_Documentation/	Entry point to Java from Yahoo!.
http://java.sun.com/docs/	Entry point to a wide variety of Java information.
http://www.well.com/user/yimmit/hworld.html	Examples of Java applets.

12.3.1 The Java Environment

There are two sides to the Java coin—running Java applets and applications and writing Java programs. To view Java applets from the Web in your browser or to run software written in Java, you need the Mac OS Runtime for Java (MRJ). This software comes on the Mac OS 8 CD-ROM, but you need to install it separately. The latest version is also available from *http://applejava.apple.com*. The MRJ includes system extensions and the code libraries needed to run Java programs on your Mac along with the Apple Applet Runner, which lets you view Java applets locally.

On the other hand, to develop applications in Java you need a full-fledged programming environment. Because of Java's popularity, third-party ports of the Java Development Kit (JDK) are available for almost any operating system, including the Mac OS and NeXTStep (soon to be Rhapsody). See

http://java.sun.com/cgi-bin/java-ports.cgi

Table 12–5 lists several vendors of Java development environments for the Mac OS.

Table 12-5 Mac OS JDK Ports

Location	Description
http://applejava.apple.com/	Mac OS Java software from Apple—Mac OS Runtime for Java (MRJ) and the Mac Software Development Kit (SDK).
http://www.metrowerks.com/	Metrowerks CodeWarrior.
http://www.symantec.com/vcafemacpde	Symantec's Visual Café.
http://www.roaster.com/roaster/	Roaster Technologies Roaster Integrated Development Environment.
http://www.visix.com/products/vibe/de/	Visix Software's Vibe programming environment.
http://www.imcinfo.com/ActionLinehome.html	IMC's ActionLine Java Web development tool.

These Java development tools consist of the following components:

- class libraries—libraries needed by the Java compiler
- a Java compiler
- a Java interpreter
- a Java debugger
- a Java applet viewer

With the exception of the Java applet viewer, these are standard components for any programming environment. The need for an applet viewer is explained with the help of Figure 12–1.

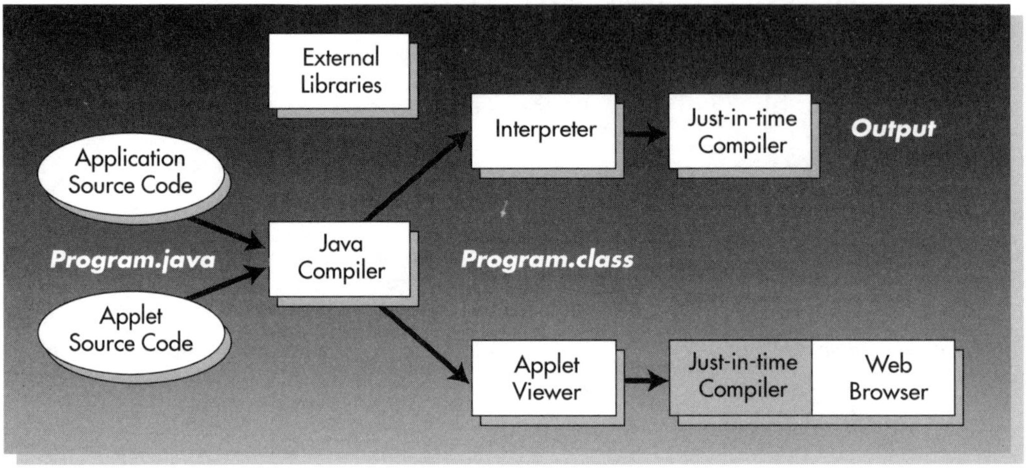

Figure 12-1 Java Components

The first thing to understand is that there are two types of Java source code; one written to be run as an application and one written to run as an *applet*. We have met the term applet at other points in this book. Recall that an applet is Java code that runs from within a Web browser. (The Apple Applet Runner lets you test your applets before making them part of a Web page.) An application runs as a stand-alone program on your Mac. As we shall see in Section 12.3.2, the main difference between an applet and an application is the libraries you use as part of your code.

Either way, the source code—shown in Figure 12–1 as the file *program.java* (*.java* is the standard file extension for Java code)—is compiled, which produces a file, *program.class*. The file *program.class* is in machine-independent *byte code* and will run on any computer for which a Java interpreter, such as the MRJ, is available. If your source code produces an applet then, as we shall see in Section 12.3.3, that applet can referenced within an HTML file and passed to a Web browser (or to the Apple Applet Runner). Web browsers that can make sense of Java code have their own built-in Java interpreters.

Machine-independent byte code is a major feature of Java, but the price you pay for independence is performance. This may or may not be a problem; it depends on the application. Because the code is not optimized for specific hardware, it will be a problem for a CPU-intensive application, but less of a problem for a simple display program. Enter the *just-in-time compilers*. Just-in-time compilers take the Java byte code and convert it to more efficient machine-specific code just prior to running the application in order to take advantage of specific hardware features. At the time of writing, just-in-time compilers are starting to appear in Web browsers. The impact of just-in-time compilers is considered in Section 12.4, which summarizes our colleagues' and our experiences with Java to date.

You should now have some sense of the various Java components and be ready to consider some of the major features of Java. We will then move on to a couple of simple examples of writing, compiling, and using Java, both from an application and an applet standpoint.

12.3.2 Java Features

The major features of Java should give you some idea why there is considerable excitement about Java. Other languages have some of these features, but only Java has them all. This section is heavy on the technical terms but should give you some idea of the power of Java. In a nutshell, these features, taken together, indicate that Java is an evolutionary step in programming. Java retains the best features of previous languages, while discarding those features affecting portability, security, and ease of programming. Moveover, it is designed specifically for use via the Internet.

Network Ready. Java was designed with the network in mind. In addition to stand-alone applications, self-contained blocks of code are easily transferred from the server using the http protocol and subsequently executed on the client. As we saw in the previous section, these blocks of code are called applets and can be executed by Java-ready browsers such as Netscape Navigator version 2.0 and above.

Assuming a Web browser is Java ready and can interpret an applet, how it handles the applet is browser and configuration dependent. Most browsers will not permit the applet, when read as part of a remote URL, to read or write to the client disk, since this poses a security risk. Browsers that access the applet as part of a Web page that is a local file often behave differently. And browsers have the ability to enable and disable features of Java.

Hardware Independent. As indicated in the previous section, hardware independence is a great feature of Java. When you compile a piece of Java code, you are not compiling it into machine-specific code, but rather into byte code. This is possible because Java is statically typed, which is a fancy way of saying that you declare all objects (numbers, variables, arrays, etc.) in Java to have an explicit data type (for example, char or int) and that data type is defined explicitly by the language to have a specific storage requirement. For example, an integer is 32 bits and a long integer 64 bits. When running an applet, it is the byte code that is passed from the server to the client; thus, the client must be running a Java interpreter to use the Java code.

GUI Independent. Only a single Graphical User Interface (GUI) need be developed for Java applets and applications—a major accomplishment because up to 90 percent of the coding effort can be expended on interface development. That interface can be displayed and used on all Macs, UNIX platforms, and PCs, since all these platforms support Java-ready browsers. In the future, more computing is likely to be done through Java-ready browsers. At the time of writing, idiosyncracies do exist in interface look and feel depending on the operating system and browser type and version, but these are slowly disappearing with every new JDK and browser release.

Extensive Class Libraries, Language Support, and Documentation. Java is enabling the use of the Internet, and, conversely, the Internet is enabling the use of Java. This is possible because Java is evolving with the Internet, rather than predating it. For example, there are extensive Java-shared *class libraries* and applet libraries being developed and shared. The documentation covering these developments is available worldwide, since it is written in HTML and available on the Web. Table 12–6 indicates where to find useful Java libraries.

Table 12-6 Java Libraries

Location	Description
http://applejava.apple.com/	Apple's Java site.
http://java.sun.com/products/JDK/	The Java Developer's Kit (JDK) from Sun Microsystems Inc.
http://www.jars.com/	Starting point for locating useful applets.
http://the-inter.net/www/future21/java/applets.html	Applets that can be simply used to enhance the appearance and usability of Web pages.
http://www.mexred.net.mx/~huibert/Java/MAE/-MAEEn.html	Work-in-progress Java library to emulate the Mac OS interface within applets.

Standard Compliant. The hardware-neutral and portable language platform of Java is known as the Java Virtual Machine. The Java Virtual Machine is based primarily on the POSIX interface specification, an industry-standard definition of a portable system interface.

Support for Threads. For the purposes of this discussion, threads can be thought of as lightweight processes. A process is the element to which the operating system allocates resources (e.g., CPU time and memory). A process has a certain overhead that must be incurred when it is started. In this era of multiprocessor computers, a process can be broken down into threads of execution that are executed simultaneously and, therefore, in less wall clock time than on a single processor. The overhead in starting a thread is less than that of starting a process, hence the term "lightweight." Java supports threads and the results can be seen in applications that can simultaneously download multiple animation sequences while scrolling and displaying graphics.

Java supports multithreading at the language level with the addition of sophisticated synchronization primitives to manage concurrent and dependent threads of execution. The language library provides the *Thread* class, and the run-time system provides monitor and condition lock primitives, again necessary to synchronize multiple dependent threads of execution. At the library level, Java system libraries have been written to be thread safe. That is, the functionality provided by the libraries is available without conflict to multiple concurrent threads of execution.

Object Oriented. *Classes and inheritance* are of proven value in shortening the software development cycle, since, if done properly, these object-oriented features make it easier to reuse code. The downside is that you need to put more thought into the initial design, so you have bits of code that you can reuse. Those "bits" come in the form of classes. Classes have attributes, that is, variables with static or dynamic values, and methods, code that performs some function. Classes, with their associated attributes and methods are inherited, modified, and reused for a variety of purposes. An object is an instance of a class.

Encapsulation hides complex programming in objects that have a simple calling interface and, hence, can be used in a straightforward manner.

Polymorphism implies that the same message is sent to different objects. This results in behavior that is dependent on the nature of the object receiving the message.

Strong typing helps make Java portable. Other than the primitive data types, everything in Java is an object. Even the primitive data types can be encapsulated inside library-supplied objects, if required. There are only three groups of primitive data types, namely, numeric types, Boolean types, and arrays.

Security. The following features help define the security features of Java.

- Memory layout is determined at run time and is not defined by the code itself. Without a knowledge of how the application maps to memory, interfering with the application is made more difficult.
- The notion of pointers to other memory locations does not exist in Java and, hence, interfering with memory mapping is difficult.
- The byte code verifier and vetter analyze byte code coming across the network. Furthermore, networked byte code is treated differently than local byte code by memory partitioning.
- There is user-level control over what byte code is run and from what machines.

12.3.3 The Simplest Application

Let us look at our simple "Hello World" example in Java:

```
/*
* File: HelloWorld.java
*/
public class HelloWorld {
    public static void main(String args[])   {
          System.out.println("Hello World!");
    }
}
```

If you are a C++ programmer or, to a lesser extent, a C programmer, the features of this example will be apparent. If you are not, note the following

- Comments are contained within /* ... */.
- The first thing we have done is to declare a class called "HelloWorld" which is public. By being public it is accessible to other classes but has the requirement that only one public class is available per file and that the file be called, in this example, HelloWorld.java.
- Next, we have declared a method main. Since it is public, it is available to other methods. Since it is static, it is shared by all instances of this class and (in principle) could be invoked as HelloWorld.main.
- System.out.println() is a method that takes as an argument a single string that is output to standard out (stdout), usually the display screen.

Your Mac programming environment of choice will compile HelloWorld.java into a file of byte code called *HelloWorld.class.* This file can be executed on any computer that supports a Java interpreter—the code is machine independent. If you run HelloWorld.class from your Macintosh, you should see "Hello World!" appear on your display screen.

12.3.4 The Simplest Applet

What we have so far is an example of a Java application; a Java applet has a slightly different structure. Here is the same application, coded as an applet:

```
import java.awt.Graphics;

public class HelloWorldApplet extends java.applet.Applet
{

   public.void.paint(Graphics g) {
         g.drawstring("Hello World!", 5, 25);
   }
```

You should see similarities and differences between the applet and the application.

- The import statement was not found in the Java application and is used to gain access to classes from the JDK to handle the applet itself and to draw to the screen.
- We have declared a public class, as was true of the application. Here, however, we extend a class java.applet.Applet, which implies that the HelloWorldApplet takes on the characteristics of the basic applet supplied with the JDK.
- The paint() method is used to display the text string "Hello World!" to the screen, The paint() method replaces main() in our Java application example.
- More specifically: The paint() method takes an instance of the Graphics class as its single argument. We then use the drawstring() method from the Graphics class to display the string. The string is displayed on the screen starting at 5 pixels across and 25 pixels down. As we shall see in the subsequent example, there are other methods of the Graphics class that we could have used to control font size, color, and so forth.

Just as with the Java application, the applet must be compiled, producing a file of byte code *HelloWorldApplet.class* that can be included in a Web page and executed by a Java-ready browser when the Web page is loaded. To include the applet in an application, use the <APPLET> ... </APPLET> HTML tags.

```
<HTML>
<HEAD>
<TITLE>A Simple Java Applet</TITLE>
<!-- File: HelloWorldApplet.html -->
</HEAD>
<BODY>
<P> Here is my Java Applet: <BR>
<APPLET CODE="HelloWorldApplet.class" WIDTH=125
    HEIGHT=30> </APPLET>
</BODY>
</HTML>
```

Note the following:

- The CODE attribute of the <APPLET> tag defines the name of the applet file.
- The WIDTH and HEIGHT attributes of the <APPLET> tag define the space reserved on the Web page (in pixels) to display the applet.

Applets can also be viewed with the Apple Applet Runner by opening the file HelloWorldApplet.html (or dragging and dropping the file onto the Applet Runner icon).

12.3.5 More Complex Applets

Let us take this simple applet to the next level. First, we give more details on how to control the look of text produced by an applet; second, we show how to pass a parameter from HTML to an applet.

```
import java.awt.Graphics;
import java.awt.Font;
import java.awt.Color;

public class HelloNameApplet extends java.applet.Applet
{

Font f = new Font("TimesRoman", Font.BOLD, 24) ;
String name;

public void init() {
     name = getParameter("name");
     if (name == null) name = "Phil" ;
           name = "Hello " + name + "!" ;
     }

public void paint(Graphics g) {
     g.setFont(f);
     g.setColor(Color.red);
     g.drawString(name, 5, 30);
     }
}
```

This applet code can then be used as follows:

```
<HTML>
<HEAD>
<TITLE>Another Simple Java Applet </TITLE>
<!-- File: HelloNameApplet.html -->
</HEAD>
<BODY>
<P> Here is my Java Applet: <BR>
<APPLET CODE="HelloNameApplet.class" WIDTH=125 HEIGHT=30>
<PARAM NAME=name VALUE="Fred">
</APPLET>
</BODY>
</HTML>
```

Note the following:

- We have imported additional classes to handle fonts and color.
- We have created an individual font object (f) using the "new" constructor of the Font class. That font object has attributes that define it as a 24-point, bold, Times Roman font.
- The init() method will get the parameter "name" from the HTML file. If name is not defined, the string "Phil" will be used.
- The "name" variable will have a text string "Hello " prepended to it and the text string "!" appended to it.
- The complete text string will be displayed in red, starting 5 pixels to the right of the upper-left-hand corner of the assigned applet space and 30 pixels down.
- The <PARAM> tag defines parameters to be passed to the applet for use. The attributes NAME and VALUE define the name-value pair to be used by the applet.
- If the <PARAM> tag had been missing, the Web page would contain "Hello Phil!"

Examples like these can be found in the introductory chapters of most books on Java or in the on-line information. They are not included here to attempt to teach you Java. Rather they are intended to provide the context for when and how to use Java to supplement the information you are providing through the Web.

12.3.6 Grinding Your Own: JavaBeans

If you are going to make extensive use of Java applets on your Internet server, you no doubt would like to reuse as much of your Java code as possible. While Java's object-oriented features provide some degree of reuse, you will still have to modify or customize your Java classes whenever you write a new applet.

JavaBeans, an extension of the Java environment, offers a way to create customizable software "building blocks" that are written once and can then run anywhere—in different applets or on different computer platforms. In more technical terms, JavaBeans is a *component model* or component architecture, which defines a set of interfaces for creating interoperable software components. By combining the components in new ways, developers can build new software applications much more quickly. JavaBeans, therefore, allows Java programmers to create the "blocks" out of which to build a wide array of applets.

Individual JavaBeans components, or Beans, have different functions, of course, but all Beans share several distinguishing characteristics, according to Sun's JavaBeans documentation:

- **Introspection** enables a builder tool to analyze automatically how a Bean works.
- **Customization** lets a developer use a builder tool to customize the appearance and behavior of a Bean.
- **Events** allow Beans to communicate and connect together.
- **Properties** let developers customize and program with Beans.
- **Persistence** enables developers to customize Beans in a builder tool and then retrieve those Beans, with customized features intact, for future use.

Properties, events, methods, and persistence are standard features of a component model, and JavaBeans adds introspection and customization to make the programming task easier. In particular, these characteristics mean that Beans can be manipulated visually in a builder tool to construct new applets or applications from the Beans you create—all without writing any code. A JavaBeans-enabled builder tool maintains Beans in a palette or toolbox. To develop with these building blocks, you select a Bean from the palette, drop it into a form, customize its appearance and behavior, and compose it and other Beans into an applet that meets your requirements. (If you really want to write code, though, you can use text-based tools to manipulate Beans through programming interfaces.)

JavaBeans is part of the Java Development Kit (JDK) 1.1; therefore, any JDK 1.1-compliant browser or tool, including those supporting MRJ 2.0, implicitly supports JavaBeans. Table 12–7 provides some links to further JavaBeans information.

Table 12-7 JavaBeans Information

Location	Description
http://java.sun.com/beans/	Sun Microsystem's JavaBeans site.
http://java.sun.com/docs/books/tutorial/javabeans/	Sun's JavaBeans tutorial.
http://jars.developer.com/listing-JavaBeans.html	The JavaBeans listings from EarthWeb's JARS Java resource.
http://www.symantec.com/vcafemacpde/index.html	Symantec's Visual Café for Java is a builder tool that supports JavaBeans development.

12.3.7 Java Servlets

Java servlets are to Web servers what Java applets are to Web browsers. Servlets are another option, in addition to CGI scripts or server plug-ins, for extending the power of your Web server. They are already supported by many popular Web servers, including Quid Pro Quo and WebSTAR for the Macintosh. For example, a servlet might take data in an HTML order-entry form and apply the business logic used to update a company's order database, perhaps using the Java Database Connectivity interface (Section 13.2).

Because servlets run on the server and not on the client (as applets do), they are freed from some of the tight security restrictions that limit them in browsers. In addition, since you always know where a servlet will run (your server), servlets avoid the headaches that result from applets that look and feel different on different client platforms despite Java's cross-platform intentions. Other features of servlets make them advantageous for non-Web applications: They can run as stand-alone applications, be written to listen to non-HTTP requests, and be chained together with one servlet calling another.

This brief discussion only touches on the highlights of Java servlets. Table 12–8 provides links to additional information to get you started writing servlets.

Table 12-8 Java Servlet Information

Location	Description
http://www.developer.com/news/techfocus/-021698_servlet.html	A good introduction to how Java servlets might be used from developer.com.
http://webreview.com/97/10/10/feature/	Web Review's feature on servlets.
http://java.sun.com/products/java-server/servlets/	Sun's Java servlet page.
http://java.sun.com/products/jdk/1.2/docs/ext/servlet/-servlet_tutorial.html	A servlet tutorial from Sun.
http://www.newatlanta.com/	New Atlanta Communications sells a Java Servlet API implementation for the Mac OS.

12.4 Developing with Java and JavaScript

On first glance, Java and JavaScript are compelling for any software developer. Java, particularly, has all the features one would like to see in a programming language and, hence, has generated a great deal of excitement. This is evident when visiting the Internet section in any bookstore—there are many books on Java. A downside of this rise to fame is that there has been little opportunity for the product to mature. Bugs and nonuniform behavior are common. Nonuniform behavior implies, for example, graphical user interfaces that appear different from one hardware type to another—or even appear different from one release of a Web browser to another on the same hardware platform. We anticipate this situation will improve with each new release of the JDK.

Another issue to consider is performance. As an experiment, Phil's colleague Ilya Shindyalov took a commonly used scientific algorithm, which he had coded in C++, and converted it to Java (a trivial process). The Java code ran ten times slower than the C++ code using the same input data set and hardware. Using the just-in-time compiler made the Java code approximately ten times faster, roughly equaling the performance of the C++ code. Thus, *the just-in-time compiler is important for CPU-intensive applications written in Java.*

So for now, if you are running a production server that targets the widest possible audience you may want to experiment with using Java and JavaScript to enhance your pages while ensuring that the pages work whether the browser supports these language capabilities or not. (You can turn off the Java and JavaScript features of your browser through the preferences dialog.) On the other hand, if you want to run a cutting-edge server that pushes the envelope of Web functionality, then JavaScript and especially Java are poised to take off as the underlying software matures and becomes more widely distributed.

▼ ▼ ▼

At this point your server should be fully operational and you should be excited at the prospect of what you might do with Java and JavaScript. Now we turn our attention to another burgeoning area of Web publishing—serving databases.

• CHAPTER • 13

Data Buffet (The Global Database)

Ingredients

- Databases
- Database connection methods
- Tools for serving databases

For some diners and chefs, single helpings of à la carte menu items only serve to whet the appetite. The only way to experience the full range of tastes is through a smorgasbord of appetizers, entrees, and side dishes. Diners can then eat their fill of exactly the amount and variety of dishes they crave.

Chapter 8 discussed what you need to consider in laying out the files stored in your ftp archive and the pages on your Web site. However, the information many organizations want to put on the Web is likely to be the same as (or a subset of) the information they spend time tracking and keeping records on. Businesses keep records of products, schedules, invoices; universities compile staff, faculty and student directories; and scientists record the sequence of amino acids in proteins, to name just a few examples.

To share this information on the Web, a trivial solution would be to create a page in which to display as formatted text all the available information at some point in time. You would probably need to update this page on a regular basis, whenever the information changed. Interested users could scan the text for the information they seek or use the find option on their Web browser. A second solution might be to create a separate Web page for each item you track and a list that linked to all the individual pages. You could then add new pages, remove outdated ones, or change the information with a little more flexibility. Web users can then peruse the list and search individual pages for the items they are interested in.

13.1 Serving Databases

You could do these things, but you would be reinventing the wheel. In all likelihood, your organization uses computers for keeping these sorts of records and performing the basic functions of adding, updating, deleting, and searching records. The Web offers a new interface for interacting with these collections of data.

13.1.1 What Is a Database?

We would like to give you at this point a precise, technical definition of exactly what a database is. But we can't. A database, according to a textbook on the subject—the fourth edition of C.J. Date's *An Introduction to Database Systems*—is "essentially nothing more than a computerized record-keeping system." (A database is also used to refer to the collection of records being kept.) That general description covers everything from the largest commercial packages for storing millions of complex records in hundreds of indexable files to a few dozen lines of code designed to store a couple hundred items in a plain text file.

Taking the notion of a database a little further, we introduce the concept of a Database Management System (DBMS). As the name suggests, a DBMS provides additional tools addressing such features as security, multiple query languages, forms generators and so on. This distinction is not important here. Just consider the following common features relevant to our discussion:

- The data are stored as a set of *records*, each of which stores data about a single item being tracked.
- The database provides ways to add, update, delete, and retrieve records from the database. Retrieval operations generally allow users to search for individual records or sets of records based on the contents of the records.
- The data in the database are *integrated*. Integrated means the records are both unique (nonredundant) and unified (because a single database may consist of many files).
- The data are meant to be *shared*. Shared means that the records are of interest to more than the person or persons doing the adding, updating, and deleting of records in the database.

In any discussion of databases, you will also likely encounter the term *relational database* and its associated RDBMS, or Relational DBMS. A relational database can be defined as a database in which all the data are represented as tables. Most large commercial software packages, such as Oracle, are relational database systems. Another common database format is the *flat-file* format, in which database records are stored simply as lines in a single file. The trade-off is search and retrieval power versus complexity. Relational databases typically offer lots of power and flexibility but a steep learning curve. Flat-file databases may not handle as many records or complex searches, but they are usually easier to use.

Helping you choose your DBMS is beyond the scope of this book. For now, we will assume you have data in a database, and now you want to know whether you should put them on the Web.

13.1.2 Why Serve Databases?

The features of databases themselves answer the question "Why serve databases on the Web?" We'll discuss the features in reverse order.

- **Shared.** Your organization is tracking these records because they are meant to be shared, either within the organization on an intranet—for example, staff office directories—or to the entire world through the Web—as with products in a mail-order catalog. The Web is the ultimate form of sharing your databases.
- **Integrated.** The data are organized in such a way that elements can be uniquely and efficiently searched and retrieved. For example, when a customer wants to place a new order, it is also possible to find the previous orders by that customer and track the shipment of the current order. A single Web interface can incorporate all these elements.
- **Methods to add, update, delete, and retrieve records.** Because the database system includes these functions, you would like to avoid having to provide the identical capabilities, particularly the retrieval (search) methods, when placing this information on the Web. Database search methods let users find just the information they want, while the other methods ensure they always find the latest information.
- **Records.** In creating its databases, your organization probably placed considerable effort into developing logical records that effectively describe the information. This same logical structure will likely also translate to an effective presentation on the Web.
- **Efficiency.** A database will be more efficient than a basic file lookup.

In discussing databases and the Web, we should also point out that databases, like the Web, are client-server applications. The client sends requests to the server to add, delete, update, or retrieve records; the server processes these requests, stores, changes, or deletes the necessary data, and returns the results to the client. Placing databases on the Web, therefore, amounts to providing a client interface in the form of a Web page.

Before the discussion becomes too pedantic, we'll let these reasons suffice for your wanting to serve databases on the Web. Table 13–1 gives several other sources of basic database information. Now that you know you want to serve up your databases, you just want to know how.

Table 13-1 Database Information

Location	Description
http://www.mactech.com/articles/mactech/Vol.11/11.06/-Client-Server-Database/text.html	A discussion of databases as client-server applications.
http://www.mactech.com/articles/mactech/Vol.12/12.12/-Tightwads-Flat-File-db/text.html	A discussion of the merits and disadvantages of relational versus flat-file databases.
http://cdr.cs.uiuc.edu/pubs/de97tutorial/index.htm	A classroom tutorial (slides from a lecture) on databases and the Web.
http://w3c2.com.au/steve/is3.html	A student report on databases and the Internet.

13.2 Database Connection Methods

Serving your databases on the Web requires, not surprisingly, that you extend the functionality of your Web server application. You want your server, after all, to serve not only HTML pages, but also database records. And you provide database methods in the same ways you add other extensions to your server, namely, CGI scripts or plug-ins. (Recall from Section 4.3 that server applications, including WebSTAR and Quid Pro Quo, can be extended via W*API or MOSAPI plug-ins.) Conversely, you might also use a database program with built-in Web-serving features that runs alongside your regular Web server, much like the Phantom search engine from Section 6.4.1

Digging one level deeper, CGI scripts and plug-ins typically use one of two methods for communicating with the DBMS:

- **Native methods**, in which the server communicates directly in the interface supported by the DBMS. These methods work most efficiently but require changes to the server software to interact with different DBMS software.
- **Open Database Connectivity (ODBC) calls**, in which the server sends database requests from a single set of commands and software drivers provided by the DBMS translate those commands for a particular database. ODBC offers a more general solution and works with databases for which you might not have native methods; however, the price of generality is somewhat slower performance.

Therefore, in choosing how to connect your database to the Web, there are several factors to consider. First, does your organization use one or several DBMS products to maintain the databases you want to serve? If only one database is used organizationwide, you will likely get better performance using CGI scripts or a Web server plug-in that uses native methods. On the other hand, if your organization uses a variety of DBMSs, you should probably look to ODBC-based server additions for the widest applicability.

If you are creating a new database and choosing the DBMS to use with an existing Web server, you have similar choices. The preferred route as far as performance goes would be to choose a DBMS for which the plug-in or scripts use native methods. Table 13–2 has pointers to more information on ODBC.

13.2.1 Java Database Connectivity

Another way to serve databases on the Web is to write Java applets for performing this task and include within the applets the commands for accessing the DBMS. In the same way that ODBC provides a standard interface to a variety of databases, the JavaSoft team at Sun Microsystems has created the *Java Database Connectivity (JDBC)* interface, which provides Java programmers with a uniform interface to a wide range of relational databases, and provides a common base on which higher-level tools and interfaces can be built. JDBC is now a standard part of the Java Development Kit distributed by Sun.

As with ODBC, a key concern about JDBC is certainly JDBC's performance and its ability to scale when the number of users grow into thousands accessing the database at the same time. Table 13–2 also has links to more information on JDBC.

The other drawback to JDBC, of course, is that it is only a programming interface and not a complete database-to-Web solution. If you don't want to write your own code, JDBC is not for you. However, you may want to file this away for future reference, as more Java-based applets and applications become available from commercial software houses. In the next section, we discuss some existing tools for putting your databases on the Web now.

Table 13-2 Database Connection Methods

Location	Description
http://www.microsoft.com/data/odbc/	Microsoft's ODBC page. Microsoft defined the ODBC standard.
http://www.bf.rmit.edu.au/Oracle/odbc.html	A commentary on using ODBC with Oracle.
http://www.synergex.com/odbc/odbc_man.htm	Synergex develops ODBC drivers and includes useful ODBC information at its Web site.
http://www.cs.hut.fi/~las/odbc.html	A no-frills listing of ODBC calls and functions.
http://www.simba.com/products/products.html	Simba creates ODBC and JDBC drivers for popular databases.
http://java.sun.com/products/jdbc/index.html	Sun's JDBC database access API.
http://www.webadvisor.com/jdbc.html	A description of JDBC and links to other JDBC information.

13.3 Products and Tools

Now that you have a little background on how databases can interact with the Web, it's time to make the connection. Table 13–3 lists a number of Macintosh tools for publishing databases on the Web. To a greater extent than with other components of your Internet server, you will find a definite difference between the low-cost options and the full-featured commercial options. Chances are, if you aren't already running a DBMS on your network, you will have to pay for the database. The cost of publishing databases once you have the DBMS also varies.

Free. At the lowest cost, it is possible to serve up a database for next to nothing. If you are comfortable with Perl and customizing and porting your own scripts for the Mac OS, then you might want to visit the Perl home page. There are Perl scripts for accessing most popular DBMSs. Table 13–3 even lists a free set of scripts for creating simple, flat-file text databases. Don't underestimate the power of flat-file text databases, however. In the same way that e-mailing the contents of a Web form (Section 11.5.1) can serve many purposes, so can the ability to store and search records from a flat file. A registration database for a conference, staff directories for small to medium organizations, a site map of available URLs within your Web site are just a few possibilities. (Chances are that your search engine software maintains the index to your site in a flat-file database.)

Table 13-3 Web Database Connectivity Tools

Location	Description
http://www2.starnine.com/extendingwebstar/-database.tmpl	StarNine's listing of database tools for extending WebSTAR (and other servers that support WebSTAR plug-ins).
http://www.inlink.com/~perlguy/simple/	A tutorial and free set of Perl scripts for creating simple databases in flat text files.
http://reference.perl.com/query.cgi?database	Listing of Perl scripts for interacting with various DBMSs.
FileMaker Pro	
http://www.filemaker.com/	FileMaker Pro version 4.0 has Web-serving capability built in.
http://www.blueworld.com/lasso */http://www.blueworld.com/lasso/lasso_lite/lite.html*	Lasso and free Lasso Lite from Blue World Software put FileMaker Pro databases on the Web. Lasso includes Java classes for accessing FileMaker Pro.
http://www.everyware.com/products/tango/-tangofm.html	Everyware Development's Tango for FileMaker puts FileMaker databases on the Web.
http://www.macweb.com/webfm/	Web Broadcasting's Web FM for publishing FileMaker Pro databases.
ODBC	
http://www.everyware.com/products/tango/-tango_info.html	Everyware Development's Tango Enterprise for connecting Oracle, FileMaker, or any ODBC database to the Web.
http://www.ndev.com/ndc2/products.htm	WebDBC from Storm Cloud Development links any ODBC database to the Web.
http://www.webink.com/	WebInk's Webink ODBC extends the Webink environment to include access to ODBC databases.

Table 13-3 Web Database Connectivity Tools *(Continued)*

Location	Description
4th Dimension	
http://www.acius.com/	4th Dimension by ACI US.
http://www.datacraft-inc.com/pages/dw_main.html	DataWave from DataCraft serves 4th Dimension databases on the Web.
http://www.isis-intl.com/s7p.html	Isis International's System 7 Pack extends 4th Dimension so that you can write scripts for it.
http://www.fsti.com/productinfo/netlink.html	Foresight Technology's NetLink/4D lets you use 4th Dimension as an asynchronous CGI (ACGI) program for your server.
http://www.mdg.com/	WebServer4D, and WS4D/CGI connect 4th Dimension databases to the Web.
Other Databases	
http://www.canto-software.com/cumulus_info.html	Cumulus from Canto Software manages digital media files.
http://www.purity.com/websiphon/	Purity Software's WebSiphon works as an HTML preprocessor, letting you include SiphonScript database commands directly in your HTML files. Works with Verona flat-file database (included).
http://www.provue.com/proVUE/-ProductsWebVUE.html	ProVUE's WebVUE lets you put Panorama (also from ProVUE) databases on the Web.
http://www.icnc.com/icn/index.html	Andrew Warner's WebFox for publishing FoxPro databases.
http://www.webclerk.com/	An integrated database and server application for conducting sales on the Web.

Moderate Cost. For slightly greater functionality and more complex databases, we recommend FileMaker Pro 4.0. The latest version of FileMaker Pro has Web publishing features built in. So for the price of a fully featured DBMS, you also get Web publishing capabilities. (In fact, most DBMSs these days have Web publishing built in.) There are also a number of tools and some free CGI scripts for adding Web publishing capabilities to older versions of FileMaker Pro and extending the Web features of version 4.0. In Section 13.4.1, we show how to install and use a FileMaker Pro Web-database solution.

In this realm, you will get a general DBMS and Web-publishing set of tools. You will have to create the databases you wish to serve and describe how you want the databases to appear to Web clients. There will be less work than programming, but you will be able to customize the tools to almost any Web-database publishing task.

High End. At the high end of Mac OS Web-database publishing are a number of tools that provide ODBC connectivity to commercial RDBMSs such as Oracle and SyBase. If you need a relational DBMS and all the associated bells, whistles, and power for a large organization, or you want to publish data from an existing RDBMS, a UNIX server or other platform, you may want to explore these options. (Or you could reconsider the free Perl scripts options described previously.)

Also in this category are customized packages and environments, such as those from WebInk and WebClerk. If you have a specific database-serving need, for which you want a well-developed set of tools, you should look to these products. However, you will not have the generality of some of the other solutions.

13.4 Examples

In this section, we show how to serve databases on the Web with two low-cost solutions. The first involves a combination of commercial software and freeware, FileMaker Pro and Lasso Lite. The second is a free set of database-handling CGI scripts written in Perl, which offer the basics of managing a simple, flat-file database.

13.4.1 FileMaker Pro and Lasso Lite

FileMaker Pro by FileMaker Corporation is a popular, inexpensive DBMS for the Mac OS. You may already be using a version of FileMaker for your database needs. To get existing or new FileMaker databases on the Web, you have two options:

1. Upgrade to FileMaker Pro 4.0, which has Web-publishing capabilities built in.
2. Use one of the tools that enable you to publish databases from FileMaker (version 4.0 or earlier) on the Web.

For this example, Dave had FileMaker Pro 3.0 installed on his Macintosh at work and was looking for an inexpensive—preferably free—solution that wouldn't expire after 30 days. His second requirement was that it be easy to install and begin using the demos. Lasso Lite from Blue World Communications fit the bill (see Table 13–4).

Table 13-4 Lasso Lite

Home page	*http://www.blueworld.com/lasso/lasso_lite/lite.html*
Downloads	*http://www.blueworld.com/lasso/lasso_lite/-ll_download.html*
Documentation (also included with download)	*http://www.blueworld.com/lasso/lasso_lite/-readme.html*
E-mail discussion group	*http://www.blueworld.com/lists/lasso/*

To install Lasso Lite (assuming you have already installed your Web server software and FileMaker Pro) takes only a few steps.

1. Download and unstuff the Lasso Lite .hqx file.
2. Double-click the Lasso Lite installer. Tell the installer where to put the Lasso Lite folder. A likely choice, although not necessary, is inside your Web document root folder.

3. To run the provided demos right away, move the Lasso Lite folder (optionally renaming it from LassoLite_1.x.x to simply LassoLite) into your Web folder hierarchy.
4. The Lasso Lite ACGI is ready to run. (The full Lasso product also comes as a Web server plug-in.)

To test Lasso Lite using one of the examples provided by Blue World, first open the database file in the example directory. Then use your Web browser to look at http://<your.host.name>/LassoLite/Examples/<ExampleName>, where you fill in your host name and the demo name. Dave's installation included an employees database and a discussion forum.

Besides testing your installation, the examples also provide the quickest way to publish your own FileMaker files. Lasso and Lasso Lite work as HTML preprocessors; you embed commands within form tags and as special Lasso tags that specify database fields and operations directly into HTML files. The example files include extensive comments explaining how the various tags and format files work. (Lasso and Lasso Lite use format files, HTML files with embedded commands as placeholders for database fields and data, to specify how to display database records and database search results, or "hit lists.")

As an example of database serving, Dave modified the employees example to create a simple calendar program that his group at SDSC (External Relations) could use over the Web. With Lasso Lite and FileMaker 3.0, the calendar allowed anyone to add an event to the calendar or search the calendar. (Lasso Lite does not support deleting or updating records.) Rather than going through the search and format files in great detail, we show what the client sees when using the calendar database. Figure 13–1 shows the opening form, which allows a user to perform a simple date search to get, for example, the week's events.

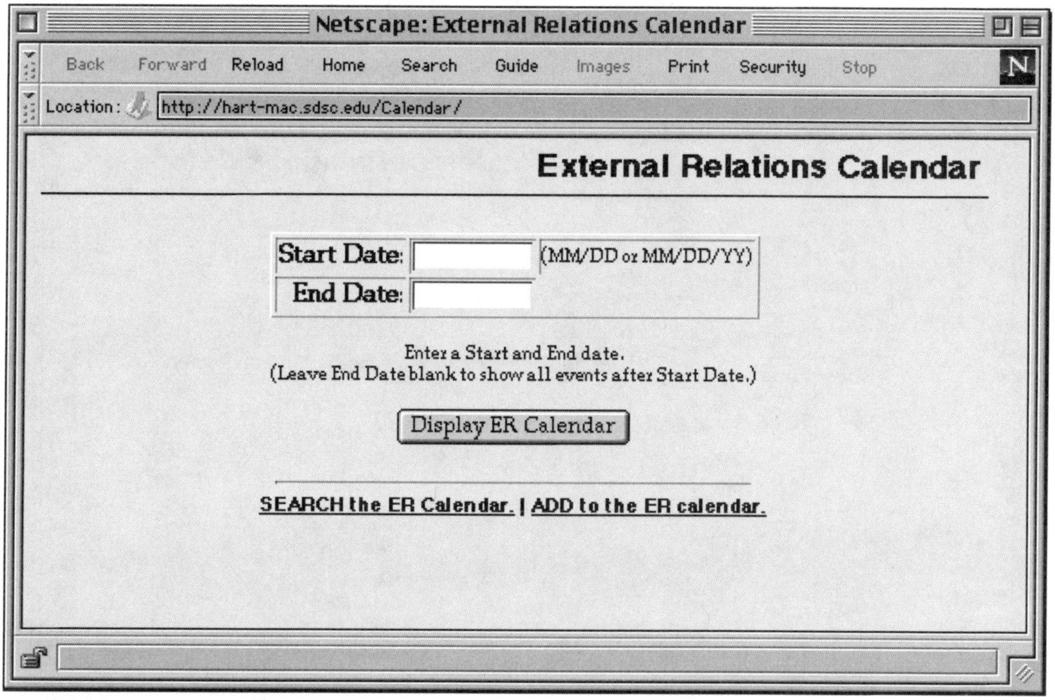

Figure 13-1 Lasso Lite Search Form

Figure 13–2 shows the beginning of the "hit list" of matching records resulting from a search for all events after February 11.

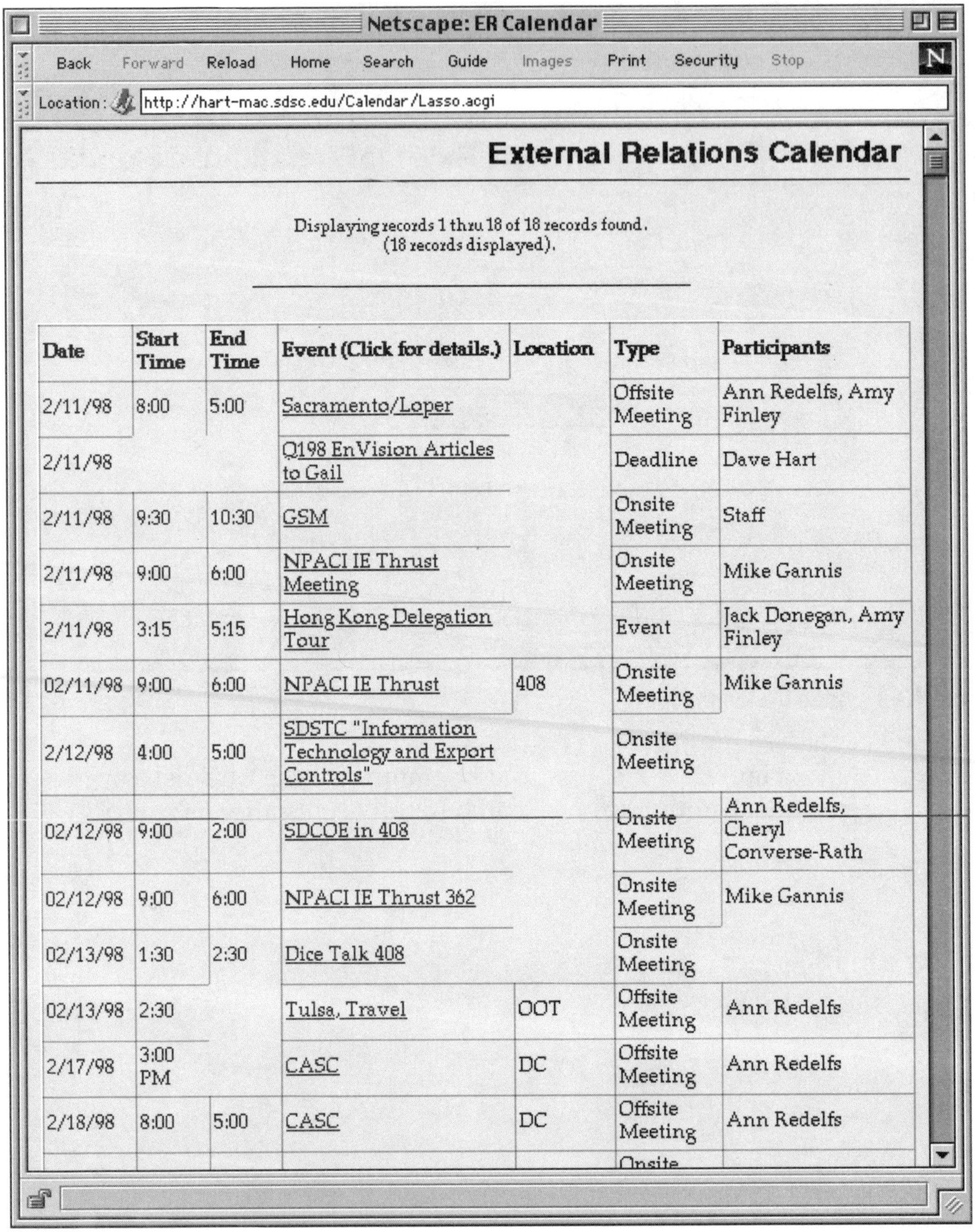

Date	Start Time	End Time	Event (Click for details.)	Location	Type	Participants
2/11/98	8:00	5:00	Sacramento/Loper		Offsite Meeting	Ann Redelfs, Amy Finley
2/11/98			Q198 EnVision Articles to Gail		Deadline	Dave Hart
2/11/98	9:30	10:30	GSM		Onsite Meeting	Staff
2/11/98	9:00	6:00	NPACI IE Thrust Meeting		Onsite Meeting	Mike Gannis
2/11/98	3:15	5:15	Hong Kong Delegation Tour		Event	Jack Donegan, Amy Finley
02/11/98	9:00	6:00	NPACI IE Thrust	408	Onsite Meeting	Mike Gannis
2/12/98	4:00	5:00	SDSTC "Information Technology and Export Controls"		Onsite Meeting	
02/12/98	9:00	2:00	SDCOE in 408		Onsite Meeting	Ann Redelfs, Cheryl Converse-Rath
02/12/98	9:00	6:00	NPACI IE Thrust 362		Onsite Meeting	Mike Gannis
02/13/98	1:30	2:30	Dice Talk 408		Onsite Meeting	
02/13/98	2:30		Tulsa, Travel	OOT	Offsite Meeting	Ann Redelfs
2/17/98	3:00 PM		CASC	DC	Offsite Meeting	Ann Redelfs
2/18/98	8:00	5:00	CASC	DC	Offsite Meeting	Ann Redelfs
					Onsite	

Figure 13-2 Results of Calendar Search

Figure 13–3 shows a detailed event record, displayed by selecting one of the events from the hit list.

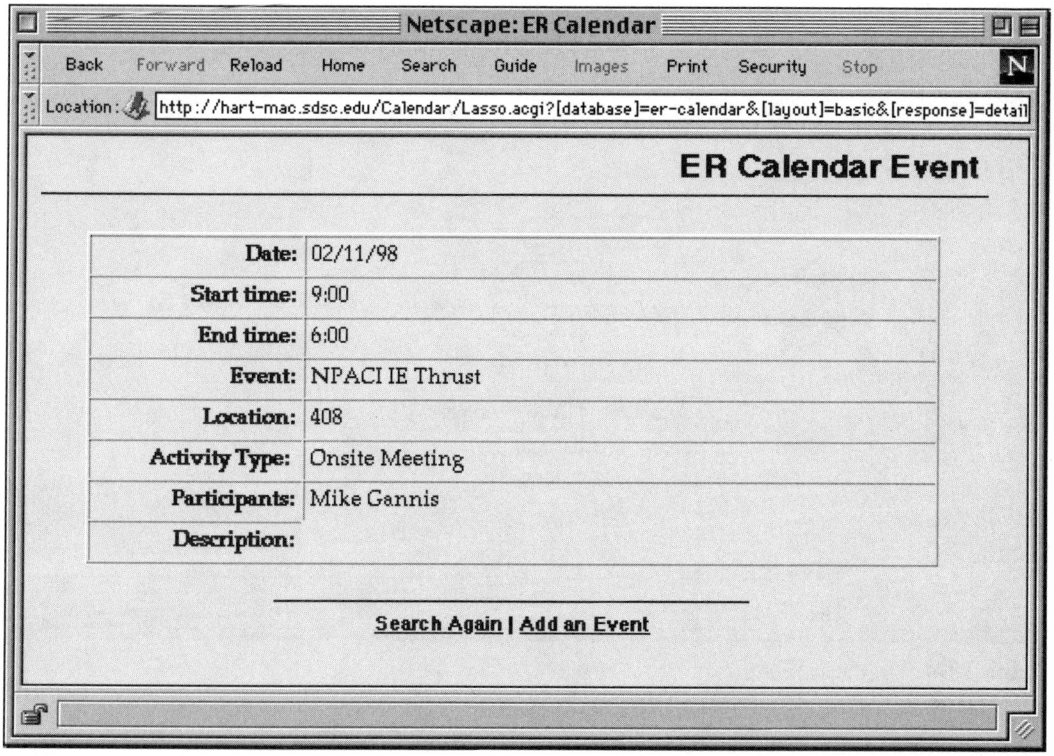

Figure 13-3 Detailed Event Record

Finally, Figure 13–4 shows the form for a more complex search of the calendar, which allows searches on most of the fields. The Lasso-tagged HTML files for the calendar example are available from the book's Web site.

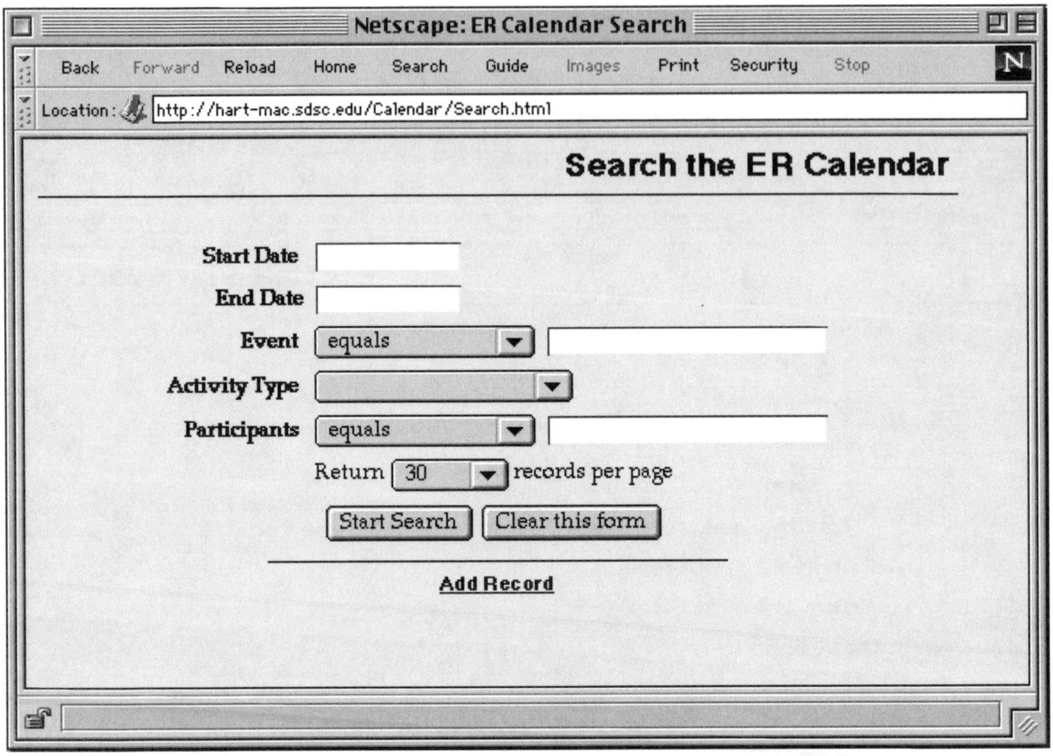

Figure 13-4 Full Search Form

13.4.2 Perl Flat-file Database

If you plan on serving only small databases with ASCII text records, you may find that a simple flat-file database system will meet your requirements with a minimum of fuss. Here we provide such a database system, implemented as a collection of Perl CGI scripts.

This example is based on the Simple Perl Database by Brent Michalski at

http://www.inlink.com/~perlguy/simple/

However, this set of scripts presents several issues for a Mac Web server. Primarily, the file-locking code, written for UNIX, did not work in MacPerl (or at least in MacPerl on Dave's Mac). The second issue is more subjective. The original code used the cgi-lib.pl library, and although cgi-lib.pl works and is available for the Mac, most CGI

Perl scripts these days have moved toward the object-oriented CGI.pm package. (CGI.pm also happens to be included with the MacPerl distribution.) So Dave ported the scripts to MacPerl using CGI.pm. We present the code below, and it is also available on the book's Web site.

The DBMS consists of six files:

- add.cgi—CGI script to add a record to the database.
- search.cgi—CGI script to search the database.
- modify.cgi—CGI script to modify a record.
- delete.cgi—CGI script to delete a record.
- database.pl—A set of file and database subroutines.
- Simple.pm—The package that defines the format of database records.
- phonebook.data—The database file.

Customizing the scripts for your own use involves changing Simple.pm to reflect the record format, deciding on a name for your database file, and modifying the four CGI scripts where they refer to Simple.pm, phonebook.data, and the field names. You should not have to modify database.pl.

To get this Perl DBMS up and running in MacPerl, you need to install the CGI extension that comes with the MacPerl distribution. (Move the file "CGI script" from the MacPerl CGI folder to the MacPerl Extensions folder.) Then save the four .cgi files as CGI scripts, and save database.pl as plain text. When passed the proper field values from a Web form, you will have a working database.

We'll start with the add.cgi script. (For now, assume the database.pl and Simple.pm files work.) The important line to note here is

```
use CGI qw/:all/;
```

"Use CGI" tells Perl to use an external package, in this case the CGI.pm package. The "qw/:all/" tells Perl also to import all the predefined shortcuts for working with CGI, forms, and HTML. In addition to simplifying the syntax later on, it automatically performs all the reading in and parsing of the query string passed to the script from the Web form. So now all you have to do is add the record. In brief, the script gets the system time and uses that as the unique key for the record to be added, creates a record by concatenating the key with the form field values, and adds it to the file.

```
#!perl

####################################################
# This file adds a record to the datbase.          #
####################################################

## Use the CGI.pm package and import all the HTML and
## CGI shortcuts. The first call to any shortcut --
## here the call to 'param' -- automatically creates
## a new CGI object, and reads and parses the
## form input. Very cool.

use CGI qw/:all/;

## Get the database subroutines.
require "database.pl";

$key=time();

$t="|";

$record=$key.$t.
        param('name').$t.
        param('email').$t.
        param('phone').$t.
        param('notes');

&AddRecord("phonebook.data","add.html");
```

Now here's the search.cgi script. The comment lines should explain the gist of this method: The key from the search form is passed to the search subroutine (in database.pl) and all the matching records are displayed. You need to modify the "print" statements to change how the records are displayed.

```
#!perl

################################################
# This file is for searching the datbase.      #
################################################

## Use the CGI.pm package, importing all HTML
## and CGI shortcuts. Automatically reads and
## parses the form input.

use CGI qw/:all/;

## Get the database subroutines.
require 'database.pl';

## Gets the "key" from the search web form.
$search=param('key');

## Call the search subroutine to find matches.
## Matches returned in $array.
&search("phonebook.data","Simple");

## Count the number of matches.
$count=@array;

## Start output HTML. header, start_html, p, hr, etc
## are all shortcuts imported from CGI.pm
print
  header,
  start_html(-title=>"Search Results",
             -BGCOLOR=>"#FFFFFF",
             -BACKGROUND=>"$background",
             -TEXT=>"$font"),
  center(h2("Search Results"),
  p("There were $count matches to your search!")),
  hr, p,
  "<BLOCKQUOTE>\n",
  "<TABLE BORDER=1 CELLPADDING=3>",
   TR( th("Name"),
       th("E-mail"),
       th("Phone"),
       th("Notes"));
```

```
## Loop $count times and display each match
## in a separate table row.
for($x=0;$x<$count;$x++) {

     $name=$array[$x]->name;
     $email=$array[$x]->email;
     $phone=$array[$x]->phone;
     $notes=$array[$x]->notes;

     print TR( td($name), td($email), td($phone), td($notes));
  }

## Finish the HTML.
print
  "</TABLE></BLOCKQUOTE>\n",
  hr,
  center(h3(a({-href=>"search.html"}, "Search again."))),
  end_html;
```

Next, the modify.cgi and delete.cgi records are very similar, so we'll show them both in succession. Both take a search string for identifying the record to modify or delete, let the user choose from multiple matches if necessary, and let the user make changes or confirm the deletion as appropriate. Since each of these steps involves a separate call to the script, the lines "CGI::delete_all()" are required to clear the query string parameters across invokations. (The "CGI::" is necessary because the delete_all method is not one of the imported shortcuts.)

```
#!perl

##########################################################
# This file is for modifying records in the datbase.    #
##########################################################

## Use the CGI.pm package, importing all HTML and CGI
## shortcuts. Form input is automatically read and parsed.
use CGI qw/:all/;
```

```
## Get the database subroutines.
require 'database.pl';

## Sets $search to the "key" from the web form.
## &search returns an $array of matches.
$search=param('key');
&search("phonebook.data","Simple");

## Count the number of matches returned.
$count=@array;

## If count was greater than 1, display all the matches
## so the user can pick one.
if($count > 1) {

  ##  Clear the past form values to make sure the
  ##  search key does not replace the record key when
  ##  modify.cgi is called the next time.
  ##  Since delete_all is not a shortcut, we must specify
  ##  the CGI package.

  CGI::delete_all();

  ## Call the subroutine that handles multiple matches.
  &multi("modify.cgi","name","email","phone");
}

## If count was 1 AND we didn't pass 'changeit' in via the
## QUERY_STRING, this means we have found 1 match.
## Now display the record to let the user make changes.

elsif(($count == 1) && (param('confirm') ne "changeit")) {

  ## Read in the first element of the results array.
  ## We have already verified there was only one match.
  $key=$array[0]->key;
  $name=$array[0]->name;
  $email=$array[0]->email;
  $phone=$array[0]->phone;
  $notes=$array[0]->notes;

  ##  Clear the past form values.
  CGI::delete_all();
```

```
   ## Display the data in an HTML form.
  print
    header,
    start_html(-title=>"Modify record",
               -BGCOLOR=>"#FFFFFF"),
    center( h2("Modify Record"),
    p("Make changes to record below, and press Modify button to
save changes.")),
    hr,
    start_form("POST", "modify.cgi"),
    hidden(-name=>"confirm", -value=>"changeit"),
    hidden(-name=>'key', -value=>$key),
    center(
     table({-border=>"1", -cellpadding=>"3"},
      TR( th("Name:"),
          td( textfield(-name=>'name',-value=>$name))),
      TR( th("E-mail:"),
          td( textfield(-name=>'email',-value=>$email))),
      TR( th("Phone:"),
          td( textfield(-name=>'phone',-value=>$phone))),
      TR( th("Notes:"),
          td( textfield(-name=>'notes',-value=>$notes))),
      TR('<TD COLSPAN=2 ALIGN=CENTER><INPUT TYPE=SUBMIT
VALUE="Modify"></TD>'))),
    end_form,
    end_html;
}

## When user has modified the record, we
## call WriteChange to save the changes.
else {

  $t="|";  ## field delimiter.

  ## Create the $record from the form input.
  $record=param('key').$t.
          param('name').$t.
          param('email').$t.
          param('phone').$t.
          param('notes');

  &WriteChange($search,"phonebook.data","","","modify.html");
}
```

```
#!perl

###########################################################
# This file is for deleting records in the datbase.      #
###########################################################

## Use the CGI.pm package, importing all HTML and CGI
## shortcuts. Form input is automatically read and parsed.
use CGI qw/:all/;

## Get the database subroutines.
require 'database.pl';

## Sets $search to the "key" from the web form.
$search=param('key');
&search("phonebook.data","Simple");

## Count the number of matches returned.
$count=@array;

## If count was greater than 1, display all the matches
## so the user can pick one.
if($count > 1) {

  ##  Clear the past form values to make sure the
  ##  search key does not replace the record key when
  ##  modify.cgi is called the next time.
  ##  Since delete_all is not a shortcut, we must specify
  ##  the CGI package.

  CGI::delete_all();

  ## Call the subroutine that handles multiple matches.
  &multi("delete.cgi","name","email","phone");
}

## If count was 1 AND we didn't pass 'changeit' in via the
## QUERY_STRING, this means we have found 1 match.
## Now display the record to let the user make changes.

elsif(($count == 1) && (param('confirm') ne "deleteit")) {
```

```
  ## Read in the first element of the results array.
  ## We have already verified there was only one match.
  $key=$array[0]->key;
  $name=$array[0]->name;
  $email=$array[0]->email;
  $phone=$array[0]->phone;
  $notes=$array[0]->notes;

  ##  Clear the past form values.
  CGI::delete_all();

  ## Display the data in an HTML form.
  print
    header,
    start_html(-title=>"Delete Record",
               -BGCOLOR=>"#FFFFFF"),
    center( h2("Delete Record"),
    p("Click the Delete button to confirm.")),
    hr,
    start_form("POST", "delete.cgi"),
    hidden(-name=>"confirm",-value=>"deleteit"),
    hidden(-name=>'key',-value=>$key),
    center(
     table({-border=>"1",-cellpadding=>"3"},
      TR( th("Name:"),
          td( textfield(-name=>'name',-value=>$name))),
      TR( th("E-mail:"),
          td( textfield(-name=>'email',-value=>$email))),
      TR( th("Phone:"),
          td( textfield(-name=>'phone',-value=>$phone))),
      TR( th("Notes:"),
          td( textfield(-name=>'notes',-value=>$notes))),
      TR('<TD COLSPAN=2 ALIGN=CENTER><INPUT TYPE=SUBMIT
VALUE="Delete"></TD>'))),
    end_form,
    end_html;
}

## When user has confirmed the delete request,
## call DeleteRecord to do the deed.
else {
  &DeleteRecord($search,"phonebook.data","","","delete.html");
}
```

The Simple.pm file specifies the Simple database format. You can use the Simple.pm file as a template for defining a different type of database. Note that each of the previous scripts refer to the "Simple" database type, you must edit them to refer to your new database.

```
package Simple;   # This is case-sensitive!

sub new {
  my $class = shift;
  my $self = {};

  if (defined $_[0]) { $self->{key}    = shift; }  # Don't
modify!
  if (defined $_[0]) { $self->{name}   = shift; }
  if (defined $_[0]) { $self->{email}  = shift; }
  if (defined $_[0]) { $self->{phone}  = shift; }
  if (defined $_[0]) { $self->{notes}  = shift; }

  bless $self, $class;
  return $self;
}

sub key {   # Don't modify!
  my $self = shift;
  $self->{key};
}

sub name {
  my $self = shift;
  $self->{name};
}

sub email {
  my $self = shift;
  $self->{email};
}
```

```
sub phone {
  my $self = shift;
  $self->{phone};
}

sub notes {
  my $self = shift;
  $self->{notes};
}

1;
```

Finally, the database.pl file contains subroutines that don't have to change if you want to change the database format. Note that the subroutines must be called from within a script that includes the "use CGI qw/:all/;" line. Also note that the search subroutine (used by search.cgi, modify.cgi and delete.cgi) searches all fields for occurrences of the match string.

```
##############################################
# Filename: database.pl                      #
#       By: David Hart                       #
#     Date: 27 Feb 98                        #
# Common database subroutines                #
# ported to CGI.pm package and MacPerl from  #
# Michalski's versions that used cgi-lib.pl  #
# for Unix. Original code available at       #
# http://www.inlink.com/~perlguy/simple/     #
##############################################
```

```
# Info from original version.
####################################
# Filename: database.sub           #
# By: Brent Michalski              #
# Date: 30 May 97                  #
# Last Modified: 18 Jun 97         #
# This file is used for database   #
# access.                          #
# Also, I have tacked on other     #
# commonly used functions for ease #
# of use in programming.           #
####################################

# Scripts calling these subroutines must include the
# line -->  use CGI qw/:all/;
# Mac file locking routines in the Mac::Files.pm package.
use Mac::Files;

##################################################################
### Add record
##################################################################
sub AddRecord{

  $file=$_[0];
  $returnTo=$_[1];

  open (WRITE,">>$file") || die "Error: $!\015\012";
  Mac::Files::FSpSetFLock($file);   # Lock the file
  print WRITE "$record\n";

  Mac::Files::FSpRstFLock($file);   # Unlock the file
  close(WRITE);

  print
    header,
    start_html(-title=>"Record Added",
               -BGCOLOR=>"#FFFFFF",
               -BACKGROUND=>"$background",
               -TEXT=>"$font"),
    center(h2("Record Added!"),
    hr, p,
    h3(a({-href=>"$returnTo"}, "Add another."))),
    end_html;
```

```
return;
}
####################################################################
### End of Add.
####################################################################

####################################################################
### Search subroutine.
####################################################################
# Open a file, search line by line for
# matches meeting the criteria supplied
# via a Web page.  Matches are stored
# in an array called $array[x].
#
# This routine takes 2 arguments:
# 1)  The database file name.
# 2)  The module name, which describes the record format.
#
# Calling program must put search criteria in
# the variable $search.

sub search{

  $req=$_[1];

  require ($req.".pm");
  $a=0;

  open (SEARCH,$_[0]) || die;
  Mac::Files::FSpSetFLock($_[0]);    # Lock the file.

  while(<SEARCH>)       # Loop through the file.
    {
      $_=~s/\"//g;      # Get rid of quotes.
      if(/$search/i){
        my @test=split(/\|/,$_);
        $array[$a] = new $req(@test);
        $a++;
      }
    } # End of while loop means end of file.

  Mac::Files::FSpRstFLock($_[0]);    # Unlock the file.
  close(SEARCH);

  return;
}
```

```
####################################################################
### End of Search subroutine.
####################################################################



####################################################################
### Multi subroutine.
####################################################################
# This function displays multiple matches and allows
# you to choose an action to take on them.
#
# This routine takes 6 arguments:
#   1) The action for form to take when submitted.
# 2-4) Field names to display part of each record.
#   5) Background you wish to use (optional).
#   6) Font color (optional).

sub multi{

  $action=$_[0];
  $item1=$_[1];
  $item2=$_[2];
  $item3=$_[3];
  $background=$_[4];
  $fontColor=$_[5];

  print
    header,
    start_html(-title=>"Multiple records found",
               -BGCOLOR=>"#FFFFFF",
               -BACKGROUND=>$background,
               -TEXT=>$fontColor),
    center(
    h2("Multiple Matches"),
    p("There were multiple matches...", br,
      "Please choose the item to use.")),
    hr;

  for($i=0;$i<$count;$i++) {

    $key=$array[$i]->key;

    print
      start_form(-method=>"POST",-action=>$action),
      center( table({-border=>"1",-width=>"90%"},
        TR(
```

```
          hidden(-name=>'key',-value=>$key),
          td({-width=>"25%"}, $array[$i]->{$item1}),
          td({-width=>"25%"}, $array[$i]->{$item2}),
          td({-width=>"25%"}, $array[$i]->{$item3}),
          td({-width=>"25%"}, submit(-value=>"Select"))))),
      end_form;
  }

  print end_html;

 return;
}
#################################################################
### End of multi subroutine.
#################################################################


#################################################################
### WriteChange subroutine.
#################################################################
# Modifies a file by creating a copy of the file
# and then overwriting the old one with the new.
#
# Takes 5 arguments:
# 1) Record key.
# 2) Database file.
# 3) Background for results page (optional).
# 4) Font color (optional).
# 5) URL for 'back to' link.

sub WriteChange{

  $key=$_[0];
  $file=$_[1];
  $background=$_[2];
  $font=$_[3];
  $returnTo=$_[4];
  $newfile=$file.".new";

  open (WRITE,">$newfile") || die;
  Mac::Files::FSpSetFLock($newfile);  # Lock the file

  open (READ, "$file") || die;
  Mac::Files::FSpSetFLock($file);     # Lock the file

 while(<READ>){
    if(/$key/){
      print WRITE "$record\n";
```

```
      }
    else {
      print WRITE "$_";
    }
  } # End of while

  Mac::Files::FSpRstFLock($file);     # Unlock the file
  close(READ);
  Mac::Files::FSpRstFLock($newfile);  # Unlock the file
  close(WRITE);

  rename $newfile, $file;

  print
    header,
    start_html(-title=>"Record Modified",
               -BGCOLOR=>"#FFFFFF"),
    center(h2("Record Modified")),
    hr,
    p("Back to:", a({-href=>"$returnTo"}, $returnTo)),
    end_html;

return;
}
##################################################################
### End of WriteChange subroutine.
##################################################################


##################################################################
### DeleteRecord subroutine.
##################################################################
# Deletes the record from a file.
#
# Takes 5 arguments:
# 1) Record key.
# 2) Database file.
# 3) Background for results page (optional).
# 4) Font color (optional).
# 5) URL for 'back to' link.

sub DeleteRecord{

  $key=$_[0];
  $file=$_[1];
  $background=$_[2];
  $font=$_[3];
```

```
  $returnTo=$_[4];
  $newfile=$file.".new";

  open (WRITE,">$newfile") || die;
  Mac::Files::FSpSetFLock($newfile);  # Lock the file

  open (READ, "$file") || die;
  Mac::Files::FSpSetFLock($file);     # Lock the file


  while(<READ>){

    if(/$key/){
     # Do nothing because we want to get rid of the record.
    }
    else {
      print WRITE "$_";
    }
  } # End of while

  Mac::Files::FSpRstFLock($file);     # Unlock the file
  close(READ);
  Mac::Files::FSpRstFLock($newfile);  # Unlock the file
  close(WRITE);

  rename $newfile, $file;

  print
    header,
    start_html(-title=>"Record Deleted",
               -BGCOLOR=>"#FFFFFF"),
    center(h2("Record Deleted")),
    hr,
    p("Back to:", a({-href=>"$returnTo"}, $returnTo)),
    end_html;

return;
}
###################################################################
### End of DeleteRecord subroutine.
###################################################################

1;
```

CHAPTER 14

Kitchen of the Future (Emerging Server Technology)

Ingredients

- Rhapsody
- Webcasting
- Style sheets, dynamic HTML, and XML
- Collaborative environments and CORBA

This brings us to the end of our meal. All good things must come to an end. However, with dining, the end of one meal only means that it is time to plan for the next. It's time to re-examine your menu, the wishes of your customers, and the specials at the supermarket.

14.1 Rhapsody and Mac OS X

For organizations using Macintoshes for their Internet information servers, one of the most talked-about Web developments is not some new file format, Java capability, or HTML extension, but the arrival of the first customer release of Rhapsody. In late 1996, Apple acquired NeXT Software, the developers of NeXTStep. Rechristened OpenStep, NeXTStep allowed Apple to accelerate its time line for producing a so-called "modern" and "high-performance" operating system.

As this book was going to print, Apple announced a shift in its plans for Rhapsody and the Mac OS. The original Rhapsody plan described a dual operating system future: Rhapsody for the high-end server market and the Mac OS for the bulk of the Apple market. Even though the Mac OS would work alongside Rhapsody (in the so-called Blue Box), this plan was a plan of divergence. Developers really wanted it all—the modern, high-performance benefits of Rhapsody and the familiar, installed user base of the Mac OS. Enter Mac OS X.

The new plan is a plan of convergence: Mac OS 8 will see some substantial upgrades to versions 8.5 and 8.6 in late 1998 and early 1999, while the first (and probably last) Rhapsody customer release remains on track for late 1998. Then, later in 1999, Rhapsody and the Mac OS will converge as Mac OS X. Mac OS X will run existing Mac OS applications without changes and include Rhapsody's modern, high-performance features. And developers will still be able to take advantage of Rhapsody's so-called Yellow Box to develop applications that will run on both Macs and PCs.

Apple's plan will let you follow two paths with your Mac Web server. On the one hand, if you have a high-volume, heavy traffic site, Rhapsody's features may make it a worthwhile upgrade for your Mac Web server while you wait for Mac OS X. On the other hand, continuing with your Mac OS-based server will provide a nearly painless upgrade path to the performance of Mac OS X. All that having been said, we now describe some of the features of Rhapsody (and eventually Mac OS X) that your Web server will benefit from.

In the technically driven world of operating systems, it's important to remember that "modern" refers to low-level issues such as preemptive multitasking and memory protection and not to a system's modern user interface and ease of use. "High performance" describes the performance of system tasks and not the day-to-day productivity of the system's users.

However, as an organization's Internet serving needs grow, these performance issues do take on greater importance. Ideally, then, what you would like is an operating system that combines the Mac OS ease of use with the low-level performance of UNIX.

With a Mach *kernel* and UNIX as its base and a Mac-like graphical user interface on the surface, Rhapsody has the potential to offer an express drive-thru for the clients of your Internet information kitchen. What follows is an overview and some technical details of Rhapsody that were available at the time of writing. Assuming Apple continues to meet its delivery deadlines, the customer release of Rhapsody should be available by the time you read this. Table 14–1 lists some sites with the latest Rhapsody news.

Table 14-1 Rhapsody and Mac OS X sites

Location	Description
http://developer.apple.com/macosx/	Apple's Mac OS X site for developers.
http://www.rhapsodyos.com/	Rhapsody news site maintained by Jason Caron and Jason Mortis, including list of applications that have been announced for Rhapsody.
http://www.mediabox.net/rhapsodic	Rhapsodic!, another Rhapsody news site.
http://www.stepwise.com/	An OpenStep/Rhapsody developer site, including Web and ftp sites with OpenStep and Rhapsody software and information.
http://devworld.apple.com/rhapsody/rhapdev/-rhapsody.html	Apple's Rhapsody developer's site.
http://www.apple.com/macos/rhapsody/	Rhapsody information on Apple's Mac OS site, including some screen shots.
http://www.macosrumors.com/rhapinfo.shtml	Mac OS Rumors Rhapsody information site.
http://www.macnn.com/rhapnet/	MacNN's RhapNet.
http://www.kagi.com/inai/rhap/	The Rhapsody User.

14.1.1 Rhapsody Features

Because it combines the best of both the Mac OS and UNIX and so as not to steal the thunder from the successful release of Mac OS 8, Apple has promoted Rhapsody first as an industrial-strength operating system and targeting high-end server applications and applications in publishing, multimedia, Internet and intranet content development and publication, corporate application development, higher education, and engineering and scientific research. Rhapsody has several key features that should make it attractive to organizations serving information to the Internet or an intranet.

High Performance and Stability. Rhapsody will be a stable, modern, fully preempted and memory-protected multitasking environment with built-in capabilities for symmetric multiprocessing. If you don't understand the technical terms, it is enough to know that these are the main drawbacks that detractors of the Mac OS have highlighted in complaining that the Mac OS is not "modern."

In a nutshell, *preemptive multitasking* describes an operating system, such as UNIX, with a scheduler that can switch between running applications, each of which gets its turn for access to the processor. In contrast, the Mac OS has *cooperative multitasking,* in which applications must be coded to allow themselves to give up the processor to another application.

Memory protection describes a system by which the operating system prevents one process from corrupting the memory of any other. UNIX and Windows NT have strong memory protection, while Microsoft Windows 3.1, Windows 95, and the Mac OS do not, although Mac OS 8 offers a limited form of protection.

Symmetric Multiprocessing (SMP) applies only to systems with more than one CPU. SMP operating systems allow any application to take advantage of any or all processors in a system interchangeably.

Internet/Intranet Support. The Mac OS has its strengths in certain areas of Internet usage—access, creation, and delivery—but is often criticized for the speed of its networking capabilities, among other things. Rhapsody, on the other hand, will have complementary strengths in the area of Internet serving, UNIX-style networking and communications, and built-in support for Java.

QuickTime Multimedia. The components of the QuickTime Multimedia Layer (QTML) have become de facto standards for multimedia creation and playback—especially on the Internet. The QTML will be incorporated into Rhapsody. The QTML includes QuickTime, QuickTime VR, QuickDraw 3D, and QuickDraw GX typography.

Ease of Use. Rhapsody will preserve the familiar "look and feel" of the Mac OS user interface, while incorporating improvements from both Apple and NeXT. The NeXTStep environment had a graphical user interface that was as well regarded as the Mac OS interface.

Rapid Prototyping and Application Development. The object-oriented NeXT environment enables streamlined application development, and this feature will remain in Rhapsody. To give you some idea of the potential power of Rhapsody, a popular NeXTStep demo is to build a working word processor—with features similar to and exceeding SimpleText—in about five minutes.

Compatibility. Rhapsody offers PowerPC-native compatibility for the Mac OS and is designed to ensure that existing Mac applications and peripherals can work without modification. The next section covers this in more detail.

14.1.2 Web Serving on Rhapsody

So, should you move your Internet server to Rhapsody when the customer release hits the shelves? More to the point, will you be able to? For Macintoshes used primarily as client systems, the Mac OS will likely be the best bet for most Mac users.

On the other hand, your busy Internet server demands the full power of your hardware for networking and server applications. With Rhapsody, you will have a UNIX environment (BSD 4.4) for this and other high performance applications. At the time of writing, applications such as the Apache Web Server, IRCii, Perl, and Lynx had been ported to and were already running on Rhapsody. The growing list of promised Rhapsody applications at *http://www.RhapsodyOS.com* included other key software such as Social Engineering's Quid Pro Quo, Tenon's WebTen, Purity's WebSiphon, Stalker Software's Communigate Pro messaging server, Symantec's Norton Utilities, and Dantz's Retrospect.

The software will be available to run an information server under Rhapsody, but whether it will pay for your organization to switch depends on how well a Mac OS server is meeting your needs. At the time of writing with only a developer's release of Rhapsody available, few details existed on Web-serving performance for Rhapsody. However, we'll leave you with comments by Social Engineering's Chris Hawk in an interview on MacNN's RhapNet (see Table 14–1) describing tests with a Rhapsody port of Quid Pro Quo.

> Our Rhapsody server performance is excellent—able to completely saturate our 10 BaseT network from an 8600/300. The Mac OS server running on the same machine does not even come close. Apple has said repeatedly that the Rhapsody DR1 release is not optimized, but I'm still very pleased with the performance of the Rhapsody network stack. CGI performance is good, and even Java servlets run pretty quickly despite the early state of the Rhapsody virtual machine. All in all, I think that Rhapsody is going to make a fantastic server platform.

14.2 Webcasting

From the first days of Usenet newsgroups and Gopher, the Internet was seen as a source of information, and that users (clients) would search out and request the information they wanted to have. As originally conceived, the Web continued this idea; Web sites would allow users to visit and view the information they want to find. In doing so, the Web avoided the major downfalls of the television paradigm for distributing information. Namely, with television, viewers have no control beyond changing channels over what information they receive and when. TV viewers are, for the most part, at the mercy of the content providers at the broadcast or cable channel. With the Web, on the other hand, users can get exactly the information they want whenever they want it.

It has not taken long for major commercial organizations to realize that while the Web search-and-find method of information gathering works well from the client's perspective, it does not work well from the perspective of the information providers, who want to send information to clients when it's best for the provider. In other words, the Web needs to be more like television. (Not that Dave is in any way cynical about this development.)

Numerous technologies have been introduced to allow information providers to "push" information to clients. Not surprisingly, the technologies have names reminiscent of television—channels, multicasting, and netcasting, to name a few. The common thread is that, rather than users going to Web sites and collecting information, the Web sites "push" information to users who have tuned into, or subscribed to, those Webcasts.

The technologies in Table 14–2 can be broken down into two main categories, which for our discussion we will call channels and multicasting. Channels refer to methods for having Web-based information delivered to clients rather than waiting for the clients to visit the Web site. Multicasting allows live events to be "aired" over the network to clients who have tuned in.

Table 14-2 Webcasting Sites

Location	Description
http://www.microsoft.com/ie/press/whitepaper/pushwp.htm	A Microsoft white paper on push technologies.
Channel Technologies	
http://www.microsoft.com/ie/ie40/features/actchannel.htm	Description of Microsoft's Active Channels in Internet Explorer.
http://developer.netscape.com/one/netcaster/	Netscape's developer site for Netcaster.
http://www.pointcast.com/	The PointCast Network.
Webcasting	
http://www.yahoo.com/Computers_and_Internet/-Communications_and_Networking/MBONE/	Yahoo! Collection of MBONE links.
http://www.mbone.com/	The MBONE Information Web.
http://www.ipmulticast.com/	The IP Multicast Initiative Web site.
http://www.real.com/server/internet	RealNetworks software for streaming audio and video over the Internet.

14.2.1 Channels

The channel technologies are in the greatest state of flux because each depends on a competing standard. Microsoft's Active Channels and Netscape's Netcaster in particular are caught up in the browser war between Navigator and Internet Explorer.

Active Channels. Internet Explorer 4.0 introduced the ability to receive information over "Active Channels," which describes both the specialized content some Web authors develop specifically for Internet Explorer 4.0 and to the four ways 4.0 can deliver it: in full-screen mode, as a screen saver, on the computer desktop, and through e-mail. When users subscribe to sites containing Active Channel content, an icon appears on the channel bar. Click the channel icon, and the content will be displayed in one or more of the four possible ways, depending on how the Web developer designed it. Full-screen mode is the most common option and gives content developers a larger "window" in which to work. Screen-Saver mode cycles through Active Channel content when the computer is idle. With desktop items, tickers or "minipages" any size or shape are placed directly on the Active Desktop. Channel Mail delivers pages directly to the user's mailbox. Active Channels are built with the Channel Definition Format (CDF), which Microsoft proposed to the World Wide Web Consortium as a channel standard.

Netcaster Channels. Netscape developed its own channel technology that uses open standards-based technologies such as Dynamic HTML, JavaScript, and Java. Netcaster is the component of Netscape Communicator that allows clients to receive these channels. Netcaster requires no server-side changes, no changes to existing Web site content, and no new files, formats, or protocols to learn or maintain. Channels can be viewed on- or off-line, in a browser window or as a full-screen "Webtop." Channels can incorporate animations such as tickers, swooping text, and changing layers of information and be tailored to the platform's screen resolution.

PointCast Network. PointCast, Inc., was one of the companies that started the idea of "push" technology that was quickly picked up by Netscape and Microsoft. PointCast developed client software (in the same way that Active Channels requires Internet Explorer 4 and Netscape Channels requires Netcaster) to view information updates in a window or in a PointCast SmartScreens, which replace screen savers with news, personalized stock tickers, weather reports and other information the user requests.

14.2.2 Multicasting

A problem with Web channels is that information providers must send an individual copy of a message to each subscriber; the server must also remember everyone who has subscribed to a channel. In more technical terms, this is called point-to-point unicast. Clearly, this is not the most efficient use of network bandwidth.

IP multicasting is a more efficient protocol for accomplishing the one-to-many communications goal. IP multicast enables sources to send a single copy of a message to multiple recipients who have requested the information. IP multicast is also more efficient than the familiar television concept of broadcasting, which in the networking arena means that one copy of the message is sent to all nodes on the network whether or not anyone at that node wants to receive the information. Because only one copy of a multicast message will pass over any link in the network and copies of the message will be made only where paths diverge at a router, IP multicast yields many performance improvements and conserves bandwidth.

Currently, the IP multicast protocol has been implemented in the MBONE, or IP Multicast Backbone, on the Internet. The MBONE is a virtual network of IP multicast-based routers that make possible "real-time" communications over the Internet. The MBONE routers are responsible for distributing and replicating the multicast data stream to their destinations as opposed to individual IP hosts.

Software such as Real Networks' RealSystem server allows you to send your own Internet broadcasts, taking advantage of IP multicasting to minimize the bandwidth such broadcasts can consume. While the client-side players are free, the server components for these broadcasts cost several thousand dollars.

▼▼▼

Despite Dave's dislike for turning the Web into television, there are situations where Web channels or multicasting may provide a useful connection between an Internet information provider and a group of users, for example, analysts monitoring the companies in a particular industry. If your organization has such a need, you may want to explore some of the possibilities listed in Table 14–2.

On the other hand, it is not yet clear which of the competing technologies will become popularly adopted, or whether such services are or will become popular enough to merit the additional effort of providing continuously updated information via the Web. After an initial flurry of hype, push technology has lately been downplayed by the computer press.

14.3 Beyond HTML

Amid all the discussions and debates and technologies competing to be Web standards, one common point of agreement has arisen among those creating Web applications: HTML has become a limiting factor to the Web's growth and evolution. Because HTML allows for only the most basic structural and presentation formats, extending the functionality of a Web site involves adding server-side preprocessors (Section 10.5), JavaScript logic (Section 12.2), Java applets (Section 12.3), or client-side plug-ins.

The problem with adding new work-arounds to the limitations of HTML is that the Web has begun moving farther from the original aim of platform-independence just as the platforms for Web browsing are beginning to move away from the traditional computer and monitor: WebTV, palm-top personal organizers, Apple Newtons and eMates, and browsers for the sight or hearing impaired. With these issues in mind, a number of new standards to replace or subsume HTML have arisen.

- *Cascading style sheets* for HTML documents parallel the style sheets familiar to users of word processors or page layout applications.
- *Dynamic HTML* combines HTML, style sheets, and scripts to animate Web pages.
- *XML*, the Extensible Markup Language, allows data providers to define new markup languages appropriate to a document's content.

14.3.1 Cascading Style Sheets

With the recommendation for the HTML 4.0 specification, the World Wide Web Consortium has included support for Cascading Style Sheets (CSS). HTML style sheets parallel the use of style sheets or paragraph styles as they are used in word processors like Microsoft Word or Corel WordPerfect and desktop publishing programs like Quark XPress.

The primary advantage of CSS is the separation of presentation information (the styles) from the structure information (the HTML tags). As a result, the HTML for pages that use CSS will typically have fewer HTML tags because many of the directives used for defining how a section should look, such as the <FONT> tag, appear in the CSS file, not the HTML file. Another advantage of CSS is that an organization can specify the look of its Web pages once—headlines will be in 18-point, chartreuse, sans serif font, paragraphs will have black, 11 point text, be indented 1 pica, and justified—and all pages can link to the same style sheet, guaranteeing the same presentation across the site. Table 14–3 provides some sources on cascading style sheets.

Table 14-3 Cascading Style Sheets

Location	Description
http://www.w3.org/Style/css/	The W3C cascading style sheet site.
http://www.htmlhelp.com/reference/css/	A guide and tutorial to CSS from the Web Design Group.
http://www.stars.com/Authoring/Style/Sheets/	Another CSS tutorial from the Web Developer's Virtual Library.
http://www.yahoo.com/Computers_and_Internet/-Information_and_Documentation/Data_Formats/-HTML/Cascading_Style_Sheets/	The Yahoo! section on CSS.
http://www.hexmac.com/hexmac/engl/webtools/cssedit/-cssedit.html	HexMac's CSS Edit, a commercial CSS1 editor available as a stand-alone application or BBEdit plug-in.
http://www.g-foods.com/w2css/	A Microsoft Word macro for converting Word documents to HTML with CSS. At time of writing, Macintosh version was still forthcoming.

CSS will likely become more widely used very soon. Both Netscape Navigator 4.0 and Microsoft Internet Explorer 4.0 support the use of CSS, but neither supports the full CSS specification, which is still under development.

For a better description of how to get started with CSS, consult the sites in Table 14–3. However, the general idea is straightforward.

1. To link an external style sheet to an HTML document (this is the most common use of style sheets), include the <LINK> tag in the <HEAD> section of your HTML file:

```
<LINK REL=StyleSheet HREF="style.css" TYPE="text/css">
```

2. Create the text file "style.css" in your favorite text editor. Here is a very simple style sheet. This style sheet redefines the HTML tags <BODY>, <P>, <A>, and the six header tags.

```
/* The page will have black text on a white background. */

BODY {    background: #ffffff;
          color: #000000;    }

/* Headers will be dark blue in a sans serif font. */

H1, H2, H3, H4, H5, H6 {
          font-family: Verdana, Arial, Helvetica, sans-serif;
          font-weight: bold;
          background: transparent;
          color: #111199; }

/* Normal paragraph will have the first line indented
   one pica and be justified. */

P    { text-indent: 1pc;
       text-align: justify; }

/* Links will be dark blue, active links red,
   visited links gray. */

A:link    { color: #000099; }
A:active  { color: #FF0000; }
A:visited { color: #666666; }
```

3. Code your HTML document without the extra attributes and font tags normally used to create these effects. Here is a bare-bones HTML file that uses this style sheet.

```
<HTML>
<HEAD>
<TITLE>CSS Example</TITLE>
<LINK REL="STYLESHEET" HREF="style.css" TYPE="text/css">
</HEAD>
<BODY>
<H1>Header level 1</H1>

<H3>Header level 3</H3>

<P>Style sheets let you use the same styles in many
documents.</P>

<P>Updating the style sheet automatically updates the look
of all the pages using that style sheet.</P>

<HR>
<A HREF="http://www.w3c.org/Style/css">See the W3C CSS page
for more information.</A>

<H6>&copy; 1998 David Hart.</H6>
</BODY>
</HTML>
```

4. Place the HTML file and the file style.css in the same folder and view the HTML file with your Web browser. Remove the .css file to see how the file would be displayed in a browser that does not support style sheets.

This example is only the tip of the CSS iceberg. Another use of CSS, as browsers begin to improve support for the specification, includes precise positioning of text and other elements. For designers of Web pages, this promises to be one of the most appreciated features of style sheets. Look at *http://www.w3c.org/Style/css* with Navigator 4.0 or Internet Explorer 4.0 to see style sheets in action.

HexMac's CSSEdit (see Table 14–3) was the first program for editing style sheets. Astrobyte's BeyondPress extension to Quark

XPress (see Table 4–17) can also produce HTML documents with style sheets. CSS functionality will likely be introduced in future versions of most HTML editors, once the browsers implement the CSS standard better.

14.3.2 Dynamic HTML

While cascading style sheets have begun to converge on a standard—to the point that both Netscape and Microsoft are supporting them—the document standard known as *Dynamic HTML (DHTML)* remains a much greater point of contention. (Dynamic HTML is not to be confused with "dynamically generated HTML" that is produced by CGI scripts or database queries.)

In some respects, DHTML is not much more than existing HTML, plus style sheets, plus some JavaScript to add some programming logic to the pages. However, as yet there is no standard DHTML—defined at least in part as DHTML that works the same in both Navigator and Internet Explorer—because of the lack of standards for scripting, CSS, and even HTML tags. Both Netscape and Microsoft claim to offer the best implementation based on the most open standards. It will be up to the World Wide Web Consortium (W3C) to sort this one out. Table 14–4 has some links to DHTML information.

Table 14-4 Dynamic HTML Information

Location	Description
http://www.w3.org/DOM/	The World Wide Web Consortium's page on the Document Object Model, a proposed Dynamic HTML standard.
http://www.microsoft.com/workshop/author/dhtml/	Microsoft's Dynamic HTML site.
http://www.dhtmlzone.com/	Macromedia's Dynamic HTML Zone.
http://www.insideDHTML.com/	Inside Dynamic HTML by Scott Isaacs.
http://www.all-links.com/dynamic/	Large index of Dynamic HTML links.
http://developer.netscape.com/library/documentation/communicator/dynhtml/	Netscape's Dynamic HTML information for developers.

According to the W3C, "'Dynamic HTML' is a term used by some vendors to describe the combination of HTML, style sheets and scripts that allows documents to be animated." In Dynamic HTML, JavaScript code is used to react to the mouse movements of the client user and act upon the elements of an HTML document. For the most part, therefore, DHTML affects the look and feel of a Web site; DHTML is HTML with a makeover.

Based on the W3C definition, there are three concepts behind DHTML: cascading style sheets (Section 14.3.1), JavaScript (Section 12.2), and a *document object model*. The Document Object Model (DOM), again according to the W3C, "is a platform- and language-neutral interface that will allow programs and scripts to access and update dynamically the content, structure and style of documents. The document can be further processed and the results of that processing can be incorporated back into the presented page." In other words, the DOM is how JavaScript "sees" the page when carrying out its instructions. The W3C received several submissions from member companies (read, Netscape and Microsoft) on the way that the object model of HTML documents should be exposed to scripts.

The three main DHTML concepts—CSS, DOM, and JavaScript—are common to both Navigator 4.0 and Internet Explorer 4.0, though the level of support and the specifics of the DOM differ in the details. However, when it comes to formulating a DHTML standard, the technical differences between Netscape's and Microsoft's DOMs become a major stumbling block. These differences currently manifest themselves in the "tricks" required to write JavaScript that runs the same on both browsers and most likely mean that one of the browsers will have to make substantial internal changes to support the final DHTML standard.

Also caught up in the DHTML fray is the ability to include custom fonts with Web pages. Both Netscape and Microsoft have (of course) latched onto completely different standards. As a recommendation, therefore, we suggest you look into DHTML, try out some simple, cross-platform JavaScript additions, and experiment with CSS, but avoid committing yourself to a particular technology before the W3C indicates which way the wind is blowing. Table 14–5 summarizes the similarities and differences between the competing DHTML standards, with both Netscape and Microsoft claiming to be the most open.

Table 14-5 Points of DHTML Agreement and Contention

Common DHTML Elements (Standards Organization)	Netscape-only Elements	Microsoft-only Elements
Cascading Style Sheets (W3C)	Bitstream fonts	OpenType fonts
Document Object Model (W3C)	Event capturing model (top-to-bottom model)	Event bubbling model (bottom-to-top model)
ECMAScript—standardized JavaScript (ECMA)	JavaScript	VBScript
	<LAYER> tag	Direct Animation controls
		Data binding

14.3.3 XML

If DHTML is HTML with a makeover, then XML is HTML on steroids. If you want to *do* something—specifically, perform more general types of computations, perhaps off-line—with information collected or distributed on the Web, HTML and even DHTML will not help. That is where the *Extensible Markup Language (XML)* comes in.

An explanation of the HTML family tree might clarify matters. HTML is derived from the Standard Generalized Markup Language (SGML), an international standard for defining and describing a document's structure. In other words, SGML is a language for defining markup languages—like HTML. Because SGML is so complex, the originators of the Web used SGML to define the much simpler, static HTML. As originally conceived, therefore, HTML was designed to describe a document's *structure,* not its appearance. This is why HTML has six header levels (for levels of sections and subsections) and such "orphan" tags as <BLOCKQUOTE>, <AU> (author), <CITE>, and <FN> (footnote).

As the Web has evolved, HTML has been adopted and used ingeniously to describe a document's appearance, which it was never designed to do. DHTML—with its cascading style sheets, font control, and document scripting—is being developed primarily to address HTML's failings for describing appearance.

On the other hand, XML returns to the Web's roots as a means for distributing structured data. XML is a subset of SGML for defining custom markup languages. In a fashion similar to the way external style sheets are linked to HTML documents, XML documents will link to Document Type Definitions (DTDs) that define the markup tags used in the document. HTML is an example of such a markup language, and as XML becomes more widely adopted, HTML will become essentially the "default" DTD. (XML will also support style sheets through the Extensible Stylesheet Language [XSL], which is a subset of the more powerful Document Style Semantics and Specification Language [DSSSL]. We mention these terms only because you will see them in reading about XML and didn't want them to surprise you.) Table 14–6 lists links to on-line XML resources.

Table 14-6 XML Information

Location	Description
http://www.w3.org/XML/	The W3C XML pages.
http://www.ucc.ie/xml/	An XML FAQ.
http://webreview.com/97/05/16/feature/	*WebReview* article "The XML Files."
http://www.sun.com/sunworldonline/swol-02-1998/-swol-02-xml.html	February 1998 *SunWorld* article, "What's the point of XML?"
http://sunsite.unc.edu/pub/sun-info/standards/xml/why/-xmlapps.htm	"XML, Java, and the Future of the Web" by Jon Bosak of Sun Microsystems.
http://www.sil.org/sgml/xml.html	Good source of XML links, FAQs, and information.
http://www.yahoo.com/Computers_and_Internet/-Information_and_Documentation/Data_Formats/-XML/	The XML section at Yahoo!

There are many benefits to specifying a document's structure because knowing the structure implies you also know something about what the data in the document *mean*. In particular, you can write programs that use structural information to analyze and process an XML document. XML will make new categories of applications possible.

1. Applications that require the Web client to mediate between two or more differently structured databases. Database structure can be incorporated into an XML DTD, which an application can use to translate from one database to another. (CORBA also fills this role. See Section 14.4.1.)
2. Applications that attempt to distribute a significant proportion of the processing load from the Web server to the Web client. In fact, with an XML document and DTD, a client could send data to an entirely different computer for processing off-line.
3. Applications that require the Web client to present different views of the same data to different users. WebTV, palm personal organizers, and other nontraditional Web browsers can be programmed to make more intelligent decisions about displaying XML documents.
4. Applications in which intelligent Web agents attempt to tailor information discovery to the needs of individual users. Because XML documents incorporate more meaning into documents, you can write "robots" that can seek out relevant Web-based information.
5. Application-specific browsers designed for a particular DTD. Biologists might have an XML browser for exploring molecular databases, and social scientists might have an XML browser for statistical viewing of survey or census data.

The second category of applications listed above meshes well with the ideas behind Java. In addition to downloading XML-structured data, a client could also download a prepared Java application for client-side processing. While Java is not the only language in which you might write XML processing applications, it is not unreasonable to say that Java is to XML as JavaScript is to DHTML.

XML will arrive on the Web in the near future. XML does not replace HTML, but work is going on to produce XML versions of HTML (and other popular DTDs) now that the specification for XML 1.0 has been completed. The W3C issued an XML 1.0 recommendation in February 1998.

However, you do not need to scrap or rewrite existing HTML files, even though XML is not backward-compatible with existing HTML documents. To be ready for XML, you should make sure that your HTML documents conform to the W3C HTML 3.2 (or later) specification; such documents can easily be converted to XML. In other words, your HTML should be well formed, which means you should not use "sloppy" HTML, for example, without quotes around attribute values or without end </...> tags. Many HTML authoring tools already produce almost (but not quite) well-formed HTML, which will be readable as "DTD-less" (default) XML. As the XML specification is finalized, authoring tools will be revised to produce well-formed HTML.

14.4 Group and Collaborative Environments

In addition to extending the Web's use for broadcasting and processing, developers are also extending the Web for collaborating among groups. A *collaborative environment* tries to replicate a local environment from a collection of remote groups and the Internet. However, we must also remember that "collaboration" is one of today's buzzwords in the computer industry and the government agencies that fund research, just as you might see the terms "enterprise solutions" or "partnership." In a very broad sense, the Web is, by definition and original intent, a collaboration environment. It was developed to allow physicists to exchange information. When you add the capabilities of CGI and databases, you have a collaboration environment that's virtually equivalent to getting a group of people together for a meeting in the same room. Not quite.

The difference between the Web and a meeting in a conference room (or even a videoconference or conference call) lies in the nature of the interaction. With meetings and phone calls, the interaction is immediate. One person's question, statement, or overhead transparency generates responses—questions, nods of agreement, or quizzical looks, for example—from the other participants.

On the other hand, many Web collaboration projects are efforts to define Web forms, pages and processes that mimic as closely as possible the methods by which groups of people work on the same task. The nature of the Web is such that these environments lack immediate feedback. A message is posted to a threaded message area, or a document is made available in a restricted download area for comments. This sort of collaboration can provide useful tools for limited tasks and may be the most cost-effective solution for a large, geographically dispersed group. Yet, most such projects are supported by telephone calls or meetings outside the Web-based components.

There may, in fact, be no completely satisfying, computer-mediated environment for collaboration, but that has not stopped new tools from being developed. For our discussion, we will highlight several collaboration environments that are under development. (To be fair, most of these tools also require telephones so the collaborators can hear one another; real-time audio is not yet a very cost-effective or efficient use of Internet bandwidth.) Table 14–7 lists some pointers to information on Web collaboration.

Table 14-7 Web Collaboration

Location	Description
General Collaboration Information	
http://www.hypernews.org/HyperNews/get/www/-collaboration.html	The HyperNews archive on Web Collaboration projects, including a list of sites and a message board.
http://www.w3.org/Collaboration/	The W3C pages on Web-based collaboration.
Collaboration Projects	
http://www.cerc.wvu.edu/nlm/nlm.html	Collaboration Technology for Health Care-related Projects at West Virginia University
http://www-itg.lbl.gov/MMC/mmc.html	The Distributed Virtual Microscopy and Microcharacterization project at Lawrence Berkeley National Laboratory.
http://www-ncmir.ucsd.edu/CMDA	The Collaboratory for Microscopic Digital Anatomy (CMDA) at UC San Diego.
http://mice.sdsc.edu	The Molecular Interactive Collaborative Environment (MICE) project at SDSC.
http://collaborate.farallon.com/www/look/ldownload.html	Farallon's Look@Me applet allows person-to-person collaboration from within your Internet browser or as a stand-alone applet.
http://trurl.npac.syr.edu/tango/	The Java-based Tango collaboratory from the Northeast Parallel Architectures Center at Syracuse University.
http://www.ncsa.uiuc.edu/Indices/Software/Research.html	The Habanero, ISAAC, and POS software development work at NCSA.

14.4.1 CORBA

While it does not specifically target network collaboration, the Common Object Request Broker Architecture (CORBA) will likely form the basis for many future Web and Internet developments, including collaborative environments. CORBA is a middleware standard for distributed objects being developed by the Object Management Group (OMG). The OMG is a consortium formed by 13 companies in 1989 and now comprising more than 800 software vendors and end users, including Netscape, Microsoft and the W3C, to promote object technology in distributed computing systems and to reduce the complexity, lower the costs, and speed the introduction of new software applications.

If you're not familiar with the concept of "object-oriented programming," we've probably lost you already, since "distributed object technology" refers simply to an object-oriented view of applications on a network. For the purposes of our discussion, it is enough to picture the world of CORBA in the client-server computing terms we have been using throughout this book. In this case, CORBA can be considered a standard way to create new servers and new clients such that other clients and servers can communicate with them through a well-defined interface.

The central component of CORBA is the Object Request Broker (ORB). (If it helps, you might think of CORBA as the Common *Server* Request Broker Architecture, and the ORB as the *Server* Request Broker.) The ORB encompasses all of the communication infrastructure necessary to identify and locate servers (objects), manage connections, and deliver data. The CORBA ORB is a framework that allows applications to communicate with one another no matter where they are located or who has designed them. Table 14–8 provides links to more detailed information on CORBA.

Table 14-8 CORBA References

Location	Description
http://www.omg.org/news/begin.htm	A good starting point for learning about CORBA.
http://www.omg.org/	The Object Management Group, an industry organization to define and support CORBA.
http://www.acl.lanl.gov/CORBA/	CORBA documentation at Los Alamos National Laboratory.
http://corbaweb.lifl.fr/	The CorbaWeb project at the Laboratoire d'Informatique Fondamentale de Lille (LIFL) in France.

All this is well and good, but how does CORBA affect the Web and Internet collaboration? The Web is an example of a specific client-server relationship: Clients send http requests to Web servers, and the servers respond with the appropriate documents. Usually these documents are in formats that the client browser (and plug-ins) can interpret—HTML, GIFs, JPEGs, QuickTime movies, and so forth.

However, if the Web client tries to communicate with, say, an electron microscope, the http request format, which is designed for requesting documents, does not map well to the sorts of tasks an electron microscope can perform. Thus, the telemicroscopy projects described in Section 14.4.4 originally defined custom microscope session server software, client software, and protocols between them. CORBA and ORBs provide flexibility. With a CORBA server, any number of CORBA clients can be written to make requests of the server.

As the Web continues to grow, inefficiencies in http have led to a W3C activity for HTTP-NG, or HTTP Next Generation. This future Web protocol will be optimized for Internet use, more efficient than HTTP 1.1, and likely provide direct support for remote service invocation models such as CORBA. In this sense, CORBA is like the CGI, except that the "scripts" you run with CORBA might be somewhere else on the network, not only on your server. While this will have no immediate impact on the construction of your Internet server today, CORBA will open up all sorts of interaction and collaboration possibilities for the future.

14.4.2 Person-to-Person: Look@Me

Farallon's Look@Me is a freeware applet that lets you collaborate with another user by providing a real-time view of your collaborator's screen. You can watch the screen activity taking place on the computer of another Look@Me (or Timbuktu Pro) user from within your Internet browser or as a stand-alone application.

With Look@Me, you can collaborate on tasks such as editing documents, reviewing presentations and graphics, or providing just-in-time training and support. However, it is not a complete Web collaboration tool. For starters, Look@Me does not necessarily use the Web, instead using a direct TCP/IP connection to the other user. Second, you will need a telephone to discuss what is happening on your collaborator's screen.

14.4.3 Virtual Worlds: MICE

Despite the inherent limitations of computer-mediated collaboration, there are some advantages in the Web for collaborators. You can, for example, hold your meetings inside a molecule. The Molecular Interactive Collaborative Environment (MICE) project at SDSC, led by Phil in his role as SDSC computational biologist, is developing the technology to create virtual worlds in which collaborating researchers and students can meet to explore the structures of proteins.

MICE is actually a specific application of the more general ICE, or Interactive Collaborative Environment. ICE uses the Virtual Reality Modeling Language (VRML) to build virtual worlds—molecules in the case of MICE—and server technology that lets users exchange Virtual Reality Behavior System (VRBS) commands with collaborators. Normal VRML worlds are single user environments; a client downloads a copy of the world and explores the world in a local browser. ICE extends the Web server to keep track of the users who have "connected to" a VRML world. While each client has a separate copy of the world, users can take control and zoom, rotate, or pan through the world and all collaborating users see these movements on their screens. Because ICE uses the Web, some elements of the world can be hyperlinked to information that gets displayed in the Web browsers of the collaborators.

ICE also has the potential to be used as a distance learning tool. As part of MICE, students at Southwest High School in San Diego are evaluating the project and exploring molecules over the Internet with faculty at the University of California, San Diego. Because ICE is based on the VRML standard, any 3-D world on any topic can be the subject of collaborative exploration.

14.4.4 Tele-instrumentation: CMDA and MMC

Two projects listed in Table 14–7 are extending Web collaboration beyond the realm of networked computers. In both University of California, San Diego's Collaboratory for Microscopic Digital Anatomy (CMDA) and Lawrence Berkeley National Laboratory's Microscopy and Microcharacterization (MMC) platform, researchers can collaborate in real time not only with one another but also with a computer-controlled electron microscope.

While the projects differ in their implementation details, both accomplish similar goals. Because electron microscopes are expensive and relatively scarce scientific instruments, researchers must often schedule time to examine their specimens and travel to the site of the microscope to view the high-resolution images. When researchers are collaborating on a project, they must all travel to the microscope. While the Web can't make more hours in the day, CMDA and MMC are working to make it possible to eliminate the travel to and from the microscope location. With their GridManager and WebScope software, respectively, the geographically separated researchers can control the specimen stage and capture detailed images over the network. Another common feature of both projects is their use of CORBA to communicate between the client users and the microscope control server.

In other words, the collaborative environments created by these projects include not only the human researchers, but also the necessary real-world instruments. The same concepts will also likely be extended to other expensive, scarce instruments, such as telescopes or particle accelerators.

▼▼▼

We could speculate further, but computing technologies not even on the horizon will likely lead to changes on the Web that might seem like magic today. What we will say is that some changes are imminent—Rhapsody, style sheets, Dynamic HTML, and XML are on the way. You may want to put these techniques on the back burners of your Internet kitchen and prepare to use them effectively when they hit the shelves.

• EPILOGUE •

Food for Thought

The feast is over and you should be full. The nature of the human condition is such that tomorrow you will be back at the table wanting another helping. A good cookbook should still have something delicious to offer.

The large, yet select, group of URLs provided in this book resulted from an extended period of Internet surfing. This surfing has left us with two lingering feelings.

The first feeling is sheer awe at the ever-increasing amount of information that is available. The Internet has already become a great reference source for the average family. What is currently lacking is a fast, cheap, and convenient delivery mechanism akin to television. This will come through cable modems, blanket satellite coverage, frame relay, or by some other yet unimaginable medium. At that time we will see a quantum jump in usage, and correspondingly, a quantum jump in the amount of information available to the average family at home. Where the Internet differs from television is that anyone is able to broadcast. Phil can't wait to have such things as his son's little league game schedule and price comparisons from the local supermarkets at his fingertips. Dave will like it when the Web becomes more accessible away from his desktop computer, and he can order up movies-on-demand and get his information without having to sit in front of a keyboard and monitor all day.

The second feeling is that the quality of the material is improving. This has happened since the commercial sector has appreciated the value of the Internet as a tool for providing information and, of course, selling their products. A small business can now be competitive in a world market, which leads to diverse and quality products available to consumers. Macintosh software, particularly from shareware programmers and small developers, is one example of a product category that is taking advantage of the Web.

If these trends continue, it is not hard to image that future generations will have a large part of human collective knowledge at their fingertips and that the Internet will become an increasingly important part of people's lives. It is our hope that, in a small way, this book and the associated Web site will help you provide some of that knowledge and continue to be a useful reference source for some time.

We have so much to offer each other, and with the Internet, there is less excuse than ever for not giving of ourselves.

• APPENDIX • A

Internet-based Resources for Learning the Mac OS

The following are popular Internet-based sources for learning about the Mac OS. If your time is limited, start with the EvangeList Web sites.

- Apple's Mac OS Web sites

  http://www.macos.apple.com

  http://macos.apple.com/macos8/

  http://macos.apple.com/macos/macos_tech.html

  http://macos.apple.com/macos/other_os_info.html

  has the latest news, developments, software, and updates for the Mac OS and Mac OS technologies

- The EvangeList Web sites at

  http://www.evangelist.macaddict.com/

  http://www.evangelist.macaddict.com/apple_tech.html

  http://www.evangelist.macaddict.com/support.html

contain links to all things Macintosh, including Apple Technologies and technical support, on Apple's Web site and elsewhere on the Web.

This is probably the best starting point for Macintosh information on the Web, as it includes links to all the sites listed here and many others.

- The Macintosh Extension Guide

  http://www.madison-web.com/ext/

  is a listing and description of all the available Mac OS control panels and extensions tucked away in the System Folder. For each control panel or extension, this site tells you who needs it, which Mac OS versions use it, and what it does.

- Jon Wiederspan's Macintosh Internet Resources Directory at

  http://host.comvista.com/Internet.tfm

  In searching for Mac OS Internet tools, Dave highly recommends this site. If you're running a Mac Internet server or developing Internet information on a Mac, you can find the tools you need here.

- Nexus Mac Resources at

  http://www.go-nexus-go.com/macresources/

  offers an extensive searchable index of Macintosh-related resources available through the Web and Usenet newsgroups.

- MacHome Journal at

  http://www.machome.com/

  http://www.nowonder.com/machome/techsupport.html

  began offering free tech support via e-mail to Macintosh users at the MacHome/No Wonder Tech Support page when Apple began charging for its telephone technical support. After filling out a Web form, you are promised an e-mail response within 24 hours.

- For a third-party look at Mac OS 8, see

  http://www.macos8.com/

  which includes OS 8 incompatibility issues, an in-depth look at OS 8, as well as information on customizing and optimizing your Macintosh.

- There are a wealth of other Macintosh Web resources. Here are just a few:

MacCentral:	*http://www.maccentral.com/*
MacDirectory:	*http://www.macdirectory.com/*
MacInTouch:	*http://www.macintouch.com/*
MacFixIt:	*http://www.macfixit.com/*
Mac-Managers:	*http://www.mrmac.com/mac-mgrs.html*
Yahoo!:	*http://www.yahoo.com/Computers_and_Internet/-Operating_Systems/Macintosh_OS/*

- And finally, to get a head start on Rhapsody, you might want to visit these sites:

  Apple's Rhapsody info:

  http://macos.apple.com/macos/releases/rhapsody/

  Mac OS Rumors Rhapsody Information Archive:

  http://www.macosrumors.com/rhapinfo.shtml

  http://www.macosrumors.com/rhapsodyapps.shtml

  The Rhapsody OS news site:

  http://www.rhapsodyos.com/

While there is a wealth of information out there on learning or brushing up on the Mac OS, the question to ask is whether this information is better than an introductory or more advanced Mac OS book. The short answer is yes and no. Yes, because there is a wealth of information, much more that can be contained in a single book. No, because this information may be repetitive and not exactly to the point (also true of some books, but not this one, of course).

As far as the Mac OS is concerned, it would seem that at the time of writing the Macintosh community is taking full advantage of the Web for promoting, troubleshooting, and discussing the Macintosh platform and Mac OS. And even before Rhapsody hits the shelves, the Web has the latest information on that next-generation operating system as well.

• APPENDIX • B

HTML Reference Guide

At the time of writing, the W3C had just finalized the HTML 4.0 specification, and neither the Netscape nor Microsoft browsers supported the latest specification. (Most likely, they will both release new versions when the CSS definition is finalized.) If you wish to write HTML that conforms strictly to the standard for a particular version of HTML refer to

http://validator.w3.org/

http://valsvc.webtechs.com/

http://www.cast.org/bobby/
(Also checks for a page's accessibility to people with disabilities.)

http://www.ozemail.com.au/~dkgsoft/html/

Alternatively, if you do not care about the standard, it is suggested that before you invest heavily in the use of an HTML tag, you check its functionality, first with the Web browser(s) you use, and then with the Web browsers you anticipate being used to access your information server.

This is not a summary of all the features of HTML 4.0 or 3.2; Chapter 9 covers where to go for that information. Rather, it is intended as a quick reference to the major features of HTML. If you need more details in a hurry refer to the Yahoo! page on HTML

http://www.yahoo.com/Computers_and_Internet/Software/-Data_Formats/HTML/Guides_and_Tutorials/

or see the W3C's HTML 4.0 specification page:

http://www.w3.org/TR/REC-html40/

The nomenclature used in this appendix, which extends the conventions used throughout this book, is as follows:

```
<IMG ALIGN={TOP/MIDDLE/BOTTOM/LEFT/RIGHT}  SRC="filename">
```

Curly braces {} indicate one of a number of options is permissible—in this case delimited by slashes (/). Common attributes to each tag are provided. HTML tags and their attributes are in uppercase, variables are in lowercase. Where necessary, variables are surrounded by double quotes (").

B.1 Page Layout

<BANNER> ... </BANNER>	Region of text that does not scroll (browser dependent).
<BODY> ... </BODY>	Main body of the document.
<DIV> ... </DIV>	Standard sections of a document.
<HEAD> ... </HEAD>	Document header information.
<Hn> ... </Hn>	Header level where n=1-6.
<HTML> ... </HTML>	Entire HTML document.
<RANGE {attributes}>	Define a section of content for use by a STYLE.
<STYLE {attributes}> ... </STYLE>	Define a style (internal CSS definition).
<TITLE> ... </TITLE>	Appears in the Web browser's title field.

B.2 Paragraph Layout

 	Line break, i.e., begin a new line.
<P>	Paragraph break, as but leave a blank line.

B.3 Text Layout

<ABBREV> ... </ABBREV>	An abbreviation.
<ACRONYM> ... </ACRONYM>	An acronym.
<AU> ... </AU>	Name of an author.
<BLOCKQUOTE> ... </BLOCKQUOTE>	Text quoted from some other source; left and right margins are indented.
<B> ... </B>	Bold.
<BIG> ... </BIG>	Big print.
<CITE> ... </CITE>	A citation.
<CODE> ... </CODE>	An HTML directive.
<DEL> ... </DEL>	Text deleted since a previous version of the document.
<DFN> ... </DFN>	A definition.
<DIR> ... <LI> ... </DIR>	Directory list of items.
<DL> ... <DT> ... <DD> ... </DL>	Definition list, where <DT> is the term and <DD> the definition.
<EM> ... </EM>	Emphasize text.
<FN> ... </FN>	A footnote.
<I> ... </I>	Italics.
<INS> ... </INS>	Text inserted since a previous version.
<KBD> ... </KBD>	A keyboard key.
<LANG> ... </LANG>	Language.
<LH> ... </LH>	The header for a list of elements.
<MENU> ... <LI> ... </MENU>	Menu of items.
<NOTE> ... </NOTE>	Admonishment—a note or warning.

<OL> .. <LI> .. </OL>	Ordered (numbered) lists.
<PERSON> ... </PERSON>	Name of a person.
<PRE> ... </PRE>	Preformatted text, i.e., text is presented literally, except hyperlinks are interpreted.
<Q> ... </Q>	Quotation.
<STRIKE> ... </STRIKE>	Strikethrough text.
<SAMP> ... </SAMP>	Include sample output.
<SMALL> ... </SMALL>	Small print.
<STRONG> ... </STRONG>	Place strong emphasis.
_{...}	Subscript.
^{...}	Superscript.
<TAB>	Force a tab.
<TT> ... </TT>	Typewriter font.
<U> ... </U>	Underline.
<UL> ... <LI> ... </UL>	Unordered (bulleted) list.
<VAR> ... </VAR>	Define a variable.

B.4 Links

<A HREF="URL">anchor_text </A>	A link via anchor_text to another HTML document designated by URL.
<A NAME="anchor_name">anchor _text </A>	A named point in an HTML document to which other links point.
<A HREF="URL#anchor_name">anchor_text </A>	A link via anchor_text to a point #anchor_name in URL.

B.5 Images and Figures

<CAPTION> … </CAPTION>	Descriptive label for a table or figure.
<CREDIT> ... </CREDIT>	Credit a figure.
<IMG HEIGHT=n WIDTH=m ALIGN= {TOP/MIDDLE/ BOTTOM/LEFT/RIGHT} ALT = "image_description" SRC="URL">	In-lined image defined by URL, either a GIF or XBM, ALIGNed with respect to text, and ALT displayed in text-only browsers.
<OVERLAY>	Superimpose an image on a figure.

B.6 Miscellaneous

<!-- comment_string -->	Comment completely ignored by browsers, regardless of content.
<!--#command VAR="variable"-->	Execute command with the associated VAR (server dependent).
<!--#INCLUDE FILE="filename"-->	Include the contents of FILE (server dependent).
&ascii_equivilent;	Use a character literally, e.g., < for less than (<).
<ADDRESS> ... </ADDRESS>	A closing address on a Web page. Has nothing to do with postal addresses.
<BASE HREF="URL">	Base part of a URL prepended to all relative URLs in the document.
<HR SIZE=n WIDTH="m%">	Insert a horizontal rule of optional thickness SIZE and covering WIDTH percent of the browser window.
<ISINDEX>	Describes a database or searchable index.
<LINK REV="RELATIONSHIP" REL="RELATIONSHIP" HREF="URL">	Identifies the e-mail address of the document owner; it is not displayed in the browser.
<META attribute_value>	Meta information provided between <HEAD> … </HEAD> tags, e.g., to define the expiration date of a page.

B.7 Table Layout

<TABLE BORDER= n ALIGN= {LEFT/RIGHT/CENTER/ JUSTIFY/CHAR} CELLSPACING= n CELLPADDING= m BGCOLOR= #bbffee> </TABLE>	Define a table with optional BORDER of thickness n. ALIGN contents in cells, leaving CELLSPACING between CELLS and CELLPADDING between text and cell edge. Optionally set the background color of the table with BGCOLOR.
<CAPTION ALIGN = {TOP/BOTTOM}> </CAPTION>	Define a centered, optionally ALIGNed caption.
<TR ALIGN={LEFT/RIGHT/CENTER/JUSTIFY /CHAR} VALIGN = {TOP/MIDDLE/BOTTOM/ BASELINE} BGCOLOR = #bbffee> </TR>	Define a table row, vertically aligning contents (VALIGN).
<TD COLSPAN=n ROWSPAN=m ALIGN={LEFT/ RIGHT/CENTER/JUSTIFY/CHAR} VALIGN = {TOP/ MIDDLE/BOTTOM/BASELINE} BGCOLOR = #bbffee NOWRAP> </TD>	Define a data cell that optionally spans n columns (COLSPAN) and m rows (ROWSPAN). Optionally prevent contents from wrapping (NOWRAP).
<TH COLSPAN=n ROWSPAN=m ALIGN = {LEFT/ RIGHT/CENTER/JUSTIFY/CHAR} VALIGN = {TOP/ MIDDLE/BOTTOM/BASELINE} BGCOLOR = #bbffee NOWRAP> </TH>	As <TD> but for column headers only.

B.8 Forms Layout

<FORM METHOD={GET/POST} ACTION="URL"> ... </FORM>	Define a form for processing by URL using METHOD.
<INPUT TYPE=TEXT NAME="name" SIZE=n>	A text entry box of n characters with the text associated with the variable NAME.
<INPUT TYPE=PASSWORD NAME ="name" SIZE=n>	As TYPE=TEXT, but with the text not echoed for security reasons.
<INPUT TYPE=CHECKBOX NAME="name" VALUE={CHECKED/NONCHECKED}>	A checked (VALUE=CHECKED) or nonchecked (VALUE=NONCHECKED) checkbox.
<INPUT TYPE=RADIO NAME="name" VALUE={CHECKED/NONCHECKED}>	A radio button (on if VALUE=CHECKED). Radio buttons with the same NAME are grouped.
<INPUT TYPE=SUBMIT VALUE="button_text">	Send form contents to the Web server. VALUE is the text within the button.
<INPUT TYPE=RESET VALUE="button_text">	Clear a form of all information and reset radio buttons, checkboxes, etc. VALUE is the text within the button.
<INPUT TYPE=HIDDEN NAME="text" VALUE="text">	Submit a hidden (i.e., not seen on the form) NAME to the server with VALUE.
<SELECT NAME="name"> <OPTION> "option_text" <OPTION SELECTED>"option_text" </SELECT>	Pop-up menu with multiple <OPTION> tags. SELECTED defines the default <OPTION>. If SELECTED is not specified, the first <OPTION> is the default.
<SELECT NAME="name" MULTIPLE SIZE=n> <OPTION> "option_text" <OPTION SELECTED>"option_text" </SELECT>	Scrollable list of OPTIONs with SIZE rows displayed. MULTIPLE indicates multiple options may be selected. SELECTED defines the default selection, which may be more than one row if MULTIPLE is specified.
<TEXTAREA NAME="name" ROWS=n COLS=m> "optional_text" </TEXTAREA>	Scrollable text area of n ROWS and m COLS (columns), optionally containing "optional_text".

B.9 Frames Layout

<FRAMESET COLS="n,m" ROWS ="n,m"> ... </FRAMESET>	Defines a set of frames, within which each individual frame is defined with the <FRAME> tag. The dimensions of the area containing frames, ROWS, and COLUMNS can be optionally specified.
<FRAME SRC="URL" NAME="name" MARGINHEIGHT=n MARGINWIDTH=m SCROLLING={YES/NO} NORESIZE>	Display the URL in a frame of specified MARGINHEIGHT and MARGINWIDTH, with or without SCROLLING. The frame will resize to remain proportional to the overall window size unless NORESIZE is specified.
<NOFRAME> ... </NOFRAME>	Defines behavior in cases when the Web client recognizes the <NOFRAME> tag, but not the <FRAME> tag.
<A HREF="URL" TARGET="name">	Update the target FRAME with URL.

B.10 JavaScript

<SCRIPT LANGUAGE="JavaScript" SRC="JavaScriptCode.js"> ... </SCRIPT>	Block of JavaScript code. Use either the LANGUAGE or SRC attributes; LANGUAGE if the code is embedded; SRC if it is in a separate file with the extension *.js*.
<INPUT TYPE={BUTTON/CHECKBOX} NAME="name" ONCLICK="JavaScript function">	As the regular <INPUT> tag but with the ONCLICK attribute to define the JavaScript function to be executed.

B.11 Java

<APPLET CODE="code.class" WIDTH=n HEIGHT=m ALIGN={TEXTTOP/TOP/ ABSMIDDLE/MIDDLE/BASELINE/ ABSBOTTOM} HSPACE=n VSPACE=m CODEBASE="directory"> ... </APPLET>	Include an applet called code.class, optionally from the directory CODEBASE. Reserve a WIDTH of n pixels and a HEIGHT of m pixels for the applet on the Web page. ALIGN the applet with respect to the text on the Web page. Leave HSPACE (horizontal space) and VSPACE (vertical space) between the applet and the Web page contents.
<PARAM NAME="name" VALUE="value">	Pass the VALUE associated with NAME to an applet. The <PARAM...> tag lies between <APPLET> ... </APPLET> tags.

Glossary

A general and more extensive list of terms is available from

- Free On-line Dictionary of Computing

  http://wfn-shop.princeton.edu/foldoc/ (US)

  http://wombat.doc.ic.ac.uk/ (Europe)

- Dictionary of Dictionaries

  http://www.refdesk.com/factdict.html

- The Cook Report—An Internet Monthly

  http://pobox.com/cook/glossary.html

Note: The definitions here relate to how the terms are used in this book and may differ slightly from the definitions used by others.

Anonymous ftp A mechanism to get files from or put files to a remote computer when you do not have an account on that remote computer.

Applet Code written in the *Java* language that is downloaded to the client via a Web browser and executed. Frequently used to support animation and continuous *client-server interaction*.

AppleScript A scripting language that is part of the Mac OS, used most often for controlling applications and other elements of the system. It can be used to write *CGI programs*.

AppleTalk A local area networking protocol for connecting Mac OS computers and printers.

ASCII American Standard Code for Information Interchange. A set of 8-bit binary numbers representing the alphabet, punctuation, numerals, and other characters used in text representation.

Attribute A modifier, for example, WIDTH or ALIGN, to an HTML *tag*, such as <IMG>.

Binary file Any file that is not a text file, that is, produces indecipherable output when forced to display as text.

Bit-mapped display A display that supports addressing of pixels (points on the screen) rather than specific characters on a line of length 80 or 132 characters.

Byte code Machine-independent code generated by the *Java* compiler.

Cascading Style Sheets (CSS) An emerging standard for specifying the presentation of an *HTML* document via style sheets, similar to those used to apply paragraph styles in word processing applications.

CERT Computer Emergency Response Team. A government-funded group that, among other things, produces bulletins of known security problems on the more popular operating systems and issues patches (fixes) from the vendors and others. See *ftp://-info.cert.org/pub/* for further details.

CGI Common Gateway Interface. A means of passing information from a Web client browser to a CGI-compliant script residing on a Web server. The *CGI script* will invoke some action, such as the generation of HTML pages that are sent back to the client browser.

CGI program Used interchangeably with *CGI script*. Strictly speaking, a CGI script uses an interpretive language and a CGI program uses a compiled program.

CGI script A file containing an executable program written in an interpretable language, (for example, Perl) that is invoked by the Web client and executed on the Web server.

Character decimal reference A way to refer to special characters in HTML documents. The format is "&#xxx;" where "xxx" is replaced by a three-digit decimal (base 10) number.

Clickable map An image that has a series of *URLs* mapped to different regions of the drawing, thereby providing visual navigation.

Client The user or application making a request of a service provider.

Client-server computing A general type of computer interaction in which a requestor (client) sends a request to a service provider (server) and the server returns a response to the client.

Collaborative environment A technology that tries to replicate a local meeting environment from a collection of remote groups and the Internet.

Common Gateway Interface See *CGI*.

Common log file format A standard file format produced by popular Web servers when logging access to the server.

Component model Also component architecture. A definition of a set of interfaces for creating interoperable software "building blocks." JavaBeans is an example of a component model.

Content document In an HTML *frames* context, the HTML documents that are used to fill each frame. See also *Layout document*.

Cookie A small file with which server-side programs such as *CGI scripts* can store information about a *client* on the client's machine. Cookies are used to overcome the Web's stateless interaction.

CORBA Common Object Request Broker Architecture. A middleware standard espoused by the Object Management Group for creating general and interoperable components of client-server applications.

Database An electronic record-keeping system (also *DBMS*), or a set of records kept by such a system.

Database Management System (DBMS) An electronic record-keeping system that provides functions to add, update, remove, and search for records.

Dedicated connection A connection to the Internet that is maintained at all times (barring technical difficulties). Dedicated connections are usually faster than *nondedicated connections*.

Document object model A platform- and language-neutral way for a Web client to "see" a Web document. This affects how user interactions with the document are handled by *JavaScript* instructions. Netscape and Microsoft use incompatible document object models in their version 4.0 browsers.

Document root directory The top-level directory recognized by the Web server that contains documents to be served. All documents served are found in this directory (folder) or below it in the folder hierarchy. Symbolic links (aliases) to files being served outside this tree may be allowed. Support for symbolic links is Web server dependent.

Domain Name Server (DNS) An Internet server that translates a text host name (your.host.com) into a unique *IP address*.

Dynamic HTML (DHTML) An emerging standard for Web documents that combines *HTML, cascading style sheets*, and standardized *JavaScript* to create animated pages. The standard depends on having a standardized *document object model.*

FAQ Frequently Asked Questions. A useful means of quickly answering the most obvious questions on a particular subject by way of a list server, Web site, or news group.

File extension Any characters following (and including) the last period in a file name.

Filter Software that converts information in one format to the same information in another format.

Flat-file database A database that stores its records one after the other, possibly but not necessarily in text files.

Frames A way to separate a browser window into independently controllable subwindows. Introduced by Netscape, frames have become part of standard HTML. See also *Layout document, Content document.*

Ftp File transfer protocol. Part of the *TCP/IP stack* of protocols controlling file transfer between two computers.

Ftp archive Files accessible by *anonymous ftp*, hopefully organized in a way to make it easy for a user to find information.

GIF Graphics Interchange Format, developed by CompuServe. A popular graphics format supported by Internet information servers.

Gopher Text-based predecessor to the Web. Used a protocol different than *http*, but supported the idea of *hyperlinks*.

GUI Graphical User Interface. The hardware and software needed to address by way of a mouse or some other pointing device an individual point on the display device and solicit a particular response.

Helper applications Applications configured and subsequently invoked from a Web browser to process a *MIME type* not recognized by the browser itself.

Hit A single access to an information server, for example, the downloading of a single Web page or graphic image from a Web server; a single mail message sent to a list server; a single file transfer using ftp. The number of hits is an approximate measure of the amount of activity on a server.

Home page A particular Web page that represents the starting point for viewing a specific body of information.

Host A computer on the Internet with a unique name and/or *IP address*.

Hotlist A list of *URLs* to which the user refers frequently and which are maintained by the client Web browser. Called "Bookmarks" in Netscape Navigator and "Favorites" in Microsoft Internet Explorer.

http HyperText Transfer Protocol, the protocol used by the *World Wide Web*.

Hyperlink (or hypertext link) A virtual connection between two pieces of information accessible via the Internet.

HyperText Markup Language (HTML) "The language of the Web" used to define Web pages.

Information service A type of electronic mail service in which a user sends a message to a server, which sends the appropriate reply, possibly a canned response or a file, back to the user.

In-line image A graphic that appears within a line (as if it were an ASCII character) of an *HTML* document.

Internet Conglomeration of interconnected computer networks all using the *TCP/IP* protocol.

Internet Service Provider (ISP) A company that provides its customers with access to the Internet. ISPs may also provide various levels of Web-serving capabilities.

Intranet Conglomeration of interconnected computer networks within a specific organization.

IP address A number and associated name by which Internet hosts are recognized.

IP multicasting An efficient Internet protocol for sending the same information signal to many clients.

ISDN Integrated Services Digital Network. A fast, dedicated network connection available through many telecommunications companies.

Java Object-oriented programming language designed by Sun Microsystems Inc. with network access and portability in mind.

Java servlet An extension to a Web server that is written in *Java*. Servlets perform many of the same capabilities that *CGI scripts* and server *plug-ins* do.

JavaScript Scripting language designed by Netscape Communications Inc., to enhance Web pages viewed with Web browsers.

JDBC Java Database Connectivity. Methods that provide *Java* programs with a uniform interface to many different *database* programs.

JPEG Joint Photographic Expert Group. A common Web graphics format supported by most browsers. It produces smaller files but its compression scheme can lose information.

Just-in-time compiler A compiler that takes *Java byte code* and converts it to more efficient machine-specific code. This is done at run time.

Kernel The lowest-level core of an operating system, through which higher-level components communicate with the hardware.

LaTeX Word processing markup language derived from TeX.

Layout document In the context of HTML *frames*, the document that tells the browser how to separate the browser window into frames. See also *Content document*.

Line interface An interaction with the computer on a line-by-line basis. You enter a text string followed by <enter>. The <enter> signifies that the computer should process the line(s) and produce a response. Contrast this to a *GUI*.

Link See *Hyperlink*.

List server Software that distributes e-mail messages to lists of users. A user subscribes to the list and thereafter any e-mail postings sent to the list are forwarded to the user. This continues until the user unsubscribes from the list. Also called a *list service*.

List Service See *List server*.

Markup The act of adding information to a document to control how it will be formatted for a printer or display device.

Metacharacters Characters that have a role is specifying *HTML* syntax, such as "<", ">", or "&".

Methods Also called *procedures*. A term loosely taken from object-oriented programming and meant to imply a piece of reusable code for performing a specific task.

MIME type Multipurpose Internet Mail Extension. A standardized method of assigning types to documents. It was originally developed for use with mail messages, that is, mailers could recognize specific types of documents embedded in mail messages by their MIME types. This same mechanism has now been adopted as the mechanism for assigning and detecting the formats of Internet documents.

Mirror site An information server that keeps a current copy of all or part of the information found on another information server. The prime purpose of a mirror site is to make the same information easily accessible from different global locations, thereby avoiding slow Internet connections.

Moderated list A list available on a *list server*, where each incoming message to that list is examined by the person referred to as the list moderator, before being optionally broadcast to all subscribers to that list after possible modification.

MRJ Macintosh Runtime for Java. This addition to the Mac OS provides a *Java* virtual machine for the Mac, as well as a stand-alone applet viewer, the Apple Applet Runner, and example *applets*.

Name resolution The process by which the Internet's hierarchy of *domain name servers* translates domain names into *IP addresses*.

Netiquette Undefined rules for how to behave when accessing the Internet. Common sense on the Internet.

Network computing The ability for clients to perform computations using code or instructions received via the Internet (or a smaller network).

NNTP Network News Transport Protocol. The protocol used to access Usenet newsgroups and associated articles.

Nondedicated connection A network connection that is sometimes interrupted, as with a dial-up modem.

ODBC Open Database Connectivity. Methods that allow programs to access many different *database* applications through a standard interface.

PC Personal Computer. Usually used to refer to any computer using the Intel 386, 486, Pentium, or other Intel chip.

Plug-in A Netscape term for an application that "plugs in" to the Netscape browser and extends the capabilities of the browser. For details, refer to

http://home.netscape.com/eng/mozilla/2.0/handbook/docs/-appans.html#C13

PPP Point-to-Point Protocol. A protocol used to support asynchronous connections to the Internet, typically over telephone lines.

Procedures See *Methods*.

RDBMS Relational *DBMS*. A database system for storing a *relational database*.

README The name of a file commonly found in *ftp archives* and software distributions. Usually contains information important to the installation or information that was written too late to be placed in the formal documentation.

Relational database A *database* in which all data are organized in terms of tables and relationships between tables. See also *RDBMS*.

Relative anchor A *hyperlink* reference within the current *HTML* document.

Rhapsody The next-generation operating system from Apple, based on NeXT Computer's NeXTStep operating system.

Rich Text Format (RTF) *ASCII*-based text interchange format developed by Microsoft Inc. Works well for exchanging text between word processing systems that read and write RTF but is not so good for exchanging graphics and mathematical equations.

Robot See *Web robot*.

Secure Sockets Layer (SSL) A Netscape-defined protocol supported by high-end Web servers that allows the data exchanged between clients and the server to be encrypted. Often used in electronic commerce, to protect private information such as credit card numbers.

Server A computer system or application that provides a service in response to requests from clients.

Server-Side Include (SSI) An instruction inside an *HTML* document that the Web server carries out before sending the document to the client.

SLIP Simple Line Interface Protocol. A communication protocol with similar functionality to *PPP*.

SHTTP Secure Hypertext Transport Protocol. Extension to e-mail that provides privacy and authentication over the World Wide Web.

SGML Standard Generalized Markup Language. Used by the publishing industry to describe the final appearance of a document. *HTML* is a subset of SGML.

SMTP Simple Mail Transport Protocol. The e-mail protocol used on the Internet.

Stateless interaction When a server application does not "remember" information from past client requests, particularly which clients made which requests. The plain vanilla Web—without *CGI scripts*, *cookies*, and so forth—is an example of stateless interaction.

Style Guide A reference document and possibly software templates that define common characteristics to be used in developing Web pages.

Swapping In virtual memory, the moving of memory pages (i.e., 512-byte chunks of information) between physical memory and disk.

Tag In *HTML markup*, an instruction embedded within a document that tells the browser how to display portions of the content. See also *Attribute*.

TCP/IP Transmission Control Protocol/Internet Protocol. The protocol suite that allows communication on the Internet. That is, all computers connected to the Internet support this protocol.

TCP/IP protocol stack The specific protocols included in *TCP/IP*.

Text file Any file that comprises characters from the *ASCII* character set. See also *Binary file*.

URL Uniform Resource Locator. A global reference point to a piece of information. That information can exist in a variety of formats. All Web browsers recognize and display the contents of URLs.

Usenet newsgroups Discussion groups on the Internet, each centered around a specific topic. There are currently about 15,000 Usenet newsgroups. Users post messages by e-mail to newsgroups and review newsgroups either via e-mail or special newsreader software.

Virtual Reality Modeling Language (VRML) Can be thought of as a 3-D version of HTML. VRML defines 3-D worlds and behaviors through which the user navigates using a VRML browser.

Web See *World Wide Web*.

Web browser Client software capable of reading, interpreting, and displaying information in *HyperText Markup Language (HTML)*.

Web client Software resident on client hardware for interpreting Web pages downloaded from a Web server.

Web form A particular type of Web page for sending information to the Web server for processing.

Webmaster The generic name given to the person responsible for maintaining Web pages on a Web server.

Web page A discrete piece of information read by a Web browser. That information resides between <HTML> and </HTML> tags and is usually contained in a single file.

Web robot Software that moves around the Internet gathering and indexing Web pages. Most commonly used to support Internet search services like Yahoo!, Alta Vista, and Magellan.

Web server Computer running software (or the software itself) capable of serving requests from Web clients for documents in *HTML* format.

Web site Computer maintaining a set of Web pages with a related theme.

WYSIWYG What-You-See-Is-What-You-Get. Usually refers to an editor that allows you to work with the document in the form it will appear on the printed page.

World Wide Web Computers attached to the Internet that support the *http protocol* used in global information exchange.

WWW An acronym for *World Wide Web.*

XML eXtensible Markup Language. An emerging standard for creating markup languages customized for marking up the structure of particular types of data to be served over the Internet. A subset of *SGML.*

Index

N

O